B-52 Stratofortress

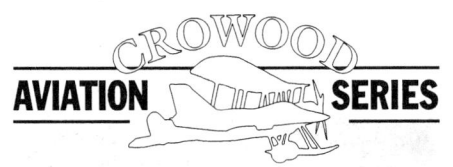

Boeing B-52
Stratofortress

Peter E. Davies and Tony Thornborough
(with Tony Cassanova)

The Crowood Press

First published in 1998 by
The Crowood Press Ltd
Ramsbury, Marlborough
Wiltshire SN8 2HR

© Peter E. Davies and Anthony M. Thornborough 1998

All rights reserved. No part of this publication may be reproduced or transmitted in any form or by any means, electronic or mechanical, including photocopy, recording, or any information storage and retrieval system, without permission in writing from the publishers.

British Library Cataloguing-in-Publication Data
A catalogue record for this book is available from the British Library.

ISBN 1 86126 113 6

Dedication
This book is dedicated to five decades of B-52 flyers and fixers.

Photograph previous page: although it was externally similar to those of previous B-52s, the B-52G wing was an integral fuel tank with ailerons replaced by seven-section spoilers on each wing.
R. W. Taylor Collection via Chesneau

Typefaces used: Goudy (*text*),
Cheltenham (*headings*)

Typeset and designed by
D & N Publishing
Membury Business Park, Lambourn Woodlands
Hungerford, Berkshire.

Printed and bound by Butler & Tanner, Frome.

Acknowledgements

The authors have been fortunate in being able to call upon the expertise and experience of a representative selection of the many thousands of people who have been associated with the B-52's first half-century. We are extremely grateful to the following individuals and organizations for their enthusiastic support and guidance:

Guy Aceto (AFA Magazine), Air Force Association, Robert F. Amos, Alvin Atkins, USAF (Ret), Jim Benson, Lt Col Temple H. Black, USAF, Capt Linda Blaszek, USAF, Col Don Blodgett, USAF (Ret), 1st Lt Peter J. Bloom, USAF, S/Sgt Shawn M. Bohannon, USAF, M/Sgt Frank J. Borchardt, USAF, M/Sgt James Brooks, (57th Wg), Mike Buchanan, Capt Danny A. Burnett, USAF (Ret), Lt Col Donald F. Campbell, USAF (Ret), USAF, Canadian Forces, Charles Canter, Col Floyd L. Carpenter, USAF, Kerry Cassanova, Roger Chesneau, Lt Col Charles Chiesa, USAF (Ret), James Cichocki, USAF (Ret), M/Sgt Larry Clavette, USAF, Andrew H. Cline, Capt John Colletta, USAF, Capt Michael Contratto, Capt Yvonne Cooper, Simon Cooter, T/Sgt Robert Crawford (Pentagon History Office), Lt Col Mike Crider, Col 'Rusty' Dean, USAF, Capt Leo Devine, USAF, M/Sgt Robert S. Devino, USAF, Mike (and the late Vera) DiCarlo, Charles Dobson, Barbara Donnelly, Robert F. Dorr, Dixie Dysart, S/Sgt Dan Elkins, USAF, Maj Juel F. Enger, USAF (Ret), Andy Evans, Ted Ewbanks, James R. Ferguson, Col Charles Fink, USAF (Ret), S/Sgt Scott Franks, USAF, T/Sgt Gary Freeman, USAF, Maj Ron Funk, USAF, David Gaudet, Lt Col Clifford B. Goodie, USAF (Ret), B Gen Tom Goslin, USAF, M/Sgt Michael Harvey, USAF, Ace Hobby (Niagara Falls), Robert H. Hopkins III, Capt Jonny Iverson, USAF, Lt Col Tom 'T. J.' Johnson, USAF, Maj Mike Joy, USAF, Ken Kimmons, Tom Krumenauer, Peter S. Kuehl, USAF (Ret), Col Jim Kwiatkowski, USAF, Donald J. Laing, Fred C. Lange, USAF (Ret), Dan Lapham, USAF (Ret), Anne Lapstra, Dale Lawhorne, 917th Wing, Capt Brooks R. Lieske, USAF, T/Sgt Brandon S. Lindsay, USAF, Lockheed Martin Skunk Works, Col Michael Loughran, USAF, Capt Mark Lulka, USAF, A1C Marcus MacDonald, Sgt Bradley D. Martens, USAF, Charles D. Martin, USAF (Ret), Lt Col Robert McAnally, USAF (Ret), Lee McTaggert, Scott Matthewson, Capt Timothy W. Mers, USAF, Larry Milberry, Maj John Miller, USAF, Capt Zane Mitchell, USAF, Maj Tony Monnitti, USAF, S/M/Sgt Thomas Moore, USAF, Capt Grey L. Morgan, USAF, Frank Mormillo, Lt Col Charles Nagy, USAF (Ret), Len Neath, Capt Robert F. Newton, USAF (Ret), Capt Dave O'Donnell, USAF, Michelle Page, Greg Paprocki, USAF (Ret), Maj Ed 'Otto' Pernatto, USAF (Ret), Tim Perry, Marlow Peters, Tam and Thanh Pham, Rick Radell, Mary Ramey, 1stLt Ellen Rasmussen, USAF, Raytheon/Texas Instruments, Chris M. Reed, Maj Gordon Rees Williams, USAF (Ret), M/Sgt Rose Renolds, The Retired Officers Association, Dave Riddel, RAAF, David Robinson, Lt Col Brian C. Rogers, USAF, Capt. David R. Ross, USAF, Col Philip A. Rowe Jr, USAF (Ret), Capt Brad Rupert, USAF, Carl Sahre, Ron and Dick Shatzel, Sgt Terrance Somerville, USAF, Daniel Soulaine, Gregory S. Spahr, Capt Bruce Sprecher, USAF, Ronnie Starling, USAF (Ret), Ed Stouffer, SrA John Taylor, USAF, Doug Thar, Jeff Thurman, BGen Jules Thurn, USAF (Ret), Maj Bruce Townsend, USAF, Chad Troxell, USAF (Ret), Lt Col David G. Underhill, AUS (Ret), Mike Valenti, Vanwell Publishing, Nick Veronico, T/Sgt Jeff Wallace, USAF, LtCol George Waskosky, USAF, Maj Barney Welch, USAF, Maj Vance K. Wilkinson, USAF (Ret), Jeff Wilson, Ken Winter, Scott Wonderly, M/Sgt Dave Wright, USAF, Richard Ziegler (Boeing). Special thanks are due to Ron Thurlow, USAF (Ret) for his tireless research efforts on behalf of this project. We are also grateful to The B-52 Stratofortress Association, a non-profit making organization which exists to stimulate interest in the B-52 and to enable contact between those who have been involved with the aircraft. Their contact address is 498 Carthage Drive, Beavercreek, OH 45434-5865, USA.

Contents

Foreword: Lt Col Brian C. Rogers, USAF		6
Introduction		7
1	BIG, BAD AND BEAUTIFUL	9
2	MORE GUTS, LESS TAIL	39
3	*ARC LIGHT* OVER THE JUNGLE	63
4	*LINEBACKER* Send in the B-52s	81
5	SIOP 'BUFFs'	101
6	DESERT DESTROYER	121
7	GOING GREY	135
Appendix I	B-52 Production	140
Appendix II	B-52 Operational Units	142
Appendix III	Named B-52 Aircraft	146
Appendix IV	B-52 Deployments to the United Kingdom	155
Appendix V	B-52 Colour Schemes	157
Appendix VI	B-52 Attrition	160
Appendix VII	Laboured Landings	163
Appendix VIII	B-52 Maritime Operations by Tony Cassanova	164
Glossary		170
Notes		172
Index		174

Foreword

The story of the B-52 Stratofortress encompasses far more than just a story of a warplane that has soldiered on in front-line service for more than forty years in the face of astounding change, that none could have imagined back in October 1948, when the XB-52's final design proposal was hammered out by six Boeing engineers huddled in a motel room in Dayton, Ohio. It is a story of thousands of factory workers in Seattle and Wichita, who understood the meaning of 'quality' many years before it became a modern industrial mantra. It is a story of visionary strategists, tacticians and staffers at every level of the U.S. Air Force who conceived ways to adapt this remarkable airframe to fulfil dozens of new missions while countering generation after generation of threats. It is a story of incredibly dedicated, persistent maintainers who fought through the new bomber's many teething pains in the 1950s and then went on to toil quietly, faithfully and often lovingly for decades, 'bending wrenches' in the deep snows of K. I Sawyer and Kincheloe, the bone-chilling winds of Minot, the steaming summers of Blythville and Barksdale, and the tropical outposts of Anderson, U-Tapao and Diego Garcia when the time came to drop iron in anger. It is a story of the thousands of combat crews who silently sat out the nuclear alert of the Cold War for more than thirty years, honed their skills year after year on those 'routine peacetime training missions' and, when called to battle, gallantly fought their way through the missiles and anti-aircraft artillery over places like Hanoi, Haiphong, H-2, Taji and Basrah.

Most of the weapons and tactics associated with the B-52 over the years were unimaginable when the first B-52B was delivered to Strategic Air Command on 29 June 1955. From the low-altitude terrain avoidance tactic, to conventional 'iron bombing', to maritime operations, night vision goggles and today's precision guided direct attack and stand-off weapons, the B-52 has proven remarkably adaptable to each 'new wave'. That the B-52 has adapted so well to these astounding changes is a testimonial to the dedication and vision of its designers, builders, maintainers, aircrews and managers.

Peter Davies, Tony Thornborough and Tony Cassanova have done an impressive job of telling many of these important Stratofortress stories. Their work is a fine chronicle of the B-52's impressive contribution to the advancement of airpower.

Brian C. Rogers
Bossier City, Louisiana
February 1998

Introduction

'Contact Moscow Control'. Did I ever think I'd hear those words, especially while flying a B-52? Not on your life! But, when the air traffic controller uttered them, that's when it truly dawned on me that I was on board a B-52, coasting into Russia, a country into which I'd prepared to fly for my entire military career – yet hoped I never would. If that wasn't enough to blow my mind, then the 'Backfire' bomber, which passed under us a few minutes later, certainly was.

Forty years previously, when the B-52 was entering operational service as the new 'flagship' of the Strategic Air Command's airborne nuclear arsenal, few could possibly have imagined that the venerable 'BUFF' would ever undertake such a goodwill visit to Russia. Fewer still would seriously have grasped the notion that the machine could continue to be at the cutting edge of American long-range airpower in the mid-1990s, and beyond. Brig Gen Dave Young, 2nd Bomb Wing Commander was at the controls that day, part of a fifty-strong contingent of personnel from Barksdale's 2nd BW and the 458th Operations Group at McGuire AFB, New Jersey. They arrived in time to join Russia's 50th Anniversary World War II Victory

A 2nd BW B-52H shows off the full range weaponry which it is uniquely able to carry. 2nd BW/HO

celebrations in Moscow and Ryazan, home of Soviet Long Range Aviation. (In 1944, 2nd BW B-17s had been the first Allied aircraft to bomb Germany from bases inside Russia). After five days of celebrations, sight-seeing and 'a few toasts of vodka to seal friendships and recognize important historic moments', Brig Gen Young observed that the trip had been a 'valuable exchange between military professionals. Because the barriers to communication are dissipating, hopefully we can work through our future differences in an amicable manner. I am absolutely convinced that if we could take the entire 2nd Bomb Wing to Russia for one week our action line would never ring again'.

Despite the hugs and exchanges of cigarettes and C-rations when American and Soviet troops met across a defeated Germany in May 1945, a great divide ensued within two years. As the Iron Curtain descended across Europe and Soviet paranoia precipitated a crisis when its leaders attempted to starve Berlin into submission, China too succumbed to its own communist revolution. The West could only react to these perceived threats to its own security through a policy of deterrence by expanding its fledgling nuclear arsenal, the exclusive province of air power, which had proved so decisive in defeating Japan. Air power would continue to attract 'big bucks'. From this melting pot was forged the B-52 Stratofortress.

To the military planners and manufacturers, who in the post-war world inherited a huge industrial-military base, such a précis of history might seem naive. However, this book is not about the politics of the last half-century. Rather, it is about a machine which was designed to meet the exigencies of the Cold War, but which has been crucial to international relations and military strategy for over forty years. Three generations of aircrew have flown the B-52 and they have witnessed many changes in the doctrines affecting its operations. This book also tells part of their story and shows how the B-52 and its crews were so decisive during the conflicts in Vietnam and the Persian Gulf. It describes the aircraft's almost infinite adaptability to new requirements, not only for the vast arsenal of nuclear weapons that have come and gone while the B-52 has kept on flying, but also new ranges of weapons systems, including 'non-lethal' devices designed to incapacitate an enemy before swords are joined. From a production run of 744 aircraft a mere six dozen remain active, the other ninety per cent having been reduced to scrap. But the aircraft is still a key player in America's airborne strategic arsenal (contrary to popular misconception) and forms much more than a stop-gap in the new Global Power Projection force as it pioneers new weapons which are still several years 'down the road' for its spanking new stablemates, the B-1B Lancer and B-2A Spirit. The B-52 is far from being branded as an aged *destrier*, ready for the retirement pasture even though critics point out that its airframe (originally constructed for a 5,000-hour fatigue life) has long since reached obsolescence. Also, the B-52 community itself contains a vast body of institutional knowledge and wisdom which will be relevant for as long as manned bombers are required.

Boeing has helped to ensure that the aircraft have been kept 'fit' and the company believes that they are 'as solid as a rock' and theoretically sound enough for operations well into the twenty-first century. Airframe hours for the surviving B-52Hs average roughly 14,000 hours, with individual bombers flying less than 400 hours per year. Studies indicate that, with careful structural monitoring, they could still be 'strong jets' in the year 2030. Comparisons with Boeing's equally well-built and even harder-worked tanker/transport products bear this out. However, the B-52's chances of staying in the Air Force that long would be greatly increased by a commercial off-the-shelf (COTS) re-engining programme, using four large turbofans. Avionics updates and many weapons-systems upgrades have kept the bomber 'current': you can hang just about anything on or in a B-52, including the burgeoning families of new munitions which continue to emerge. Without the contribution of the surviving B-52 units, newer heavyweight attackers will be unable to meet their operational goals on the USAF's 'Bomber Road Map' at the turn of the century using those new weapons. Integrating many of the new systems on board the B-52 has proved both easier and cheaper, allowing it to act as 'pathfinder' for new technologies.

The last B-52H rolled off the Boeing Wichita line in October 1962 at a fly-away cost of $8,965,597, according to the manufacturer. Recently, the Brookings Institute placed a current cash value on the aircraft in Fiscal Year 1995 money. It estimated each bomber at $260-400m in its 'all up' nuclear alert configuration, depending on the weapons load, but *discounting* operations and maintenance costs. It is still a 'big league' type and the bean-counters at the General Accounting Office and Capitol Hill would not tolerate the operational costs of an old aircraft unless they felt it was still viable. In simple terms, the B-52 represents fantastic value for taxpayers' dollars.

Its value in other contexts is more difficult to measure. To the many thousands who have flown it the B-52 has been astonishingly flexible and hardy, outliving many of its supposed successors. In military service it has fostered an emotional attachment which puts it alongside the B-17, Mustang and Spitfire in many flyers' memories. The B-52 has become an invaluable bridge between the jet age pioneers and today's 'super-tech' air force, even with all its 'crow's feet', warts and draggy appendages. Nobody is under any illusions that this is a slick performer: it is a doughty war-horse which often requires great physical strength to rein it in. Its crews are real Knights of the Stratosphere.

When the last 'BUFF' bows out of front-line service it is likely that NASA and the USAF will continue to require the aircraft's unique capability as an airborne launch platform for new generations of lifting bodies or orbital vehicles, taking the B-52 into its sixth decade of service, or even longer.

**Peter E. Davies and
Anthony M. Thornborough**
*Bristol, England,
February 1998*

CHAPTER ONE

Big, Bad and Beautiful

The YB-52 (49-0231), identical to the XB-52 but instrumented for flutter testing. It was not radically different from the 'back of an envelope' sketch by six Boeing designers at the Cleve Hotel, Dayton over a weekend in October 1948. Realizing that their turboprop bomber design was unlikely to satisfy USAF requirements the team rapidly came up with a totally different approach. USAF/NASM

On 29 June 1955, Brig Gen William E. Eubank Jr, 93rd Bomb Wing Commander, flew the first of his Wing's shiny new Boeing Stratofortresses (B-52B 52-8711) from the Boeing factory at Seattle, Washington, south to its new home at Castle AFB, California. The 93rd BW would receive most of the fifty-strong B-52B production run up until March 1956, 'bedding down' the base and its new machines for their role as global strikers and 'Stratofortress Schoolhouse'. Secretary of the Air Force, Quarles, praised the machine as 'the most formidable expression of airpower in the history of military aviation'. He was not wrong. The aircraft would provide the backbone of long-range American airpower for the ensuing forty years!

Origins of the Stratofortress

The origins of the venerable B-52 can be traced to November 1945 when Air Materiel Command defined the characteristics for the Army Air Force's new post-war heavy bomber, which was to offer a speed of 300mph at 34,000ft, and be capable of carrying a 10,000lb-payload over a 5,000-mile radius. Requests for proposals resulted in submissions from Boeing, Martin and Consolidated Vultee during February 1946. In June, Boeing's design was selected as the most promising, and shortly after was assigned the designation Experimental Bombardment Number 52 (XB-52).

It was the start of of an immense programme that would see the new Boeing concept undergo many radical metamorphoses before the familiar shape of the aircraft, as it is known and loved today, finally took fruition in the minds of its designers. Originally conceived as the Model 462, a straight-winged aircraft powered by six 5,500shp Wright XT-35 Typhoon turboprops weighing some 360,000lb and offering a radius of 3,100 miles, in the space of twenty-eight months it rapidly matured into a much heavier, faster and more aerodynamically refined machine known as the Model 464-49 of October 1948. It now featured a 35 degree swept wing married to no fewer than eight of the radical new Pratt & Whitney axial-flow J57 turbojets, and weighing some 330,000lb. The interim evolutionary milestones ran as follows:

Oct 1946
Boeing proposes a four-engine, 230,000lb Model 464 version, ousting the earlier Model 462 offering which was deemed deficient in range.

Dec 1946
Boeing asked to revise designs for a four-engine, 480,000lb version offering a 12,000-mile range, and responds with two designs: the 464-16 capable of carrying a 10,000lb atomic weapons load, and the 464-17 optimized for 90,000lb of conventional weapons. The Air Force selects the 200-ton dash 17 proposal featuring a 205ft span and powered by four 8,900 shp T-35-W-3 Wright turboprops.

Sept 1947
Boeing has developed its own 'flying boom' aerial refuelling system which solves the problem of bomber range. A 445mph, 400,000lb Model 464-29 is evolved, featuring a more tapered 205ft-span wing with 20 degrees of sweep, retaining the four T-35 powerplants.

Jan 1948
Boeing fights criticisms from the office of the Secretary of the Air Force regarding continued woes with its design and submits the Model 464-35, employing contra-rotating propellers and a more swept wing with a span of 185ft. Weight was reduced to 280,000lb, with the design offering a top speed of 500mph and ceiling of 41,000ft. Endorsed by the Air Force, construction of two XB-52 prototypes was authorized – until October 1948, when there came a drastic change of plan. The USAF then decided it wanted an all-new jet-powered bomber design, partly due to development problems being incurred with the T-35 Typhoon.

Innovation was necessary if Boeing was to ward off the competition from Northrop's XB-35 and jet-powered YB-49 'flying wings', funded as private ventures and both engaged in flight tests by October the previous year. But for the determination of Boeing Engineering's Vice President Ed Wells and his team, who were prepared to go back to their drawing boards and a clean sheet of paper time and time again, the B-52 programme might well have foundered in its infancy. Model 464-49, the first outwardly to resemble the eventual production model, was actually conceived in a hotel room in the Van Cleve, just up the road from the Air Force Project Office at Wright-Patterson Field, Ohio. Legend has it that one of the team went to a local hobby store, picked up some balsa wood, and knocked-up a display model in time for the Monday morning meeting, three days later, when the team submitted their 33-page proposal. Boeing was asked to stop work on the turboprop dash 29 and proceed with its new 464-49 design instead.

After the early trials and tribulations the sponsors grew increasingly delighted with progress and by April 1949 an XB-52 mock-up had been completed. Further exhaustive wind-tunnel tests and engineering studies resulted in the definitive XB-52 configuration: the Model 464-67, weighing some 390,000lb, with an unrefuelled range of 3,785 miles (later expanded), which exuded the sleek performance the Air Force was seeking. C-in-CSAC Gen Curtis LeMay was particularly supportive of Boeing's 464-67 design and by February 1951 long-lead funding was already in place for production of thirteen machines.

The one and only XB-52 (its sister was to be refined into a YB-52 service test model) was completed at the Seattle-based Boeing factory and rolled out to the flight test hangar amidst great secrecy on the rainy night of 29 November 1951, its vertical tail folded to starboard and the entire machine shrouded beneath protective wraps. Bearing the serial 49-230, it subsequently underwent many essential static tests, and would not fly until 2 October the following year. The honour of the first flight lay with YB-52 49-231, which 'elevated' off its four 'trucks' amidst tumultuous applause on 15 April 1952, crewed by Boeing Project pilot 'Tex' Johnston and Lt Col Guy M. Townsend. Following the two and a quarter hour flight, which culminated in a smooth touch-down at Larson AFB near Moses Lake in central Washington State, 150 miles east of the factory, 'Tex' Johnson announced, 'I am convinced that this is not only a good airplane; it is a hell of a good airplane!'.

Immediately following formal delivery to the Air Force, both aircraft were bailed back to Boeing for continued tests, to be joined two years later by the first trio of B-52As which were also engaged in ongoing development work. Known as the Model 464-201-0, these introduced a nose stretched by 4ft, able to accommodate bulky mission avionics and a new side-by-side seating arrangement which replaced the Stratojet-like tandem cockpit used previously. It was also equipped with a receptacle for the newly perfected 'flying boom' method of aerial refuelling, and added a pair of 1,000 USgal external tanks, and offered a ceiling of 46,700ft and top speed of 490kt – more than sufficient to haul the new range of nuclear weapons to target. Rolled out on 18 March 1954, when Gen Twining described the machine as 'the long rifle of the air age', the aircraft was powered by P&W J57-P-1W turbojets offering 10,000lb thrust dry (11,400lb with water injection).

By May 1954 the order books had swollen to eighty-eight B-52s, which included fifty of the first true operational variant – the Model 464-201-3, or B-52B. The type made its maiden flight on 25 January 1955, when 52-0004 took to the skies. Gross weight rose to 420,000lb, while there were two different tail gun and allied fire control configurations, one combining the MD-5 with twin 20mm cannon, before production reverted to four 0.50 calibre machine guns linked to an A-3A FCS. With series production underway, the unit price of the aircraft fell rapidly, levelling out at around a quarter of the costly B-52As which carried a staggering pricetag of $29,383,466 apiece!

The 'hand made' XB-52 copilot's instrument panel. Six main flight instruments are above a fuel panel and between eight sets of J57 'steam gauges'. Boeing

To modern observers the aircraft does not seem revolutionary, but only because it set a pattern which others followed and, to some extent, because its shape has become so familiar over the decades.

On the other hand, its structure was and remains conventional in design philosophy: four braced steel longerons strapped to a huge wing carry-through structure supporting the engines and landing gear, all skinned in aluminium and magnesium alloys 'but manned by iron men', as the saying goes. More than twenty subcontractors supplied airframe components to Boeing, accounting for 56.7 per cent (by weight) of the finished aircraft. Several of the larger units, including the Cessna horizontal tail, Goodyear fuel cells, side panels and wing stub components, Aeronca gear doors, rudder, ailerons and elevators and Fairchild rear fuselage and outer wing assemblies, were trucked or railed to the final assembly factories where the mandatory stipulated minimum 0.02in tolerance guaranteed a smooth fit of parts. There was no doubt that this was made less fraught by some twelve years of American experience of geographically displaced series bomber production.

In terms of flight control systems and accessories, the B-52 also partly built upon the B-47 in using main landing gear that was incorporated into the fuselage, with mere outriggers on the wings to provide extra stability on landing and to stop the wingtips from scraping the runway during all-up, heavy take-offs. This meant the wing design was not compromised. From a pilot's perspective, dealing with four 'trucks' in lieu of more conventional undercarriage presented no real difficulty. Both the fin and horizontal tail offered full trim as well as rudder/elevator control, making the beast highly manageable in skilled hands. Roll control was through conventional ailerons fitted at mid-wing on early B-52s, and spoilers which popped-up on the upper wing skin. Flaps provided additional lift on take-off and for reducing approach speeds, while a 44ft-diameter parachute billowed out from the rear during landing rollout. Most of these features remain in use to this day in largely unmodified form. There were sufficient eager ranks of pilots and gunners to fill the new slots created by the burgeoning B-52 programme, but a number of 'situations vacant' existed.

Castle AFB: Stratofortress School

Capt Robert F. Newton Sr (USAF, retired), began his flying career as a navigator via the Air Force Aviation Cadet programme (called the Tiger program, 'because every man was a tiger, hence my nickname', he recalled). Normally reserved for college graduates, it was opened up to high school

'Crabbing' along the runway, the XB-52 demonstrates its then-secret crosswind landing gear which enabled the aircraft to face 20 degrees into wind on take-off or landing while the wheels went straight ahead. To the 'backseat' crew this sensation was 'like being in a car skidding sideways'. Boeing via Chesneau

Specification – XB-52–B-52A					
Engine power:	Model	Serial	Engine	Thrust (lb) (wet)	Thrust (lb) (dry)
	XB-52	49-230	J57-P-8	–	10,200
	YB-52	49-231	YJ57-P-3	–	8,700
	B-52A	52-001 to -003	J57-P-1W	11,000	10,000

NB 'wet' thrust is with water injection.

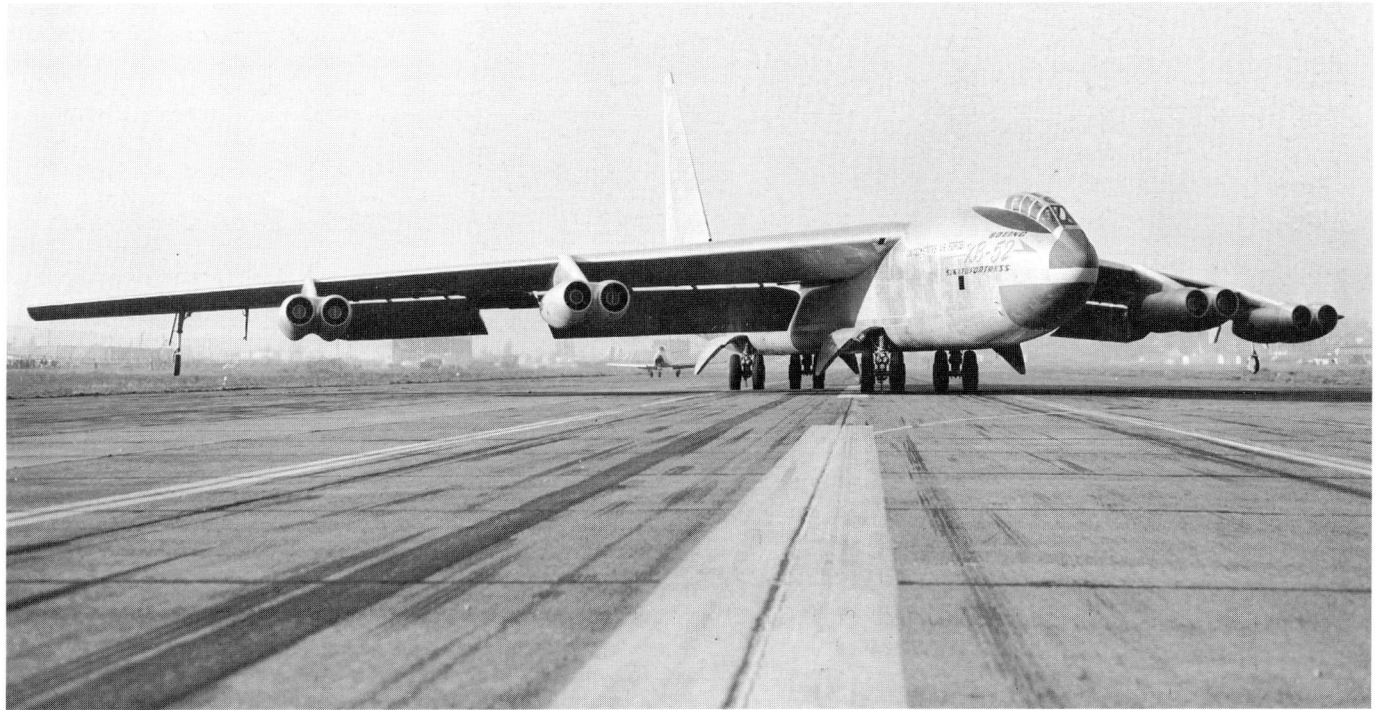

Both tandem-cockpit aircraft, XB-52 and YB-52, with their early-version tail turrets. They survived the test programme only to be scrapped for lack of storage. Boeing via Chesneau

Specification – B-52B

Dimensions:	Length 156.58ft (47.73m); height 48.25ft (14.71m); wingspan 185ft (56.39m); wing area 4,000sq ft (371.2sq m); tailplane span 52ft (15.85m); main undercarriage track 11.3ft (3.4m), outriggers 148.45ft (45.25m); distance from top of fuselage to ground 17.45ft (5.32m)
Operating weights:	Empty 172,285lb (78,148kg); combat 272,000lb (123,379kg); max take-off 420,000lb (190,512kg)
Fuel capacity:	37,550 USgal (204,843l)
Performance:	Max speed 546kt (1,012km/h) (at 20,000ft/6,096m) Service ceiling 47,300ft (14,417m) Combat radius 3,110nm (5,760km) Take-off run 8,200ft (2,500m) (at sea level, typical)

Engine power:

Serials	Engine	Thrust (lb) (wet)	Thrust (lb) (dry)
52-004 to -013	J57-P-1W	11,000	10,000
52-8710 to -8716	J57-P-1W or J57-P-1WB	11,000 11,400	10,000 10,400
53-366 to -376	J57-P-29W	12,100	10,500
53-377 to -391	J57-P-29WA	12,100	10,500
53-392 to -398	J57-P-19W	12,100	10,500

Armament and bombing/navigation systems (original configuration):

Serials	Guns	Fire control system	Bomb/nav
52-004 to -013	4 × 0.5 M-3 (600 rounds each)	A-3A	MA-6A
52-8710 to -8716	2 × 20mm M24A-1	MD-5	MA-6A
53-366 to -391	2 × 20mm M24A-1	MD-5	MA-6A
53-392 to -398	4 × 0.5 M-3	A-3A	MA-6a

graduates in 1955 and Robert Newton became one of the first to qualify. Progressing to bombing/photo recon school 'since at that time SAC was the hot command for advancement', he flew T-29 trainers equipped with the basics of the original B-52 MA-6A bombing and navigation kit.

While in training a colonel came into the class one day and asked for volunteers to go to B-52 training and I was the only one that volunteered. I went to an interview with another colonel and that was the last I heard from them. The reason I volunteered was, as I knew from talking to some B-47 crew members, that the navigator there worked harder than a one-armed paperhanger. When graduation came, everyone got an assignment but me, but a week later I was sent to Castle AFB for B-52 crew training.

What they did there was take an ex-B-47 crew and the gunner off a B-36 with a new navigator and ECM operator and mould them into a crew. There is a big difference between a 180kt aircraft and one that goes 444kt and they wanted to know if I could hack it. I qualified into the aircraft quite easily because my radar navigator taught me that you didn't navigate this aircraft, you aimed it. After the school was over and I became the first 2nd Lt to become a crew member I found out I was an experiment to see if it could be done, and opened the doors for every new navigator that came behind me.

Training at Castle ultimately embraced all three of its squadrons as they matured, but fell first to the 4017th Combat Crew Training Squadron, which served as a 'sausage machine' for the force. Five weeks' worth of ground instruction were interspersed with about forty hours' flying time as a knitted crew. It was not much for a sophisticated bomber, but SAC was reliant on the 'old heads' pulling things together, combined with discriminating crew selection and most gained experience in a 'hands on' manner after being assigned an operational posting.

Bombing was the name of the game and the more experienced crewmen helped hone the skills of their minions, based on their time in the big prop bombers and Stratojets. It also helped that the MA-6A bombing and navigation package introduced in the B-52B was based on the 'K-3A System' (the 'K-system') that had been developed for the B-36 Peacemaker, and was familiar to most. It was a mechanical analogue computer that number-crunched using a system of cams and gears and clutches, like a brass counting machine (that shared much with those sketched out by Leonardo da Vinci in the sixteenth century!). Designed and manufactured by the Sperry Company, it was the first real application of mechanical robotics, powered by stacks of little electric motors. Values derived from radar and other data could thus, with considerable manual intervention to input values like speed, altitude and so on, be used to coax the computer into deriving navigation solutions for great circle routes (curved earth, spherical trigonometry) and shorter, 'straight' legs to help the crews get to the target with minimum meandering. Radar was thus employed to plot radar significant waypoints – prominent landmarks – to help the crew stay on track,

At Seattle the workforce takes a break to watch the roll-out of the first production Stratofortress, 52-001, with its fin folded down, on 18 March 1954. via Ron Thurlow

(Below) **The first of three B-52As (52-001) makes its maiden take-off on 5 August 1954. All three were bailed back to the Company for development work, the third becoming NB-52A (52-003), used for X-15 launches.** via Ron Thurlow

backed by celestial navigation methods to enable regular fixes to be made, both providing further values that could be inputed into the computer-cum-counting machine. Robert Newton explained that the radar had a 25-mile crosshair range. 'We had to take wind runs to kill drift and it only had one offset, a means of bombing a hidden target by aiming at a point [visible on radar] and cranking the difference in distance into the computer. For the bomb aiming computer they took the same computer they used to train the 16in guns on a battleship and turned it upside down.' The radar set folded out from the wall, near the ladder where crews gained access to the navigators' dungeon below. An optical bomb sight was also featured in the MA-6A, optically linked to a porthole below so that the navigator was not obliged to unstrap from his seat and enter some other-worldly space that would dazzle his eyes.

With effort, and good crew coordination (a key to success), the system worked surprisingly well, despite its bulk. Matched to weapons offering a prospective yield measured in megatons of striking power, slight inaccuracies were tolerable if not always tolerated. During Operation *Redwing Cherokee*, when B-52B 52-0013 made the first air drop of a US hydrogen bomb at the Bikini Atoll in the Pacific on 21 May 1956, the Mk 15 bomb fell short of its target by three miles due to an error in timing. Packing a 3.75 megaton warhead, it nonetheless demonstrated the USAF's ability to deliver weapons of mass destruction where it hurt. JB-52B *The Tender Trap* (52-0004), was rigged to measure the effects during the *Redwing* series of flights and confirmed – as everybody already knew – that the USAF had a decisive weapon system combination in its hands. Turning that capability into an equally accurate conventional weapons delivery would be an altogether new problem for future engineers, tacticians and crews in the years ahead.

Snoopin' Stratofortresses

It was during the Spring of 1956 that improved models flowed off the lines. The previous December had already witnessed a quantum leap in production with the first key milestone met. Seattle had rolled out its first B-52C (54-2664) while Boeing Wichita rolled out its premier B-52D (55-0049), the first to be produced at the Kansas Plant, home of the famous

An evocative view of a 2nd BS, 22nd BW crew dashing for the door. RB-52B 52-8711 was SAC's first B-52, delivered to Castle AFB on 29 June 1955. It was preserved at the SAC Museum, Offutt AFB. *Boeing via Chesneau*

Stearman. The aircraft first flew on 9 March and 14 May respectively. The two models were virtually identical except that the 'D lacked any provisions – wiring buses and attach points – for the weapons bay reconnaissance modules. Outwardly, during January 1955 the USAF had decided to delete the R-for-recce prefix from its snooping RB-52B/C variants, although the capability remained very much in place with twenty-seven B-52Bs and all 35 dual-capable C-models rigged for reconnaissance duties. One of three purpose-built two-man pressurized capsules could be hoisted into the bomb bay of these aircraft, loaded for either photo reconnaissance (complete with K-38 or K-17C cameras in tri- and multi- camera stations and two dozen M-120 'photo flash bombs'), Sigint (signals intelligence, using RF-spectrum recorders to record emissions from radars and communications arrays) or 'weather reconnaissance' duties using sampling equipment and cameras, the former fed by five scoops which collected particulate debris and gases for later analysis in the laboratory, after being flown downwind of known Soviet nuclear detonation trials. Ironically, most of the 'weather' missions were flown by the B-52D variant which never was supposed to undertake reconnaissance in the first place. The capsules resembled petrol wagons mounted on a pallet, hoisted to fit flush with the B-52's belly in lieu of its normal bomb load and doors, and 'plumbed' into the aircraft's oxygen and electrical system through pigtail umbilicals, taking approximately four hours to install. All featured downwards-firing ejection seats. Little is known about these missions even forty years later, and the 'RB-52' mission was very much played-down after the B-52C/D Stratofortresses' service introduction.[1]

The two newcomers to the B-52 lineage introduced thermal-reflecting white paint on their undersides to mitigate electromagnetic interference to the electronics during nuclear missions (though serious 'nuclear hardening' came much later, as newer, lightweight electronics that could 'fry' replaced the old electro-mechanical devices) and, of course, to shield the crew. Uprated P&WA dash 19 or dash 29 engines packing a total of 84,000lb dry thrust compensated for the upwardly revised 450,000lb take off weight, and external tanks were increased to 3,000 USgal expanding fuel capacity to 41,700 USgal to feed them. Otherwise, the B-52C/D variants retained the rudimentary MA-6A bombing and navigation package. The first B-52C to be assigned to operations

Buff Power: the P&W J57 Engine

Background

Pratt & Whitney began their design of the JT3/J57 at the dawn of the jet age in 1947 with their X-176 turbojet. In 1949 the company's veteran Chief Designer, Andy Willgoos and Leonard S. Hobbs (who later won a Collier Trophy for his J57 work), turned it into the high-powered, economical engine which airframe designers wanted for the new generation of supersonic jet fighters. It first ran as the JT3 in June 1949 and as the military JT3A in January 1950. It was the first jet engine to develop more than 10,000lb thrust. Design work began on a larger version, the J75 (which was to power the weighty, double-sonic F-105 and F-106 fighters) and a smaller variant, the J52 for the Navy's A-4 Skyhawk and A-6 Intruder attackers and for cruise missiles such as the AGM-28 Hound Dog. The J57 was probably the most important US jet engine of the 1950s and its development was undoubtedly spurred on by its selection in 1948 for the B-52.

Construction

The basic J57 comprised two multi-stage, axial flow compressors, eight Iconel can-annular combustion chambers and a three-stage turbine. Each 14ft-long engine weighed over 4,000lb and generated 11,200lb dry thrust in its JT3C/J57-P-43WB version. Afterburning versions could push out more than 16,000lb. In the B-52, extra thrust of up to 2,500lb per engine was generated by a water injection system which sprayed mineralized water into the compressor air intake and into each engine's diffuser stage to cool and increase the density of the air, 'kidding' the engine into thinking that it was handling a greater airflow and generating an automatic fuel-flow increase. Large pumps in each nacelle delivered the water from a 1,200-gallon tank behind the crew compartment at a rate of 40,000lb per hour and 400lb psi or more. The consequent plumes of smoke and water vapour, together with prodigious noise, characterized the take-off of most B-52s thereafter. For the most powerful variant, the J57-P-43WB (B-52G), three triangular 'sonic suppressers' were mounted at the end of the exhaust duct, not to reduce aircraft speed (though they did slightly) but to moderate vibration fatigue in the rear half of the aircraft's wing when water injection was switched on. Unlike most turbojets of the period, if a J57 turbine disintegrated it tended to throw debris out through the jet efflux, rather than outwards through the engine casing. Capt Robert F. Newton described an unusual way of cleaning carbon deposits out of a J57 without taking it apart. 'First we would start the engine and run it up. Then a man would stand next to the inlet with a barrel of pecan nut shells and, at a given signal would throw handfuls of shells into the intake and let them go through the engine.' However, the J57's appetite for other substances was limited. 'In the winter of 1960 we had a big snowstorm at Griffiss AFB. They had to move the B-52s so that the ramp could be snow-ploughed but there was no way to tow the planes because of the snow so it was decided to taxi them. They started the engines up without cleaning the snow and ice out of the inlets and the result was sixty-four ruined engines.' Fred Enger remembered another non-standard use of the B-52's jet power at K. I. Sawyer AFB: 'The place has an average snowfall of 180 inches per year so winter operations were very interesting. The first winter [1961] they tried blowing the snow from one B-52 by using another with its engines running. As you can imagine this did not work out too well.'

J57 Variants

USAF Designation	T.O. Thrust: Wet/Dry (lb)	Application in B-52
J57-P-8	not used/10,200	XB-52 (49-0230)
YJ57-P-3	not used/8,700	YB-52 (49-0231)
J57-P-1W	11,000/10,000	B-52A (three)
(W signifies water injected version)		B-52B (in p/n batch 4-13)
J57-P-1WA	11,000/10,000	B-52B (in p/n batch 14-20)
J57-P-1WB	11,400/10,400	B-52B (in p/n batch 14-20)
J57-P-29W /WA	12,100/10,500	B-52B (in p/n batch 21-46)
		B-52C (in p/n batch 54-63)
		B-52D (or J57-P-19W)
		B-52E (or J57-P-19W)
J57-P-19W	10,500/12,100	B-52B (in p/n batch 47-53)
		B-52C (in p/n batch 64-88)
		B-52D (or J57-P-29W)
		B-52E (or J57-P-29W)
J57-P-43W/WA	13,750/11,200	B-52F (or J57-P-43WB)
J57-P-43WB	13,750/11,200	B-52G

Notes:
The J57-P-29WA differed from the J-57-P-29W in having double the capability of water flow for water injection and doubled hours at 'water rate' (10,000hr).
- the J-57-P-19W differed from the J-57-P-29W in having titanium compressors.
- the J-57-P-43WA/WB had a 40,000hr water rate 'life' and stronger accessory drives for oil, fuel and water pumps.
- p/n batch indicates production unit number and allows for some aircraft in each batch being fitted or retro-fitted with later models of the engine.
- from the J57-P-19W onwards production was shared with Ford Motors whose engines were designated J57-F-19W, and so on.

Specification – B-52C

Dimensions:	Length 156.58ft (47.73m); height 48.25ft (14.71m); wingspan 185ft (56.39m); wing area 4,000sq ft (371.2sq m); tailplane span 52ft (15.85m); main under carriage track 11.3ft (3.4m); outriggers 148.45ft (45.25m); distance from top of fuselage to ground 17.45ft (5.32m)
Operating weights:	Empty 172,637lb (78,308kg); combat 272,000lb (123,379kg); max take-off 450,000lb (204,120kg)
Fuel capacity:	41,550 USgal (226,664l)
Performance:	Max speed 546kt (1,012km/h) (at 20,000ft/6,096m) Service ceiling 47,300ft (14,417m) Combat radius 3,305nm (6,120km) Take-off run 8,000ft (2,438m) (at sea level, typical)

Engine power:

Engine	Thrust (lb) (wet)	Thrust (lb) (dry)
J57-P-29W or J57-P-19W	12,100	10,500

Armament and bombing/navigation systems (original configuration):

Serials	Guns	Fire control system	Bomb/nav
53-399 to 54-2687	4 × 0.5 M-3	A-3A	AN/ASQ-48(V)
54-2688	4 × 0.5 M-3	MD-9	AN/ASB-15, MD-1 AN/APN-108

Specification – B-52D

Dimensions:	Length 156.58ft (47.73m); height 48.25ft (14.71m); wingspan 185ft (56.39m); wing area 4,000sq ft (371.2sq m); tailplane span 52ft (15.85m); main undercarriage track 11.3ft (3.4m); outriggers 148.45ft (45.25m); distance from top of fuselage to ground 17.45ft (5.32m)
Operating weights:	Empty 170,126lb (77,170kg); combat 293,100lb (132,950kg); max take-off 450,000lb (204,120kg)
Fuel capacity:	41,550 USgal (226,664l)
Performance:	Max speed 551kt (1,021km/h) (at 20,000ft/6,096m) Service ceiling 46,200ft (14,082m) Combat radius 3,305nm (6,120km) Take-off run 8,000ft (2,438m) (at sea level, typical)

Engine power:

Engine	Thrust (lb) (wet)	Thrust (lb) (dry)
J57-P-29W or J57-P-19W	12,100	10,500

Armament and bombing/navigation systems (original configuration):

Guns	Fire control system	Bomb/nav
4 × 0.5 M-3	MD-9	AN/APN-108

was allocated to the 42nd BW at Loring AFB, Maine, on 16 June 1956, the same month that Castle began to receive B-52Ds. The strategy was six bases operating three fifteen-strong Stratofortress squadrons apiece, and within three months of the first Seattle-built B-52D taking to the skies the projected inventory – based on advance orders – had already been set at 603 aircraft under eleven Wings. With the 205 B-52C/Ds joining the force it seemed that SAC was unstoppable.

One EWO's World

Globally expanding Air Force contingency plans imposed newer and greater challenges. These, combined with the Stratofortress' nuclear mission, stipulating strict timing and accurate bombing, dictated that no less than half of its crew comprised rated navigators to help manage the workload. Two sat strapped in downwards-firing ejection seats (never a popular arrangement) in the lower deck, one acting as offensive systems specialist working as Radar Bombardier (known as 'Radar' or 'RN') and the other plotting courses and keeping a fix on aircraft position ('Nav'), in 'dimly illuminated, cramped stations with precious little room to work'. The third was located in the back of the main upper cabin, eight feet behind the AC and copilot, further trained in the arcane art of listening to enemy radar emissions and replying with jamming. Known as the Electronic Warfare Officer (EWO), despite his expertise he was usually just one step up the hierarchy from the gunner.[2]

Col Philip A. Rowe Jr (USAF retired), graduated a 33-week-long Electronic Countermeasures School at Keesler AFB, Mississippi, to join the burgeoning Stratofortress programme in 1957, serving as EWO and Navigator on B-52Ds with the 92nd BW at Fairchild AFB, near Spokane, Washington. Of his 4,000+ hours' flying time in some thirty-three aircraft types, including five years on the B-58 Hustler and 168 combat missions in the RF-4C Phantom, he described his Stratofortress experiences as the most 'challenging' and 'educational'. His memories are illuminating and form much of the rest of this chapter.

> In the early 1950s, at the height of the Cold War, many of us who went through navigation training, as either aviation cadets or student officers, were blessed with instructors who acquired their skills the hard way. Those fellows were the seasoned combat veterans of World War II. They mastered through necessity the basics of dead reckoning, celestial navigation and general airmanship. They were skilled in the fundamentals because they had to be. Systems and aids to navigation that modern crewmen take for granted did not exist for those pioneers and our mentors. From them we learned the essentials upon which to build our own skills.
>
> We were called 'bubble chasers' too, though that was not really a pejorative term.[3] Indeed, many of us used spirit-level sextants and octants to make celestial observations. The process of

B-52B 53-0373, the first of its kind, uses drastic measures to reduce speed for a refuelling by a KC-97G. These early trials, and the later Steeltrap tests, evolved the refuelling techniques which enabled the B-52 Alert force to operate. USAF via Thurlow

computing and plotting celestial lines of position changed markedly in the post-World War II era, especially with the introduction of two advances in technology. The H.O. 249 tables, along with an improved Air Almanac made it simpler and faster to compute our star, sun and moon observations and to transform observed and calculated data into accurate position information. But perhaps the greatest improvement was the periscopic sextant, the technological breakthrough that freed navigators from hand-held sextants that necessitated peering through astrodomes. On the upper forward flight deck the EWO inserted the periscopic sextant into the receptacle next to the bunk. He and his navigator worked as a team on these celestial practice legs, for the EWO took the star, sun or moon observations necessary to determine the plane's position. His measured azimuth and elevation angles were reported to the navigator down below, who would then compute and plot the lines of position on the charts to establish the 'fix'. It was a great improvement. No longer would navigators have so much difficulty finding stars or the sun through a bubble dome. Now they could peer through their own periscope at celestial bodies important for navigation. Gone was the correction for astrodome distortion too. The biggest advantage to the new sextant was the calibrated azimuth ring which permitted direct readout of relative or true bearings to the stars. Determining airplane true heading became a snap.

There were some unusual uses for the instrument, however, that its creators probably never anticipated. One widely practiced use was scanning the aircraft structure itself. Setting the optical elevation angle to very low values often enabled the navigator or others to see the upper surfaces of the wings, the fuselage or other parts of the plane not visible to the pilots up front or to the tail gunner in the rear.

On one occasion, Col Rowe used the periscope 'to determine the extent of smoke and flames' threatening the crew and aircraft following an in-flight fire. 'It was easy to watch the billowing smoke trail and the flames consuming the engine'. Other uses included providing 'a good view of ice building up along the leading edge of the wings and up and down

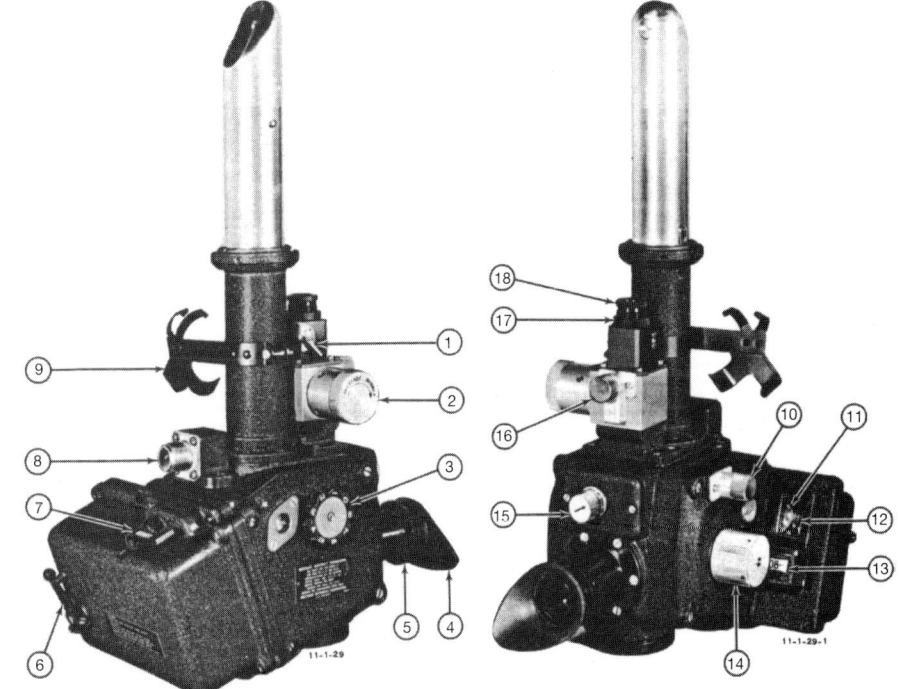

1. heading scale shutter lever
2. bubble adjustment knob
3. filter control knob
4. eyepiece
5. eyepiece focus adjustment ring
6. averager rewind lever
7. averager actuating button (lever)
8. electrical connector
9. watch clip
10. dial lamp
11. half time dial
12. averager indices
13. altitude counter
14. altitude knob
15. rheostat knob
16. bubble light
17. projection lens lock ring
18. projection lens adjustment ring

Periscopic sextant.

the vertical stabilizer of the tail. The pilot was kept informed of the situation as the layer of ice potentially altered wing performance'. Phil Rowe also contends that despite 'scoffing remarks of other crew members', he saw the first Russian Sputnik satellite through the mildly telescopic optics of the periscopic sextant. 'That too was never an intended use for such a fine instrument.'

The EWO enjoyed primary access to a large console of equipment, which in the pioneering days, was very much 'hands-on', requiring great skill. ACs such as Phil's, Capt Ray Grant, expected the crew to know every little nuance of the aircraft and quizzed them repeatedly on 'what if?' scenarios, but the electronic countermeasures (ECM) business was strictly the EWO's bailiwick – something he had to know in addition to his general knowledge of the aircraft and the navigators' equipment.[4]

Ape Alternators

First impressions are usually the most vivid, and Phil Rowe's introduction to the Stratofortress, which he titled 'What in the World Was That?', is particularly poignant in the B-52's evolution:

Early in the B-52 program at Castle things were very difficult. Airplanes were blowing up and that was downright scary. The problem was exploding air-driven electrical power alternators. They were located in the fuselage just aft of the crew compartment, right below a large fuel tank. Crews were briefed on the technical elements of the problem. The early design alternators were supposed to shut down automatically when over-speed conditions arose, as when the airflow regulating valves allowed too much high pressure engine bleed air into the alternator turbines. Unfortunately, on some recent flights the regulator valves failed to close and the bleed air kept coming into the turbines, driving them faster and faster. Eventually the turbines or other alternator parts simply failed, shattering and throwing material everywhere. One of those places happened to be the fuel tank immediately above the alternator. Bad news. Planes were destroyed and crews were lost or injured.

Officials briefed us on the situation and we were told to be alert for unusual electrical system problems while on one of our early training flights. We were told that the probabilities were very low that we would experience difficulties, but that was only of minimal reassurance. We were still nervous. No, we were downright fearful. At least the navigators and the EWO were. Maybe the pilots didn't seem so apprehensive (or wouldn't admit it).

The first such operational loss occurred on 16 February 1956, when 93rd BW B-52B 53-0384 caught fire halfway through its sortie, resulting in loss of control which ended in a terminal dive. The aircraft broke up into pieces in the skies near Tracy, California, and only four of the eight flight members got out. A grounding order ensued and all surviving affected aircraft received modifications, while Boeing and its supplier simultaneously addressed the issue on the production line. However, the problem continued, possibly as a result of the existence of two different alternator suppliers and the inherently bad design itself – air being piped from the engines to the fuselage, to drive electrical-generating systems. Another machine (53-0393) was lost in September, following an in-flight fire. Some reckoned the problem very nearly killed off the entire Stratofortress programme. A reporter named P. D. Eldred had interviewed crews at Castle during a temporary 'low' in morale resulting from these incidents, and SAC, fearful of the repercussions, immediately instigated what it described as a 'counteroffensive' – Operation *Quick Kick*. Eight B-52s from Castle and Loring, refuelled by KC-97s, circled the entire North American Continent on 24–25 November 1956, calming frayed nerves. They successfully traversed 12,271 miles in thirty-one hours.

However, the calm turned to a maelstrom when five days later, on 30 November, Capt Doddard's crew (in B-52B 52-8716) crashed on take-off at Castle. Col Charles 'Chuck' Fink was his IP (Instructor Pilot), and recalled that 'He lost both aft alternators at night during flap retraction, and needed cockpit lights and electrics but [the B-52Bs] had no transfer power relay'. Having lost its systems bus, the heavy Stratofortress turned into a brick and fell.

B-52 missions took them over many snowy landscapes such as this. B-52B 53-0394, Power Flite leader, was later preserved at the USAF Museum, Wright-Patterson AFB. Boeing via Chesneau

Loring AFB's 42nd BW(H) converted from the B-36 (visible in the background) to B-52Cs in June 1956, trading up to the B-52D a year later. USAF via Thurlow

All ten men onboard sadly perished. Sad, but mad as hell, Col Fink and the other two ACs first to qualify on B-52s were authorized to show off the bird. The end product was Project *Power Flite*, undertaken in January 1957 – although with hindsight that display of power was primarily a response to Soviet leader Nikita Khruschev's brash statement to Western diplomats the previous November, which translated as 'We will bury you'. *Power Flite* made it abundantly clear that the Soviet heartland was open to an American nuclear counterattack. Inevitably, it also honed Soviet rocket development yet

RB-52B 52-8716 cruises over the clouds in 1955 at the start of a brief career, curtailed by a crash at Castle AFB the following year. Boeing via Chesneau

Project *Power Flite*

The planning for *Power Flite*, a round-the-world, non-stop flight, began just before Christmas 1956, when 93rd BW operations officers met with Maj Gen Archie Old, Commander of 15th Air Force, who would serve as mission commander and ride aboard the lead aircraft. Five aircrews were hand-picked on 7 January by Brig Gen William E Eubank, 93rd BW commander, comprising nine-man teams – the normal crew of six, plus a reserve pilot and navigator, and an aircraft crew chief. Lt Col James Morris was nominated as AC of the lead B-52 *Lucky Lady III* (53-0394) – Morris had been copilot on the global-trotting prop-driven B-50 *Lucky Lady II* in 1949. Modifications to the five B-52Bs – selected from the available fleet at Castle – included installing additional bunks, twenty-man life rafts and cooking facilities. Three crews and their machines would perform the endurance mission, with the other two acting as airborne reserves for the first few legs.

All five aircraft roared down Castle's runway just after midday on 16 January, seemingly in perfect order. However, one of the primary aircraft, *La Vittoria*, refused to retract one of its outriggers, and although this eventually tucked back into position of its own accord, the machine's AAR receptacle became blocked with ice over Newfoundland, forcing it to land at Goose Bay. One of the 'spares' took up position while the other left formation over North Africa, after the Casablanca refuelling, and recovered at RAF Brize Norton in England, as planned. *Power Flite* continued flawlessly, using Great Circle legs, taking the trio from French Morocco to Saudi Arabia, Sri Lanka – including a simulated bomb run on a railway crossing in Malaya – en route to Manila, then Guam, the North Pacific and home. All three crews recovered at March AFB, California, instead of just the lead – fog at Castle creating the diversion. The total distance flown was 24,325 miles apiece, exactly 45 hours and 19 minutes after their departure.

The aerial refuelling feat was paramount to the success of *Power Flite*. Col Chuck Fink, who commanded *Lonesome George* (53-0398) recalled that there were five refuelling areas encompassing a staggering ninety-eight KC-97 tankers and crews! Drawing gulps from the prop-driven tankers meant refuelling altitudes of 15,000ft. The National Aeronautic Association recognized *Power Flite* as the outstanding mission of 1957, and the 93rd BW received SAC's sixth Mackay Trophy. As Gen Curtis LeMay told the crews during the presentation of their DFCs, the accomplishment was a 'demonstration of SAC's capabilities to strike any target on the face of the Earth'. The B-52 had come of age.

These three B-52Bs took part in the Mackay Trophy winning Power Flite **in January 1957. 53-0394** Lady Luck III **was the lead ship.** Boeing via Chesneau

---

further – in this instance the SAM (surface-to-air missile), command-guided by groundborne radar installations. Within two years Russia was mass-producing the SA-2 Dvina, known in the West as the 'Guideline', later to become the B-52's principal combat adversary.

Back in the 'States, Phil Rowe recalled that it took several years for the B-52's alternator problem to be fully resolved, creating some scary moments for his crew.

Three hundred miles off the California coast on a routine daytime navigation mission, we were just about to alter course for a practice bombing run with a turn east toward San Francisco, when it happened. It was a loud screeching noise that seemed to shake the whole forward crew compartment. 'What was that?', our navigator blurted over the interphone. He was the only one who vocalized what we all felt, but the five of us up front surely knew something not good had just happened. The sound was loud, penetrating, and really got our attention. We just knew it had to be alternator-related. The copilot calmly told us that the right forward alternator had come off line. His cockpit instruments showed that it was no longer powering the main bus. The rest of the crew sat silent. Nobody said a word for several seconds, though it seemed longer. 'The other alternators are okay. Power on the bus is coming from the remaining alternators', the copilot added. 'We appear to have lost one though.' 'Nav, you better go back and take a look', the pilot suggested. He wanted the navigator on the lower deck to get out of his seat and move toward the hatch leading to the forward wheelwell and the bomb-bay. A window in that small door would let him see into the equipment area where the alternators were. 'Nav? Did you hear me? Go check those alternators.' A pause and the lack of the navigator's response was deafening. Soon the radar operator, sitting just to the left of the navigator responded. 'I'll go, pilot. The Nav is a little shook up.'

The radar operator put the pins into the proper slots to safety his downward ejection seat, then unbuckled his lap belt and harness, before easing out of his seat and moving toward the starboard side, in the galley area. He carried a flashlight and pointed it through the small window of the hatch, allowing him to look aft into the equipment bay. He connected his interphone cord to the adjacent galley area jack.

Then he acknowledged that he was looking through the window. 'Don't see much, pilot', he reported. 'There's no fire or any sign of an explosion. Wait a second. It does look like there's a little smoke back there. It's hard to tell.' 'Okay, Radar. Look carefully to your right and up a bit', the pilot urged. 'Do you see anything out of the ordinary?' 'Nope. Just a little smoke, and I'm not sure where it's comin' from.' 'Nav. Give me a heading straight back to Castle', the pilot quickly ordered. By then the navigator had settled down a bit and responded, 'Have it for you in a second, pilot.' Then, in less than two minutes he called, 'Heading one-two-five to Castle.' And a few seconds later he gave the pilot an estimated arrival time.

We were back on the ground at Castle Air Force Base in about an hour, greeted by an armada of fire trucks with flashing lights and two ambulances. The blue station wagon of the squadron commander greeted us too. We were instructed to park the plane just off the main runway and not to taxi all the way to the parking ramp. The pilot set the brakes and began to shut down systems and the six engines. He did it in record time and then said, 'Crew, let's evacuate the airplane. Now.' That command was really not necessary, for we intended doing just that. The navigator's hatch opened, exposing the short ladder for crew members to scamper down to the ramp below. The copilot was quickly followed by the radar operator and then by me, the EWO. We all expected the navigator to be the first one out of the airplane, but he didn't come for what seemed an eternity.

Then the pilot come down the ladder, followed slowly by the navigator. The fire department urged us to get back away from the plane, for they too observed light smoke coming from the forward wheelwell and the alternator area. But the navigator wasn't moving very well. He walked awkwardly. The pilot began laughing, despite what could have been disastrous. He watched his navigator and soon laughed uncontrollably. Something about the navigator was not right. 'What's so funny?' the copilot asked. 'It sure can't be that we missed being blown to bits by a failed alternator.' 'He crapped in his pants', the pilot said, haltingly and with some difficulty because he was laughing so hard. 'He's okay, except for that.'

The fire department told us that the alternator had indeed failed, but we were lucky that *this* time the regulator valve shut it down before it disintegrated. That was our fourth flight in the new B-52s. It was quite an introduction to the Stratofortress, and one that our navigator would probably never forget.

Some time later the alternators were replaced on all of the B-52s, incorporating a safer 'hard drive' design specifically chosen to prevent overspeeding, as described later.

Pernicious Plumbing

The still shiny, new aircraft also suffered from fuel pipe leaks which manifested themselves in a most worrying manner, resulting in other grounding orders. Three

Space is tight on the Wichita production line in 1955 with the first B-52D (55-0049) nearing completion in front of some of the 1,341 B-47Es which were also made. USAF via Thurlow

This view gives some idea of Boeing's workload in the mid-1950s as SAC rapidly acquired its huge bomber force. These B-52Ds left the line on their scheduled date and work continued in the open air. 56-0625 crashed at McCoy AFB in 1972. Boeing

successive projects attempted to address the problem, beginning with *Blue Band* in September 1957, under which CF-14 aluminium clamps were fitted throughout the fleet, but failed to work due to unexpected stresses. *Hard Shell*, which substituted CF-17 stainless steel clamps was completed the following year, but still did not cure the problem. The final solution, which did seem to work, was to add safety straps to the clamps under Project *Quick Clip*. Again, Phil Rowe takes up the story after his crew had joined the 92nd BW at Spokane, the first of the 'Big Wings' to form with the Delta model beginning in March 1957. From his own perspective the problem was far from a trivial one:

seat. From that all-metal armless stool, that pivoted 360 degrees, I could see a lot more than from my regular place behind the ECM console. And I could look outside left or right through small windows. The view was much more interesting than I was used to. What a great place to take pictures!

Along the cabin ceiling, forward and left of the swivel seat, ran a large manifold (pipe) from the aerial refuelling receptacle atop the fuselage to the main fuel tanks where our on-loaded jet fuel was transferred. The manifold had several twists, turns and connector joints, plus a plunger switch which from time to time I was tasked to close to check out part of our plane's refuelling indicators. This description is important for what was about to happen.

was very wrong. I was being sprayed with jet fuel, very cold and wet, spewing from a leak at one of the manifold's connectors. 'Pilot, we've got a fuel leak back here!', I shouted over the interphone. 'You better disconnect. It's pouring into the cabin – and all over me.'

The instructor pilot turned around and saw me scrambling to get out from under that shower of fuel. He echoed my plea and quickly we disconnected from the tanker's boom. Perhaps five gallons of fuel, though it seemed like more, slopped around the upper deck of our bomber. Most of it was behind the jump seat. It wasn't as bad as it first appeared, but still it was something we had to either fix or stop by aborting the refuelling process. The IP and I grabbed for some rags and paper towels to mop up the sloshing fuel before it

With 98 per cent rpm, oil pressure at 42psi on all engines and throttles almost fully open, ND-52B 52-005 banks away after take-off. Boeing via Chesneau

Fibreglass fashion-wear for the 'downstairs' crew members; a B-52B navigator and R/N attempt to carry out their business in high-altitude pressure suits, which were only required above 50,000ft. Boeing

From my seat behind the pilots, on the upper deck of our B-52, I couldn't really get a good look at the process of inflight refuelling. I was curious to see what went on, but as the EWO, I faced a console that precluded forward visibility. So, if I wanted to see what was going on while we joined up with KC-135 tankers, I had to unstrap and move forward.

I had a choice of using a small swivel seat or the jump seat between the pilots. The swivel seat was primarily used for taking celestial observations with the periscopic sextant and located about half-way between my console and the pilots. The jump seat, between the pilots, was occupied on the day of our problem by an instructor pilot (IP). I moved on to the swivel

The huge KC-135 came closer and closer as my pilot eased our Stratofortress forward into position below and aft of the flying gas station. The U-shaped pattern of director lights on the tanker's belly helped guide us in, one set of lights indicating whether we were too close or too far out, and the other telling us whether we were too high or low. The last time I looked we were positioned just right.

'Clunk', resounded the hardware above me as the tanker's boom slammed into the receptacle. There was no doubt that the two planes were now joined. Soon the fuel would flow down from the tanker, through that big manifold and into our thirsty B-52. No sooner had the fuel begun to flow than it was obvious something

dripped down onto the electronic gear below. Down there sat the navigator and radar operator with all kinds of electrical equipment. A cabin fire might result quickly if that stuff couldn't be contained and cleaned up. Fortunately, all my ECM gear was inactive and turned off.

Fortunately also, nobody was smoking, and that sometimes happened, precipitating disaster, despite it being prohibited.

I tried to wipe what I could from my jacket and left leg of my flight suit. Boy, was that stuff cold. I was lucky that I didn't get wetter. Luckily too that kerosine-like fuel is not very caustic. It is a bit slimy and smelly though. And it is, by design, combustible. In a few minutes we managed to clean up most of the mess. The pilots were still flying in formation behind the tanker, trying to decide what the real problem was and what to do about it. We still needed that fuel from the tanker to continue our mission. I checked out the manifold as best I could, holding my flashlight in several positions to see if I could identify the source of the leak exactly. Nothing appeared obvious about it. There was no clear gap in the seal between connector joints, and the fuel had sprayed so wildly that everything was dripping and the source could not be pinpointed. We had no tool kit on board, so I could not attempt to tighten the many bolts at the several manifold connectors. And none appeared loose as I grabbed and twisted one and then another. It was a mystery.

The three pilots decided to connect again with the tanker, after first advising its pilot of our problem. We eased forward once more and the boom loudly clunked at it slammed into the receptacle. The IP and I watched anxiously to see if we could locate the source of the fuel spray, before things got very wet again. And just as the fuel began to flow we saw the problem area. On the upper side of one connector a small hole spewed fuel once more. It went everywhere. Quickly the IP advised my pilot to disconnect from the tanker, this time before very much fuel sprayed about the cabin and on us. 'Yep, it's still leaking', I declared of the all too obvious problem. 'We'd better not try that again.' The pilots decided not to try that again, I thankfully learned. Again I got busy with the rags and remaining paper towels. We stuffed them into a metal trash can stowed on the lower deck. We aborted that part of the flight and flew a shortened training mission, but continued only after verifying that no fuel had descended on to the equipment below. I never did turn on my ECM gear. It was one I will never forget, though I still wonder how much fuel we would have dumped into the cabin if I had not been sitting forward that day. That problem could have been much more serious, of course. And we were fortunate that no fire resulted from all that fuel sprayed into the cabin full of electronic gear.

But another problem on a different flight came closer to costing my copilot his life. We were nearly back at our Washington B-52 base, cruising along smoothly at 35,000ft, when it happened. The window in front of the copilot suddenly cracked and crazed over completely. Only the inner laminate of the multi-layered glass prevented the whole thing from imploding on to the pilot's face.

Quickly, the copilot and the pilot lowered their protective helmet visors. That would offer them some measure of screening from flying particles if the window failed completely, and help deflect the wind blasts that might follow. The pilot eased the throttles back to reduce our airspeed and lessen the pressure on the fractured window. If only it would hold until we got on the ground. I was glad that time that I did have a huge and heavy console in front of me, for if things began to fly about the cockpit I would have that between me and the debris or wind blast.

Within an hour we were safely back on the ground, none the worse for wear except for my copilot's frayed nerves. He didn't get his usual view of the runway as we touched down and rolled out to a stop on the taxiway. But at least he didn't have to pick bits of glass from his skin or suffer the likely cuts and bruises that could have ensued. We were lucky that time.

In fact, of the many mishaps we experienced in the B-52, from broken windows and interior fuel sprays to loss of an engine over Montana and a wing fire with it, that rugged old bird always brought us home. It suffered a variety of problems and mishaps, but in many ways was very forgiving.

Alert

Despite these operational hazards, which were, perhaps, to be expected with such a great stride in performance and huge expansion programme, crews took to the aircraft well. By November 1957 the last six B-52Ds were accepted, equipping five operational Bomb Wings, each of which was working up towards an AUE (Authorised Unit Establishment) of forty-five Stratofortresses and beginning to contribute towards SAC's newly instigated 'One-Third Ground Alert' system whereby aircraft were maintained on fifteen-minute alert with weapons loaded, all but a few switches away from being cocked-ready, and crews standing by for immediate take-off. Evaluated by B-47 units that year under Projects *Try Out*, *Watch Tower* and *Fresh Approach*, the programme became official in October 1957 and was gradually expanded into the B-52 force (reaching full implementation by May 1960). Phil Rowe recalls the tension:

> For years, during the height of the Cold War, Alert duty was a way of life for SAC flight crews. They were ready to go to war at any moment, day or night 365 days a year. As a retaliatory nuclear response, our planes were loaded with a variety of weapons, each capable of annihilating whatever targets they were sent to strike. Crews bore an awesome burden, knowing each airplane carried so potent and destructive a payload. SAC's power was enormous, reflecting the best that our defense industry could produce.

Another view along the Seattle pre-flight line with B-52Es in the final stages of completion in 1957. Boeing via Chesneau

The concept of Alert duty evolved as a response to the growing threat from the Soviet Union. At the flight crew level, down in the trenches, the men felt more the tension and the pressure of SAC headquarters than the 'enemy', for in those days the standards were high and rigours of training, regulations and procedures from SAC headquarters daunting. Life for SAC aircrews was one of unrelenting tension. Alert duty for [us] began in 1957 with the Lebanon Crisis. What followed became a lifestyle of SAC Alert.

Two very different kinds of activity existed. First was Ground Alert, with bombers placed near the end of the runway, ready to take off, which began clumsily and awkwardly. Logistical problems involving equipment and personnel were gradually overcome.

Alert duty took its toll on crews and support personnel. Some men could not stand the constant pressures or the extended family separations. Others did not like the lifestyle, finding it too restrictive and stifling of other pursuits. To look forward to a career pulling Alert duty, despite the rationale of national security and patriotism, held little appeal. Many left the service at the first opportunity. Others looked for assignments outside SAC.

Airplanes too suffered from extended Alert duty. It has long been known that the best way to keep airplanes airworthy is to fly them frequently. Placing planes on the Alert parking spots for weeks or months at a time resulted in mechanical problems. Security rules and procedures complicated even routine maintenance and servicing of loaded and ready planes. Even simple tasks required both flight crews and line maintenance people to be present.

Tension was rife in SAC where schedules, timing, checklists and strict discipline dominated a flyer's working day. Censure for not meeting such everyday pressures (which people invariably discovered to be intolerable work practices) ranged from open humiliation to spot demotions complete with scissors-on-buttons and epaulettes (the authors knowing one such individual, who turned up a quarter of an hour late for duty when he was not even expected to fly that day). The LeMay 'Spot Promotion' system, which rewarded those whose faces fitted and who did their duty, similarly caused resentment amongst those not directly connected with bomber duties – tanker crews, for example, were subject to the same reprimands but got no rewards for doing their duty. It was hardly surprising that practical jokes were not uncommon. Raconteur *par excellence* Phil Rowe remembers one such occasion.

To say that [our AC] Captain Ray was unique doesn't go far enough. Ray was eccentric in the extreme. When I knew him, he was one of the oldest captains in the US Air Force, a gray-haired curmudgeon with just a touch of sadism, especially towards junior officers. He was my aircraft commander in the early days of B-52 bombers. No sterner task-master ever drove me harder to learn and perform my crew member duties. Ray was said to chew on nails, a real grump at times, who was not fun to be around. Despite his credentials and recognized piloting abilities, he was respected but just unpopular.

Ray was the butt of jokes among his peers, for with his thick glasses, gray hair and tall, lanky build, he was likened to Ichabod Crane or one of Dickens' characters. Some said he was the best instrument flying pilot in the outfit, because he had to be. With those thick eyeglasses, they said he couldn't see out of the cockpit and had to master the instruments.

A joke that Ray's colleagues played on him deserves telling. It happened in the early days of SAC ground alert, when B-52 bombers were fully loaded, ready to go to war, and flight crews lived in a special dormitory not far from the runway. In those early days, when SAC was learning how to maintain an Alert force, there were a number of temporary measures flight crews had to accept. In our case, that meant being quartered in an old World War II wooden, two-storey barracks for a week at a time. Boredom was a problem, sometimes overcome by pranks played on other crew members.

The system of button-activated klaxon horns, to send crews scurrying to their planes, had not been established. Our signal to scramble for the planes came from a hand-activated bell, rung by an enlisted man, who stayed by the telephone night and day. If he got the message from our Command Post to alert the flight crews, all he did was ring the bell loudly.

One quiet Sunday afternoon, while we were on alert, Captain Ray passed the time by taking a nap on his cot in the barracks. Others read the newspaper, watched television or played horseshoes, just outside the building. Our World War II vintage jeep-like vehicles stood at the ready, parked in front of the barracks, backed-in for a quick get-away. If the bell rang, we'd grab our gear, tumble out of the building and jump into the vehicles for the short drive to our airplanes. We had to be able to take off within fifteen minutes of the alarm bell.

Ray slept soundly that warm spring afternoon, oblivious to the noisy television and the clanking of horseshoes just outside his open window. Unbeknownst to Ray, his pilot colleagues were about to play a joke which would, to say the least, disturb his slumber. Collusion by the rest of us was an essential part of the trick. Quietly, stealthily the entire Alert force of 60 officers and men slipped out of the Alert barracks. Only Ray and the enlisted man on duty, by the bell, remained. Even the Alert vehicles were removed to the back-side of the building, making it appear that all had left. One vehicle, loaded with its six-man flight crew, was positioned to drive away from the barracks on cue.

On a signal from one of the pilots, the enlisted bell ringer did his thing. He loudly clanged the bell for all he was worth. The building resounded with bell ringing. Ray jumped up from his bed, bleary-eyed. He grabbed his flight jacket, donned his cap and carried his boots, as he scampered down the hallway and bolted out the door. The pre-positioned single vehicle, now about a block down the street, began to speed away, making it look like the last of the crews was heading for the runway. Ray was sure that he had missed his ride, and that even his own crew had abandoned him in their zeal to get to the airplane. He tried to put on his boots and run down the street at the same time. It was a comical sight, like something from an old Mack Sennett movie. Ray's desperation was obvious.

He stopped running and just stood there, forlornly in the middle of the street. We could only imagine what he was thinking at that moment. Some of us, watching from behind the bushes at the side of the barracks, could not contain our laughter. Ray heard the giggles and turned to stare at us, now realizing that he'd been had. He was suddenly aware that the joke was on him. And he became furious.

It isn't fit to include here all the things he said about his fellow crew members. If we ever had an old grump to contend with in the past, it was nothing like what we faced in the next few days. Captain Ray did not like being the butt of a joke, even a creative one like that.

For the most part, the crews' daily itinerary while on Alert meant checking and re-checking – everything. For routine missions crews checked their aircraft, reported back, then went out to fly.

Early in the B-52 program, with memories of the lumbering B-36 still fresh in our minds, we followed the long-time practice of lengthy pre-flight of our airplanes. I mean really lengthy. For a typical training flight we began the process of checking out aircraft equipment and systems over four and a half hours before each scheduled take-off. SAC policy for crews in the heavy bombers required extensive preflight checks. Just before 0400 hours, well ahead of our planned 0840 take-off, we'd arrive at the squadron area to pick up our gear. That gear included more stuff than Aunt Bessie needed for a wedding. That was but a part of the preparation for routine training missions. We had already spent the whole day earlier on mission planning and briefings to the senior squadron staff to describe each and every aspect of the scheduled mission.

There were six of us on the crew, not including any extras that frequently came along. Extra people might include an instructor pilot, or evaluator if this was a check ride. And there might be an instructor/evaluator navigator or similar extra for the electronic warfare and gunner's positions. Seldom did we carry more than nine folks, but there could be more.

Regular and extra crew members carried a briefcase, a parachute (plus three spare parachutes – two for the forward compartment and one for the aft tail gunner), one or more flight lunch boxes each, and heavy clothing. Two large thermos jugs and one small one were added too. Then there would be one or two sextant cases, each half the size of a footlocker. And, of course, there were sometimes whole footlockers full of spare parts [for the avionics]. That last item depended upon how important the mission was. We quite literally filled the whole back of the crew bus with stuff to bring along. In the earliest days, before 1958, we additionally carried duffel bags with extra clothing, shaving kits and such ... just in case we landed someplace other than our home base. Add six to nine duffel bags to the load.

Upon arrival at the airplane, parked way out in the boonies a mile or so from the squadron buildings, we'd immediately unload the equipment and line it up under the wing. Each man would place his own stuff in front of where he would soon stand for inspection by the pilot in command, the AC or aircraft commander. Six to nine men would soon be ready for final briefing by the AC and be subject to inspection to make sure everything needed was present and in good condition. The process was much more easily endured if the weather was good. Such was not always the case.

Then the crew would separate and the loading process began. Most of the stuff went into the forward crew compartment where five of the six would fly, plus others if extras were coming. The tail gunner flew all alone in the aft compartment. Some of the stuff not needed in flight might be stored in the '47 Section' aft of the rear landing gear and forward of the gunner's position. No wonder the B-52 grossed out at 450,000 pounds or more!

Then it was time to start the 'Exterior Inspection', that important stem to stern examination of the aircraft's external parts. The two pilots usually divided the exterior walk-around checks, one taking the starboard side and the other the port side. The EWO and the tail gunner checked their exterior portions of the plane too, things like radomes, radio antennae, guns and ammo compartment doors, chaff dispenser ports and such. Ground power carts were not yet started, so there was no electrical power or cooling air supplied to the interior equipment. Only in severe winter conditions would there be special carts running to pump warm air into the cockpit or essential equipment areas. Soon it was time to climb aboard. Each man headed for his assigned crew station. The two pilots headed for the upper flight deck, followed by the EWO and any extra folks. The gunner went his own way, aft to the tail of the plane and his separate world. The fuselage in between forward and aft compartments was not pressurized in flight, or heated and cooled either. Each man followed his own printed checklist, carefully sequentially positioning switches on equipment, attaching helmets and oxygen masks to the communication and life support systems. An hour or more might pass between the time the crew first arrived at the plane and the first systems were powered up with the help of ground equipment. There was much more to do.

The Power-Off checklists completed, it was then time for electrical and pneumatic carts to be started or readied. Soon the crew would complete system checks without engines being started or depending upon aircraft generators (alternators). Confirmations over the interphone to the AC would be made to report each crewman's readiness to proceed. Next would be engine starts and system checkouts on aircraft power. All systems would be exercised and checked, all except those which involved actually moving the plane. Some systems could not be tested for safety reasons. Such systems included high-powered electronic transmitters, armaments and things like gear doors and retraction mechanisms, of course. They must await in-flight conditions.

And then everything was shut down. Engines were stopped and electrical power turned off. The Power-On and systems checks were completed. Discrepancies noted would be entered into the aircraft systems and equipment logbook. Things that had to be fixed before the scheduled training flight would get attention by maintenance personnel. Very few discrepancies would be allowed to remain as open items. Safety of flight and mission critical items had to be fixed, else the flight might be cancelled. Sending B-52 crews off on eight-hour training missions is expensive, so all must be in order to preclude wasted effort.

After the plane was completely powered down, just the way it was before the crew arrived, then there would be a few moments for a coffee break, another crew briefing and a report by the pilot to the Wing Headquarters Command Post about the status of the plane. Was it or was it not ready to go? Or how long would it take to get necessary repairs made? Getting things ready for an on-time take-off became a high-interest item for the crew, the maintenance people, and the Wing Commander too.

About forty-five minutes before the scheduled take-off, the crew would return to the airplane, climb aboard and start the checklists all over again. Only this time they would continue on through all pre-take-off phases and finally move the airplane to the end of the runway.

A lot of work was done by a lot of people to get that big bomber to the ready line at the end of the runway. Ground crew, flight crew, maintenance teams and others all contributed to getting things that far along. And still the airplane was on the ground, but not for long. At 0830 the huge Stratofortress roared down the runway, accelerating and getting closer to that all-important on-time take-off.

Just getting off the ground was fraught with tension. For safety purposes many runways were extended beyond 12,000ft to accommodate the lengthy take-off roll of the 225-ton all-up, fully fuelled and armed bombers. Copilots would often call out the point of no return while the wheels were still rolling on the concrete. From the vantage point of the end-of-runway (EOR) where the thrust gathered into thunder, beginning the roll, a trundle gave way to a delicately balanced roll as the machines, in turn, seemed to miniaturize, then seemingly disappear before they rose again, as mere specks trailing swirls of smoke to give any visual indication that they were airborne. An imaginary tiger clawed grey streaks in the blue as the flight climbed over the horizon. Each and every take-off represented hours of grind on the part of both ground and air crews, and hours more yet to come.

'Non-flyers may think that it was merely kicking the tires and roaring off into the wild blue yonder for another glamorous flight. It was certainly a heck of a lot more work than that. Now you have a small inkling of that involved and lengthy process that preceded every mission.'

Chromedome

The inescapable logic of shortening reaction times and making bomber assets more invulnerable to missile attack by keeping a number in the air, ready to be routed to

Suitably inscribed, Wichita's first B-52D, 55-0049, over the flat Kansas terrain. A non-standard SAC sash, extending around the whole nose, was later added to the 'roll-out' logo. Boeing via Chesneau

their targets, was recognized by Gen Thomas S. Power in 1957. Successor and former Vice-Commander to the legendary Curtis LeMay as CINCSAC, Gen Power presided over a continued expansion of SAC up to his retirement in 1964. At that time the Command had charge of over 2,000 aircraft, 875 ICBMs and over a quarter of a million personnel. B-52 strength, at forty-two squadrons, was over 600 bombers.

Airborne Alert trials were conducted by the 42nd BW during 1958 under Operation *Head Start* and the 92nd BW in 1959, with five B-52Ds from each Wing. Other units became involved as SAC worked towards the objective of keeping over a fifth of its B-52 force airborne in an emergency. The *Chromedome* programme was expanded to all operational B-52 Bomb Wings – principally those at Loring, Westover, Fairchild and Ellsworth – in March 1959, when costs also were heavily scrutinized. In July 1959, the Fairchild Wing was tasked to fly nine round-the-clock missions a day under Operation *Steel Trap*.

The whole airborne Alert process was wearisome for crews and aircraft. Phil Rowe takes up the story again:

Unlike our normal practice of reporting for a training mission four and a half hours before take-off, we didn't have to show up for our airborne Alert flights but one hour early. That's because fellow crews performed the B-52 pre-flight checks for us. It sure helped. Ordinarily, an eight-hour routine flight meant a fourteen-hour day or longer, with preflight, the mission itself and then post-flight de-briefings. For a 24-hour airborne alert flight, normal practice would have made for thirty-hour days. Much too much.

Crew schedules for airborne Alert duty were planned ahead months at a time. Typically, a crew flew a series of four 24-hour missions, from mid-day one day to mid-day the next, with 48-hours in between flights. Then, they were given a week off, before returning to squadron duty. For the next week they performed mission planning and pre-flight checks for planes readied for airborne Alert. Finally, crews started the cycle over again. The 24-hour sorties were a great way to build flight time, with some crews logging two dozen or more missions each six months. Each Alert mission included two aerial refuellings, keeping the planes adequately fuelled to reach their targets, no matter when the 'go code' was received. The routes flown depended on where the aircraft came from and where their assigned targets might be. The 92nd Bomb Wing flew over northern Alaska and then down the Pacific coast to the Straits of Juan de Fuca. They'd fly the circuit twice in a day. The Lebanon Crisis of the late fifties and the Cuban missile fiasco of the early sixties were two of the toughest periods for SAC crews. Some pulled forty-five days of continuous Alert for the former, but most believed that chances of an actual war mission scramble were greater during the latter period of tension.

A dozen B-52s, fully loaded with weapons, armament and fuel, headed down the taxiway for a noon lift-off. We couldn't be airborne any too soon for our sister ships that were still aloft. If we were delayed, our counterparts could not land, so that the Alert force would not be degraded by missing airplanes.

At intervals of two minutes, we took the active runway and roared off into the Washington skies. Soon, lined up in a loose trail formation, one-mile apart and stacked up 500-feet, the lead ship flew slightly below optimum cruise altitude and the last one slightly above, for our gross weights. We turned west and headed out over the Pacific, a string of birds loaded with nuclear destruction we hoped would never be needed.

Our crew flew twenty-eight of the noon-to-noon missions over a seven-month period. The first half dozen missions were really tiring, for we hadn't yet mastered our pacing. None of us got much sleep, until the routine became more comfortable after several flights.

Down on the lower deck, we stored quite a bit of stuff for that mission. Three wooden footlockers were stowed in the galley area. One, double-locked with two combination padlocks, held the war-mission folders. We would not open that box, unless we got an authentic 'go code' radio message. Another footlocker held spare parts of the K-System (MA-6A) radar bombing equipment. In those days of vacuum-tube electronics and analog electro-mechanical computers for navigation and bombing calculations, spare parts were the order of the day. Many times we'd have to remove and replace circuit boards or vacuum tubes to keep the system running. The third box was the most

Steeltrap

The 4238th SW, based at Barksdale with the B-52F, was one of the first units to pioneer the airborne Alert mission. Maj Jule F. Enger checked his log book for details of one of the earliest of these:

The first flight I took on the *Steeltrap* testing programme was on 4 May 1959. The mission time was 24hr 30min. My crew flew seven of these between 4 May and 20 June and we learned a lot about refuelling, with KC-97s out of Goose Bay and over eastern Canada. The refuelling track had a westerly heading and that was a mistake as the Northern Lights made the horizon seem to be at a 45 degree angle at our right and this made refuelling almost impossible for some. My AC, Vernon McCardle, just could not do it. I took over and, with difficulty, got the fuel. They changed the refuelling track to a southerly one after our second flight. SAC came up with a recognition system [for successful refuellings] and that was pins which were labelled 'One Gulp'. I think I got the most – five. In mid-April 1960 our crew and four or five others were sent TDY to Columbus AFB to support the test of flying four airborne alerts a day; two every twelve hours. We flew in trail formation, with aircraft No. 2 500ft higher than Lead, north to the middle of Hudson Bay then back to refuel on a southerly heading towards the base so that the tanker could offload his fuel and dive into Columbus. We took the maximum load of 80,000lb from the tanker and intercepted our track north and back up to Canada. The process was then repeated with one aircraft leading on the northbound leg and the other on the south to give a break for the navigators. Average flight time was around 24hr 30min. I personally flew 196.15 hours between 16 April and 8 May 1960.

In August 1961 the *Thule Monitor* missions began, using *Chromedome* B-52s on 'guard duty' near the BMEWS station at Thule in case it was hit by a surprise Soviet nuclear attack. The B-52 would have been able to confirm whether the break in contact with the station was due to an attack or merely communications problems. This continued until 1968. Fred Enger flew *Thule Monitors*:

We called it 'Thule Watch', because that was what it was. The flights were twelve hours on station, plus flight time up and back: for us it was around twenty-two hours. We would relieve the southbound crew some 200-250 miles south of Thule AFB and bore holes for the next twelve hours except for the two tankers from Alaska. We used to look at the station out in the Greenland ice, though we could not see it often because of cloud. When we did it was interesting to see all the activity. I think they called it Little America. Sometimes, to pass the time, we would follow the Pan Am polar flight 707 as it came from London to Tokyo.

Robert Newton flew *Thule Monitor* and remembered:

Twenty-two hour missions where we acted as a radio relay plane in case they couldn't use ground communications. We would fly a 300-mile bowtie pattern over the base. The first mission flown by another outfit almost turned into a disaster. When you go that far North the true North Pole and the Magnetic Pole are in opposite directions and you can't use a regular compass. You have to use a free-running gyro and polar navigation and at a certain point crank an artificial heading into it so your directions come out right. Well, the navigator didn't do this and they went 1,100 miles off course and came close to violating Soviet airspace.

Normally, SAC regulations were hard on B-52 navigators when flying over the USA:

One thing that inspired us to be good navigators was that if you were more than ten miles off course or five minutes out of your time limit they would scramble fighters up to identify you. If this happened it was an automatic $10,000 fine for you and the pilot plus the cost of sending the fighters up.

---

important, to us at least. It was full of inflight meals especially created for SAC's finest aircrews. There were meals for all five in the forward cabin, sorta like today's TV dinners, but much more de luxe. The steak meal was my favourite.

In the aft compartment, way back where the tail gunner rode, all alone, 100-feet from the rest of us, was another food and beverage supply. The gunner had a galley in his lonely little world that faced backwards.

On the upper deck of the forward crew cabin, just to the right of my seat, and about eight feet aft of the pilots, was the only bunk on the plane. On the early Alert missions, I was able to get to the bunk before any of the others. But, after about the tenth mission, I had to be really quick to beat the copilot to it, or I slept on the cold floor, atop an air mattress. We were required to keep two people awake at all times in the forward cabin. That meant one of the two pilots, plus one of the remaining three, which included the radar bombardier, the navigator and me. Back in the tail compartment, our gunner could sleep whenever he wanted, though he was frequently interrupted by intercom checks to make sure he was still alive and kicking.

During take-off, landing and the two aerial refuellings, we all had to be awake and in our seats. Out of the 24-hours aloft, it was common for us to each get a full eight hours of sleep, once we got the routine down. Someone in headquarters had the bright idea to give EWOs, like me, enough training in the pilot's flight simulator to be able to monitor the fuel, electrical and hydraulic systems in the front cockpit. The plan, intended when one pilot was asleep, was that one non-pilot could sit up front to keep the other pilot awake, and help monitor things. But since they never asked the two navigators to participate, that usually meant that the EWO did that job.

On one of the twenty-eight missions, my limited pilot training came in handy. Our autopilot failed, just after climb-out, and the bird had to be hand-flown for the full twenty-four hours. I got about five hours at the controls on that flight. For a guy who'd only flown light planes, that '52 seemed like a Mack truck, and about as responsive.

One of the strangest and most interesting things occurred on two successive missions, along the same part of the west coast, just off the Queen Charlotte Islands. We were flying south, parallel to the Canadian coast, over water, our B-52s in trail formation. It was routine for the radar operator to monitor the one-mile spacing of planes ahead of us on his scope. B-52s looked like bright dots on the radar screen, clearly visible against the blackness of the ocean below.

Suddenly, and unexpectedly, another radar return appeared off to our 2 o'clock position. It was about fifty miles away when first spotted, and heading straight for the formation. The radar operator alerted his pilot to be on the lookout for another plane, but none could be seen. The target flew diagonally across our string of bombers, passing just ahead of our plane and then disappeared to the rear. Nobody ever got a visual sighting, just the radar image. Even our tail gunner turned on his radar, but he never saw anything. Strange.

The phenomenon visited us on the next flight, down the same part of the coast. That time, the radar operator turned on his scope camera to successfully capture the images. He wasn't seeing things. We radioed our sister ships to verify the target. They too, only saw it on radar. We never learned what it was, but there was much speculation about it.

Viewed from the Top

Flying at high altitude was a new experience for many flyers who had been honed on cloud-bobbing heights. First, there was the sheer exhilaration of being at 40,000ft or more – a capability which earned the B-52 its official name Stratofortress – even though it didn't quite reach those dizzy heights. It was a good name, and in relative terms, sat well with its Boeing bomber predecessors' names of Flying Fortress, Superfortress and Stratojet which had already earned their spurs. Phil Rowe, our eloquent EWO, recalled the wonder.

In the early days of jet planes, back in the 1950s, the skies above 25,000ft were uncrowded. Boy, that was nice. The few bombers and fighters who flew that high seldom had to worry about other traffic. What folks today now accept as normal high altitude cruising for commercial jetliners and numerous military aircraft, used to be unique and special.

It was the summer of 1957 when the 92nd Bomb Wing got its first brand new B-52Ds. Each of the three squadrons had but one airplane for months, though they'd eventually get 15 per unit. Newly trained flight crews took turns flying those enormous shiny birds. That was an exciting and fascinating time. The last of the 92nd's old B-36s were gone and learning the all-jet Stratofortress was a real challenge. It was great fun too. I remember well when cruising at 40,000 or even 50,000 feet was new territory, and how thrilling it was. There in the wild blue yonder, above the clouds, the weather and most other traffic, you could see for ever. The deep blue sky was almost unreal, unlike the murk at lower altitudes. Zipping along at 600 miles per hour, with the ground slipping along below us at more than eight miles per minute, the sensation was almost ethereal. Looking up at the stars from way up there invoked even more amazement. For me, it was awesome.

A unique and interesting phenomenon experienced back then, in the late fifties, was watching the sun rise in the west from 45,000ft. We were returning to our Washington State air base from Massachusetts, cruising across Canada's prairies, well above 50 degrees north latitude, when it happened. It was after sunset when we took off, but the farther north and westward we flew, the brighter the sky gradually became. Soon we noticed the sun rise ahead of us, from the west. That was weird. Yet, at that latitude and at our speeds, we were over-taking the setting sun.

On other flights, up and down the west coast of Oregon and Washington, we discovered other phenomena of interest. In the early evening, while watching the sun set over the Pacific, we learned that our high altitude twilight occurred almost an hour later than for folks on the ground. It was pitch black below us, but still light up where we were. That was quite something for those of us who'd begun our flying days in propeller-driven planes seldom going above 15,000ft. It's a wholly different experience at 40,000ft and higher. It's a shame that wonderment and awe are considered 'uncool' today.

There were, of course, serious aspects to high altitude flight – equipment checks were thorough, and crewmen were required to report at regular twenty-minute intervals, confirming they had taken a sip of oxygen. Cabin pressure was only half an atmosphere (7½lb psi) and 'hypoxia' could all too easily result without a supplemental intake, causing crewmen to lapse into unconsciousness. For special recce missions where the 'cruise climb' profile climaxed at 50,000ft, partial-pressure suits became the norm, with visors screwed in place above 45,000ft. But day-to-day practice bombing missions required just as much attention to detail:

Our new Stratofortress took off at dawn for a training flight from our Spokane, Washington air base. The weather was perfect, clear and crisp that October morning. After climb-out we levelled off at 30,000 feet to begin the first of two celestial navigation legs, each planned for about 1,200 miles. The first was to end near the air refuelling control point (ARCP) for a rendezvous with a KC-135 tanker.

Our tail gunner, Ken, faced aft in his own little cockpit, way back there about 100 feet behind the rest of us in that enormous winged aluminum wonder. His view of the world was where we had been, but at least he had one. The two navigators and the EWO didn't even have windows from which to view the bright blue skies or the magnificent western mountains of Montana down below. It was Ken's job to regularly initiate routine oxygen and interphone checks, reporting to the pilot, our aircraft commander, every half hour. Ken would declare, 'Gunner, oxygen check', to start the process. Then, in turn, each crew member would chime in with his crew position and the acknowledging words that all was working and the oxygen system was up to par.

After about two hours into the first celestial leg, Ken was uncharacteristically remiss in starting one of his oxygen check reports. But it wasn't until he was about ten minutes late than anyone noticed. That was the copilot, who inquired, 'Gunner. You okay back there?' The AC didn't seem too worried and suggested that old Ken was probably dozing, bored with the view or something. 'Hey, Ken? Wake up back there. Are you all right? Oxygen check, Ken.' But still no answer. Now the whole crew began to worry. Maybe he was asleep, or in trouble. It could be that his cabin pressure had failed and he had passed out for lack of oxygen. Or perhaps his oxygen supply had run out, a leak or some other problem. What was wrong back there?

The AC kicked the rudder pedals. That would shake the huge bomber's tail, tossing Ken left and right in his little rear-facing world. If Ken was asleep that would get his attention. Of course it would also jostle him about so that he'd spill his coffee or dump his meal, if he was eating back there. If he was merely asleep, or perhaps temporarily off interphone briefly to go to the 'can', that rudder jolt should get his attention and quickly have him inquiring, 'What the hell is going on?' Yet all was silent. Not a word from Ken. This could be serious. 'Better let down to low altitude, to where the air is thick enough to breathe and support life', the AC declared. 'Copilot, you get us traffic clearance for an immediate descent. Tell them that we've got an emergency situation.' While the copilot got on the radios to request descent clearance, the AC already started down. We'd have to descend to at least 13,000 feet. 'Navigator? What's the minimum safe altitude, clear of the mountains, for descent?' The AC commented too that he sure was glad that there were no clouds below us. He could descend in the clear.

'EWO, Phil. I want you to get ready to go back to check on Ken.' I'd kinda expected that and was already inserting my injection seat pins and doffing my parachute harness. I knew well what the job entailed, and answered, 'Roger. On my way down to the lower deck.' I would wait down below for word that we were low enough to no longer need cabin pressurization. It took about 15 minutes to get down to the safe altitude. I was waiting in the galley area, now on interphone next to the coffee jugs. In fact, I'd already gotten myself a cup of hot coffee and obtained a small portable, walk-around oxygen bottle to take with me.

'Okay, Phil. We're levelling off at 13,000ft now', announced my pilot. 'We're de-pressurizing the forward cabin, crew. Stay on oxygen, we may be at this altitude for a while.' The AC was reminding us that even at 13,000ft we'd still need some oxygen for a sustained period there. As soon as I felt the cabin pressure dumped, actually raising the pressure from 8,000ft equivalent to the actual 13,000ft, I opened the small hatch on the starboard side next to the galley. I was about to head aft along the little catwalk in the bomb bays and then climb into the '47 section' behind the aft wheel well. From there I'd work my way all the way aft to the gunner's compartment. Yes indeed, I was nervous. It was the first time that I'd taken that trip while we were airborne. I'd only done it once before, just for practice. And that was on the ground. But I crawled out there, with a flashlight in one hand and that walk-around bottle in the other, to go see what the matter was with Ken.

It was cold, dark and noisy back there in the bomb bay. I never realized just how noisy it would be, nor did I remember that everything would be so cold from our prior cruising at 30,000ft. But my mind was on two things. First and foremost I had to get back to check on Ken, and at that moment it was just as important to me not to fall off that narrow catwalk and plunge on to those bomb bay doors. They were all that stood between me and a heck of a fall.

Finally, and thankfully, I reached the entry to the 47 section. That huge section, of the fuselage controlled and monitored various aircraft systems. I ducked down below the huge metal boxes holding the chaff which is meant to confuse radars. And finally I got to the bulkhead and entry door to Ken's aft station. There was a small window in the door with a streak of sunlight.

I peered into Ken's world, that separate pressurized compartment. I could see Ken. He was in his seat, but he wasn't moving. Carefully, I reached for the lever which would de-pressurize his compartment, for unless I took that step it would be dangerous to open that door. The lower pressure of 13,000ft altitude in the 47 section would suck out the air in Ken's compartment, if I could even get the door open against whilst nodding his head. As I got within reach of him, we could talk to each other more easily. 'What the hell are you doing here?' he demanded. 'We didn't hear from you, Ken. We didn't know if you were dead or alive. Are you sure you're all right?' 'Yes, yes... I'm okay,' he responded. He grinned a little and continued, 'My interphone must be dead. I've called and called you guys, but got no reply.' 'Well, you'd better come forward with me. The AC and the crew are really worried. In fact, bring your stuff, 'cause you're riding up front the rest of this flight.' He nodded in agreement. Soon the two of us made the dark, noisy and cold journey forward. 'Pilot, radar. They're both coming forward. Ken's all right', the radar

B-52E 56-0640 of the 6th SAW landing at Walker AFB, New Mexico. The base operated three B-52 squadrons and a CCTS beginning in 1957. USAF via Thurlow

between the aft wheel well area and the tail gunner's compartment, was still thirty feet or more long. And that was the noisiest and darkest part of the journey. In the bomb bay, at least, I had some light from the crack between the big doors and a dim bulb on the wall. But back in the 47 section it was pitch black. My flashlight was essential. I was able to almost stand upright there, as I passed the racks of ECM transmitters, the numerous cables and black boxes which the differential pressure. I heard the whoosh of air as Ken's compartment de-pressurized and I could safely open the door.

Just as the air began to flow out noisily, Ken suddenly moved. He turned around and looked at me, surprised and startled, as an unexpected visitor entered his domain. We looked at each other for a few seconds. I shouted, 'Are you all right?' but in the din of noise back there I couldn't be sure that he had heard me. 'Yes,' he shouted back, operator reported over the interphone. 'Thank God, he's okay.'

Soon we re-closed the forward pressure hatch. The pilot once more pressurized the forward crew compartment, and all six of us could relax a bit. We climbed back up to cruise altitude and were able to still make our rendezvous with the tanker. All's well that ends well. But I sure as heck never wanted to make that journey aft again. It was no fun at all.

Tail Guns

Turret and associated equipment.

1. ammunition chuting
2. azimuth drive motor
3. azimuth magnetic brake
4. elevation servo pump
5. elevation relief valve
6. elevation drive motor
7. elevation magnetic brake
8. pressure sump
9. calibre 50 M3 machine gun (typical 4 places)
10. demand boosters
11. hydraulic filters
12. intermediate boosters
13. azimuth servo pump
14. azimuth relief valve
15. ammunition roller
16. breakaway joint

A 'quad 50' turret with side-skins removed for maintenance. Ammunition feed guides snake back to the M-3 guns. Frank Mormillo

Boeing's bombers, from the B-17E onwards, defended their tails with guns which were either manned by a 'tail-end Charlie' gunner or remotely controlled. A pair of 0.50cal machine guns was added to the rear end of the B-47B, controlled by the copilot using an A-2 fire control system (FCS) which gave him a radar scope in the rear cockpit, connected to a gun-laying radar above the gun position. He could fire the guns manually or rely on the ballistic computing capability of his A-2 system. Later B-47Es had a pair of M-24A-1 cannon instead and the improved General Electric A-5 FCS.

Although the necessity for guns in military aircraft was in widespread doubt it was decided on 21 October 1949 to revert to the 0.50cal gun (with modified Arma system) and the manned, rear 'turret' position for the B-52. Testing of the rear armament was conducted in RB-52Bs, using four M-3 'point fifties' in a quadmounted configured Bosch Arma turret. Initially, the A-3A FCS was tested and eventually installed in the B-52A, though RB-52B 52-0009 tested the twin M-24A-1 20mm installation of the B-47E, with the A-3A, as a stop-gap for a proposed 30mm twin-gun installation which, in 1950, would have been available for another five years. This 20mm fit, though with the later MD-5 FCS, was installed in thirty-three production B-52B/RB-52B aircraft, partly because of strikes and delays affecting Arma's 0.5 installation. The rest of the B-52B production run, most B-52Cs and a number of early B-52Ds, used the 'quad fifty' and A-3A set-up (63 units delivered). A later FCS, the MD-9 appeared in most B-52Ds from September 1955 and remained in use through the B-52E and B-52F series. The quad fifty arrangement was 'hard to maintain,' (according to a 1961 AFSC Report). 'Possibly the most persistent fault lay in ammunition feeding and the ejection of spent cases and links.

All the fire-control systems operated in a similar way. The gunner could select 'Search' mode, which enabled him to pick up fighters at 8,000 yards out. The 'Track' antenna could be locked on to a target from around 6,000 yards. The system enabled the gunner to break lock on target and switch to another quite easily. At optimum range he could then use the guns' total of 2,400 rounds to deter pursuers. If the radar 'went down' (as early sets so often did) the gunner could use a periscope sight for manual back-up.

With an effective range of 3,500ft each 'point 50' could pump out 750 rounds per minute velocity of 2,850fps. Although of World War II vintage the gun could still cause lethal damage to a thin-skinned fighter with relatively few 5.4 inch-long bullets. Ammunition was stored in a large rectangular tank which had to be winched out below the rear fuselage on two internal hoist cables for replenishment.

The gunner's compartment offered cramped accommodation and a view which was best through his 'greenhouse' roof and to the sides, but quite restricted in the rearward direction. His ride was lonely and uncomfortable, particularly in turbulent air when his position at the rear of the aircraft caused him to be thrown about more than the forward-cabin occupants. 'The "Boeing Bounce" is what they called the rough ride in "tall-tail" B-52s', recalled gunner Danny Burnett. 'The tail moved about three feet for every foot the nose moved and it was considered a sign of macho to have had a helmet cracked on your head from the ride. One of my friends had a cracked vertebra in his neck on one flight to go with his split helmet'. It is sobering to think that one gunner, M/Sgt Tolbert, flew 450 missions in Vietnam in those conditions.

Tail Guns

tions. On 'Guns' right side were controls for the chaff dispensers and on his left the handle which caused the whole of the turret, aft of his 'greenhouse', to separate cleanly from the aircraft and allow him to escape in an emergency. Lacking an ejection seat, the gunner simply leapt out of the hole left by the turret, making sure that he departed quickly before the aircraft adopted a nose-down trim attitude after losing a substantial chunk of its rear end. If the turret failed to fall away he had the somewhat dubious option of asking the pilot to lower the right landing gear, inching along the narrow walkway to the rear wheel well and dropping out past the huge undercarriage unit.

Major re-design of the airframe for the B-52G gave the gunner an ejection seat and re-located him to the main crew cabin (*see* Chapter 3). The 'quad 50' turret was retained (and all 30mm replacement gun project were cancelled) but with a new FCS using the AN/ASG-15 system with a search antenna covering 160 degrees (azimuth) and 120 degrees (elevation). The track antenna dish, viewing 25 degrees in azimuth and elevation was located, as it was on earlier versions, in the more pointed radome between the guns. Initially an RCA orthicon TV camera was installed in a transparent blister under the search radome to give visual back up to the radar and limited identification of targets. Capt Danny Burnett reckoned gunners found it 'only good for telling when the drag chute deployed on landing, or if the sun was out'. It was replaced by an AN/ALQ-117 antenna during the Phase VI ECM updates. During 1979 the STC modifications to the ASG-15, researched by Danny Burnett, replaced vacuum-tube electronics with 'nuclear-hardened' solid-state components. In the late 1980s B-52Gs were scheduled to receive the improved AN/ASG-33 FCS using a single search-and-track antenna in the upper radome 'lobe', giving a search range of 20,000yd (a distance which had only been possible against very strongly radar-reflective targets with earlier systems). This planned re-fit also offered electrical rather than pneumatic gun-charging and a VHS video recorder to store radar images from the FCS.

RB-52B (52-8713) exhibits the flattened lobe of its A-3A fire-control system and the twin M-24A-1 20mm cannon fitted to thirty-three B-52B/RB-52Bs. USAF via Thurlow

---

SAC eventually discontinued the airborne alert missions. They were horrendously expensive, wore out planes and equipment, and really only protected a fourth of the bomber fleet. It was limited nuclear deterrence at best.

As early as September 1959 a Joint SAC and Air Materiel Command team concluded that maintaining the airborne Alert system at full tempo for the next five years would cost $4 billion. A series of 'off the shelf' airborne alert concepts were evolved instead by that November, including '1/8th Alert' and '1/16th Alert' – downsized to '1/39th Alert' system in December 1960, involving a dozen sorties a day, and implemented from January 1961 under Operation *Coverall*, later Operation *Clear Road*. Implementation was at the discretion of 'higher authority' (the President and Joint Chiefs of Staff), and was put into effect during times of tension. The practice continued until 1968 when *Chromedome* was discontinued in favour of round-the-clock Intercontinental Ballistic Missile silo alert.

Only a Few More 'Tall Tails'

Castle AFB continued to host crew training, this momentous task being undertaken by the three resident Bomb Squadrons while simultaneously holding down the 'RB-52 mission' and absorbing B-52D models. In turn, the resident CCTS shifted more towards ground academics and administrative support. The Wing would continue to accomplish this training feat well into the future.

Specification – B-52E	
Dimensions:	Length 156.58ft (47.73m); height 48.25ft (14.71m); wingspan 185ft (56.39m); wing area 4,000sq ft (371.2sq m); tailplane span 52ft (15.85m); main undercarriage track 11.3ft (3.4m); outriggers 148.45ft (45.25m); distance from top of fuselage to ground 17.45ft (5.32m)
Operating weights:	Empty 172,720lb (78,346kg); combat 291,750lb (132,338kg); max take-off 450,000lb (204,120kg)
Fuel capacity:	41,550 USgal (226,664l)
Performance:	Max speed 551kt (1,021km/h) (at 20,000ft/6,096m) Service ceiling 46,200ft (14,082m) Combat radius 3,320nm (6,148km) Take-off run 8,000ft (2,438m) (at sea level, typical)

Engine power:

Engine	Thrust (lb) (wet)	Thrust (lb) (dry)
J57-P-29W/WA or J57-P-19W	12,100	10,500

Armament and bombing/navigation systems (original configuration):

Guns	Fire control system	Bomb/nav
4 × 0.5 M-3	MD-9	AN/ASQ-38(V) AN/ASB-4A, MD-1 AN/APN-89A, AJA-1

By December 1957, inventory strength had leaped from 97 to 243 big shiny fellahs. The same month the 6th BW at Walker AFB at Roswell, New Mexico – coincidentally, the sixth Bomb Wing to form with Stratofortresses, and the last to adopt a three-squadron force comprising an AUE of forty-five aircraft – began to equip with the new B-52E. This model, which first flew on 3 October 1957, was outwardly similar to the B-52D but featured many on-line improvements to ECM, and more significantly a new AN/ASB-4 analogue radar navigation and bombing computer, which formed the heart of its new AN/ASQ-38 Offensive Weapons System.

The Q-38 represented a quantum jump over the older MA-6A, chiefly because it represented a truly integrated system. Originating with Perkin-Elmer, a research and development company, the core AN/ASB-4 computer was designed to be both lighter in weight than its predecessor and offer modular architecture, to facilitate maintenance needs and soon became known as 'black boxes'. Instead of using manually inserted data derived from other sensors it was interfaced with them, among which was the Raytheon search and tracking radar that was boresighted with the GPL Doppler radar. This provided ground track angle and ground speed data plus autopilot, gyro (for aircraft attitude), bomb damage assessment camera, astrocompass, temperature and pressure sensors (to furnish airspeed and altitude) and an all-important ballistics data storage system which held the characteristics of the B-52s' various weapons. Radar bombing crosshairs and navigation read-outs were similarly linked in the cockpit, making it easier to locate targets on radar and to update the navigation computer by means of button-pushing.

The fledgling IBM, under the skilful leadership of its founder, T. J. Watson Sr, constructed the AN/ASB-4 and integrated it with the other subsystems at its new purpose-built Owego, New York Military Products Division, while Boeing was responsible for installing the complete Q-38 computer and sensor suite on its production lines. Curiously, its modular design enabled the engineers to package the electrical components into off-the-supermarket shelf metal cans originally designed for beer, fruit or vegetables! It saved a great deal of money. Relay frames joined the 'beer cans' together, interconnected with cables with blowers keeping the valves from sizzling. Operational flight tests were initially performed on a B-47 at Lake Charles, Louisiana, in time for the system to be incorporated into B-52E production. It was installed as standard on all subsequent production and retrofitted into earlier builds, with all surviving B-52Ds receiving the upgrade.

Capt Robert F. Newton, after qualifying in the MA-6A-configured Stratofortress, was sent back to bombing school to be taught the ASQ-38 system for operational assignment to the new B-52E. 'Compared with the MA-6A the ASQ-38 system was a totally electronic system. It featured a fifty-mile [radar] crosshair range [double that of its predecessor], and a Doppler radar that automatically killed the drift and kept the crosshairs on target, plus two offsets to cross-check your accuracy. All the components came in containers and could be replaced in flight with spares we carried onboard. We called it "beer can" maintenance.' His impressions of the aircraft were very positive. 'I was absolutely thrilled at being able to fly on [the B-52] and sitting down in that dark hole working my head off posed no problem for me. In fact, if they asked me to go back and do it again I wouldn't even pack my bags; I would go to the nearest base and say, "Take me, I'm yours". Now some people did have a problem with it, but these people were lousy navigators and, as the saying goes, they couldn't find their rear end with both hands. The difference between working with the MA-6A and the ASQ-38 was like night and day. Most functions with the old system had a lot of manual work involved and with the new system you just entered the information and pushed a button to update everything.'

Bombing techniques were expanded too. 'Primarily we used the radar bombing system to drop one or multiple drops on high or low targets. There were several cities and towns designated with several targets. We did not drop anything. Everything was scored by Radar Bomb Scoring sites tracking us in and we turned on a radio tone. When the tone stopped, a needle lifted off a chart and we called down several pieces of information so that they could score in feet and direction and how close we came. The next technique we used was heading and timing where the targets were too close together for the radar navigator to acquire the second or third target. We did this by me giving the pilot the heading after the first drop and starting a stop watch. Then at the right time we would break the tone and get a score. I got so good at this that I could actually beat my RN's score which just about drove him up the wall!'

The dramatic demise of B-52D 55-0102, burned out in a ground fire at Loring AFB in June 1958. USAF via Thurlow

Low-level target ingress tactics down to 500ft AGL began to be honed in earnest with the introduction of *Oil Burner* (later *Olive Branch*) Strategic training routes established over sparsely populated areas, to which electronic scoring systems would be added so that the crews' performance – navigation timing and bombing accuracy – could be scrutinized based on RBS techniques, as just described. The sites encompassed training corridors set aside in cooperation with the FAA, and were formally announced in 1959. Most exist to this day, though it is important to appreciate that high altitude cruise to the let-down coordinates and en-route AAR (air-to-air refuelling) replenishment remained contrail-generating exercises. Short and terrifying low-level excursions were part-and-parcel of the mission, when the aircraft would bend and creak like jet galleons.

Robert Newton continues. 'The last technique we used was fixed angle bombing. This was where we picked up a target, and by correcting direction and using a stop watch, we could literally talk the plane into the right position to make the drop without using the computer. On one mission we had twenty simulated drops. For the second drop we got a boondocker (bomb score out of the magic circle). We knew we had to make up for it on the rest of the mission and we did so by getting four shacks (a bomb exactly on target) which is the equivalent of hitting "four home runs" in one ball game. We did this by using all the techniques described above. Another amusing thing that would happen was that the radio tone would fail. We corrected this by taking a deep breath and whistling into the radio until the equipment indicated a bomb drop. You can imagine how we struggled for breath towards the end. If you want to try it, just try whistling for twenty seconds.'

'The way to describe the workload on these practice missions is hours of boredom interspersed with moments of panic. The typical practice mission lasted ten to twelve hours. It was called a profile mission because we did everything in the same order as it was a real war mission. We would take off and then meet a tanker and take a token load of fuel. Then we would do a two-hour celestial leg ending up at the entrance to a low-level route with two hours of low level navigation ending up at an RBS site and then make some bomb runs.' The periscope sextant used in previous models had also given way to a new automatic astro-tracker supplied by Kollsman (which apparently was removed when it was discovered that when insects impacted the dome its performance was degraded severely). 'When flying at low level we flew about 280kt and stayed straight and level (about 500ft above the terrain) until we

From March, 1964 the Air Mail deployments by Reflex B-47s to Guam were taken over by B-52Bs of the 22nd BW and 95th BW. USAF via Thurlow

1950s Era B-52-compatible Nuclear Bombs

The USAF was in the process of transitioning from atomic to more powerful thermonuclear gravity weapons at the time of the B-52's introduction in 1955, and thus both categories were employed at the beginning of the aircraft's career.

The early atomic and thermonuclear devices had to be armed in-flight using manual assembly procedures, customarily the responsibility of the navigator. Capt Robert Newton recalled that 'the first weapon I would have carried was the Mk 4 atomic bomb. It was rated at about 50 kilotons and we carried two internally. It was armed manually by going into the bomb bay in flight, taking a ball of radioactive material mounted on a cone out of a container called the birdcage, screwing it on the end of a pole and inserting it into the nose of the bomb. Then we took the pole off and inserted a block of high explosives into the empty space and put the nose shield back on. We had to practice this technique quite frequently on the ground. The next weapon (Mk 5) was essentially the same except they had an electro-mechanical device that did the same thing we did manually to arm the bomb.' Arming was accomplished on receipt of the 'go code', which authorized the crew to cross the Arctic Circle and proceed to their targets. The AC would depressurize the cabin (the bomb bay was unpressurized), having previously shut down the air conditioning system, which quickly turned the aircraft into a deep freezer for its occupants. Repressurization would then ensue after arming.

A retard or drogue parachute was later added to most thermonuclear weapons so that the crew could egress the drop zone to evade the weapon's shockwave. More complex, automated fuzing options came with later weapons, and are described in Chapter 5.

Mk 4/5 Latter entered National Atomic Stockpile May 1952. Weight approx. 3,150lb. 150 built. *See* above for further details.

Mk 6 Entered stockpile July 1951. Weight approx. 8,000lb. 60 kiloton yield. Two in bomb bay. 1,100 built through 1955. In the stockpile until 1963.

Mk 15 Entered stockpile April 1955. Thermonuclear (hydrogen) bomb measuring some 12ft long with weight approx. 7,600lb. 3.75 megaton yield. Two in bomb bay. 1,200 built through early 1957. Retired 1965. First live weapon to be dropped from a B-52, during Operation *Redwing Cherokee* on 21 May 1956. Retired during 1965.

Mk 17/24 First thermonuclear weapon for the B-52, based on the equally short-lived B-36 Peacemaker's *Mk 14*. 20ft-long and weight approx. 43,000lb. 15 megaton yield. One only in bomb bay. The two models used different triggers but were otherwise similar.

Mk 36 Parachute-retarded derivative of the Mk 21. Entered stockpile April 1956. 12ft-long and weight approx. 17,500lb. 9–10 megaton yield. Two in bomb bay. 275 converted from Mk 21s for use by B-52s, alongside approximately 675 new builds. Ousted Mk 17/24 interim thermonuclear heavyweights but retired by January 1962.

Mk 39 Drogue-parachute version of Mk 15, later adapted with 'laydown' retard parachute as the Mod 2, of which 700 were built between 1957 and 1959. Weight approx. 9,500lb. Retired during 1966.

Another gleaming '52 emerges from the factory. In the foreground, a B-52F has its scoop-like drag 'chute door open. To the right of that is the open rear fuselage entry door and to its left, an ammunition bay access door. Guns are yet to be installed.
Boeing

made our bomb runs. Occasionally we would make high speed runs at 325kt and it became a real wild ride. Just as I was leaving they started getting terrain avoidance radar and we humped and dumped over the hills and mountains and it became a real roller-coaster ride.'

This radar enhancement was incorporated as part of Project *Big Four* – which included installing an updated search radar and reorientating the Bomb-Nav-System with extra modes for the low-level 'legs' of the mission, by means of a newly developed terrain-avoidance computer and associated terrain displays for the AC and copilot, known as the 'dark face tube' and showing a lingering trace of the profile of the terrain ahead. Doppler processing was similarly improved to provide more accurate drift and velocity feedback and new low altitude radar altimeters were added. Initiated in 1959, it took four years to complete, but was essential to low-level prowess.

Structural improvements were also needed to match the new low-level portion of the mission, which although modest in the overall profile, placed a disproportionately huge strain on the airframe, particularly in terrain-hugging operations over rugged topography where factors such as mountain turbulence could literally tear an aircraft apart. B-52D 56-0591 *Tommy's Tigator*, a heavily instrumented Hardtack nuclear bombing trials veteran, was bailed to Boeing to wring-out stresses incurred in low-level flight. Sadly, and unpredictably, it crashed on 23 June 1959 in severe turbulence and all aboard perished. The crash investigators concluded that the horizontal stabilizers had been overstressed and broke at 425kt, resulting in loss of control. The Stratofortress's 'red line' was subsequently reduced to 390kt Indicated Airspeed (or

Unusually tight formation by a pair of B-52Es on a low-level exercise at Nellis AFB in the late 1950s. USAF via Thurlow

Specification – B-52F	
Dimensions:	Length 156.58ft (47.73m); height 48.25ft (14.71m); wingspan 185ft (56.39m); wing area 4,000sq ft (371.2sq m); tailplane span 52ft (15.85m); main under carriage track 11.3ft (3.4m); outriggers 148.45ft (45.25m); distance from top of fuselage to ground 17.45ft (5.32m)
Operating weights:	Empty 172,150lb (78,087kg); combat 291,750lb (132,338kg); max take-off 450,000lb (204,120kg)
Fuel capacity:	41,550 USgal (226,664l)
Performance:	Max speed 553kt (1,025km/h) (at 20,000ft/6,096m) Service ceiling 46,000ft (14,020m) Combat radius 3,345nm (6,195km) Take-off run 8,000ft (2,438m) (at sea level, typical)

Engine power:	Engine	Thrust (lb) (wet)	Thrust (lb) (dry)
	J57-P-43W/WA/WB	13,750	11,200

Armament and bombing/navigation systems (original configuration):

	Guns	Fire control system	Bomb/nav
	4 × 0.5 M-3	MD-9	AN/ASQ-38(V) AN/ASB-4A, MD-1 AN/APN-89A, AJA-1

0.90 Mach, whichever came first), while Boeing and the IRAN Depots continued to evolve safety enhancements for the airframe under carefully drafted Engineering Change Proposals (ECPs), to beef-up the airframes – measures which still exist to this day, although monitored in concert with ultrasonic sounding and other techniques requiring minimal airframe dismantling.

With Global reach within their grasp the 'Knights of the Stratosphere' never seriously undertook overseas alert in those days, *Reflex* being an assignment of the shorter-legged Boeing B-47 force which, with hindsight, shone and faded like the strike of a match. One hundred B-52Es were built (fifty-eight at Wichita and the remainder in Seattle), the last three being accepted in June 1958, also equipping the 11th BW at Altus AFB, Oklahoma from January 1958, the first of three Wings with an AUE of thirty aircraft and two squadrons apiece.

Production very rapidly switched to eighty-nine of the 'F' which made its debut on 6 May 1958 and closed-out production of the 'tall tail' series, with the first operational examples deployed to the the 7th BW at Carswell AFB, Texas, in the Spring, followed by the 2nd BW at Barksdale AFB, Louisiana, during August (the last three of the pioneering Bomb Wings to form, all nominally assigned thirty aircraft each). More significantly, the forty-fourth Seattle-built 'F' signalled the end of B-52 production there, allowing the Plant to focus on the KC-135 Stratotanker and allied commercial aircraft production, which would establish them as the premier international jet airliner manufacturer.

Chiefly, the Foxtrot model differed from its predecessors in that the dangerous air-driven alternators were replaced by hard drive versions built into the port side of each pair of its uprated J57-P-43 equipped engine pods, the cost of which was doubtless absorbed in its fly-away price of $6,485,404 a copy. Otherwise, it was a B-52E.

Earlier models were progressively upgraded with this package during IRAN (Inspect and Repair, as Necessary) major overhauls, alongside field installation kits undertaken by Air Material Command. IBM Q-38 Contract Technical Services Personnel (CTSP) teams handled the avionics upgrades and support, making the aircraft a much more capable one and greatly homogenizing the operational fleet's avionics.

Veteran crews remained astonished at the growth rate in new systems (always

Former Crew Chief Alvin Atkins, recalled, 'We would fly our low-level bomb runs through the valleys between the mountains in Tennessee and Kentucky at night at about 800ft. One of our planes came back with what looked like a 30-30 bullet hole through the horizontal stabilizer. It had missed a control cable by half an inch.' Boeing via Chesneau

resulting in reams of new paperwork to digest), and also at how much the IRAN process, in particular, really involved substantial 'tear-downs'. In reality, there always existed several B-52 plants to meet the workload – two, then one, putting them together to begin with, and at least two taking them apart and putting them back together again, the latter under Air Force jurisdiction. Depot maintenance was initiated as early as April 1956, as Project *Sunflower* at Boeing Wichita, and

B-52D 55-0093 sails serenely through clear skies on a pre-delivery flight. Its relatively brief service career ended in July 1958 when it crashed on approach to Loring in very different weather. Boeing

High and Mighty – the North American X-15

Built of stainless steel and titanium with a skin of nickel alloy called Iconel-X, (melt point: 1,200 degrees F), the extraordinary X-15 research craft was designed for speeds of Mach 3.5 above 100,000ft, partly to investigate the problems of surface heating from air friction. The short duration of the rocket motors used to power many of the X-series research aircraft necessitated an air launch from a larger aircraft. For the X-15 the Convair B-36 was nominated as mother-ship, but it was close to retirement by the time the X-15 was ready to fly. Instead, the B-52 was proposed, partly because the X-15's Reaction Motors XLR-99 rocket powerplant was running late and the early flights had to be made with a pair of the less powerful LR-11 motors used in the Bell X-1. With the B-52's advantage in height and speed the shortcomings resulting from a total thrust of only 17,000lb were somewhat mitigated. The B-52's undercarriage configuration meant that the usual under-belly mounting for the X-craft had to be replaced by an underwing pylon for the X-15A. This arrangement forced the pilot to enter his confined cockpit before take-off, rather than just prior to launch and it denied him the chance of scrambling back into the mother-ship in the event of a fire on engine ignition, as had happened on several previous X-launches. The specially designed pylon was located between the inner starboard engine pod and the fuselage.

Curtis LeMay was reluctant to release any operational B-52s from his burgeoning SAC Wings so one of the three B-52As (52-0003, later named The *High and Mighty One*) and RB-52B 52-0008, were selected in 1959 and became an NB-52A and NB-52B respectively. Modifications included a liquid hydrogen tank in the B-52 to top up the X-15A's fuel supply as it boiled off on the climb to launch altitude, a long jettison pipe for the fuel behind the B-52's forward undercarriage bay and two 'blisters' on the starboard side of the forward fuselage. One was an observation port and the other housed cameras to record the launch. A slot was cut in the right wing's rear edge to accommodate the X-15's thick tail fin.

Free-fall gliding tests from the B-52 began on 8 June 1959 after a series of flight tests 'on the pylon'. The first powered flight followed in September 1959 but a rear fuselage fire in the X-15A caused extensive damage. Fifteen flights were made by the B-52s and their pyrotechnic payload that year, though only one achieved all its objectives. Nine were total aborts. However, thirteen successful launches were made in the first four months of 1960 using B-52 crews which included an RAF exchange officer, Sqn Ldr J. Miller. The first ground test of the XLR-99 motor in X-15A 56-6672 was carried out by Scott Crossfield in June. A fuel system fault caused an explosion which took the forward fuselage containing Crossfield (who survived) on a brief twenty-foot journey at a measured acceleration of 50g. The second X-15A was retro-fitted with the new engine instead, flying in November 1960 and completing two years of successful tests which included a speed record of 3,063mph and a record altitude of 169,000ft on 30 March 1961. By April 1962 these had been superseded by a new record of 246,700ft and on 27 June Joe Walker hit 4,159mph in an X-15A. Walker qualified for astronaut's wings on 17 January 1963 having climbed above fifty miles to reach 271,000ft. However, his best was to follow on 19 July when he blasted off from his NB-52 to reach 347,800ft.

In order to increase potential speed and altitude still further two large fuel tanks were added under the X-15 containing liquid hydrogen and anhydrous ammonia, allowing an extra fifty-five seconds burn time and acceleration to speeds close to 5,500mph. As the X-15A-2 this variant first flew on 28 June,1964. After the conclusion of the very successful X-15 programme on 24 October 1970 both NB-52s continued in NASA service as launch aircraft for a wide variety of powered and unpowered underwing research craft. NB-52A 52-0003 ended up at Pima Museum while NB-52B 52-0008, which first flew on 11 June 1955, remained in service in 1997 after thirty-eight years in its unique role. Of the 199 X-15 launches, 106 were made from '008. It also launched 128 of the 144 wingless lifting body flights leading to the Space Shuttle and conducted drag 'chute and booster rocket recovery trials for that programme. Additionally, it was responsible for F-111 capsule 'chute tests and Pegasus space booster missions (it is the first aircraft to send a satellite into Earth orbit). Although '008 is kept going, sometimes with parts scavenged from museum B-52s, it has under 3,000 hours flying time and could provide many more years of service.

The High and Mighty One **lifts off with its X-15 payload.** USAF via Ron Thurlow

concurrently under Project *Yellow Rose* at San Antonio Air Materiel Area, at Kelly AFB, Texas, with eleven aircraft refurbished under Fiscal Year 1957 funds, the start of a huge rework programme.[5]

IRAN also included a new paint job, including enlarged US Air Force logos and the hallmark anti-flash white introduced on the bellies of the B-52Cs. 'It always looked great until a Stratofortress stumbled into an icy thunderstorm, when the white peeled and chipped and in a single mission the jet would return looking as if a hundred gremlins with little chisels had vandalized the paintwork.'

Dispersal of SAC's 'Big Wings' across many more bases from 1957 onwards, to complicate the USSR's ICBM targeting, meant that further B-52 production was diverted to twenty-two Strategic Wings created between 1957 and 1959 and scattered around CONUS, each operating a solitary fifteen aircraft-strong bomber squadron, supported by its own tanker squadron. The first to form was the 4123rd SW at Carswell AFB, Texas on 10 December 1957. Of the Bomb Wing establishments, all but the training nuclei at Castle – and 6th BW at Walker, which with its newer Q-38 aircraft was one of the first to prepare crews for the low-level, radar-evading tasking for stand-off semi-covert missile launch – were similarly downsized to mostly just one squadron of bombers each, helping to 'feed' these many new SWs with their spare two squadrons' worth of B-52s. This also eased-in the similarly expanding KC-135 Stratotanker cadre by permitting the SWs to absorb these without placing undue stress on the new tanker crews, who could work-up alongside their bomber compatriots. The civil engineering impact was massive too, with a huge runway-lengthening programme spanning the United States that almost matched Roosevelt's 1930s impetus in terms of men at work and concrete mixed and poured.

The operational inventory continued to soar, with 488 B-52s on strength by the end of 1959, the year when SAC reached peak aircraft strength with a staggering 3,207 aircraft, maintained and flown by just over 262,600 officers and airmen.[6] Stratofortress strength, however, was still rising with the addition of two more, but rather different models, in which the gunner's station would be moved up to the main double-decker cabin complex, where he could fire his tail guns by remote control and share coffee with the rest of the crew.

Sidewinder Shoot-down

On 7 April 1961 B-52B 53-0380 *Ciudad Juarez* rose from the runway at Biggs AFB, Texas with Capt Don Blodgett in the left seat. It completed the first navigation leg of its training sortie and then prepared itself to offer some interception practice for a pair of F-100A Super Sabres of the 188th TFS, New Mexico ANG, the first Air Guard unit to fly the type. 1st Lt James W. van Scyoc and Capt Dale Dodd received instructions from *Blush First*, their ground control interception station, to steer towards the B-52's position as it approached Albuquerque and complete their armament safety checks. Each F-100A, with its smart black and yellow 'sunbeam' markings, carried a pair of AIM-9B Sidewinders on a dual pylon under its left wing.

After five simulated missile passes followed by tail-chase gun 'attacks' van Scyoc, the 188th's Safety Officer, hauled his fighter round for a final Sidewinder practice. He was closing with the bomber when his No. 2 AIM-9B suddenly left its rail, homed on to the B-52's left inboard engine pod and exploded, severing the wing. Capt Blodgett, who had always had reservations about these intercepts, explained to the authors what happened then:

I heard van Scyoc call, 'Look out! My missile's fired'. We were on autopilot and I grabbed the controls just as the missile hit. There was a tremendous shudder and the aircraft banked left steeply. Electrical equipment in the right side of the cockpit caught fire. My copilot ejected with the aircraft in a 90 degree bank and in all the confusion I didn't realize he had gone. I tried to reach the alarm bell control between the two seats to order the crew to bale out, while holding the controls with my left hand to maintain full right aileron and rudder. I didn't realize the wing had gone and the aircraft wasn't responding at all; it began to spin down into the clouds and I still wasn't sure that I had hit the alarm. Later, my crew chief said he had seen the red light flashing as he sat on the steps to the lower cabin. With g-forces building up tremendously, pinning me to my seat I could not raise my right hand from its position near the bale-out alarm but could move it sideways to the ejection handle. The hatch fired and the seat threw me up fifty feet with the B-52 at 600kt. The slipstream tore off my helmet as I left the aircraft. There was another explosion and I went through a ball of fire – it felt like being in an oven. Immediately after that I went through a 'bath' of JP-4 fuel as the fuel tanks had broken up in this second explosion. At least this put out the fire but now I was soaking wet with fuel and still on the ejection seat. Assuming a seat malfunction (they told me afterwards I was holding on to it) I reached out to unfasten the lap belt when suddenly I flew out of the seat. However, the interphone cord wrapped around my left leg so now I was going down through the clouds with a 650lb seat hooked to my leg. I thought it would rip my leg off and I managed to claw the cord free. By now I was falling in a cloud of debris – and a blizzard. I released my survival gear pack, which also automatically released the survival raft. This was suspended about 40 feet below me and, with all the updraughts in the clouds due to the bad weather it acted like a sail, pulling me round in a 180 degree arc. I thought, if I hit the ground sideways, this is it! I couldn't get to my knife to cut it free but I soon got out of the turbulence and began to fall straight.

When I ejected, my left arm hit the hatch putting a big gash in it. The blood was pouring out of this and I was holding this with my right hand, trying to stop the bleeding. Suddenly I saw something white and I hit the ground in a downswing of the parachute and a 30kt wind. It felt like jumping off a two-storey building. I hit so hard that everything in my survival kit; the radio, mirrors etc. was broken apart from the survival rifle. My original intentions were to get the radio going and tell that fighter pilot what I thought of him! I thought everybody must be dead except me. I was still soaked in JP-4, in a 30kt wind at 30 degrees F. I was cold! I tried to stand but when I put my weight on my right foot there was excruciating pain. I found later that I had knocked a two-inch piece out of my pelvis. Also, when I hit the ground I landed on my left arm. There was cactus and pine needles on the ground which packed the wound with needles stopping some of the bleeding. I was going to start a fire but couldn't get the matches to work – which was a good thing as I was still soaked in fuel. I lay there and looked at my watch which had stopped at 12 noon when I hit the ground. I kept firing a three-shot distress signal with the rifle every so often. At 3pm a figure came towards me and I recognized my gunner, S/Sgt Ray Singleton who had landed in a tree half a mile away. He had third degree burns to his hands and face and I put the socks from my survival kit on his hands. He helped me a little further up Mount Taylor [on which they had landed at 7,500ft rather than the 4,000ft Don originally assumed] and we laid out our 'chutes. At 5.30pm the cloud cover opened up and at that moment a T-33 flew directly overhead and saw us. I guess you could call it a miracle. In about 30 minutes an HH-43 helicopter picked us up.

Just as they took off Ray spotted another parachute belonging to the EWO, Capt George D. Jackson, who had fractured his back. All three were flown to hospital. However, five other crew were still missing and assumed dead as van Scyoc had seen no parachutes. That night and most of the next day foul weather made searching impossible, though the bodies of the two navigators, Steve Canter and Pete Gineris were discovered in the 75ft-crater caused by the B-52's crash. Holes in their helmets indicated that they had died from hits by the Sidewinder's fragmentation warhead. Student EWO, Glen V. Bair, also died. Crew Chief S/Sgt Manuel Mieras, who was perched on the steps when the missile hit and had no idea how he got out, had broken a leg on landing, made a crutch and hobbled to a shepherd's hut where he played cards for 36 hours until rescued. The final crew-member, copilot Capt Ray C. Obel, had ejected at 30,000ft using his bail-out oxygen bottle to survive as a 150kt jetstream carried him much further down the mountain. He was found two days later with a fractured back.

The Board of Investigation found that a tiny amount of moisture had seeped into a cracked plug in the missile's firing circuit and although it had subsequently malfunctioned it had somehow allowed the firing signal to pass to a second missile. Don returned to service after ninety days and went on to a varied career in Flight Safety.

CHAPTER TWO

More Guts, Less Tail

Super Strat

When the last Seattle-built B-52, a B-52F (c/n 17467, serial 57-0072) was eased out of the factory on 24 February 1959 the company had already established a second production line at their Wichita, Kansas facility. There, a total of 1,644 B-29 Superfortresses had been assembled in a factory which was erected in 1943 as Plant II to relieve the Seattle line where the B-17 was still in production. Wichita began to turn out B-52s in 1955 as a second source for SAC's main bomber and manufactured sixty-nine B-52Ds, fifty-eight B-52Es and forty-five of the F model. No. 57-0072 was the 277th B-52 to be completed at Seattle, Stratofortress production then continuing exclusively at the Kansas site, where a switch was made to a substantially redesigned variant that Boeing had proposed during a period of phenomenally rapid progress in aircraft design.

In the mid-1950s, SAC had invested in the delta-winged Convair B-58A Hustler, a programme whose enormous cost restricted its numbers to only two operational Wings. Concern over the formidable technical and development difficulties posed by this sustained-supersonic, low-level penetrator prompted Boeing to explore the possibilities of an improved B-52 as a fall-back proposal. Initially, Boeing considered a B-52 with much more powerful J75 turbojets slung beneath a new wing. As the design team debated further revisions for this, the Model 464-253, from March 1956 onwards they also concentrated on revised crew stations but retained the basic airframe. Minimal funds were allocated to the study because it seemed that SAC would be able to engage in even more spectacular technical advances than the B-58A. To replace the B-52 after 1965 it envisaged a bomber powered by 'zip' fuel (ethyl borane), with supersonic dash capability, for which Boeing's WS-110A proposal was in competition with a North American design. A second long-range, supersonic-cruise bomber requirement (WS-125A) was allocated to Convair and based on massive nuclear engines. By mid-1957 this over-ambitious project had evaporated, defeated by the weight and shielding problems of an airborne nuclear powerplant, but the WS-110A competition was eventually won by North American in December, 1957.

B-52H 61-0023 hauling a pair of Hound Dogs, with all three wearing the white 'thermal reflective' finish specified in 1956. Boeing via Thurlow

Their extraordinary Mach 3 XB-70A Valkyrie bomber demonstrated some outstanding features but was eventually downgraded to a research programme in January 1962.

In the meantime, Boeing Seattle had refined their 'Super B-52', or B-52G, which was presented to the USAF on 15 August 1956 and approved by the Air Staff on 29 August. Their fall-back initiative had not been in vain. Although the USAF offered a 'minimum change' mandate, the B-52G included some significant internal changes reflecting new roles for the aircraft. Valkyrie was cancelled partly because at high-altitude even its Mach 3 performance would not protect it from the anticipated Soviet missiles. It was limited to Mach 0.9 at low altitude and it possessed no stand-off capability with the new air-to-surface missiles such as GAM-77 Hound Dog and GAM-87A Skybolt which were under development. Compromised as a high altitude bomber by the same highly effective Soviet defences as XB-70A the B-52 was re-configured as a stand-off missile launcher which could release a pair of Hound Dogs with large nuclear warheads up to 750 miles from the target. To reduce its vulnerability further the B-52 was substantially re-engineered to cope with the stresses of low-level penetrations with Hound Dogs and free-fall 'nukes', if the USAF pursued that strategy. Boeing's success in seeing the B-52 through this transitional period, with so many more glamorous though ephemeral options available to the USAF, was crucial in establishing the bomber as the grand old survivor which out-lived them all.

Boeing (Wichita) took on some impressive aims for the new B-52G. Essentially, they sought a 30 per cent range increase via a re-designed wing with integral fuel tanks and a 15,000lb reduction in empty weight. Maintenance man-hours were to be cut by a quarter and internal ECM improved considerably. The new 'wet' wing was a total re-design using 80ft-long sculpted and etched extruded panels bolted to the internal structure and sealed within to form fuel tanks between the forward and aft main spars. Creating fuel-tight spaces with the wing structure flexing at the tip in an arc measuring up to 18ft required some very effective sealant. Fuel capacity was increased to 46,000 gallons; 8,719gall more than the earlier bladder-type wing tanks. Initially, this was a selling point for the B-52G concept as it

Hound Dog

A B-52G with a pair of needle-nosed Hound Dog missiles underwing was an impressive sight. Each 10,150lb missile was really a pilotless jet aircraft as long as a two-seat TA-4F Skyhawk and powered by the Skyhawk's J52 engine. North American Aviation began development of this stand-off weapon in 1956 as Weapon System 131A, later designated GAM-77 and then AGM-28A. The first powered flight occurred on 23 April 1959, and by October the missile's Autonetics inertial guidance system had been proven in test flights using B-42E 56-0631 as launcher. Category III operational testing continued with B-52Gs when the weapon, nicknamed Hound Dog, joined the USAF on 21 December 1959 with the 4135th SW at Eglin AFB. The first production missile was launched on 1 March 1960. The type was eventually supplied to twenty-nine SAC units by the end of FY 1963 for use on B-52Gs and a number of B-52D, 'E and 'F variants with the appropriate pylons and control equipment. Service entry was relatively untroubled. One of the early proving flights covered 10,800 miles when an Eglin B-52G flew to the North Pole and then successfully launched its missile off the coast of Florida. SAC was convinced that its new side-arm could survive a trans-Polar combat mission to a Soviet target.

Hound Dog's underslung P&W J52-P-3 turbojet, developing 7,500lb of thrust at sea level, was a smaller version of the B-52's J57 engine. Its tanks could be filled from the B-52's own fuel system and the engines of both pylon-mounted missiles could occasionally be used to provide additional thrust for take-off, making the B-52 a ten-engined leviathan. (Lt Col Don Campbell remembered a copilot at McCoy AFB who managed to flame out all ten in a single mission, though not all at the same time.) Take-off use was restricted partly because the missile was prone to FOD damage. Its INS was linked to the bomber's navigation and astro-tracker systems and updated in flight or re-programmed to some extent. After release from its 'mother' it could fly up to 700 miles at speeds up to Mach 2.1 and altitudes of 500 to 55,000ft. Its stubby 12ft-span wing and canard foreplane made it manoeuvrable enough to jink in flight and divert towards other targets in feint attacks.

Accuracy was improved in the AGM-28B which had a better N-5G INS and a Kollsman astro-tracker fitted to the missile itself rather than the launch pylon. Hound Dog presented a very small radar signature and had a good chance of delivering its large W28 thermonuclear warhead in the target area. Meanwhile, the 'mother' B-52 could return to base without exposing itself to the enemy defences, or more likely follow up the missile in the hope that its explosion would have degraded those defences sufficiently for the bomber to release its own free-fall nuclear weapons.

Hound Dog remained in use until 1976, its career having been prolonged by the cancellation of the GAM-87A Skybolt and it replaced that weapon on the B-52H too until an alternative could be produced. Hound Dogs were initially white-painted and later received camouflage to match the B-52's 'low-level' scheme. They bore USAF serials in six production batches:

59-2791 to 59-2867 for XGAM-77 (77 built)
60-2078 to 60-2247 and 60-5574 to 60-5603 for AGM-28A (200 built)
60-6991 to 60-6699 for XGAM-77A (9 built)
61-2118 to 61-2357 and 62-0030 to 62-0206 for AGM-28B (417 built)

Total production was 703 units.

Capt Robert Newton flew as B/N on Hound Dog-equipped B-52s:

The copilot operated the engine and electrics and I programmed and launched the missile. We started the (J52) engine on the ground and kept it in 'idle ' for electric power to the missile for the entire mission. We never used them for additional take-off power because we had water augmentation and a typical take-off roll was 8,000 to 9,000ft. Hound Dog's purpose was to fly out ahead and destroy enemy fighter bases in our path. Programming was relatively easy once you got all the initial information entered. After that you picked out radar points and used the bombing cross-hairs to update its position. We were able to 'score' them by making a simulated launch and letting the missile guide just as if we were making a simulated bomb-run. We also 'dropped' them on very close targets which made for a 'double shuffle' when switching from one missile to the other. You knew it was near its target when the dials started running wild; you started a stop-watch and fifty-five seconds later you stopped the bombing radio tone. Every unit with Hound Dogs had to make an annual live launch at Eglin AFB. As far as I was concerned, for its time it was a wonderful thing to work with.

Don Campbell added, 'On training missions we'd take off, fire up the Hound Dog engines, programme them, simulate a launch, shut down the Hound Dogs and then land. We flew with it a lot and because we trained with it so much I really think we just wore them out. When I got into the ALCM business I remember saying that we screwed up the Hound Dog by flying it all the time and was told that this was recognized and was not going to happen with the ALCM.'

Lt Col Bob McAnally explained that, 'Each Hound Dog had a celestial navigation system on board with which you tried to acquire sight of a particular star for each system. We had a plotter that would advise navigators of what stars would be available for their headings, and whether or not the auto-sextant in the Hound Dog could acquire the stars. If you could get both of them to lock-on then you could use them to cross-check against each other. However, if you could only lock-on one missile you would have to cross-feed from one to the other and that automatically degraded some of the information because it was old analogue signals.'

Hound Dog-equipped B-52H 60-0017 with the 450th BW in the mid-1960s at Minot AFB. USAF via Thurlow

Low-slung Hound Dogs under this B-52G show why the use of their engines to boost the bomber's take-off posed a FOD risk. Boeing via Chesneau

was estimated that a range increase equivalent to an expensive KC-135 fill-up would greatly reduce operating costs, partly offsetting the $49m price label on each B-52G. In fact, the extra capacity was reduced to an overall 330 gallons of usable fuel when it was decided to replace the bulky 3,000gal external wing tanks. Non-jettisonable 700gal tanks were used instead and their function was partly to counteract flutter. Weight-saving of over 5,800lb in the wing structure came partly via the elimination of the normal aileron mechanism. Instead, lateral control was achieved by a set of seven hydraulically-operated, comb-like spoiler segments above each wing, operating in groups of four and three. For airbrake mode all segments could be raised in unison.

Much of the overall weight-saving came from a major re-design of the fuselage, despite a one-foot increase in length (to 147½ft) to house new ECM equipment. To reduce aerodynamic loads on the rear fuselage in low-level flight there was a 91-inch reduction in the height of the vertical stabilizer. This stubbier fin had been tested on the first B-52A. In practice, the short fin combined with spoilers-only lateral control induced a tendency to Dutch-roll and low level handling was more sensitive than on earlier B-52s. Raising the spoilers also caused a slight pitch-up movement which was considered a real problem for inexperienced pilots when flight-refuelling. A later modification (used on the B-52H) the 'Airbrake 1' position gave a 10 degree independent movement on the outer spoiler sections for minor corrections, particularly during flight refuelling. The spoilers were powerful control devices. A B-52G from Robins AFB (28th BS) was landed using only throttles and its spoilers after total failure of the elevator controls. This feat won Crew E-21 the Mackay Trophy for 1982.

Specification – B-52G

Dimensions:	Length 157.58ft* (47.73m); height 40.67ft (12.4m); wingspan 185ft (56.39m); wing area 4,000sq ft (371.2sq m); tailplane span 52ft (15.85m); main under carriage track 11.3ft (3.4m); outriggers 148.45ft (45.25m); distance from top of fuselage to ground 17.45ft (5.32m)

* Length with Phase VI ECM is 160.91ft (49.05m)

Operating weights:	Empty 158,737lb (72,003kg); combat 302,634lb (137,275kg); max take-off 488,000lb (221,357kg)
Fuel capacity:	47,975 USgal (261,713l)
Performance:	Max speed 551kt (1,021km/h) (at 20,000ft/6,096m) Service ceiling 46,000ft (14,020m) Combat radius 3,785nm (7,010km) Take-off run 8,150ft (2,484m) (at sea level, typical)

Engine power:

Engine	Thrust (lb) (wet)	Thrust (lb) (dry)
J57-P-43WB	13,750	11,200

Armament and bombing/navigation systems (original configuration):

Guns	Fire control system	Bomb/nav
4 × 0.5 M-3	ASG-15	AN/ASQ-38(V) AN/ASB-16, MD-1 AN/APN-89A, AJA-1

The design team's deliberations on revised crew quarters resulted in further weight saving. Cabin positions were re-organized around a 'battle stations' idea which moved the gunner from his traditional tail-end seat to a new, rear-facing position, with Weber ejection seat, alongside the EWO. The move required little re-organization of the forward crew compartment apart from the installation of a television link to the ASG-15 fire control system which replaced the previous optical and radar system. However, over 1,000lb was saved by removing all the troublesome oxygen, intercom, air-conditioning and pressurization lines to the old 'gun-turret', 130ft further aft. Reduced weight at the tail-end also lessened the aerodynamic load on the rear fuselage and enabled the brake chute compartment to be moved from under the tail-gun position to a new, upper fuselage receptacle behind the rudder. A 44-foot diameter ribbon parachute deployed from a canister fixed to the interior of an upward-opening door. In Capt Danny Burnett's opinion, 'the gunners almost universally thought it was

The presence of an F-86F chase-plane shows this to be an early test flight for the first B-52G (57-6468), later preserved at Offutt AFB with its appropriate nickname on retirement – Eldership. Boeing via Chesneau

a great idea to move the gunner forward. The rest of the crew usually would rather have had the extra eyes looking for people trying to kill them. The biggest drawback was that he now became chief of 'food services', picking up and delivering the flight lunches to the crew members since he was the least busy during a mission. There was a 'hot cup' at the gunner's position though it must have been put there for a contortionist or masochist as it required a good amount of twisting to reach it while strapped in or not.'

Crew comfort generally was enhanced by making the seats a little more bearable for long-range flights, increasing the provision for big, silver 'hot cup' dispensers of soup or coffee and revising the unpopular cabin heating system. Previously this had over-cooked the pilots while everybody else was sometimes numb with cold. Maj Rees Williams, who flew most B-52 variants, found that the B-52G, 'had better air-conditioning, and the cabin was more comfortable at high altitudes and low power settings'.

In addition, the opportunity was taken to automate and modernize a number of flight deck instruments and electrical systems. Folding rudder pedals could be stowed in deeper foot-wells allowing the pilot to rest his heels on the floor while taxying. Better forward visibility, especially for flight refuelling, resulted from lowering the floor, moving the pilots' seats and front panels forward a few inches and tilting the instrument panels a little. Pilots no longer had to strain backwards to view the flight refuelling process though it was still a very 'physical' business in the B-52G, with great stamina needed from the pilot to hold his aircraft in position for over half an hour while it absorbed up to 160,000lb of JP-4 fuel. Power setting adjustment during refuelling was done using throttles number 4 and 5 which stuck up higher than the others in the unique bunch of 'poker chips' which formed the B-52's eight-lever throttle array.[7]

Inevitably, there were still gripes among crews who had to spend so long in such confined working environments where it was virtually impossible to stand upright. The cabin heating, lack of storage space and cockpit lighting systems often aroused adverse comment. Both pilots were given slightly larger ejection hatch windows and electrically demisted cabin windows. A real electric oven could be installed rather than the microwave usually provided.

Another welcome bonus was a slightly more efficient urinal arrangement, though this was never exactly socially acceptable!

Although the J57-P-43B engines of late-model B-52Fs were retained in the B-52G, a revised water injection system was used, supplied from a larger 1,200gal tank of distilled water situated behind the gunner and EWO's positions. In most B-52 variants prior to the B-52H the enormous increase in noise caused by the use of water injection on take-off induced ultrasonic fatigue and cracking in parts of the flaps. Usually, 'water in' was selected at 86 per cent of throttle movement with the aircraft moving at around 70kt, giving a perceptible increase in acceleration as the full 110,000lb thrust from all eight engines was felt.

Water injection was restricted to outside temperatures above 40 degrees F to avoid freezing within the system. This was a disadvantage for SAC, many of whose bases were placed as far north as possible in the USA to shorten approaches to the trans-polar SIOP routes. Malfunctions in the system occasionally caused an excess of water to 'put out the fire' in an engine, necessitating an abort if this occurred around the 4,000ft marker on the runway. Dry take-offs were possible at a calculated 'dry capable' weight, usually somewhere below 360,000lb. Each engine pod had a single water pump serving both engines with coolant water so loss of a pump on a take-off over 'dry capable' limits meant an abort if pushing the throttle to the 'dry' engine pressure ratio (EPR) one more time did not re-engage the water. Decision time was 113kt or 'S One'. Water normally cut off after 110 seconds, sufficient to get the aircraft to around 1,500ft AGL with the flaps rolling in.

Boeing's original weight-reduction goal was more than realized with an overall saving of 15,420lb in empty weight. At the same time a 42,000lb increase in gross weight was possible, together with 900nm more range at altitude compared with the B-52D/F (rather less than the 30 per cent range increase originally desired). B-57G 57-6468, the first of the most-produced B-52 variant to be rolled out, was flown by Ray McPherson on 26 October 1958. In all, 193 B-52Gs came from Wichita, the last emerging from the factory on 23 September 1960 for delivery to the USAF on 7 February the following year. Travis AFB's 5th BW received the first service specimen on 13 February 1959 with the 42nd BW as the second unit to convert from B-52Ds.

Constant Alert

The short-tailed B-52G entered SAC squadrons at a time of considerable expansion. SAC's original production target of 603 B-52s, equipping eleven Bomb Wings, each with three squadrons, had been increased by Cold War pressures to 744 aircraft, sufficient for 42 squadrons. In order to present the USSR's ICBMs, the first of which had been test-launched in August 1957, with a more complex and demanding set of targets it was decided to disperse SAC's bomber resources across an additional thirty bases. The extra B-52s also made it possible to accelerate re-equipment of the remaining B-36, and some B-47 Bomb Wings. The build-up of B-52 Strategic Wings at thirty-eight air bases was completed by 1963. SAC's justification for the massive growth of its bomber and missile capability (ICBMs entered SAC service in 1959) was the supposed 'gap' in the number of these weapons compared with the USSR, which allegedly (though inaccurately) put the USA at a disadvantage. The bombers' main alert role was confined to the USA and constituted a major part of SAC's declared intention of having up to a third of its forces on 15-minute readiness at any given time. By mid-1961, President J. F. Kennedy was able to claim that a half of the bomber fleet could be put on alert status if required. Although this state of readiness varied and was periodically affected by other demands, notably the Vietnam War, it continued until 18 September 1991 when a general stand-down was ordered.

Capt Robert Newton flew in B-52Es before being assigned to the B-52G at Griffiss AFB: 'Once you completed training you were assigned as a crew to a specific base and given a crew number in the order that you were assigned there. After a check ride you became combat-ready and you would be assigned a war mission and go on full alert. The first target our crew was assigned was the Kremlin. What a shocker for a 2nd Lieutenant! The base alert facility had dining rooms, classrooms and recreation rooms above ground. The sleeping facilities were below ground, known as the Mole Hole or Rat Hole. We were on alert for seven days and then got three-and-a-half days off.' There were gradations of ground alert status. 'If it was an Alpha Alert you went to the aircraft and just reported in on the radio after you got

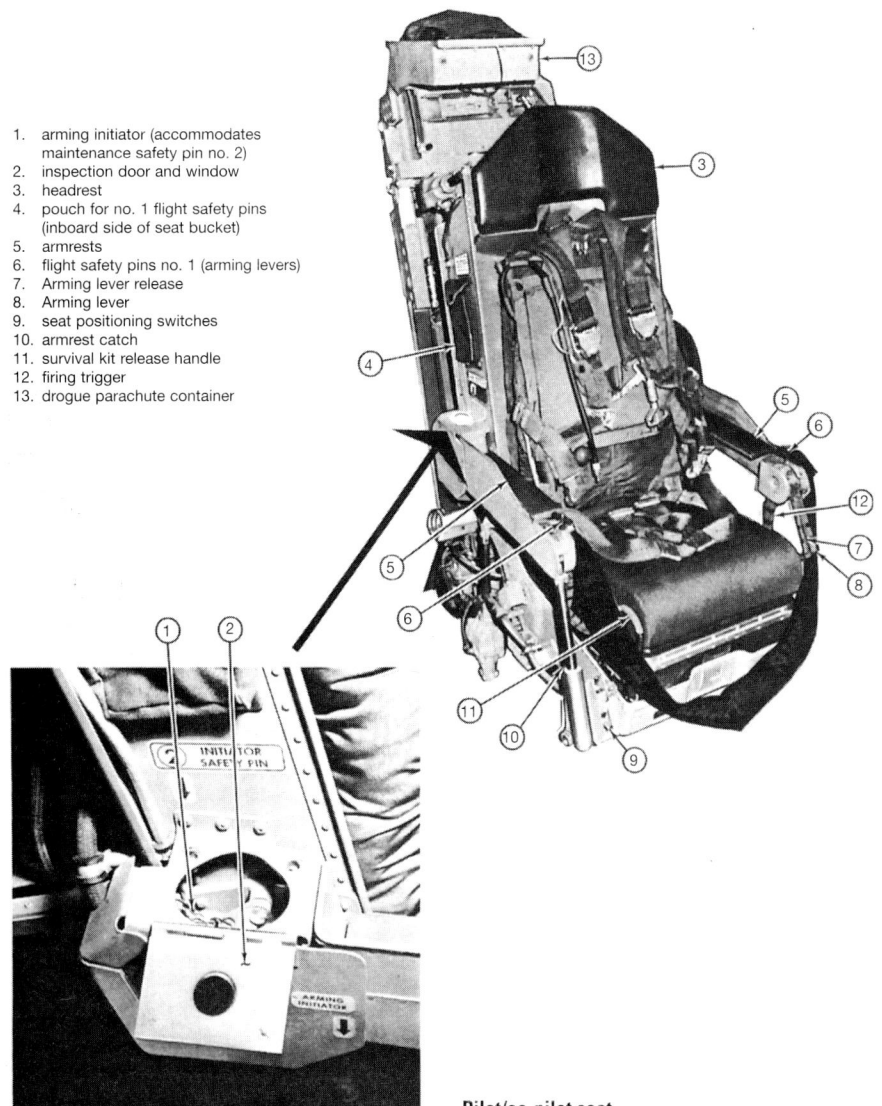

1. arming initiator (accommodates maintenance safety pin no. 2)
2. inspection door and window
3. headrest
4. pouch for no. 1 flight safety pins (inboard side of seat bucket)
5. armrests
6. flight safety pins no. 1 (arming levers)
7. Arming lever release
8. Arming lever
9. seat positioning switches
10. armrest catch
11. survival kit release handle
12. firing trigger
13. drogue parachute container

Pilot/co-pilot seat.

Jim Cichocki vividly recalled having to pre-flight aircraft at 2am in conditions where the wind-chill factor was measured in seconds and many men wore bandages on frostbitten hands. One of the most exposed jobs for an assistant crew chief was having to pre-flight from outside the aircraft with a headset but no other head protection. With only two of the base's five hangars available for the routine maintenance of thirty-two B-52s and KC-135s, most such work was done outside in all weathers. Jim rated re-packing the B-52H's drag chute as a particularly taxing job. Unlike the tall-tailed B-52s' it was stowed above the rear fuselage, requiring a tall working platform and several men.

Throughout the early 1960s between six and twelve airborne alert bombers were plying their monotonous routes over the Atlantic or north to the Arctic at any hour of the day or night. As a demonstration of the B-52's range capability Col T. R. Grissom flew a 5th BW example for 10,000 miles in 19hr 47min without refuelling during Operation *Long Jump* on 13 December 1960.

Cuban Crisis

If SAC ever needed justification for its colossally expensive airborne alert programme it had a perfect demonstration of its psychological value during the Cuban Missile Crisis of October 1962. Following Soviet Premier Nikita Kruschev's precipitate decision to base Il-28 'Beagle' bombers and SS-5 nuclear IRBMs in Cuba, a mere 100 miles from the American mainland, President Kennedy ordered a naval blockade of the island and the removal of the Soviet weapons. The missiles had arrived undetected because Kennedy had acceded to a Soviet request in July 1962 not to overfly Russian vessels in the area with reconnaissance aircraft. From 24 October, SAC's bomber and ICBM assets were committed, for the only time in the Command's history, to a full alert situation – DEFCON 2. (The next stage, DEFCON 1, was actual war.) Kennedy resisted pressure from the majority of his Emergency Cabinet for a major pre-emptive airstrike.

Don Blodgett flew one of the first of those sorties. 'I remember taking off for a 24-hour mission the night that President Kennedy announced the blockade. After pulling up the gear and starting to climb, I

the coded message. For Bravo Alert you started the engines and moved forward a couple of feet. If it was a Coco Alert you taxied to the runway, rolled down it to the first turn-off and taxied back to your parking spot. We hated Coco Alerts because it meant staying with the aircraft until they pushed it back into its spot, re-serviced it, fuelled it and fixed any problems. We had to stay there regardless of the weather or temperature and it generally took two hours. One time we had a blizzard and they told us the alert 'horn' would sound only if it was the 'Real Thing'. You guessed it – someone didn't get the word and in the afternoon the horn blew and we raced out to our planes. You can imagine the thoughts that go through your head when you think you are going to start a nuclear war.' Even the sombre business of nuclear alert duty had its lighter side though. 'Another thing we dreaded was having the horn go off when we were eating or in the shower. Once our ECM operator had just got to the shower and squirted green shampoo on his head when the horn blew. He raced back to the room, dressed and went to the aircraft. When he got there he ran upstairs and jammed on his helmet, forgetting the shampoo. He yelled and we all stared at him as ugly green slime oozed down his face.'

Alert duty was often an agonizing business for the OMS/FMS people. Working on B-52Hs at one of the most northerly and coldest bases, Grand Forks North Dakota,

ADM-20 Quail

One way of improving the B-52G's chances of survival over hostile territory was the McDonnell Douglas GAM-72 Quail, later re-designated ADM-20. The ADM prefix stood for 'air decoy missile', a neat summary of the task performed by the 13ft-long device, the first missile to be carried by the B-52. Containing passive and active deceptive ECM equipment it could simulate the radar signature, speed and flight pattern of a B-52 thereby confusing and diluting the effectiveness of enemy air defences. It dispensed chaff and carried an infrared 'burner' in its tail which gave a stronger IR signal than the B-52's engines. Four Quails could be carried in the rear section of the bomb bay in the B-52E, 'G and 'H, on two launchers.

McDonnell began design studies for the GAM-72 in 1955, flew a powered version in November 1958 at Holloman AFB and used a B-52D for early flight tests. B-52Gs were used extensively for Category III (operational) tests and the trials concluded in June 1960 with the launch of three Quails from a B-52G within several seconds. McDonnell rapidly developed the GAM-72A with improved DECM which could replicate more than one B-52 on enemy radar screens. Deliveries of this variant began in September 1960 and Quail became operational with the 4135th SW in February 1961, eventually equipping fourteen B-52 squadrons by April, 1962. Deliveries closely followed those of the GAM-77 Hound Dog though it remained in use for two years longer, until 1978. With both types of missile aboard the B-52 became a flying airfield with its own 'squadrons' of nuclear attack and ECM unmanned jet aircraft as well as its internal, free-fall nuclear weapons.

Quail was powered by a GE J85-GE-7 turbojet developing almost 4,000lb of thrust. This engine was developed by General Electric's Small Aircraft Engine Department at Lynn, near Boston, specifically for use in missiles but its diminutive size and weight (under 600lb) and outstanding fuel economy, soon found it wider application in the Northrop F-5 and T-38, the USN's T-2 Buckeye trainer and a wide range of executive jets. When installed in vertical pairs on specially-designed launch racks the Quail had a box-like cross section about 2ft square with all its flying surfaces retracted. When the B-52's navigator wished to launch Quails, at any altitude above 1,200 ft, he opened the bomb doors and a Quail was automatically extended into the airstream on its telescopic launch rig. The J85 fired up and a pair of aluminium delta wings extended from the 'stowed' position (folded down against the fuselage) and also 'grew' vertical and ventral fins from each wing. With 'Launch' selected by the navigator on his control panel the Quail headed off while a second missile slid down to take its place on the launch frame if required. Another pair of missiles then duplicated the procedure on the opposite side of the bay, after which the carriage assembly retracted and the bay doors closed. The entire sequence was supposed to happen within seconds but jettisoning facilities were available for missiles which failed to power up or release properly and the entire four-round package could be dumped in an emergency. As long as a missile's motor had not fired its wings could be folded and it could be drawn back up or dropped over-water. The basic success of the concept paved the way for more sophisticated multiple-launchers for B-52G/H-mounted missiles such as SRAM in later years.

Post-launch, the Quail could travel at speeds between 0.6 and 0.9 Mach for over 400 miles at high altitude, and its flight control system allowed it to change direction twice and vary its speed once in order to simulate a bomber's mission profile. Programming, according to B/N Robert Newton, 'was easy. You set it to fly high or low and timed its turns by switches and dials on a side panel. You can imagine the confusion it would cause if you had twenty planes making a penetration and launching eighty of these things. Which one of these do you aim at through all the jamming?'

Each missile weighed only 1,230lb and measured 12ft 10in long by 5ft 4in in span with wings extended. Its structure made extensive use of honeycomb and fibreglass materials. In all, 585 Quails were produced in nine serial blocks. In 1963 all Quails were modified to GAM-72B (ADM-20C) standard with a barometric switch to enable them to perform simple terrain avoidance at low altitude. Although this meant that they could follow the B-52's shift to low-level operations at this time it drastically reduced the missile's range to less than 100 miles at low altitude.

ADM-20 Serial and Production Blocks

XGAM-72-1-MC	57-5752 to 57-5775	24 built
GAM-72-5-MC	59-2232 to 59-2243	12 built
GAM-72-10-MC	59-2244 to 59-2255	12 built
GAM-72A-15-MC	60-0616 to 60-0645	30 built
GAM-72A-20-MC	60-0646 to 60-0705	60 built
GAM-72A-25-MC	60-0706 to 60-0851	146 built
GAM-72A-30-MC	61-0333 to 61-0444	112 built
GAM-72A-35-MC	61-0445 to 61-0539	95 built
GAM-72A-40-MC	61-0540 to 61-0633	94 built

A GAM-72 Quail (59-2233) with a 4135th SW B-52G at Eglin AFB. USAF via Menard/Thurlow

B-52D 56-0695 made the first powered launch of a GAM-72 Quail at White Sands Missile Range. After service with the 22nd BW and 7th BW, '695 was displayed at Tinker AFB. Boeing

felt "This is it. I'll never see my wife again."' Over the following months about 12 per cent of the B-52 force flew over 2,000 airborne alert sorties using 70 million gallons of fuel. Usually, fifty aircraft were on airborne alert. Fred Enger recalled the route of one of those sorties with the 410th BW, 644th BS out of K. I. Sawyer AFB: 'I took off on the first of the Cuban Missile Crisis flights. We flew down around Detroit, to New Jersey, up the Maine coast and across to a point north of Portugal where we picked up three tankers.' The lead B-52 took on 40,000lb of fuel from one tanker while the No. 2 B-52 remained with his tanker to take 80,000lb. The leading bomber then took his other 40,000lbs from a third tanker, completing his refuelling at the same time as the other B-52. The tanker trio then headed back to Torrejon with minimum fuel, but able to top each other up. 'We then headed east out over the Mediterranean, flew over to Corsica and Sardinia, turned west to Gibraltar and up the coast of Spain, picking up another 40,000lb of fuel from two tankers. We then went north and intercepted our original track back across the Atlantic at a higher altitude, passing the eastbound pair [of B-52s] soon after turning west. They would not let us fly across Canada since we had four atomic bombs aboard and two Hound Dogs.'

In all, the US had nearly 3,000 nuclear weapons ready to launch against the Soviet bloc. Ground alert was intensified at dispersed bases. Meanwhile, the South East USA filled up with TAC aircraft. Kruschev considered giving the Soviet Commander in Cuba discretion to use his nuclear missiles against the USA if it attempted an invasion of Cuba, changing his mind only when he realized that this order could be intercepted by US Intelligence, thereby providing a pretext for SAC's B-52s and ICBMs to be directed at Russia. The alert was ended on 21 November when Russia agreed to remove the offending weapons. However, tensions might actually have increased further if Kennedy had realized that Cuba still housed nearly a hundred Soviet tactical nuclear missiles at that time. These were not shipped out until late December 1962 in a covert operation which closed a terrifying episode that took SAC's bombers to the brink of real nuclear conflict.

Close Calls

Airborne alert, by its very nature, contained an element of nuclear hazard. Crew fatigue on extended flights increased the difficulty of in-flight refuelling, particularly when several tanking sessions were needed. This may have been a factor in the high-altitude mid-air collision between B-52G 58-0256 of the 68th BW and its attendant KC-135A on 17 January 1966 over Spain. The tumbling wreckage contained four B28 nuclear devices, two of which released their radioactive contents around the crash-site near the fishing village of Palomares. The fourth weapon sank 2,500ft into Palomares Bay and was eventually located by the USN deep-submergence exploration craft *Alvin* and *Aluminaut* and recovered over two months after the accident. Marvin McCamis, 'piloting' *Alvin*, later claimed that the search took so long because its organizers insisted on a grid-pattern search which took the recovery vessels into impossible sea-bed terrain. In fact, a Spanish fisherman had seen the bomb descending on its parachute but his report was not taken seriously until much later and the B28 was eventually discovered in the exact location that he had described. It was hauled up after an awkward moment when the recovery vehicle got entangled in its 'chute. USN search director, RADM Guest, was photographed standing over the tamed weapon, marking the end of a period of acute embarrassment and huge expense for the USA.

B-52F 57-0036 suffered a 'mid-air' with its KC-135A over Kentucky in October, 1959. Two nuclear weapons fell to earth, fortunately without severe contamination or damage. Fred Enger had particular cause to remember that painful experience:

I had flown the night before from Barksdale and I was home the next day when I heard there had been an accident. The copilot on the KC-135 was my partner in flying training, both in primary and basic, 1st Lt William Epling.

The B-52 Commander was Lt Col Milt Chatham. He had been in our outfit (the 4238th SW) and was sent to help the ex-B-36 guys, who were now on the B-52, learn more about flight refuelling. We had all refuelled on the B-47 so it was not strange to us, but the B-36 guys had to learn from scratch. Milt was then sent to Columbus (4228th SW) to be Chief of Standardization. On the night of 15 October a Command Post pilot went along on the '52. He

(Above) **B-52G 58-0170 awaits clearance for take-off at Griffiss AFB. As** Special Delivery **this aircraft later flew twenty** Desert Storm **sorties.** USAF via Thurlow

The B-52G's tail configuration, as seen in 1987 on this 2nd BW example, includes an upper lobe for the FCS search radar and a lower one containing elements of the Phase VI defensive avionics. Authors

Boeing Company photographers produced some lovely images, including this B-52H view from the early 1960s. Boeing

was to try refuelling with Milt in the right seat but got a little nervous and before Milt could do anything he pulled up into the tanker instead of pushing down. All on the tanker died and everyone on the B-52 got out except the gunner, who had been sitting back in the tail with his parachute off. I left from Barksdale the evening I heard and drove over to Columbus to be with Jan, Bill Epling's wife, and do what I could to help her through this terrible time. There were several changes after that. The primary crew had to be in their own seats during take-off, landing and refuelling, with all their gear on and parachutes hooked up.

Another aircraft (57-0166) on airborne alert crashed when it ran out of fuel in March 1961 but it was the loss of B-52G 58-0188 on 21 January, 1968 which prompted Defense Secretary McNamara to terminate airborne alert with live 'nukes'. On approach to Thule AFB, Greenland with an electrical fire in its cabin the bomber bellied-in on the sea ice and came apart. It was at first believed that one of its four B28s had sunk through the ice flow and the deep submergence team was alerted once again. Eventually, it was found that pieces of all four fire-damaged bombs could be accounted for, but the complex clean-up (Operation *Crested Ice*) took nine months and required thousands of tons of contaminated water to be stored in the USA to 'cool off'. Clearly the risks of keeping the deterrent in the air outweighed the benefits of a slightly faster reaction time to a threat which could, in any case, be more effectively monitored as satellite reconnaissance technology improved.

The Fourth Blackbird and Senior Bowl

The late Ben Rich, former boss of Lockheed's top secret Skunk Works noted in his autobiography, 'We had built a pilotless drone, the D-21, a forty-foot manta ray-shaped ramjet that was launched from B-52 bombers to streak high across Communist China and photograph its nuclear missile test facilities. It had the lowest radar signature of anything ever built at the Skunk Works.' Kelly Johnson, its designer called it the 'fourth Blackbird' which was the 'highest performing of all the Blackbird series. It flew higher, faster, and farther'.

Design of the D-21 began in 1963 as a response to the loss of several U-2 spyplanes. By June 1963 the first D-21 was rolled out of Building 199 at Lockheed's Burbank plant and fitted above one of the two A-12 Blackbird mother-ships (60-6940 and 60-6941), known as M-12s, which were converted to carry and launch it piggy-back fashion.

The D-21, built mainly of titanium, could cruise at Mach 3.3 at altitudes up to 90,000ft, powered by a 1,500lb-thrust Marquardt RJ-43-MA-11 ramjet. Its launch was supervised by a Launch Control Officer (LCO) in the rear cockpit (Q-bay) of the M-12, but its mission was flown independently and automatically with course, camera triggering points and altitude all programmed into its INS. At the end of the mission a hatch under the forward fuselage of the D-21 was ejected and parachuted at a pre-determined point where it would be snagged in the air by the Fulton 'scissors' jaws of a Mid-Air Recovery System (MARS)-equipped JC-130B Hercules. In the watertight hatch were the INS, avionics and Hycon HR335 camera with its film, ready for processing. The D-21 shell, meanwhile, devoid of its valuable contents self-destructed at a set altitude.

Flight tests of the D-21/M-12 combination, codenamed *Tagboard*, began on 22 December 1964 at Lockheed's secret Groom Dry Lake airfield and proceeded into 1966. On 3 July of that year the first separation and launch of the drone was scheduled but an 'unstart' in the D-21's ramjet as it left the pylon caused it to flop back on to the M-12's rear end, causing the loss of both. Kelly Johnson was so disturbed by the loss of a company flyer, LCO Ray Torick in the crash, that he quickly cancelled the programme.

The drone concept obviously had potential and an alternative launch vehicle was sought for a D21B with intakes modified to avoid the 'unstart' problem and a dorsal rather than ventral suspension so that the craft could fall clear of its carrier in the event of an engine problem on launch. Two B-52Hs (60-0021 and 60-0036) were modified by the Oklahoma City Materiel Centre to carry a D-21 on each underwing pylon for Project *Senior Bowl*. Boeing engineers fitted and tested the Lockheed-designed pylon and launch cradles, relying on previous experience with the Bell X-15 programme. Both B-52Hs had their flight decks modified to accommodate two LCOs in place of the EWO and gunner's stations. Two periscopes were installed in the fuselage sides in order to observe the drones on their pylons. A stellar INS/star tracker unit, four-track tape recorder, flexiwrite unit and telemetry gear with two antennas were built in to handle the relevant guidance data. In the bomb-bay some extensive pipework to provide services to the missiles precluded the carriage of other weapons. Modifications took place during 1967–68 and the two special 'BUFFs' were handed over to the 4200th Air Support Squadron at Beale AFB under CIA control.

A D-21B drone and its solid fuel booster beneath a B-52H. Lockheed Martin Skunk Works

The Fourth Blackbird and Senior Bowl (continued)

A D-21B on the pylon, as seen from a KC-135. Lockheed Martin Skunk Works

Basic to the Tagboard concept was the need to accelerate the D-21 to Mach 3.3 before its Marquardt ramjet could operate. Since this was a little beyond the means of the ever-versatile B-52 a massive booster rocket weighing 13,286lb was required – for the D-21s. Designed by Lockheed Propulsion Company, the 44.25ft booster was longer than the D-21B and its ground clearance when the assembly, with under-slung rocket, was mounted on the B-52 was a matter of inches even with its rocket fins folded up. It developed 27,300lb of thrust for a minute and a half, sufficient to kick the drone up from 40,000ft to 80,000ft over a 32-mile (horizontally measured) trajectory. Together, the D-21B and booster imposed a weight of twelve tons on each of the bomber's pylons.

The B-52H's prodigious range enabled it to launch its drones from virtually anywhere in the world and the drone's 3,000-mile radius gave it access to large tracts of 'forbidden' territory which could not officially be observed by manned reconnaissance aircraft. During the 'carrier' phase of flight the D-21's INS was constantly updated from the B-52's stellar INS and the drone could pass back telemetry data to its 'mother' during the boost phase of its journey and for the first ten minutes of cruise until it passed out of the B-52's command range. Having flown its recce sortie in radio silence it then resumed contact with the B-52 towards the end of the mission, passing back telemetry information on the performance of its various systems. In the B-52H, LCOs could then provide back-up signals in case the drone's automatic commands for fuel cut-off, hatch ejection and self-destruction were inoperative.

Flight trials with D-21s suspended from B-52H pylons began early in 1967, mainly at night for security. One unit, the first to be built, fell off a pylon on 28 September due to a faulty attachment and its booster ignited with spectacular pyrotechnic results. On its official launch on 6 November, the booster thrust the drone to the required altitude but it then dived to earth shortly afterwards, presumably because the ramjet failed to develop power. Twin D-21Bs were flown on 28 November and powered launches continued though many ended in failure partly because the mother-ship really needed another 10,000ft of altitude to provide optimum launch conditions. The first successful launch took place on 16 June 1968 when the twelfth D-21 completed a 3,000-mile flight and its hatch was recovered as planned. As the project moved into 1969 (and into expensive over-budget costs for Lockheed) the *Tagboard* vehicle at last achieved useful photo data in tests on 6 May and 10 July using D-21Bs with build-numbers 519 and 520.

These successes prompted the CIA to request Presidential approval for *Senior Bowl* overflights of Communist China to survey that country's nuclear weapons research facilities. The B-52H carriers departed Beale at night, landing at Anderson AFB, Guam from where the missions were launched. On the first attempt, on 9 November 1969, D-21B 517 went off course and crashed in Soviet Siberia. One of its radar-absorbent panels was discovered by a shepherd and passed to a CIA agent as a gift from a member of the KGB some years later. In due course it found its way back to Ben Rich's desk.

Kelly Johnson ordered revisions to the navigation programming and a second operational mission was flown using Number 523 on 16 December 1970. Although the drone completed its 2,448-mile flight the hatch was not recovered. Mission Three on 4 March 1971 succeeded up to the point of hatch recovery but this was then damaged in the water by the recovery vessel when its parachute opened incorrectly and it sank. The final *Senior Bowl* took place on 20 March 1971 when D-21B 527 disappeared towards the end of its mission. On 15 July the CIA pulled the plug on *Senior Bowl*. The 4200th ASS was disbanded and its B-52Hs returned to other units after modification. Seventeen remaining *Tagboards* out of the thirty-eight built went into storage at AMARC, from where four were taken to NASA Dryden Flight Research Center for use in projects in June 1994.

Senior Bowl had faced some extraordinary technical challenges and it came very close to success. Undoubtedly, the new generation of unmanned aircraft under development in the 1990s has benefited from the *Tagboard* experience.

Constant Development

Although the B-52G had been designed as the ultimate Stratofortress, evolution in the design of air-launched ballistic missiles encouraged the DoD to order a further variant. Studies for the B-52H (Model 464-261) began in January 1959 before deliveries of the B-52G began. Whereas the 'Golf' had been initiated to some extent as a launch vehicle for the GAM-77 Hound Dog, the H-model specifications included the requirement to carry GAM-87A Skybolt. Finding an alternative to the eight trusty J57 powerplants as used on the first 640

In typical Alert weather, B-52H 60-0025 of the 449th BW negotiates a snow-shower as it recovers to Kincheloe AFB, Michigan. USAF via Thurlow

Pristine B-52H 60-0009 with the twin launcher for Skybolt ALBMs. Boeing via Chesneau

GAM-87 Skybolt

GAM-87A, the missile which originally justified the ordering of the 102 B-52Hs to carry it, had its origins in Weapons Systems 110A and 125A of the mid-1950s, which eventually produced the XB-70A Valkyrie bomber. In May 1959 the DoD selected Douglas Aircraft as prime contractor for an air-launched ballistic missile (ALBM) as a result of the company's earlier studies for stand-off weapons to equip the WS-110A. Its genesis was extremely protracted, first as the advanced air-to-surface missile (AASM), then as WS-138A. USAF Chief of Staff Gen Thomas D. White revealed its 'Skybolt' nickname in January 1960. The following month, it was approved as a two-stage, solid-fuel air-launched ballistic missile with a range of 1,150 miles and a W59 nuclear warhead. Skybolt was to have been a joint Anglo-US project, equipping both the B-52G/H and Britain's Vulcan B.2 bomber force. Initially, the UK was to have participated in its development, purchasing a hundred from the anticipated production run of 1,000.

It was an extremely ambitious project using untried technology and the British order was in some ways a safeguard against possible cancellation pressures in the USA. Many influential figures in the defence establishments of both countries felt Skybolt was unworkable from the outset. However, to the British it seemed a safer bet, given the resources and track record of American manufacturers, than the UK's own hugely expensive Blue Streak ballistic missile, developed against a background of Royal Navy preference for the American Polaris sea-launched missile.

Britain dropped the Skybolt development option in June 1960, retaining its plan to purchase the missile. Development continued, with Aerojet General as propulsion system contractors, General Dynamics for the re-entry vehicle to contain the warhead, and Nortronics with Bendix in charge of guidance and electronics. IOC was planned for 1964 and Boeing proceeded with the B-52H, complete with Skybolt pylons, while Vulcan B.2s were modified on the production line to carry the untried weapon. In its anxiety to ensure the production of the missile on which its independent nuclear credibility depended the UK Government used the promise of a British port for the berthing of US Navy Polaris submarines as a trade-off. The USAF envisaged a NATO force with joint control of Polaris missiles as well.

Possibly the US Government felt that it was being railroaded into supporting Skybolt. Some historians have judged that the air of suspicion between the two countries which still lingered on from the Suez affair deterred Americans from allowing the UK too much freedom in acquiring advanced US weapons systems. At any rate, the submarine base agreement included no firm Skybolt production commitment in Autumn 1960. Shortly afterwards, US concern over the rising cost of the project (all to be borne by America) was made known to Prime Minister Macmillan, as were thoughts that cancellation was a possibility. Faced with acute embarrassment over the possible loss of the UK nuclear force, Macmillan told his Minister of Defence that he intended to remind the USA of its, 'heavy moral commitment to us over this'.

Meanwhile, development continued with the twin missile-launcher pylons for the B-52H and, in 1961, with drop-tests of Skybolt 'shapes' from B-52s. The first five firings of live missiles took place in 1962, although all experienced technical failures, often with the guidance system. The lack of pinpoint airborne navigation systems made it almost impossible to programme the missile sufficiently accurately with the exact geographical position of its point of launch from a fast-moving launch aircraft, or to update its guidance system later. When the US FY 62 Budget was published there was no new funding for Skybolt, only the suggestion that existing funds could be stretched. The US

The crew of B-52G 57-6477 on 19 April 1962, the day of the first successful Skybolt firing off Cape Canaveral. Lt Col Theodore Skawienski (AC and programme Director – left) is seen with Lt Col Raymond Johnson (copilot and Deputy Director), and Capt William Smith (B/N). On the right are launch operators Martin Czanan and Paul Sullivan from the Douglas Aircraft Company. USAF via Thurlow

Defense Secretary spoke of the 'considerable technical question as to the feasibility of the system' and the 'question of whether this is the most efficient system available'. Increasingly, Skybolt was referred to as a 'research and development vehicle' rather than the primary weapon for a new generation of B-52s and the whole programme was slowed down. Neither President Kennedy, who inherited the programme from the Eisenhower Administration, nor his Defense Secretary, Robert S. McNamara, had any strong inclination to foster Skybolt. Kennedy would have preferred a nuclear-free Europe while McNamara considered that the missile failed to meet his new targets for cost-effectiveness. In his estimation, the USA's doctrine of 'Massive Retaliation' had created an arsenal of nuclear weapons sufficient to destroy the Communist empires several times over. Skybolt was an expensive and redundant extra. As President Kennedy put it, 'enough is enough is enough'. 'Massive Retaliation' became 'Assured Destruction' in strategic jargon and Skybolt in his words was, 'the kind of engineering that is beyond us'.

On 19 December 1962, Macmillan and Kennedy met in Bermuda and the British were offered the improbable option of going it alone on Skybolt or the chance of acquiring Polaris with a British warhead. There was really no choice. Macmillan came away with a face-saver and Skybolt was cancelled immediately afterwards. On the same day, the missile completed its first successful flight trial. Skybolt Program Director BGen 'Davey' Jones held a press conference in which he described the 'perfect flight' and this was reported in the same papers which carried the cancellation story. Technically, his faith in the programme may well have been justified but other, stronger political forces prevailed. The B-52 force reverted to its AGM-28 Hound Dogs for another fourteen years and the new B-52Hs were retro-fitted for 'Dogs' in 1963.

(Above) **GAM-87 Skybolts on the pylons of JB-52G 57-6473, one of five JB-52F/Gs used for the programme, together with B-52Hs 60-0006 and 60-0023.** USAF via Thurlow

A J57P-43-WB engine pod on B-52G 57-6506. The bulge, lower right, houses the alternator, fitted to 'odd-numbered' engines. Ram air scoops cool the engine oil and constant-speed drives. Authors

B-52s became increasingly interesting to Boeing as the basic weight of the new aircraft began to grow once again. There was little hope of finding more powerful engines of similar size to avoid major structural changes. Pratt & Whitney had managed to push up the thrust of each J57 from 11,000lb (wet) for the B-52A's J57-P-1W, to 13,750lb (wet) for the J57-P-43WB's hung on B-52Gs. By 1959 engine manufacturers had shown renewed interest in the turbofan principle as a way to increase power and cut fuel consumption. Pratt & Whitney took their basic JT3/J57, one of the most crucial post-war jet engines, and converted it into the JT3D/TF33 turbofan, the chosen powerplant for the B-52H.

Boeing also took their chance to update many avionics and controls. Although little could be done about the basic crew 'quarters', (described by one pilot as being 'like sardines in a tin') some alleviation of the work load was devised. For the pilot there was a less tiring way to fly the aircraft via the MA2 autopilot, using his control wheel in the normal way but with reduced control forces. Radar navigators had a superior Advanced Capability Radar (ACR), also retro-fitted to some B-52Gs.

Externally, the B-52H was identifiable by its revised engine nacelles and also by the new defensive armament. In place of the proven quartet of 'fifty-cal' machine guns, Boeing put a single M61A-1 Vulcan cannon.

H-Power: the TF33 Engine

P & W's J57 powered many of the USAF's Century Series fighters as well as the A-3 Skywarrior and F-8 Crusader. It was also the driving force for the widely-used jet airliners, Boeing 707 and Douglas DC-8. Over 21,000 J57s were built. Partly to counter the threat of the more economical Rolls-Royce Conway by-pass engine as a follow-on power-plant for the cost-conscious airlines, P & W designed a simple turbofan conversion of the JT3 (its civil designation) for commercial use. Parts commonality with the J57 is between 40 and 70 per cent, depending on the variant. In its JT3D form, the engine's first three low pressure stages were replaced by a two-fan stage (initially planned as a modification kit for existing JT3 users) giving a 50 per cent increase in take-off thrust and a 20 per cent improvement in output at cruise settings. Later, heavier Boeing 707s and DC-8s used the engine, as did the Boeing C-135B and Lockheed C-141. However, the re-design was also a response to a 1956 bid from General Electric to re-engine the B-52 around their CJ-805-23; a J79 (as in F-4 Phantom) with a fan fitted behind the turbojet stage. P & W investigated further military applications of the 'turbofan' or TF33, and they also turned their other main military engine, the J52 into the JT8D which powered the Boeing 727, 737 and Douglas DC-9.

When the engine was selected for the B-52H, B-52G 57-6471 was converted to test the TF33 in July 1960 and it immediately demonstrated significant performance enhancement. Flat-rated at 17,100lb thrust it delivered 30 per cent more thrust than the standard J57 with water injection and reduced the take-off run by about 500ft compared with the B-52G. The heavy and sometimes unreliable water system, whose liquid content alone weighed 10,000lb, was eliminated adding to the B-52H's choice of bases – not all installations could supply the 1,200 gallons of distilled water needed for each fill of the aircraft's water-methanol system.

The TF33 engine. Boeing via Chesneau

An additional benefit for people living near the SAC bases was a major reduction in the fearful noise and blankets of black smoke associated with a 'traditional' B-52 take-off. Inside the B-52, the crew also enjoyed lower noise levels. So marked was the power increase and response speed that the B-52's throttles were fitted with adjustable 'maximum thrust setting' gates to prevent over-acceleration and uncontrollable pitch angles when flying a lightly-loaded aircraft in traffic patterns. Partly, this was caused by fuel flowing rearwards in the huge wing-tanks under high g, altering the centre of gravity.

Increased fuel economy was the second big bonus. In addition to having a power increase equivalent to a fifth pair of J-57s and take-off at throttle settings well below the maximum, the B-52H could offer a 13 per cent decrease in specific fuel consumption and a 1,400nm increase operational radius compared with the 3,110nm of the earlier B-52B. A B-52G with a 10,000lb-warload usually managed a 3,550nm-radius.

Mounting the engines in pairs meant a new cowling for the larger fan stages air so that they could vent their 'cold' air directly backwards over the main engine nacelle rather than mixing that air internally with the core airflow. A wider front-end cowl of greater diameter than the compressor casing for the rest of the engine enabled fan-stage air to eject rearwards through 'banana ducts' around most of their periphery. Eight spring-loaded 'suck in' doors were let into this front cowl to increase airflow for ground-running and other stages of flight where rapid acceleration was needed.

Other changes to the J57 for its TF33-PP-3 production configuration included a beefed-up third stage turbine and an added fourth stage to power the front fan stage. A new Sundstrand 120-KVA generator was installed and all engines, apart from Nos 2 and 8, had hydraulic pumps, as in the J57. Both electric and cartridge starting were incorporated.

Beginning in January 1963, cartridge starting was provided only on the Nos 4 and 5 engines, which then powered up the other six pneumatically. Two minutes were saved in the Alert duty rapid take-off routine and the aircraft's ability to self-start without ground support increased survivability in an emergency and facilitated dispersal to other airfields. From 1974 to 1976, Operation Quick Start introduced battery-operated 'cart start' on all eight engines to cut reaction times further on Alert duty. San Antonio ALC installed the starters in 185 B-52G/H models, surprisingly, taking a minimum of 1,249 man hours per aircraft because of the extensive additional electrical 'plumbing' required. Storage for eight spare cartridges was included. Simultaneous engine start generates huge quantities of smoke and soot on the rare occasions on which they are used. When the 'sailboat' engine nacelles are lowered for cleaning every 250–300 hours the accumulated dirt from the engines covers the unfortunate maintainers, making this their least-requested job.

In service the TF33 has thrown up few problems though pilots have to be aware of its stall characteristics. In crosswinds above 10kt stalls can occur while taxying, though a stall prevention system is included to operate the compressor bleed valves, stopping engine surge. On the B-52G there was a tendency for these valves to open at low altitudes, slightly reducing thrust. Early TF33s had minor difficulties with throttles whose power settings were not quite evenly aligned between the eight engines, or 'crept' to higher uncommanded power settings. There were some instances of blade and turbine case cracking or excessive oil consumption – familiar problems with early turbofans. They were addressed by Project *Hot Fan* between October 1962 and December 1964 (interrupted by the Cuban Missile Crisis) during engine PDM. TF33s had the additional disadvantage of a marked increase in frontal radar cross-section caused by their larger, highly-effective front fans. However, with an overall radar invisibility problem as huge as the B-52's this was a minor snag! With its new engines the B-52H was set for a long career. Earlier models, particularly the B-52G, had their retirement accelerated partly because the J57 was replaced in its only other large-scale user, the KC-135B by the same TF33 powerplant, making support operations for the older engine too expensive in the cost-conscious USAF of the 1980s.

In 1997, the TF33 provided the largest workload for commercially-derived engines in the maintenance depots: 0.9 million hours direct labour. The work could be 'out-sourced' or 'privatized' from the Oklahoma City Depot to a commercial organization in order to free capacity for 'military only' engines like the F100 for which there is no competitive repair market. Pratt & Whitney, Aviall and Greenwich Air services have the relevant experience with the JT3D. However, a major re-engining effort based on commercial off-the-self (COTS) leasing of Rolls-Royce RB211 engines (discussed later in the book) would radically alter the appearance and performance of the B-52H. Support for this powerplant would be provided by Rolls-Royce and Allison.

A pair of J57P-43s with lower cowls and one-piece front-fairing removed for maintenance at Seymour-Johnson-Johnson AFB in 1982. Ron Thurlow

TF33 cowls have cleaner lines than the B-52G's. Just visible on B-52H 60-0057 (410th BW) are the 'Invasion Stripes' applied for the last Marham Giant Strike in 1981. Team member Col Floyd Carpenter told the authors, 'We were soundly beaten by the RAF Vulcans but had a great time'. Authors

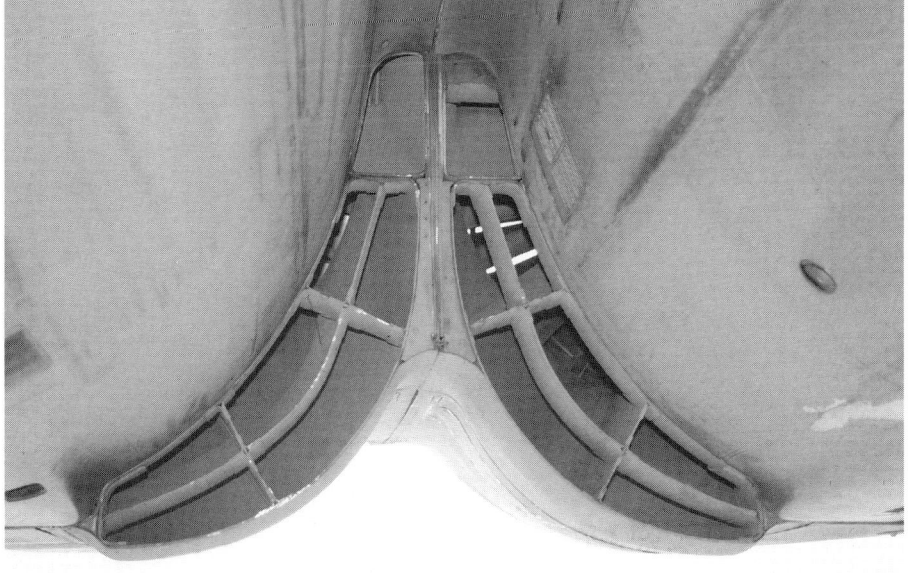

By-pass air is ejected from the TF33's front fan through these slots and others around the upper circumference of the front cowls. Authors

Self-protection: ECM

Philosophy Although the mighty B-52 was well-supplied with its own guns and deception missiles, it has always relied on a massive ECM suite as its principal means of protection. This was designed into the aircraft from the outset and it has been constantly and expensively developed during the B-52's lifetime.

Phase 0 Early B-52B/C models had this configuration which comprised two receivers to intercept hostile radar emissions (one AN/APR-9B and an AN/APR-14), an AN/APS-54 radar warning receiver and fourteen AN/ALT-6B 'brute force' CW jamming transmitters. Two AN/ALE-1 chaff dispensers were installed.

ECM 'Tech' Peter S.Kuehl: 'ALE-1 had dual dispensers on either side of the vertical stabilizer, each with a large bin which held at least 600lb of chaff. I know that I uploaded and downloaded plenty of it when we had ORIs or when the plane went on the Alert Pad as the "training" chaff had to be changed for "war" chaff. Some ECM systems had pretty common malfunctions caused by the technology of the time not being ready to do what was asked of it, for example, mechanical tuning, which today would be done electronically.'

EWO veteran Phil Rowe explained:

When I started in the EW or ECM business the equipment and tactics were similar to those used in late World War II and the Korean War. We had simple noise jammers which had to be tuned manually to coincide with enemy radar signals. Our receivers were old too, though the APR-9 was soon added. You have to know what electronic signals the enemy is using before you can develop and employ countermeasures. Advances in ground and airborne radar systems brought correspondingly advanced ECM equipment and new techniques. But the basic philosophy was to deny the enemy knowledge of your position, altitude, course and numbers. We had countermeasures for early warning and long-range radars, as well as some rudimentary techniques for protecting against tracking radars, ground and airborne. Multiple frequency radars and those that could shift frequencies to avoid jamming made the ECM operator's job more difficult. The advent of moving target indicator systems and signal processing made chaff all but useless, except for its general nuisance value.The biggest thing multiple frequencies and frequency shifting did was to make jamming more complex. Keeping a jamming signal frequency-coincident with the source radar became more challenging. Available jamming power had to be spread broadly or shifted from frequency to frequency with agility and accuracy. That was a tall order.

What is known today as 'power management'; apportioning available power to key threats automatically, very much required a 'man in the loop' forty years ago.

We used terminology descriptive of the techniques. Spot jamming was simply putting one jammer signal at the same frequency as the enemy radar, one signal at a time. The name probably resulted from the 'spot' in the spectrum that we were jamming. Barrage jamming was the technique of simultaneously jamming over a range of frequencies. It was problematical because available transmitter power had to be spread. Sweep jamming was a kind of compromise between spot and barrage techniques, automatically shifting over a range of frequencies in an attempt to put all available power into the bands requiring it. This was marginally effective because it was difficult to put the jamming exactly where it was needed at the proper time and frequency.

Arguments developed among strategists about what countermeasures to use. Some advocated denying the enemy all information about the bombers' position, course and altitude at the very earliest chances of encounter. That meant having the capability to jam both long-range early-warning radars and GCI management radars which could vector fighters at us. Others argued that you could not really do that in the first place, because multiple radars would simply triangulate on your jamming signals. The use of low flying, to deny enemy radars early indications of incoming planes was also proposed, though navigational problems had to be overcome.

Some argued that what was really important were the so-called terminal threats, since you could never really deny the enemy knowledge of your presence. A fighter's airborne radar that could acquire, lock on and track you was a terminal threat. So too was a SAM.

The EWO's command of chaff was also used for its nuisance value to fox terminal threats, from the very beginning:

Ah, yes, the good old days in B-52s and those ice-cube episodes. B-52Ds carried chaff, routinely dropped from high altitude. Chaff packets are bundles of aluminized mylar, like boxes of thin toothpicks. As the packets are opened by the slipstream the foil strips scatter to form a radar-reflective cloud intended to mask the echo returns of the bomber.In the upper aft section of the B-52 two huge hoppers held the supply of chaff bundles. A dispenser system, commanded by the EWO ejected just one or two packets or a whole stream depending on the size of the 'cloud' and necessary tactics.

Sometimes things didn't always work as planned. If the bombers sat on the flightline during rainstorms, water often leaked into the chaff hopper and soaked the cardboard bundles of chaff. When the airplane reached high altitude those chaff bundles froze into solid blocks of ice and as the dispenser began ejecting the frozen chaff bundles the strips did not scatter and the frozen blobs descended to earth still intact. Fortunately, we chose wide open, unpopulated areas to dispense the chaff. Usually, that is. I am sure that some of those big ice-cubes landed in farm pastures and even on rooftops. We never got reports of injury or damage, but the falling blocks could have been devastating. Some enterprising ground crewman came up with the idea of securing sheets of household aluminium foil with duct tape over the chaff exit ports to keep snow and water out of the hoppers. It worked beautifully.

Phase 1 In 1959–61 the equipment was updated to this standard (for B-52Ds and some B-52B/C variants) by the replacement of four of the ALT-6B jammers with a powerful barrage jamming suite consisting of two AN/ALT-13 (V) units, an AN/ALT-16 and an AN/ALT-15H high-band set.

Phases II and III in 1961–63 added an AN/ALR-18 automatic set-on receiver, a second AN/ALT-15H and an AN/ALT-15L low-band jammer, while the AN/ALT-6B CW jammer suite was reduced to five units. Flares were introduced, with six AN/ALE-20 dispensers and the rather basic pair of ALE-1 chaff-shooters was replaced by eight AN/ALE-24 versions with greater capacity (Pete Kuehl remembers this happening at Depot Maintenance in 1964–65).

Phase IV in 1964–66 brought a comprehensive upgrade in ECM capability. It also prepared the B-52 for the very tangible opposition it was to face from Soviet-built defensive systems in South East Asia. Much of the Phase III equipment was retained: the AN/ALR-18, AN/ALT-6B jammers and the AN/ALT-13 (V), ALT-15H and AN/ALT-15H and -15L barrage jammers. An AN/ALT-16 barrage jammer was also included, plus a sophisticated Tasker AN/ALR-20 panoramic countermeasures receiving set and an Itek AN/APR-25 radar homing and warning system (RHAW). Chaff and flare capability remained the same but the B-52G and B-52H were given two small underwing pylons for AN/ALE-25 forward-firing chaff rocket pods. Each Boeing-produced pod, weighing 1,100lb, held twenty Tracor AN/ADR-8 2.5 inch folding-fin rockets. They were designed to detonate several thousand feet ahead of the bomber, producing a cloud of chaff which would spoof enemy detection and missile tracking radars. The system only remained in being for about five years but the pylons were retained for other small stores. In Vietnam they appear to have been used on occasion for AN/ALQ-101 (V) ECM pods on a number of B-52Gs which had not received the early stages of the Phase VI upgrade. The ALE-25 was retired before it could be used in *Linebacker II*.

Phase V, also known as *Rivet Rambler*, was the next update and it was essentially a Vietnam War upgrade for the B-52D during 1967-69. Additions were six Hallicrafters AN/ALT-28 (or an extra AN/ALT-13 (V)) barrage jammers. Also the AN/ALT-15 jammers were replaced by an AN/ALT-32H and -32L of much greater power. With this fit, the B-52Ds (and a number of B-52Gs which received the same additions) were better able to jam the powerful *Fan Song* guidance radars of North Vietnam's SA-2 missiles and related communications equipment.

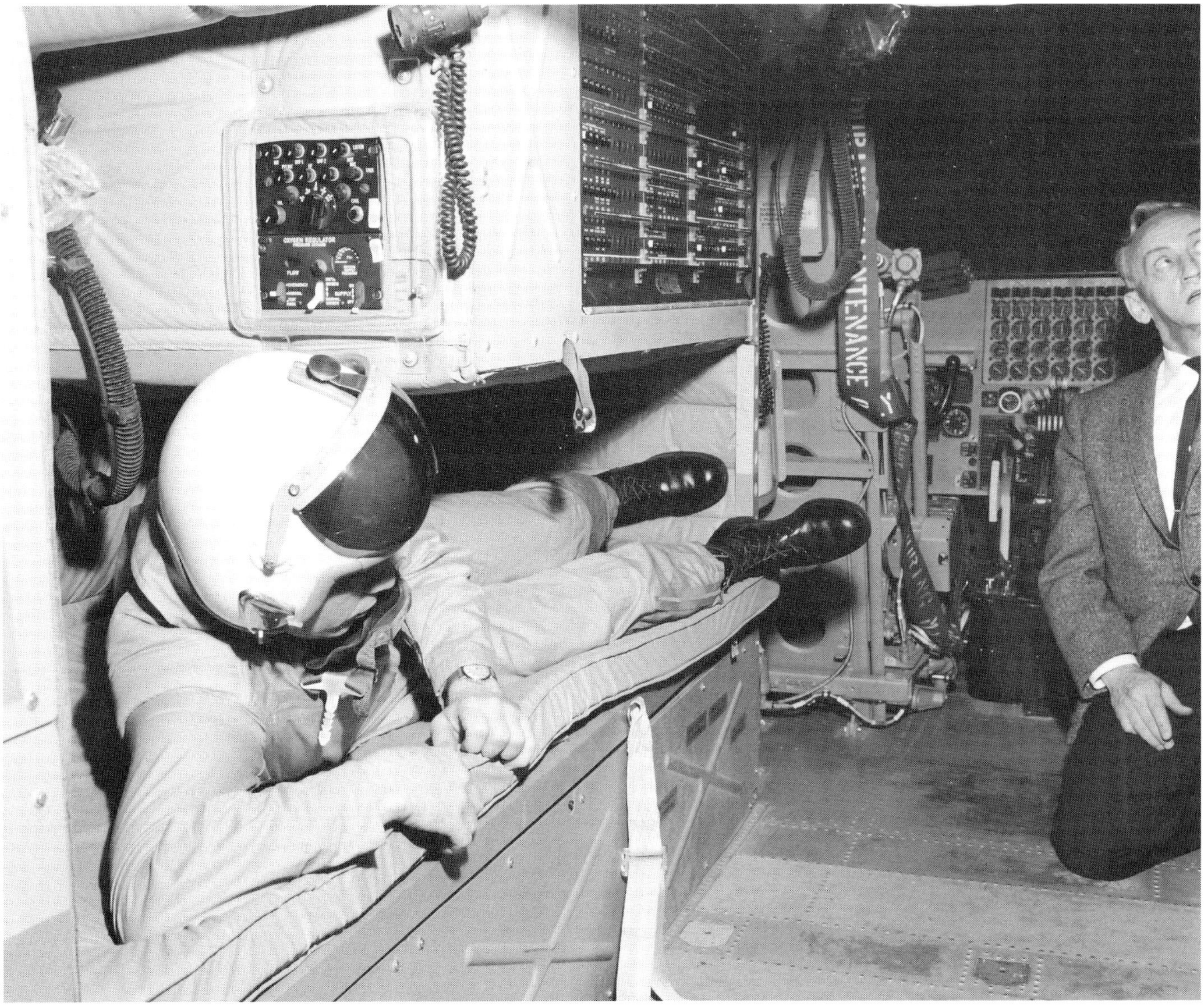

(Above) **The crew rest station on the B-52G/H. Most crew members found that you had to lie in one position. There was not room to turn over.** Boeing

B-52H Memphis Belle IV's M61 cannon with the dual search and track radars of the Emerson ASG-21 FCS above it and an ALQ-117 horn antenna below. This was the first B-52H (60-0001), rolled out in September 1961. Thirty-six years later it was the 2nd BW's flagship. Authors

Tail Stings

Developed for USAF fighters such as the F-104 and F-105, the General Electric M61-A1 six-barrel gun had been included in the B-58A Hustler to clean off any hostile fighters capable of tail-chasing that Mach 3 delta. (In fact, they did have some chance of catching it below 25,000ft where its maximum speed was around Mach 0.91.) For the B-52H, the USAF suggested the 30mm T-212 revolver gun, firing pellets but eventually specified the M61-A1 (originally proposed for the B-52 in 1950) to replace the antiquated, but still effective 'quad' 0.50 cal. armament of all previous B-52s. Its multi-barrel muzzle protruded from a flexible 'boot' around the General Electric hydraulic gun mounting. With a firing rate of 4,000rpm the gun would give a brief hose-down with the 1,240 rounds supplied, though the hitting power far exceeded that of the 0.50 machine guns, which had twice as many bullets.

Emerson Electric displaced Avco Crossley as contractors for the fire control system with their MD-7 (later AN/ASG-21), developed from the Black Warrior programme for the B-58. Its two parallel radar systems could each search for a target or track it, though only one target could be tracked for the gun at a time leaving the other system in 'search' mode. The system had only four modes, compared with 23 in the ASG-15. Gunner Danny Burnett found the B-52G's system, 'more flexible. With practice and experience it was a fairly simple matter to to isolate and work around electronic problems with the various automatic/manual and emergency modes. In all models up to the H you could tell where the guns were pointed because a turret cursor was displayed on the radar screen and you could move the turret manually if you had to.'

Unlike its predecessors, the B-52H never used its tail-sting in self-defence. In the early 1990s, after investigation of a General Dynamics proposal called Scorpion to replace the gun with rear-firing Stinger missiles, the gun was removed as a cost-saving exercise. In retrospect, many preferred the Arma 'quad' as a defensive weapon and crews (apart from gunners!) liked the old tail-turret position where the 'guy in back' could look out for emergencies ranging from MiGs and missiles to fuel leaks and engine fires.

Specification – B-52H

Dimensions: Length 157.58ft* (47.73m); height 40.67ft (12.4m); wingspan 185ft (56.39m); wing area 4,000sq ft (371.2sq m); tailplane span 52ft (15.85m); main undercarriage track 11.3ft (3.4m); outriggers 148.45ft (45.25m); distance from top of fuselage to ground 17.45ft (5.32m)

* *Length with Phase VI ECM is 159.33ft (48.56m)*

Operating weights: Empty 165,988lb (75,297kg); combat 306,358lb (139,100kg); max take-off 488,000lb (221,357kg)

Fuel capacity: 48,030 USgal (262,013l)

Performance: Max speed 547kt (1,014km/h) (at 20,000ft/6,096m)
Service ceiling 46,200ft (14,082m)
Combat radius 4,510nm (8,352km)
Take-off run 7,420ft (2,262m) (at sea level, typical)

Engine power:

Engine	Thrust (lb) (wet)	Thrust (lb) (dry)
TF33-P-3	–	17,000

Armament and bombing/navigation systems (original configuration):

Guns	Fire control system	Bomb/nav
1 × M61-A1 (1,242 rounds)	ASG-21	AN/ASQ-38(V) AN/ASB-9A, MD-1 AN/APN-89A, J-4

The first of 102 B-52Hs rolled out at Wichita on 30 September 1960 and the last was delivered to SAC on 26 October 1962, this being the 467th Wichita-built B-52 and the last of 744 Stratofortresses. Wurtsmith's 379th BW were the first unit to receive the ultimate B-52 model on 9 May 1961 though its early aircraft lacked some of the avionics for low-level flight. B-52 tooling was put into store until mid 1963 in case production had to be re-started. However, SAC's enormous growth had peaked and no further funding was voted despite a spate of structural problems resulting in several B-52 losses.

The 410th BW received B-52Hs a few months after Wurtsmith, picking up some of their aircraft direct from Wichita. Fred Enger recalled one of those delivery flights with John Morrison as AC, shortly before Fred got his own crew:

John made the approach and there was a strong crosswind from the left. He had always said to me, 'Don't do anything unless I say so'. When

Minot AFB's first B-52H, 60-0027 Peace Persuader, for the 4136th SW in July, 1961. The translucent HF antenna can be seen in the fin. '027 was lost in a crash at Minot in 1968. USAF via Thurlow

Gunners' Tales

Capt Danny Burnett was an Instructor Gunner on B-52Gs out of Wurtsmith and Fairchild from 1975 until 1980 before he became a Commissioned Officer on Minuteman missiles.

Every aircraft was required to undergo a 'fireout' periodically; a chance to actually fire the guns. Since near the West Coast the target was usually the Pacific Ocean or another large body of water, we never missed. The B-52H had a switch labelled 'jettison/fire' which led to a rather bizarre event. A Wurtsmith B-52 had a fireout over Lake Superior. The gunner got a bit lazy and set the switch to jettison, then pulled the trigger. This caused the Gatling gun to rotate and cycle the ammunition through the gun. Since he wasn't firing he neglected to 'clear the area' or have the navigator do a radar sweep to ensure that there were no vessels below the aircraft. He jettisoned the unfired ammunition which fell 27,000ft on to a Great Lakes ore freighter, whose crew were startled by the sight of it bouncing around on their deck. He never flew again.

In the B-52G it was possible to tell from feel if all four guns were firing. By putting the turret in an azimuth limit and firing you could actually move the tail over, irritating the pilot because it kicked off the autopilot and messed up the trim. Slamming it from limit to limit without firing would also knock off the autopilot.

One of my biggest complaints, before Red Flag, was that all of our air intercept training was terribly unrealistic and done at 20-30,000ft while we were supposed to be low-level penetrators. This tended to create a false sense of security for the gunners and EWs because they could see the fighters at maximum range (conversely they had no problem picking us up visually either). Fighter intercepts at Red Flag on the other hand could best be described as a nightmare, trying to pick out a radar return that was probably no bigger than two rasters wide (of the ninety-nine on our screen) and either closing in or holding position, from a radar scope 'washed out' with ground returns. While it was impossible to actually see the target elevation on the scope you could be pretty sure it was above you unless the fighter pilot had a death wish or your pilot was a chicken. The maximum range of the ASG-15 search radar was ten miles. At low level you were lucky, or really good, to see anything the size of an F-4 at more than six miles. One element of the STC mod helped this problem considerably because it allowed for blanking out the ground returns below aircraft horizon for a range set by the gunner. I flew six Red Flags (including the first at night for the B-52) and found that fighters were not that big a threat to us. Even the vaunted F-15 could be avoided or defeated. Instead we would have been cannon fodder to the AAA and SAMs. On our missions we were never 'shot down' by fighters but after most missions we were sent a rather embarrassing videotape of us in the crosshairs of a 100MM AAA gun or SAM sight. The TAC fighter pilots or Aggressors waiting for us had every advantage; they knew when we were coming, our targets and a general idea of our approach direction. We would launch a three-aircraft cell from our home base and head for Nevada. At low level entry we would orbit and one aircraft would head out, with the others following at fifteen-minute intervals. We joked that the first aircraft would wake up the defences, the second one piss them off and they would take it out on the third. On the first missions we flew at SAC 'TAC Doctrine' altitudes. The F-5 Aggressors orbited the dry lake beds and watched for our moving shadows (our SIOP camouflage really worked well in the desert environment, especially when faded) and dropped down for the intercept. After we figured their tactics out (one debrief was all it took) our next mission was a true ground-hugging wild ride where we had to pull up to turn. At one point the copilot reported fifty feet on the radar altimeter and the bottom of our No. 1 engine nacelle was missing when we landed. The aircraft covered its own shadow on the ground and the fighters had to change tactics because they couldn't 'see' us. They either 'cheated' (used AWACS) or flew really low and waited for us to pop up over the mountains and be silhouetted against the sky. With F-15 Eagles they used its radar's look-down capability to try to find us. Since our ALQ-117 didn't work against the F-15 radar (though it really messed up the radar in F-4 Phantoms and F-5s) there wasn't a whole lot we could do. Ideally for the fighter he would come up and fire a missile or two from long range and go away.

I did get four fighter kills. Unfortunately two were my own MiG-CAP who came up behind and didn't talk to us. One was an F-15 at night. Once inside the IP, while the R/N is fine-tuning the bomb-run there is limited manoeuvring before bomb release and that is when the F-15 appeared at about eight miles out in our 6 o'clock. Once I determined we could not manoeuvre to avoid him I began a bit of psychological warfare by reaching up and putting my search radar in standby mode and then sitting back and folding my arms. I was counting on a macho response from the fighter pilot and I got a better one than I hoped for. I don't think there's a fighter pilot alive who could resist the chance to avoid using a missile to shoot an aircraft down when it can be accomplished with a cannon, and now we looked pretty defenceless. While I couldn't 'see' the fighter with no fire control radar on I could get a pretty good idea of what he was up to by watching the display on the ALR-46 radar warning indicator. When the signal was good and strong, indicating a close range, I closed the action switch and hit the track button, causing both search and track radars to start radiating. I could almost imagine the F-15 pilot's surprise when the track radar locked on to him, with his RHAW gear going from 'no signal' to the continuous wave of the track radar, inside AIM-9 range and outside cannon range but inside my firing range (the 0.50 cal had a slight advantage firing backwards), and the frustration when he heard the radio call 'REDO 42 tracking bandit', meaning I was firing on the target, namely him.

There were a few practical jokes that could be played on the EWO. If the gunner caught his EWO dozing off (this really worked well on the 'not very tall') he could run the EWO's ejection seat to the 'full up' position, then pull the circuit breaker. When he woke he might find that he could not reach the intercom mike switch, much less the floor and he would flail around until he could get the gunner to re-set the seat switch. The other thing was to catch him being inattentive and move the wafer switch on his communications panel from 'interphone' to UHF, so any communications he thought were going to the crew were in reality going out to the world. Occasionally we heard some pretty wild things on the radio before the victim realized what had happened. At Wurtsmith we had the sport of 'shooting' hard-boiled eggs. At altitude, we would peel off the shell, hold the egg under the sextant port and open the port, causing the egg to be sucked out by the pressure differential. [This pastime was forbidden after it was found that eggs were blocking the ECM cooling airscoop, ahead of the tail and in the eggs' trajectory, causing ECM overheating.] The gunner's job could be mind-numbingly boring, if you let it. On a normal training sortie the gunner would actually be busy for less than twenty minutes in an eight- to ten-hour mission.

Mission planning was normally done the day before, all day. The gunner planned the defensive co-ordination exercise (DCE) with the EWO and the rest of the crew. This consisted of dropping two bundles of chaff and two 60 degree turns, to check out the chaff dispensers and the tracking circuits of the FCS. It should be noted that the gunner's activities were the lowest priority and would be the first thing dropped if there were any problems in flight. The gunner then took the navigator's paperwork, drew the pilot's chart and took lunch orders. On the day of the mission the crew bus made two stops; one at the inflight kitchen where the gunner would get the lunches and coffee, water or lemonade. The other stop was so the EWO could pick up his classified manuals. At Base Operations we usually ran into the tanker crew who would be refuelling us and exchanged insults about each others' aircraft (for example, 'Boom operators had three officers to take them to work so that they could lie on their stomachs and pass gas').

The gunner's pre-flight was a walk-around of the tail area looking for missing panels, leaks and blocked ammunition chutes on the turret. Once the aircraft was in the air it was time to start a systems check and then settle back for the rest of the flight.

---

we touched down the plane porpoised: the front gear touched down, the airplane bounced up and with a crosswind it drifted to the right. It happened again and we were close to the edge of the runway. As we were starting down for a third bounce I deployed the drag-chute, which accomplished two things. First, we were down on the runway to stay. Also, the wind then weather-vaned the aircraft back towards the centre of the runway. This broke the ice with John to the point where he said, 'Now, don't wait for me anymore'.

Rough Air = Wear and Tear

Like the B-52G, the B-52H was stressed for low-level terrain-following flight To prevent the effects of low-level turbulence from eating too far into the aircraft's original 5,000 hour fatigue life over 120 major structural modifications were made to the airframe. Each one was described in an Engineering Change Proposal (ECP) and, by 1981, 1,800 of these in total had been proposed ranging from very minor detail changes to full-scale rebuilding of components to counter the unexpectedly rapid onset of fatigue in what was largely an unexplored flight regime for heavy combat aircraft. The first of these, ECP-1000 in 1959, included among its 'Big Four' updates to the B-52G/H (including new ECM, the ACR and integrated flight instrumentation for the B-52G) a strengthening programme for various airframe components. Slightly over a year after service entry B-52Hs started to develop cracks around the wing/fuselage joints. Boeing's Project *Straight Pin* replaced corroded fasteners in the area and reamed out small radial cracks in the forgings. It was the first of many similar initiatives. Further trouble was foreshadowed by SACs 'lead the fleet' team. These were ten B-52Gs and a similar number of B-52Hs which were given accelerated operational use to keep them at least 1,000 hours ahead of the rest of the fleet in order to show up any incipient structural problems. A series of cyclic test programmes (ECP 60) from 1959 to 1961, also showed how low-altitude operations would limit airframe life. The aeroelastic properties of large airframes in turbulent conditions became the subject of intensive study.

Losses of earlier B-52 models also occurred due to structural failures at high altitude. B-52B 53-0390 of the 95th BW and B-52E 57-0018 both crashed after an over-loaded main rear fuselage bulkhead gave way due to excessive torsional loads from the tail-fin during severe atmospheric turbulence. The bulkhead had already been stiffened and fitted with doubler plates by Oklahoma AMA during programmed depot maintenance during 1960. Although these failures had occurred at high altitude the causal fatigue had probably been induced in more turbulent low-level conditions. B-52C 53-0406 from the 99th BW sustained major gust-induced structural failure involving the rear bulkhead and it fell to earth near Greenville, Maine in January, 1963 during a low-level sortie. ECP 1124 was set up to replace the bulkhead entirely and the follow on ECP 1128 required stronger skinning on the fin and upper fuselage. Autopilots and yaw dampers were adjusted to restrict loads on the tail area and the aircraft's load factors of -2g and -0g were restricted also.

Gusts of wind, particularly in the mountain passes which B-52s traversed on their terrain-following missions were sometimes so severe that an airframe could be terminally over-stressed in seconds. The first such loss was a B-52D (56-0591). Another B-52D (55-0060) hit turbulence and disintegrated in January 1964. Three days earlier, on 10 January 1964, another Boeing crew led by test pilot Chuck Fisher flew a

Open wide! A 2nd BW B-52H (60-0009) shows off its forward ECM racks (left), AN/ASQ-176 radar and ALQ-117 antenna 'horns' (below nose-art). Andy Evans

heavily-instrumented B-52H complete with two inert Hound Dogs and full internal bomb load along Rocky Mountain routes at 500ft AGL, varying their speed from 280 to 400kt. Faced with bone-jarring turbulence they climbed to 14,000ft but a violent gust of turbulence hit the bomber side-on, ripping away the rudder and 85 per cent of the fin. Fisher forced the heavy B-52 back into stable flight at 220kt and was advised of the extent of the damage by a company test pilot in an F-100 chase-plane. Three hours later Fisher and his copilot, Dick Curry, managed to put the 'flying wing' down safely at Blytheville AFB, Arkansas, so that its valuable data on dynamic structural loading could be properly analysed.

More major structural strengthening was obviously necessary if the B-52 force was to be able to withstand the stresses of airborne alert utilization and low-level penetration missions. ECP 1185, introduced in May 1966 replaced all side-skins on the fuselage on all B-52s. Paradoxically, the B-52G and 'H' which had been designed for low level work, displayed the most rapid wing fatigue. The first major failure was appalling, if spectacular. B-52G 58-0187 from the 4241st SW had only 650hr on its log book when a wing panel cracked at altitude causing a deluge of JP-4 from the fuel tank it covered. Its pilot took it to Seymour Johnson AFB for a recovery but when he extended the flaps the additional aerodynamic load broke the wing completely and the Stratofortress crashed in flames.

Partly, the problems were caused by the lighter alloys used for the 'wet' wing. As early as May 1961, ECP 1050 had to be instigated at a cost of $139.1m. An entirely new wing box using thicker alloy was installed during IRAN, wing panels were stiffened and new fasteners were installed. All B-52G/Hs (apart from the last eighteen B-52Hs which were modified on the production line) were re-worked by September 1964.

A similar programme was initiated for the surviving B-52Ds in 1972. ECP 1581, otherwise known as *Pacer Plank*, was a hidden cost of the B-52Ds' massive utilization in South East Asia. SAC was asked to select the eighty B-52Ds which had taken the least punishment while the other 48 were soon retired. As an interim measure, all B-52D wings were proof-tested; the maximum design load was applied with the wing flexed upwards by 14ft and downwards 4½ feet. There were no wing failures despite numerous small cracks in wing panels. However, *Pacer Plank* progressed and B-52Ds had most of their wings and substantial sections of the fuselage re-built, plus thirty-one refurbished wing fuel cells and other updates including better ejection seats. Theoretically, the programme's re-created B-52Ds could have remained in service until the end of the century, but the

---

My First Alert

Col Mike Loughran

After rigorous, by-the-book, and by-the-numbers training at my first tactical unit, I was finally selected for SAC alert during 1970. At the time, I was a spare crew member – that is, not assigned to a formed combat crew. On my first day of Alert, I was assigned to a real crusty major. His first words to me were something like, 'Sonny, forget all that fancy crap they told you during your training – you're with the big boys now. Do it my way and you won't get in trouble'.

My AC then proceeded to explain his way of doing things. The goal was simple – be the first ones back in the Alert shack after an Alert exercise – no cold coffee! That meant his unique way of starting engines, taxiing and then putting the airplane back on Alert status, or 'recocking'.

The normal Alert method of engine start was to fire up engines Nos 4 and 6. During this timeframe, these were the only engines with a cartridge start capacity. With No. 4 and No. 6 spooling up, a selector was moved to the 'ground start' position; after which the throttles were advanced to a high rpm to provide engine bleed air to the remaining six engines – although, these could be started with just one running engine. As the remaining engines reached the starting rpm stage, the pilot would advance the throttles for Nos 1, 2 and 3 to idle, while the copilot advanced the remaining throttles. Both pilots would monitor for correct exhaust gas temperatures and oil pressures during the start sequence before proceeding further.

When at least one of the engines with a generator (that being numbers 1, 3, 5 or 7) came up to a stable rpm, you could activate an electrical generator and continue the start. No. 5 would be the first engine to reach the appropriate rpm to operate a generator, which produced the necessary voltage to power certain components. Engine No. 5 came up to speed before the others with generators because it was closest to the air source provided by the engine No. 6, although engine No. 3 was also pretty quick. When an rpm slightly higher than idle was achieved, you could power up the generator. Well, that did not meet the 'first out, first back, no cold coffee' rule. To my absolute surprise, I experienced my first 'moving Alert' exercise with this guy. And that was even before I could absorb what he just told me about the 'no cold coffee in the cup' rule.

What this pilot had me do was to hold the generator switch in the on position as soon as there was ignition or an EGT [exhaust gas temperature] rise on No. 4 and/or No. 6. This forced the system to energize the generator immediately as it achieved the minimum rpm. This action could have sheared the drive shaft, put the generator into an under voltage shutdown mode or just cause it to 'spike' a burst of power, since the rpm was not stable and it would then sense a malfunction and shut itself down. This was a very important item since the starter valves on the rest of the engines needed ac power from the generators to operate. The end result was that not all eight engines were probably running yet!

With the checklist going 'normally' there were a few steps before telling the crew chief to pull the interphone, remove the chocks and get out of the way because we were moving. In short, it was a methodical way to make haste safely and complying with all the rules. It took a lot of power to get a 500,000lb (226,796kg) B-52H moving, especially in the winter with the weight of the jet flattening out the tyres. Sometimes the tyres even froze to the ground or to the chocks which would become jammed in front of the tyres. And it could be a real chore to break free. One technique was, just like in your car, to try and rock the jet out by adding power and chopping the throttles. Repeated attempts at this encouraged the chocks to break loose. If it was an all-out event, you just added enough power to taxi right over them.

Once the Nav/EWO team said, 'Mover', the aircraft commander told the crew chief to get the hell out of there – we were moving. He had me look out the window to make sure no one was coming our way and then we taxied! About half a million pounds of jet with maybe six of eight engines running normally. A hard and fast rule was that you had to have all engines going to taxi – but I think it was a fairly new rule. At least, that was my impression of the Wild West Alert force's view of it. It seemed to be a rule for wimps and command post pukes if ever there was one!

In the midst of this eye-opening, non-standard response to an Alert, the AC turned to me, as we were about to cross the runway hold line and said, 'Put on your damn helmet, Co. The DO [Deputy Commander for Operations] will see you and I'll get in trouble.' Events happened so fast that I had not taken off my headset and put on the bright white helmet we wore: a rather astonishing concern since up to this point this AC had virtually ignored all the rules meant for lesser men than he.

Crossing the hold line brought an application of full thrust by the left seater. We accelerated to about eighty or ninety knots. 'Got to check out the airspeed indicators, they don't register below a speed of 35 KIAS, sonny. And besides, how do you know them engines will reach full thrust unless you try 'em?' Another explanation over a cup of lukewarm coffee! He explained that the only thing that would keep him from moving was if the engines that powered the hydraulic systems, brakes or steering failed to start. He would declare, if interrogated, that the engines that were not running had simply flamed out after start. This guy just liked taxiing and viewed this as a sort of a race to the runway and back.

Pacer Plank

During a visit to Carswell AFB, Texas in Spring, 1976, Air Force Secretary Thomas C. Reed remarked of the B-52D he was inspecting, that it originated from, 'the year I graduated from college and bought my first car; come to think of it, it looks a lot like my first car'. This anecdote may be familiar but it underlines a more serious issue: war-weary 'BUFFs', particularly the 'Big Belly' B-52Ds, were showing their age. Beneath the rippled skins lay many a tired old stringer and spar. By 1973 this hard-pressed sector of the fleet had accrued double its design lifetime of 5,000 hours, but its iron-hauling capability was legendary and SAC wanted to retain the force for conventional bombing in support of NATO and in other potential trouble spots.

Engineering Change Proposal (ECP) 1581, known as *Pacer Plank* was already well under way to address the problem, especially after cracks had appeared in the lower wing skins of some aircraft. At an extra $3m per airframe (about the same cost, at the time, as a new Phantom *without* engines) the USAF decided to retain eighty B-52Ds from the surviving 128 beyond their originally-projected 1971 retirement date and refit them, under the auspices of Boeing, Wichita. Selection was based on fatigue, operational and combat histories and on the length of time since the aircraft's last PDM. Twenty-one passed outright, twenty-eight failed and seventy-nine were subjected to detailed scrutiny. One airframe was used for destructive testing to study how long a cracked piece of structure could last. All selected aircraft were proof-tested by having their wings bent to their design limits, both up and down. No 'BUFF' failed the latter ordeal.

Before the structural rebuilding under *Pacer Plank* could be started up, all B-52Ds were restricted to 1.5g manoeuvres, 290kt indicated airspeed and a 350,000lb all-up weight. The subsequent 'beef-up' was two-fold. First came the Boeing mods, which involved scrapping fifteen tons of structure per aircraft, 'enough to fill three railroad cars' and installing new replacement parts. Over 8,000 components were removed, corrosion inspections were done and updates (including improved ejection seats) were effected. Re-construction involved:

- The rippled fuselage skins in the wing root area (stations 538 to 694) were replaced with 7075-T651 aluminium alloy. Side-skins from stations 805 to 1237 were replaced with fifty feet of new 2024-T351 alloy.
- A tenth of the 'crown' skins on the fuselage top were renewed, skin joins around the cockpit windows were strengthened, different body/wing junction bonnet fairings appeared and many cables and pulleys were replaced.
- Wings were removed and wing centre upper panels were redesigned. In one of the most demanding jobs, all thirty-one wing fuel cells were re-installed, most of the lower wing skin and large areas of inboard upper skin was replaced with 2024-T351. Leading-edge skins out to the external tank location were replaced using aluminium instead of magnesium. The trailing edge assembly was renewed (partly as a result of acoustic fatigue from water-injected engines on hundreds of wartime take-offs) including flap-tracks, ribs and skins. Many stiffeners and much of the wing's internal wiring were renewed.

Pacer Plank cost $219.1m but it provided a rejuvenated 'Delta' fleet which could have soldiered on until the year 2000 with its 7,000hr 'bonus' airframe life. They even looked new, according to USAF and Boeing personnel. As a further dividend the B-52Ds gained nearly 3 per cent in cruise range and a few extra knots because the 'draggy' external re-inforcement 'Band-aids' which had sustained them for so long were deleted.

Phase 2 of *Pacer Plank* included a full PDM at Oklahoma ALC when the fleet was brought up to operational standards (using $400,000 of the overall cost per upgrade) including a new paint-job. The Vietnam-era Phase V Rivet Rambler ECM gear was updated with elements of the Phase VI Rivet Joint system for 360-degree coverage, and flight restrictions were removed. The programme was completed in February 1977, giving the Air Force a very slick batch of 'tall tails'.

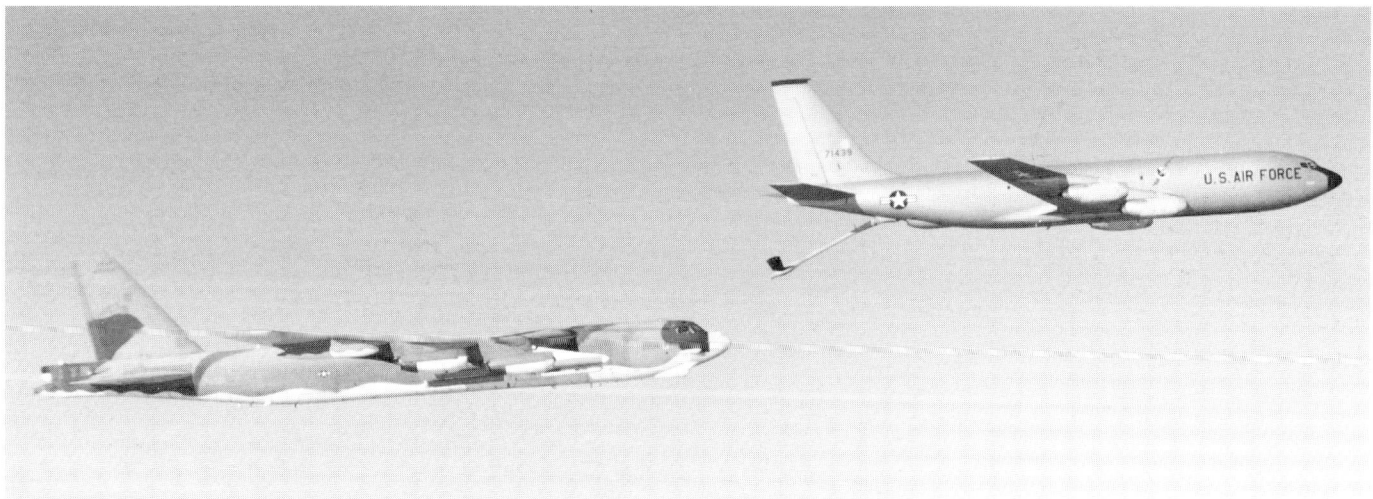

The 'BUFF's 'better half', the KC-135 tanker has always made the aircraft's strategic role possible. During the Chromedome **era, each sortie required two KC-135s. Here, B-52G 58-0204 pulls away after a fill, its extreme wing-bend showing that it has refuelled to the heaviest maximum weight of any B-52 – 567,000lb – in Exercise** Big WIP, **August 1981.** USAF via Col Mike Buck

fleet had withdrawn to its desert retirement home at AMARC by the end of 1983.

Pacer Plank and its equivalent programmes for the younger B-52s revived the fleet, giving it the stamina to perform the extremely demanding missions which were foreseen for the late 1970s and beyond. However, it did not make those flights any less fatiguing for the 'crew-dogs'. A low-level ride was usually prohibitively uncomfortable, one pilot comparing it to running an elderly car over an endless succession of speed bumps. Tight straps and strong stomachs were essential items of kit.

The cost was enormous. The five ECPs which generated these reinforcement programmes amounted to nearly $600m, not far short of twice the factory-door price of the seventy-seven B-52D/Es ordered from Boeing in December 1955. Inevitably, the weight-saving gains of the original B-52G design were soon wiped out by all the extra metal, and with other added equipment, the last Stratofortresses were the heaviest of all.

CHAPTER THREE

Arc Light Over the Jungle

The exigencies of international politics in the mid-1960s placed the B-52 in a situation which SAC planners would have considered unthinkable ten years earlier. America's prime symbol of global power was denied its primary mission and weapons, deployed to two primitive overseas bases and flown repeatedly in hundred-strong formations against a small, third-world capital in order to force its leaders to negotiate peace with the USA. This endeavour eventually required over half the entire B-52 force to fly 729 sorties in eleven days, dropping 15,000 tons of conventional bombs. Fifteen of the huge bombers fell to the enemy defences despite the presence of up to 120 tactical support aircraft for each mission, including the world's most sophisticated defence suppression units. Night after night B-52 formations flew into the lethal envelope of Soviet SA-2 'Guideline' batteries, the very missiles they would have carefully avoided in a nuclear engagement.

More extraordinarily still this onslaught constituted a tiny fraction of the B-52's role in a war to which its masters were initially reluctant to commit its immense striking power, but which (in many respects) it eventually won. Over 99 per cent (123,803 sorties) of its activity was directed at South Vietnam, Laos and Cambodia over an eight-year period. Of the 5,898 million pounds of bombs delivered by America's main strategic bomber the majority were dropped in tactical support of ground troops, often in situations which resembled the Close Air Support (CAS) function normally provided by tactical fighters. Although much of that ordnance probably did little more than disturb the ecological balance of small parts of the area for a time, to the communist insurgents the B-52 was the most feared weapon in the US armoury.

Washington's initial decision to deploy B-52s to South East Asia reflected the uncertainty of purpose and misjudgement of North Vietnamese determination which crippled America's chances of resolving the Vietnamese situation for a decade. When overt US military activity in the area began with Operation *Flaming Dart 1* on 7 February 1965, B-52 movements were part of that response. Four days later, the Joint Chiefs of Staff (JCS) decided on 'gunboat diplomacy' by positioning a sample of SAC's 'big stick' at Andersen AFB, Guam. On 9 February, fifteen aircraft from the 20th BS, 2nd BW flew to Kadena AFB and the 441st BS, 320th BW despatched another fifteen to Andersen, which had hosted a B-52B deployment the previous year.

B-52F 57-0153 tucks up its gear as it departs Andersen AFB with M117 bombs in June 1965 on one of the first *Arc Light* missions. This aircraft was the first B-52 to be delivered to Barksdale AFB on 14 August 1958. It was finally scrapped in November 1993. USAF via Robert F. Dorr

The aircraft concerned were B-52Fs, twenty-eight of which, in 1964, had fortuitously received enhancement of their conventional war capability under the Project *South Bay* modification programme, allowing twenty-four M117 bombs to be carried on two external wing racks and twenty-seven internally.[8] The bombers' presence did nothing to deter the Hanoi Government, and US policy ruled out the use of B-52s for punitive strategic attacks on the then-lightly defended North Vietnamese heartland. Partly, this reflected fear of hostile reactions from the USSR and China, but also concern about US public reaction to a military response which would have seemed grossly disproportional for a 'minor war' situation in which Washington was attempting to adopt a covert role. However, contingency plans were drawn up for a selection of strategic targets in the Hanoi/Haiphong area and the B-52F (after brief consideration of the B-47 and B-58) was pencilled in for those attacks. Several of the targets were still on the planners' lists seven years later when the *Linebacker* attacks on the area were carried out – by B-52s.

When the bombing of North Vietnam began in earnest on 2 March 1965 with the first *Rolling Thunder* strike, the task was handed to tactical fighter units to avoid the political consequences of an overtly 'strategic' assault. Senior USAF staff were convinced that this would, nevertheless, be sufficient to crush North Vietnam's aspirations towards the South of the country. From then on, the terms 'strategic' and 'tactical' became rather blurred. While single-seat tactical fighters pounded major military targets in the heart of North Vietnam the 'strategic' B-52 took on an essentially tactical role in support of US and ARVN ground forces.

This pattern was conceived largely by Gen William Westmoreland, following talks with Defense Secretary McNamara in Honolulu on 19-20th April 1965. He had been disappointed by the lack of punch from USAF tactical airpower during a combined US Army/ARVN operation a few days previously. At this early stage in the build-up of US airpower the effect of F-100 Super Sabres with a couple of 750lb bombs apiece failed to provide the 'heavy artillery' substitute which Westmoreland wanted. In the B-52 he saw just that potential, and an all-weather capability for a war zone where monsoon conditions grounded tactical aircraft for long periods. He wanted enormous firepower to catch the elusive North Vietnamese in their jungle sanctuaries, decimating their forces at a stroke and deterring further insurgency. Also, he needed the capability to destroy the enemy's base-camps without having to risk large US ground forces in the process. Usually, these bases included extensive tunnel networks for storage and shelter. Saturation bombing, to collapse these complexes was a better alternative than having US troops entering them for hand-to-hand conflict. However, locating the camps was to prove extremely difficult, and deterring North Vietnamese resolve was always far harder than expected.

Arc Light

Having received JCS authorization for 3rd Air Division B-52 attacks (coded *Arc Light*) Westmoreland and MACV began to evaluate potential targets, eventually settling on a dispersed base area in the Ben Cat Special Zone near Hanoi. In a pattern which was to become familiar in the following years, ten cells of three B-52s, each cell designated with a phonetically-distinct colour name, were rostered for the mission. They were drawn from the 9th BS, 7th BW (which had replaced the 20th BS at Andersen) and the 441st BS.

Also setting the format for years to come, the mission was guided to its target by an MSQ-77 Combat Skyspot/Combat Proof radar beacon which was flown to Tan Son Nhut airport, Saigon in June for the purpose. Based on the MSQ-35 equipment used to train SAC Radar Bomb Scoring teams, it activated a transponder in the B-52 and the Skyspot operator provided accurate navigation inputs and bomb release indications at up to 100nm range (later doubled). B-52s flew to a fixed pre-initial point (PIP) and IP, checked in with the area Skyspot operating location (OL) which would guide the first aircraft over the target by voice control and relay a bomb release 'hack' to the B/N. Skyspot enabled diversions to new, unbriefed targets of opportunity during the mission. Briefing times were reduced and targets could be chosen without the need for prominent terrain features in the target to provide radar bearings. Seven Skyspot OLs[9] were established by June 1967, bringing most of the war zone within the reach of at least one beacon. Setting up Skyspot sites was not without risk – six SAC personnel were killed by Viet Cong (VC) while surveying one of them.

From the B-52 crews' viewpoint, Skyspot was, 'just a GCA without the glide-path', according to Maj Rees Williams. 'The only addition was to ensure there was clearance for bomb release. Where one aircraft had lost an engine there were additional considerations as it had difficulty in maintaining position and climbing to bombing altitude. This required the cell leader to balance Time on Target (TOT) requirements with the need to fly slower and select a bombing altitude which the underpowered aircraft could reach.'

Back from war, the 320th BW's Thunder Express **(B-52F 57-0169) had completed sixty-eight** Arc Lights **when it returned to Mather AFB in March 1966.** MAP

Thirty B-52Fs left Andersen AFB on 18 June for the first *Arc Light*, climbing to meet their KC-135A tankers near the Philippines. The leading cells arrived at the refuelling 'race-track' too early and they began to circle to use up time. In so doing, the first cell, unused to formation flying, turned back into the path of a following cell. Two aircraft, 57-0047 and 57-0179 collided and fell into the ocean with only four of their twelve crewmen surviving. Another B-52F aborted with avionics failures and the remaining twenty-seven bombers scored indeterminate results. SAC immediately altered the five refuelling air corridors, widening them and separating them by altitude. A complex system of 'timing triangles' was also introduced to enable aircraft to 'hold' if they arrived early, turning back on to track to meet their tankers exactly on time. These modifications to the routes enabled countless air refuellings to be conducted safely during seven more years of *Arc Lights*. The KC-135As, based at Kadena, Okinawa, met their customers over the Luzon, Philippines 'track', or over the South China Sea and then usually landed at Clark AFB, Philippines to replenish themselves. B-52s normally took up to 89,000lb of fuel from their Stratotanker partners, requiring the pair to travel the track for about seventeen minutes for a full transfer. Often, this involved flying into the sun, further complicating the demanding procedure for tired B-52 crews.

Careful analysis of *Arc Light No. 1* revealed ambivalent results. In return for the $20m mission, delivering a million pounds of ordnance, the official 'score' was forty 'barracks' buildings, a communications centre and a large rice store. There were two confirmed enemy casualties, most troops having apparently withdrawn after a tip-off. *Arc Light No. 2* was postponed when it was established that the VC had decamped from the intended target area. Despite this initial lack of success, five missions were flown in July 1965 but in most of them the problem of successful BDA was apparent. Justifying the use of such mighty force against such small or indeterminate targets, McNamara told Congress that finding an accurate aim point under such heavy jungle cover was virtually impossible. Use of a random pattern of 'carpet bombing' was the only way to ensure hits.

Gen Westmoreland fully endorsed this view and advocated more extensive use of the B-52, although Gen Momyer felt the missions were wasteful of resources and wanted control of *Arc Lights* to be passed to his 7th AF (rather than SAC and the JCS) so that they could be better integrated into his overall tactical air strategy. Washington was still very sensitive about committing SAC resources in this way, not least because of the consequences for North Vietnamese propaganda if a B-52 – America's nuclear status symbol – was to be shot down. Initially, all requests and target details had to be approved by the White House and severe controls were imposed to protect non-combatants, religious shrines and friendly forces. Later, the approval process was relaxed a little, though details were still supplied to the White House.[10]

From August to December 1965, *Arc Light* responsibility fell to the 9th BS and 20th BS until the 441st BS returned at the end of the year, paired with the 736th BS. This period saw a steady build-up of *Arc Light* sorties, generally flown by smaller formations as the frequency increased. In August, 165 sorties were flown and in November, the first use of the B-52 in direct support of ground troops was approved. A 1st Air Cavalry firebase at Plei Me in the Central Highlands was surrounded by VC and a secret base housing two North Vietnam Army (NVA) regiments was discovered nearby. Over a five-day period, Guam's B-52Fs dropped 1,795 tons of bombs in ninety-eight sorties, often bombing within three miles of the Plei Me base. On 16 November, a formation of eighteen aircraft used 344 tons of ordnance to prevent an NVA counter-attack from the Ia Dang valley, saving the base. Once again, this action was to be a prototype for many similar B-52 missions in support of ground forces. Lt Col Don Campbell recalled that missions of this kind brought additional anxiety to crews: 'In October 1968, my crew was called out one night with no notice to lead a wave of B-52s on Cam Duc, a US Army Special Forces camp. On the way to the target we could hear radio transmissions from the ground describing how the NVA had penetrated the wire and were about to overrun the camp. This gave the crew and me a real chill. We put the bomb train parallel to a runway on the outskirts of the camp as directed and the radio transmissions suddenly stopped. For the longest time I lived with the belief that I had hit our own people as well as the NVA.' Two years later, Don happened to meet a former US Army helicopter pilot who had arrived at Cam Duc immediately afterwards. He reassured Don that the majority of the camp defenders had indeed escaped safely while most NVA had been caught in the open and wiped out.

Another 320th BW B-52F with thirty-five Arc Lights **chalked up. '0163 was Mather AFB's first B-52. On delivery to the California base on 4 October 1958 it was named City of Sacramento. The B-52F's engines had two bulges housing alternators and accessories.** MAP

Running on time, the Mekong Express **(B-52F 57-0144) already has twenty-five** Arc Light **scores as it heads for another target in South Vietnam. It completed another sixty-five before returning to the USA.** USAF

One of the most lasting images of the Vietnam War – a B-52F raining bombs, each one of which contained 403lb of Tritonal or Minol 2 explosive. Twenty-six years later the same M117 weapon was also the B-52's most-used ordnance in Desert Storm. USAF

Close air support (CAS) was of course a USMC speciality and it was one of the ironies of the war that an early *Arc Light* was flown in response to a USMC request for CAS. On 12 December, an NVA infantry force was shattered by B-52s as it prepared to engage Marines in Operation *Harvest Moon* near Da Nang. At Gen Westmoreland's suggestion, B-52s rather than the Marines' own tactical aircraft were called up after a request for CAS from Lt Gen Lewis W. Walt, who observed the first strike from his helicopter and was impressed: 'The overall effect was awesome to behold'. Although the bombers had not quite provided Marine-style CAS, it was 'just next to it'. The strike produced a rare example of evidence of its success too. It uncovered a network of tunnels, caves and bunkers which the Marines investigated, finding sixty Viet Cong dead.

On the same day, twenty-four B-52Fs with BLU-3 CBU and M117 bombs flew the first *Arc Light* against a target in Laos. Maj Rees Williams rated it as a fairly routine affair. 'We were briefed in greater detail and timing was stressed but it seemed like just another run to us. The wave leader aborted and the wave commander had to transfer to the No. 2 first cell aircraft. That was my crew. He confirmed what we were to do, and that was the last of the excitement that mission.' It was a covert affair supporting the ongoing *Steel Tiger/Cricket/Tiger Hound* counterinsurgency operations in eastern Laos. In an attempt to disguise this widening of the conflict Washington had not informed the Laotian Government of the strike, but news of it reached the US Press later in December, considerably embarrassing President Lyndon Johnson and the Laotian Prime Minister, Souvanna Phouma. However, it was decided to pursue the policy of covert missions in response to the enthusiastic advocacy of Westmoreland who saw *Arc Lights* as a 'major innovation' which gave the ground forces 'an unprecedented advantage over the enemy and a means to deter or counter the Asian tactic of employing mass formations on the battlefield.'

Although the 'mass formations' rarely presented themselves as targets, Westmoreland was aware that NVA and VC forces were using neutral Laos as a safe headquarters, storage and training haven from which to launch incursions across the border into South Vietnam. Their movements were extremely hard to detect under a seamless jungle cover and vast quantities of supplies were hidden in a huge cross-border tunnel network, the extent of which was only fully appreciated after the war. Enemy forces quickly learned to keep on the move to avoid airstrikes. As Gen McConnell, USAF Chief of Staff admitted, this sometimes meant that the complex twelve-hour round trips by Guam-based formations were forced to bomb where there was, 'no real enemy; no real target', but he felt it better to 'take a chance than leave them untouched'. Gen Westmoreland's influence was such that the Pentagon reluctantly accepted this logic and sanctioned the continuation of *Arc Lights* in Laos under Operation *Ocean Wave*, using smaller formations from 14 January 1966. (As Gen 'Chuck' Horner, architect of US airpower strategy in the Gulf, remarked in 1993, Gen Westmoreland, 'owned our B-52s during Vietnam and they were often misused. It was not until *Linebacker II* that we got to use them efficiently.')

Selection and approval of targets for the B-52s was a complicated procedure at this time. Each request for a strike originated in MACV's Combined Intelligence Center, Vietnam (CICV), was reviewed by its J-2 (Intelligence) and J-3 (Operations) Sections, approved by the MACV Commander and then sent to Washington for final approval by the JCS. SAC's input was at first negligible. A specialist *Arc Light* section of CICV, with some USAF representation planned each mission in detail without reference to SAC, though SAC HQ was involved in giving final approval after March 1966. The first round of targets in January 1966 was selected from a list which straddled the Laos/South Vietnam border and secrecy was maintained because William H. Sullivan, the US Ambassador in Laos, could not be sure that Souvanna Phouma would approve these missions over his country. Planners went to extraordinary lengths to disguise the purpose of these sorties. Bombing altitudes were above 30,000ft to escape visual detection, ordnance was of the same type used by tactical fighter-bombers, and tactical aircraft were included in the mission to enhance the deception for observers on the ground. For example, on the *Arc Light* of 14 January 1966, four F-4C Phantoms from the 390th TFS bombed at lower altitude just ahead of the B-52s. MACV decided to list two types of *Arc Light* target: Category 1, which would not be notified to Souvanna Phouma for permission, and Category 2, which would. It was also proposed that targets across the Cambodian border should be attacked, though this was not begun until March 1969.

Early *Arc Lights* experienced one of the most perplexing problems facing MACV – the virtual impossibility of assessing the effects of their bombing. Targets were stretches of relatively featureless terrain, divided into areas of 1×2km on the map. Each 'box' represented the coverage of a bomb pattern from a cell of three B-52s. Guided to his target by the Skyspot operator, the radar navigator in each aircraft would press his D-2 bomb release on the operator's signal and the cell then banked away for the long reciprocal journey to Guam. Dropping from above 30,000ft, often through heavy cloud, the B-52 crew saw nothing of the results although the tail gunner might have detected the long, grey scar of smoke as the trains of bombs impacted. Dense jungle precluded reliable tactical aerial reconnaissance too, though the cameras could reveal the swathes of matchwood and erupted soil caused by 150 tons of bombs exploding within a few seconds. Col Phil Rowe, by this time flying RF-4C Phantoms, described this mayhem: 'The B-52 strike zone was just a few miles north of our level-off point. We headed for it and waited for the rain of terror to stop before moving closer for pictures. Yet even from our position ten miles away, and parallel to the path of the bursting bombs, we felt the shock of the bursts blasting one after another for several miles. We could only imagine what terror existed for those poor souls on the ground. When the bombing stopped we moved in to get several strips of post-strike photography. The craters down there looked new; lighter coloured than the older ones now filled with rain water. It's interesting how you learn to judge the age of bomb craters and hillside scars by their colour.'

At one stage Westmoreland suggested that B-52s could at least remove the jungle canopy, enabling tactical fighters to follow up with more precise strikes on the targets which he hoped would then be revealed. One of the most bizarre projects of the war was Operation *Pink Rose* in which B-52s were used to drop napalm and M36 thermite bombs in an attempt to burn away the jungle cover. It was abandoned after three missions. Over South Vietnam FAC aircraft and the occasional TF-102A Delta Dagger were used to observe the raids, but they too were unable to see much apart from whether the correct target co-ordinates had been hit.

The only realistic solution was to helicopter an observation team into the area to conduct BDA on the ground. For the 14 January mission this was impossible as the area was under communist control, but MACV set up *Shining Brass* teams to evaluate subsequent Laotian *Arc Lights*, two more of which were flown in February 1966. The first, Operation *West Stream*, used twelve B-52Fs with unknown results, followed by *Back Road* on 27 February when twenty-seven bombers attacked a target in Kontum Province. For this, a *Shining Brass* team was inserted and discovered that the majority of the M117 bombs had exploded in the tree tops, while 70 per cent had missed the target area entirely. Although *Shining Brass* teams were unable to inspect many strikes in 1965-68, possibly missing evidence of severe damage to the enemy's progress, their task was often thankless. Sometimes they encountered NVA ambushes and had to be pulled out in a hurry. At one point, they were reduced to making detailed measurements of bomb shrapnel damage to tree trunks as there was no other visible evidence of damage to the supposed target.

In March, the bombers made five more attacks on suspected enemy troop concentrations or base camps near the Laos/South Vietnam border. None could be checked by *Shining Brass* because of the risk from booby traps or ambushes, but MACV assumed that they had been of military use. Using the peculiar language of that war, success was measured in numbers of sorties and tonnage of bombs in the absence of more tangible results. However, faith in the efficacy of *Arc Lights* remained strong among military leaders. Gen Lucius Clay believed that B-52s 'gave ground forces the kind of fire support no other army has ever had'. Importantly, secrecy was preserved, partly through the 'cover strike' strategy which was in force for the majority of Laotian *Arc Lights*. Each time a mission hit a target in the Laotian border area several cells of B-52s simultaneously attacked a target on the South Vietnamese side of the border in the same general area. The entire mission was officially logged as a South Vietnam *Arc Light* and briefers often informed aircrew that their targets were in South Vietnam rather than Laos. Observers who might have 'blown the whistle' on the continued Laotian night raids supposedly saw and heard only the South Vietnam portion of the mission.

In all, 406 *Arc Light* missions were flown against troops, truck parks and supply sites on the Laos border between January and June 1966. Each included three to six cells of aircraft, with cross-border cover strikes. None was actually notified to the Laotian Government for fear of disapproval and, in fact, Souvanna Phouma was not put in the picture until September of that year. Although it seems incredible that the enormous destructive effect of these missions seemed to pass unnoticed by the government of the country under attack, the vastness of the sparsely-populated terrain must be considered. In all, some three million tons of ordnance were to be dropped on Laos; three times the amount which blasted North Vietnam.

Emboldened by the apparent success of these early missions Westmoreland wanted B-52s to be used against the NVA's supply network, interdicting the flow of military provisions along jungle trails from the North before it could reach troops in Laos who were preparing to strike into South Vietnam. It has been estimated that over half a million North Vietnamese civilians were engaged in establishing and maintaining the 42,000 miles of the Ho Chi Minh trails from 1965 onwards. Vast quantities of war supplies were moved south at night using trucks, animals and bicycles on paved roads or tracks. The USA devoted a colossal military and technological effort to interdicting this operation but never came close to stopping it. The best bet was to try to interrupt the flow at bottlenecks, for example, mountain passes. Westmoreland estimated that three-quarters of the truck traffic had to go through the Mu Gia Pass, one of two main passes, which crossed into Laos from the *Steel Tiger* area of North Vietnam. Realizing its vulnerability the NVA had placed 300 AAA sites in the vicinity making it extremely hazardous for tactical aircraft. In March 1966, Westmoreland was informed that the NVA were about to transport 140mm rocket launchers along the trail. These long-range weapons would have put

B-52F 57-0163 sprinkles 'special CBU' on a suspected Viet Cong stronghold eighteen miles south of Saigon in December 1965. USAF via Thurlow

Saigon at risk so it was considered vital to prevent their delivery. This attack was seen as an escalation of the war because it was the first use of B-52s against a North Vietnamese target. It raised the propaganda spectre of a possible B-52 shoot-down and also the practical difficulty of avoiding 'friendly' road-watch teams who were hidden in the area. The aim was to bomb the steep mountain slopes each side of the pass causing rockslides to block the route. The first mission, on 11/12 April, *Rock Kick II/Rolling Thunder 50*, required thirty of the newly-deployed B-52Ds, each dropping twenty-four variable-fused 1,000lb-bombs from their internal bomb-bays, and twenty-four 750lb-bombs from wing-racks. These were delivered from 35,000ft along a three-mile section of Route 15 through the Mu Gia Pass. Accuracy was degraded by some fuzzy radar pictures of the terrain. Some damage was caused, but the army of roadworkers had the traffic flowing again within twenty-four hours after the $21m mission. For the crews, going north brought a new tension to the missions. Peter S. Kuehl, a B-52 EW technician, remembered hearing that, 'the EWs and gunners got real jumpy on their first trip north. We heard that a tailgunner opened

Pre-loaded M117s await transport to the pylons of Guam-based B-52Ds. Boeing

A BAT (Bay Assembly Transport) trailer with a B-Bay high-density bomb rack pre-loaded. The A-Bay configuration had two vertical beams with fourteen M117s; the B-Bay had three vertical beams holding twenty-eight 500lb bombs.
USAF via Thurlow

up on an escorting fighter that got a little too curious, but no harm came from it.'

A second *Rock Kick*, on 27 April, caused thirty-two road craters but these too were filled in within a day. Undeterred, Westmoreland advocated continued attacks from B-52Ds and tactical fighters against this difficult, but at least finite target. He was overruled by general reservations in Washington about wasting munitions at a time when tactical fighters were having to fly with much reduced bomb-loads because of shortages. There were also rumours that SA-2 missiles were soon to be emplaced in the pass and no further 'landslide' missions were approved until 12 December 1966. The threat of missiles at least occupied the B-52s' EWs. Pete Kuehl: 'Until the B-52s started going north the EWs didn't have a whole lot to do, although they had to be ready. On training missions we always had runs against ECM sites scattered all over the USA. With the primitive receivers that they had at the time I don't know how they handled these runs without prior knowledge of the frequencies to expect. They were equipped with the AN/APR-9 of near-World War II vintage for high bands and the low-band AN/APR-14. The latter was handy on the flight line at Ellsworth because we could tune in to TV audio while working in the EW's position.' The ordnance shortage was a real constraint on the bomb-hungry B-52 force too, limiting *Arc Light* sorties to a maximum 600 monthly for the rest of 1966. Over 60,000 tons per month were needed to supply all USAF needs in the area, requiring substantial shipments from USAFE in Germany.

Big Belly

The B-52's combat initiation by B-52F units ended in March 1966. The JCS required an increase in the 300 sorties per month which the Guam squadrons had generated, and heavier bomb-loads per aircraft. Under the $30.6m *Big Belly* Project the B-52D fleet was modified between December 1965 and September 1967 to increase its internal 500lb-bombs from twenty-seven to eighty-four (or forty-two of 750lb), with twenty-four 750lb-bombs on external wing-racks. With the maximum of 108 500lb-bombs the full load was 54,000lb (49,000lb with 750lb-bombs). A new bomb-loading system was introduced whereby pre-loaded C-clips of 500lb-bombs could be uploaded into the internal bay to save time. (In practice, experienced loaders found that they could do the job manually in about the same time. Guam teams stuck with the traditional method, whereas loaders at the newer U-Tapao base preferred C-clips.)

Big Belly increased the B-52D's armament options to include mines, and later the GBU-15 glide bomb, while retaining the mountings for a quartet of nuclear weapons. From April 1969 'psyops' leaflets were carried by one B-52 in each cell on missions over South Vietnam, releasing 50,000 propaganda leaflets in an attempt to sap Viet Cong morale. Lt Col David G. Underhill, who supervised leaflet-dropping operations in Vietnam and wanted specially-modified B-52s for the purpose, told the authors that, 'the B-52 was used to drop leaflets and specially-designed radios to North Vietnam. I had repeatedly asked for a B-52 which could drop leaflets over all of North Vietnam from high altitude. Eventually pressure on Washington led to the despatch of a B-52 to Guam without external wing shackles, making it useless for 'iron bombs' and it worked perfectly. At the peak of the Vietnam war [using other aircraft too] we dropped over one billion leaflets a month, weighing over a thousand tons.' From 1967, Guam-based aircraft began to utilize more CBU-type weapons. Each B-52 could carry two 12,750lb-Hayes dispensers which carried BLU-3B canisters and could be reloaded on the aircraft. On fifteen sorties in April 1967 2,448 BLU-3Bs were dropped. Also introduced at this time was the BLU-26B anti-personnel bomblet in ADU-272B canisters, 144 of which could be carried in two Hayes dispensers, totalling 28,908lb and 25,488 bomblets.

The extra loads ate into the aircraft's fatigue life, necessitating the *Pacer Plank* (ECP 1581) structural 'beef-up' in the post-war years. In parallel with *Big Belly* the B-52Ds received more powerful Combat Skyspot radar transponders and a coat of TO-1-1-4 camouflage. The returning

A classic shot of B-52F 57-0144 as it crosses the South Vietnamese coast after a lengthy flight from Guam. By October 1965, black undersides had replaced the SAC white finish. USAF via Robert F. Dorr

B-52Fs had been warpainted only by covering their white 'nuclear' undersides with anti-searchlight matt black. B-52Ds of the 28th BW (first with the *Big Belly*) and 484th BW deployed to Andersen AFB, Guam in March 1966 giving increased weight of fire to Westmoreland's 'long-range artillery'. On their first mission, to the Mu Gia Pass on 11 April 1966 for *Rock Kick*, they dropped 600 tons of bombs in the largest single bombing attack since World War II. Over the following seven years, eleven SAC B-52D Wings rotated crews and aircraft through Guam. Introduction of the more numerous B-52D (170 built, compared with 89 B-52Fs) enabled a steady build-up from thirty to fifty, and then seventy aircraft, allowing 800 sorties a month.

Andy and 'U-T'

The 32-mile long island of Guam had many disadvantages as a B-52 base. Situated on top of a 32,000ft column of rock rooted in the Marianas Trench it supported a single base, Andersen AFB, built for the massive B-29 force which ended the war in Japan. It had been the centre of 3rd AD operations since 1954. A second, smaller airstrip, Northwest Field, was prepared for recovery of battle-damaged or 'hung-bomb' B-52s but it was never required. The main runway, 06/24 undulated, with a dip in the middle and an uphill stretch to the northern take-off end (Pati Point) where a cliff fell 500ft to the sea. Heavily-loaded bombers, struggling for flying speed could use 200ft of that to pick up a little more energy, though two went into the sea in the attempt in Summer 1969 (56-0593 and 56-0630, which also had structural failure). The cliff also caused a powerful updraught which posed handling problems for the pilot as he sought unstick speed (S2), which was reached excitingly close to the end of the runway. Flaps were pulled in at 180kt and, with a full bomb-load, a B-52D often needed ten minutes to work up to its climb speed of 280kt and over fifty minutes to reach 30,000ft. Maj Rees Williams stated that, 'take-off on seven engines was not a problem as long as you were past the the go/no-go point when the engine was lost. The major problem was climbing to altitude and maintaining altitude and position during the bomb run. Many missions were flown on seven engines; some on six. Loss of two engines on take-off on Guam posed a real problem. It happened several times. Six engines were insufficient to climb, and in some cases even to get the flaps up until some fuel was burned. Parameters for take-off were easy. First, the acceleration was checked. If that was deficient the take-off was aborted. Then we had a go/no-go point beyond which we could or could not stop if we aborted. Problems before this point caused an abort; after it we were committed to take off or accept a crash during abort. There were times when the end of the runway looked awfully close before breaking ground if an engine was lost at decision point.'

On take-off, crew members with downward-ejecting seats were acutely aware that 700ft AGL was their minimum punch-out altitude. Rain and algae made the runway slippery, causing traction problems for tow-trucks pulling bombers on the 'down-hill' section. There were areas of gravel each end and it was not unusual to find chipped paint under an aircraft's belly after it had ploughed through part of this on take-off.

Other, less threatening hazards included the giant Guamanian toad which liked to squat on warm runways. Robert F. Newton remembered that one of the men he worked with, 'made a sport of running them down when he got bored', drawing toad 'kill marks' on his truck door for each victim. 'At the last count he was a triple toad ace. There is also a miniature deer that came up on the runways from over the cliff. I would take the truck and round them up, just like the movie *Hatari*.' Another familiar resident was the Russian 'trawler', 'cruising off the end of the cliff and monitoring our activities and take-offs, so that in all our radio transmissions everything was related to a baseball game. The ground crew and maintenance people were "ball players" and the base was the "ball park", etc. When the planes were spotted coming back from a mission we reported them to Control by saying "Beast in the East", or "Best of the West", depending on which way they were coming in to land. One day a KC-135A took off, had a problem and had to return to land. Unfortunately he was far too heavy so they gave him permission to dump 50,000lb of fuel over the ocean. There was the trawler in front of him as he began his run so he lowered the boom and dumped all the fuel on it. For two weeks we didn't have the trawler there and for some strange reason there was never a formal protest over the incident.'

Don Campbell recounted another example of the dangers from Guamanian wildlife:

While on the bomb-run during a sortie from Guam we discovered a stowaway in the crew compartment in the form of a rat. After departing Vietnam airspace we decided to deal with the rodent by depressurizing the cabin. However, we had a great deal of trouble pressurizing again and remained at 35,000ft cabin altitude for 30 to 45 minutes. We figured that certainly this had done the rat in. As the flight home progressed the pilot went back to the 'bunk' to get a little sleep. He had only been asleep a few minutes when he was awakened by the rat crawling over his leg. The gunner, safe in a separate compartment, thought the whole situation was just hilarious. The ironic thing is that a month before deploying to Guam from McCoy AFB my crew were informed that we were required to get plague immunization shots. The copilot, being an Air Force Academy graduate, dutifully went and received his shot. Soon after, we were sitting Alert and the copilot spent the next two days hugging the toilet while being violently sick. The rest of us decided we didn't want any part of this so we forged our 'shot' record. On the day of deployment a 'Stars and Stripes' headline read 'Rat Discovered in Guam with Bubonic Plague'. At the time we never gave it a second thought, but after the rat was discovered panic set in. Fortunately, it didn't bother any of us. Soon after we landed a Crew Chief reported that the rat was spotted running down the hatch and off into the jungle. The moral of the story is that rats are much tougher than B-52 crewmembers.

Guam's main disadvantage was that it lay 2,600 miles from Saigon, requiring crews to make 12–14 hour round-trips to the target. At the height of *Linebacker* it was said that there was not room on the base for all its aircraft at the same time, requiring at least thirty to be flying at any time. With the advent of the B-52D the 4133rd BW (Provisional) was established at Andersen to control B-52 squadrons on their six-month rotations.

Gen Westmoreland suggested the creation of a second B-52 base nearer the action to reduce transit times and increase the sortie rate. Sattahip Naval Base in Thailand was chosen, but known as U-Tapao ('U-T' to its occupants). On 10 April 1967 three B-52Ds from the 4133rd BW (P) arrived for Operation *Poker Dice*, led in by Maj Gen W. J. Crumm. The 4258th SW was activated in June 1966 to control the resident KC-135 tankers, and the B-52s when they arrived. At first they were restricted from striking targets in Laos or overflying that country, causing severe pressure on Guam as the Laos missions increased. This restriction was lifted on 6 December 1967 and both day and night sorties were authorized. Initially a KC-135 and B-52 Forward Operating Base with tented accommodation, 'U-T' became a Main Operating Base in January 1969 and a major building programme began. This included docks for unloading the ceaseless supply of bombs, rather than having to bring them ashore in landing craft as before. Some aircrew remembered life in the area as being a little more entertaining than on Guam. However, the rules still applied. Rees Williams: 'I even remember the Ops Officer visiting our crew just before take-off and advising some of the crew members to get a hair-cut (or to become a martyr). Flying from there was great. We had block take-off times and flew the same block for about a week.' Above all, U-Tapao, only 450 miles from the target areas, meant no tankers, shorter missions and the possibility of heavier warloads. 'Time from pre-mission briefing to post-mission briefing was about eight to ten hours – just like a normal working day.' Jim Cichocki's normal day, working on B-52Ds, included having to cool down the tail-gunners' 'greenhouse' cabins before each mission, topping off the two water-injection reservoirs (one in each wing, unlike the B-52G) and coping with sleepless nights. As one of the first maintainers on the base he arrived, in plain clothes on Government contract, to find that the accommodation consisted of tin-roofed 'hootches'. One on-base recreation for airmen after a night out was to throw handfuls of rocks on to the metal roofs.

B-52Ds could go to their full 64,000lb-fuel load, grossing 450,000lb for take-off on the improved runways, (which, like Andersen's, had a Russian 'trawler' on permanent duty at the seaward end.) 'This was an in-flight limitation. At the start of take-off they were often 20,000lb heavier to allow for water (engine-injection) and fuel burn-off.'

With a second base operating B-52s from April 1967 utilization increased rapidly. Initially, fifteen B-52s used 'U-T'. Usually they had performed *Arc Lights* from Guam, flying on to U-Tapao and remaining in Thailand for several missions before returning to Guam on the final mission.

Demands on the B-52 force rose steadily as the war escalated. By November 1967 McNamara asked for a sortie surge rate of 1,200 per month. From 5 December 1967 B-52s were permitted to overfly Laos, and Souvanna Phouma was persuaded that the *Arc Light* operations in eastern Laos were necessary. 'Cover' strikes in South Vietnam were then suspended though the attacks within a neutral country were still kept from the world's press. The Laotian Government insisted that all *Arc Lights* should be flown above 30,000ft, preferably at night and that overflights should be made within a 60-mile corridor which avoided major population centres. In so doing it merely approved existing tactics. In 1966 5,217 *Arc Lights* were flown; 650 over Laos and 280 over southern North Vietnam.

Inevitably the record of this period has to be expressed in sortie and bomb statistics, the only reliable measures for the thousands of virtually identical sorties flown from Guam or U-Tapao to indeterminate targets throughout the war zone. With the new Thai base available, *Arc Light* totals increased to 9,686 in 1967 and 20,568 in 1968. In crude terms, more bombs had fallen on North Vietnam and Laos by 1968 than on Germany during the whole of the Second World War, but without significantly weakening NVA or VC strength. However, Gen Westmoreland still regarded the B-52s as, 'so valuable that I personally dealt with requests from field commanders, reviewed the targets and normally allocated the available bomber resources on a daily basis.' Because of the elusive nature of many of the targets, particularly in Laos, many *Arc Lights* were probably little more than 'matchwood missions' against the jungle. Unlike their tactical fighter colleagues, B-52 crews had little to worry about from enemy defences. *Arc Lights* flew well above the range of most AAA. A 100mm gun could reach their altitude but was inaccurate at that height. B-52s were usually outside the MiGs' sphere of influence, though MiG activity over Laos did increase from December 1971. No *Arc Lights* were hit by the defences although they were often attacking the same targets whose AAA had brought down, for example, twenty-five *Whiplash* F-105 Thunderchiefs over Laos up to February 1968. Fighter cynics commented that the worst you could face in the cockpit of a B-52 was spilling coffee from a 'hot cup' if the air got a little turbulent. In fact, many crews had participated in stateside air-defence exercises such as *Top Rung* in 1967 and were prepared for interceptions by fighters.

Arc Light Operations, Summer 1966 to December 1968

Operation Tally Ho
A continuation of the *Tiger Hound* trails interdiction programme devised by Lt Gen William Momyer, who took over 7th AF in July 1966. It supported *Rolling Thunder* attacks in Route Package 1 including six *Arc Lights* in the DMZ supporting USMC Operation *Hastings*, August 1966.

Operation Slam
Trails interdiction *Arc Lights* in Quang Tri Province from October 1966. Acronym for 'Seek, Locate, Annihilate and Monitor'.

Operation Birmingham
April–May 1966. *Arc Lights* were used to 'soften up' enemy positions ahead of this large 'search and destroy' operation in Tay Ninh. Over 3,000 tons of ordnance, including 220 tons of CBU dropped in 162 sorties, bombing fourteen base camps. NVA resorted to more tunnelling to escape *Arc Lights*.

Suoi Da
October 1966. 225 *Arc Lights* made possible relief of a Special Forces Camp.

Operation Attleboro
8–25 November 1966. 200 *Arc Lights* delivering 4,000 tons of bombs. *Shining Brass* team reported rice stores and buildings destroyed and the (unconfirmed) death of a VC General. Like many of these operations it drove the VC/NVA deeper into Laos to retrench.

Operation Cedar Falls
8–26 January 1967. *Arcs Lights* caved in a huge tunnel complex near Saigon, causing many secondary explosions of ammunition stores.

Operation Junction City
February–May 1967. Continued *Cedar Falls*. B-52s used in direct support of ground troops for the first time rather than 'area-bombing'. 126 *Arc Lights* flown. BDA reported 2,700 VC/NVA bodies.

Operation Slam III
30–31 January 1967. Two missions totalling 30 *Arc Lights* against 'Sihanouk Trail' targets. B-52s and F-4Cs controlled by ABCCC C-130 from Da Nang. *Hornet* BDA teams discovered supply dumps destroyed by B-52s.

Operation Slam IV
February 1967. Total of 256 *Arc Light* sorties against Route 922 in eastern Laos. Many secondary explosions. From 10 February, six B-52s and six F-4Cs made nightly missions in the *Steel Tiger/Tiger Hound* areas. One third of B-52 ordnance was delayed action.

Operation Slam V/VI
June–August 1967. Concluded the programme with 110 *Arc Lights*, all with undetermined effects.

Operation Neutralize
March and September-October 1967. Major initiative to halt VC advances in South Vietnam. 820 *Arc Light* sorties including the first over North Vietnam since April 1966. B-52s targeted on NVA artillery. In September, B-52s flew 852 sorties (90 per cent of that month's total) to throw back NVA threatening the USMC base at Con Thien. *Battle of Dak To* November 1967. B-52s flew 268 of the 2,000 sorties needed to repel VC advances in Kontum Province and Loc Ninh. Thirty-two targets hit in day-and-night bombing of artillery around Con Thien with a 'body count' of over 3,000.

Operation Niagara
January–March 1968. (*See* text.)

Operation Delaware
April 1968. 726 *Arc Light* sorties against 123 targets in the A Shau Valley, west of Da Nang.

Operation Turnpike
April–June 1968. Led to development of Special *Arc Light* Operating Areas (SALOAS).

Operation Plattsburg
May–June 1968.

Defence of Saigon
June–September 1968. Particularly active (846 sorties) in June.

Operation Thor July 1968.
Operation *Thor* in Cap Mui Lay area, July 1968. 210 *Arc Light* sorties on VC threatening USMC positions near the DMZ. Over 2,000 gun positions and other structures destroyed. On 14 July B-52s made their deepest northern penetration to date, hitting supply caches fifteen miles north of the DMZ. Four days later the first *Arc Light* was flown against an SA-2 site.

Ban Laboy (October 1968) included the first use of concentrated 'pinpoint' bombing rather than 'area' bombing.

Rolling Thunder ended on 1 November, 1968 by which time B-52s had contributed 2,380 sorties, dropping 643,000 tons of bombs. In all, 35,680 *Arc Light* sorties had been mounted since June 1965, hauling 886,490 tons of explosive. The 1968 'bombing pause' freed large numbers of tactical aircraft and it was suggested that they could be used to attack *Arc Light* targets but MACV insisted that a six-aircraft B-52 mission, hitting a 2km-square target with 180 tons of ordnance in ten minutes could only be matched by between 60 and 180 tactical aircraft, and even then they could not be concentrated in the same way.

Flying the B-52 actually presented its own problems for crew. Fatigue from a succession of twelve-hour missions, with a twelve-hour break between them, was the principal drain on Andersen crews. For most members of a B-52 crew confinement to a claustrophobic, cramped position behind the cockpit was a punishment it itself. As former *Arc Light* navigator Don Laing told the authors, 'I never really liked navigating a big plane like the B-52. Part of that feeling was due to the fact that big birds that had navigators did not have windows where the navigators were, including the B-52, and we couldn't see out. Where was the fun in flying?' Don was delighted to transition to the F-111A in 1969 at a time when, 'SAC was having serious problems keeping its navigators, partially due to the gruelling job involved in navigating a B-52; extremely long hours, great pressures and being sent to Vietnam every other six months for *Arc Light* tours.' Radar navigators (RN) had one of the most demanding jobs on the 'lower deck' of the aircraft. For the attack sections of the mission an RN had to peer into his radar scope hood, operating the controls largely by touch. Exhaustion may have contributed to the second mid-air collision of two B-52s, on 7 July 1967. Maj Gen William J. Crumm, who had commanded 3rd AD since July 1965, was leading a cell of three B-52Ds in tight formation on an *Arc Light*. When the cell reached its IP it had to do a steep turn to enter the bomb-run but the third aircraft's pilot misjudged his turn and collided with Crumm's 22nd BW aircraft. Both aircraft (56-0595 and 56-0627) plummeted down, twenty-two miles off the coast of South Vietnam taking six crewmen with them, including the 3rd AD Commander.[11] Seven others were recovered. The rules on tight cell formation were relaxed after that. Early 'tall tail' B-52s required considerable physical strength to operate their unpowered controls in any sort of manoeuvre and close formation flying greatly increased that difficulty. Separation within a cell was set at 1,500yd for most *Arc Lights*.

Maj Rees Williams remembered that crew fatigue was a frequent topic among crews. 'The conversation was about different ways to ensure safety in flight. Most crews had a rule that at least two crew members must stay awake at all times. Others embellished this by requiring that the two should be in the pilots' seats. This

Jim Cichocki marshalls 'his' B-52D, 55-0080, back into its revetment at U-Tapao in 1968. '080 was one of six Loring B-52s in Operation Longlegs, a non-stop return flight to Buenos Aires in November 1957. Cichocki

B-52D's pilot and gunner put a brave face on the prospect of another Arc Light from U-Tapao. Cichocki

is where many non-pilot members got in their flying practice. The usual case was that at least one pilot was to be in those seats, but I heard rumours that this was not always the case. In addition some cell leaders required periodic radio contact with the other two aircraft. All of this was on the return trip when the pressure of the mission was over.'

Another 22nd BW aircraft was destroyed the following day. It lost power on several engines and a number of electrical systems during an *Arc Light* and its pilot attempted an emergency landing at Da Nang. The ever-present risk of VC sniper fire near the runway necessitated a much steeper approach than usual. The Stratofortress touched down nearly half-way

Trailing its 44-ft diameter drag 'chute, B-52D 56-0693, recovers to U-Tapao in 1968. It was the first B-52D to arrive at the base when 'U-T' became the second main Arc Light launch-pad in April 1967. USAF via Robert F. Dorr

Squatting ponderously on U-Tapao's runway this 307th SW B-52D awaits the order to advance throttles and take off. USAF via Thurlow

down the strip, its yellow drag 'chute ripped away and B-52D, 56-0601, crashed and exploded at the end of the runway.

An omen of the much harder life facing B-52 crews later in the war was the first SA-2 'Guideline' SAM fired at a B-52, in September 1967. On an *Arc Light* at 37,000ft over the DMZ, a safe position for a B-52 normally, the EWO of a 454th BW aircraft picked up a *Fan Song* guidance radar signal indicating that an SA-2 was 'up' and about to be launched at them.

Breaking off their bomb run and heading out to sea to increase their chances of rescue the crew sat tight, anticipating a hit. Luckily the EWO was able to use his jammers to good effect and two SA-2s exploded about 3,000ft from the bomber. However, it was a close call and a worrying sign that the North Vietnamese could move SA-2s on their ZIL-157 semi-trailer transporter-erectors into hitherto safe areas of the trails and DMZ to combat *Arc Lights*. The appearance of SAMs also hastened an

improvement programme in the B-52D's ECM fit, taking it from Phase IV to Phase V through 1967-69 with the addition of ALT-28 and ALT-32H/L jammers to the existing ALT-6B, ALT-13, ALT-15 and ALT-16 ECM suite. These updates made the B-52D the best-equipped B-52 model in this respect until the B-52G was similarly upgraded and, with the *Big Belly* it ensured that the 'D' remained in service in Vietnam long after the B-52E and B-52F which were retired from 1967 onwards.

Jim Cichocki effortlessly supports a MER-ful of 500lb bombs at U-Tapao. Cichocki

B-52 revetments and bomb storage areas at U-Tapao. USAF via Thurlow

Add Kadena

In 1968, the year in which the USAF flew an incredible 1,034,839 combat sorties in South East Asia, a third B-52 Operating Base came into use and contributed to the 20,568 *Arc Light* sorties flown that year. The Tet Offensive damaged US morale and prompted an increase in B-52 sorties from 800 to 1,500 monthly after 1st February. The seizure of the US communications ship *Pueblo* by North Korea prompted President Johnson to send another twenty-six B-52Ds in a movement coded *Port Bow*. Fifteen joined the 4252nd SW at Kadena (provider of KC-135A services for the B-52 force) during the first week of February 1968, the remainder going to Andersen. Their availability for *Arc Lights* enabled the monthly sortie rate to peak at 1,800 during July, 1969. (SAC had objected strongly to this level, which had been approved by the Pentagon on 22 June 1968, saying that, 'We cannot continue to provide 1,800 sorties and maintain our SIOP posture without additional resources.') They remained at Kadena until September 1970 when the *Arc Light* operation was concentrated at U-Tapao. Mission times from Kadena were half those for Guam-based bombers. Another bonus, Rees Williams recalled was, 'The nice thing for pilots was that the fuel offload from the tanker was not nearly so large as when flying from Guam. The weather there could present a real problem though, with wet runways and variable direction cross-winds. I experienced some "pucker time" during take-offs and landings at Kadena.' Don Campbell rated it as, 'the best deployment location, due to weather, sortie length and especially the off-base amenities'.

Khe Sanh

Of all the B-52's combat engagements in the 1960s, none illustrates the wisdom of Gen Westmoreland's faith in its capability better than Operation *Niagara*, the use of airpower in the relief of Khe Sanh. Speaking to 3rd AD personnel about the missions he said, 'I visualized your bombs falling like water over the famous falls in New York State'. At the height of the Tet Offensive in 1968, communist forces attempted to capture the substantial Khe Sanh combat base situated fourteen miles south of the DMZ and six from the Laotian border. It was one of the closest US strongpoints to enemy border territory and therefore easy for the opposition to bring up constant reinforcements. For seventy-seven days from 21st January, 20,000 troops from the NVA's 304th and 325th Divisions besieged the camp and its 6,000 USMC and ARVN occupants, whose only useful defence came from forty-six medium artillery pieces. NVA artillery, ringing the base was able to deluge shells (1,307 on the worst day) into the small base area. The use of overwhelming airpower, making Khe Sanh's surroundings the most bombed target in history, eventually enabled the base to be relieved by Operation *Pegasus/Lam Son 207*. The NVA withdrew, shattered by aerial bombardment. B-52s contributed a daily average of forty-five *Arc Light* sorties to more than three hundred tactical sorties. In all, 24,000 tactical sorties and 2,707 *Arc Lights* were needed to dislodge the NVA siege which eventually dissolved under the impact of 110,000 tons of ordnance. Over half of this fell from B-52s. *Niagara* was the largest tactical air operation of the war and the largest commitment of B-52s to an operation of this type. On many days, smaller tactical aircraft were limited by monsoon weather which did not hamper Skyspot-directed B-52s, though frequent fog-banks made BDA difficult. At the height of the battle, an *Arc Light* cell from EB-66C/E jamming aircraft was particularly valuable during *Niagara*.

Lt Col Don Campbell told the authors of the extra demands that *Niagara* brought: 'I was flying out of U-Tapao, so missions were about two to four hours in length. On one occasion I flew two sorties in one day in attacking targets of opportunity after the lengthy mission planning procedure was complete. From 15 February 1968 *Bugle Note* allowed a cell of B-52s to arrive at a predesignated 'pre-IP' every ninety minutes. They were picked up by the Skyspot operator who the directed them to an IP

Dwarfed by heavy monsoon clouds and the huge wing of B-52D 55-0107, Jim Cichocki contemplates life in Thailand. The white stripes on wing-tips and tanks were to minimize night-time ground collisions. Cichocki

appeared over the target at least every ninety minutes around the clock. Their targets were staging and assembly areas, storage and artillery positions and they prevented the NVA from formatting sufficiently to make a mass attack and overrun the base with sheer force of numbers. On one occasion when troops were caught in the open by an *Arc Light* some 75 per cent of a 1,800-man regiment were killed, according to a captured Viet Cong. The B-52s themselves were not invulnerable. Flying near the DMZ they were within the 25-mile slant range of several SA-2 batteries in the North. *Tiny Tim* ECM support, against targets around the besieged camp. My crew and I had just returned from a strike and were on our way to get something to eat when we were summoned back to Ops and informed that we were going back. We immediately briefed and boarded another aircraft. Two 'BUFF' sorties in one day was unheard of and had we been on Guam it would have been impossible. I'll always remember looking at the photography and seeing how the NVA had dug out the trenches we had buried the day before. They certainly had some nerve.'

The operation also introduced a procedure which overcame the lack of flexibility and thence to a target 'box'. In practice, it proved better to use six aircraft every three hours. *Bugle Note* later extended to all *Arc Light* areas and replaced the Quick Reaction Force of B-52s which had been maintained at their S.E. Asia bases.

Bombing in such close proximity to 'friendlies' required the B-52Ds to descend to 24,000ft and reduce speed, avoiding the effects of high-altitude winds on bombing accuracy. The normal Skyspot bombing safety limit was 3,300yd from 'friendlies', even when two Skyspot beacons were used to ensure maximum accuracy, as at Khe Sanh. An earlier experience at Con Thien

Life on the Rock

Capt Robert F. Newton was also a Maintenance Officer with responsibility for loading bombs into B-52Ds taking part in *Arc Light* missions, and for combat damage repair.

The weather at Andersen was always the same – 85 degrees in the day and 72 degrees at night, with downpours every 20 or 30 minutes. The only difference was the wind blew from the South for six months, then from the North for six months. You could tell if a man was a newcomer or not – the 'old guy' would continue to work on the plane when the rain came while the new one ran for shelter. My job was to cruise the flight line in a truck to resolve problems, sign the maintenance records and aid in radio communications. Working space was no problem for us as we did everything outside. When I first got there we had about fifty planes scattered about the base, but when the January 1968 Tet Offensive hit we had over 100 planes and we had to send some to U-Tapao. (U-Tapao in Thai means 'new land' and the land it was on was originally a swamp, but they tore down a mountain to get the earth to fill it.)

Normally it took six hours to turn a plane around for the next mission because they were very safety-conscious. You refuelled it, loaded it and then fixed it. After Tet we refuelled a plane, loaded it with bombs, changed a tyre and fixed it all at the same time, turning it around in two hours. Safety went out the window. We launched six planes in a stacked trail formation. One day some people went out to check a B-52's infrared flare system, without downloading the flares. They ignited and burned all the skin from the rear wheels to the tail. They had to send to Kadena for a horizontal tail off their 'hangar queen' so they could fix the plane.

Just to the right of one runway there was a small hill and one B-52's wing hit it on landing. It crushed the tip-tank and sheared off the outrigger. Another day I was preparing a launch and there was a truck parked in front of me. The occupant was talking to the Crew Chief. Along came a B-52 and hit the truck with its wingtip, throwing it fifty feet with the man still in it. He didn't get hurt because he was belted in but it destroyed the truck and threw debris on the taxiway. The B-52D's wing had a deep gouge in its leading edge.

We had six primary planes ready to fly the mission and one back-up. If one of the primaries couldn't go up I had to go to the plane, get the crew and transport them to the back-up. This was called a baggage drill. A crew-member flying 100 missions got a patch and when I completed my hundredth drill I got a '100 Baggage Drills' patch.

As far as bomb loads are concerned, we had our basic 500lb-iron bomb load: eighty-four internal loaded in packages like at U-Tapao and twenty-four externally, loaded individually. Sometimes they made a load of 1000 pounders or mixed them with 500 pounders. Then there were the 'BB bombs' [CBU]. They came in boxes and were pre-loaded like the 500lb bombs. They armed when the fins deployed and just striking a leaf would set them off. They were considered too dangerous. One was made in the shape of a ball [BLU-26B] and its rotation armed it. Every so often one would fall and split open. You could easily tell when it happened because the first thing you saw was everyone running out of the revetments and the rest climbing over the wall as if you had disturbed an ants' nest. Then we had to call EOD (explosives team) to go in and pick them up. Another time, some of the bombs didn't release over the target and when the plane landed they fell down on to the bomb-doors and were sticking through. Another trip to the hangar queen!

One of the most exciting things to see was called a 'torch-over'. If an engine would not start normally and the wind was right you would start the up-wind engine (of the pair) and let raw fuel pour through the dead engine. When the hot exhaust hit the raw fuel there would be a big flash of flame and it would go up the dead engine and start it.

I was able to fly on 16 missions and I was one of the few people other than aircrews to win the Air Medal during that operation. Except for the critical time of bomb-drop I sat in the various positions to give the crew a rest. Most of the time it was in the copilot's seat because I could manage the fuel panel, work the radios and other functions. On one flight I sat in the pilot's position and used the autopilot, which then failed so I flew the plane by hand. When the pilot returned to his seat he noticed I was wearing navigator's insignia and he almost fainted.

After his two *Arc Light* tours Capt Newton was assigned to a 'Spooky' unit at Da Nang flying EC-47s modified to monitor enemy radio transmissions. He still came into contact with *Arc Light* B-52s – almost too closely on one occasion.

We were patrolling north of Saigon and knew a B-52 strike was coming in. Before the strike we picked up transmissions from someone right in the middle of the strike area. Then came 648 bombs, right where he was. We had stood off ten miles so we wouldn't get caught in the blasts and after the dust had settled we went back to check the area over. Five minutes after the strike the guy was back on the air! Where he had gone to avoid the bombs is still a mystery to me. On one of my last EC-47 missions we were sent east of Saigon. We had finished our patrol and were heading back to Saigon. Then I heard an incoming strike on the radio and something told me to plot the co-ordinates (to this day I don't know why) and they showed we were right in the target box. I told the pilot to turn south immediately. Three minutes after the turn, down came the bombs and a B-52 almost got me.

Electronic warfare expert Pete Kuehl: 'There were usually rainstorms daily on Guam. The humidity 'raised Cain' with our electronic gear. On the trip back from Vietnam B-52s cruised at over 40,000ft at well below freezing, then descended to Guam where it was 85 degrees F and humid. They were required to run all the systems up before parking the bird and most of them would fail. The fix was to haul the 'black boxes' into the shop where you could pour water out of them, dry them out and put them back on the shelf. Often, if the plane didn't get worked on until later the system dried out on its own.'

Even navigators weren't immune from a little suffering in the cause of maintenance and Don Campbell reckons he was, 'the first in a long line of black-and-blue navigators that were dropped out of the bomb bay during post flight. I was walking along the bomb bay doors, checking to see that all the arming wires had been retained when... *Pow*! The next thing I knew I was on the ramp, flat on my back. There was some misunderstanding between my pilot, Bill Anderson and the Crew Chief regarding the meaning of 'Are the doors clear?'. Never again would Bill open the doors until he saw me standing in front of the aircraft.'

---

in 1967, when a cell of B-52s accidentally dropped its load within 1,500yd of USMC positions, had caused a re-think of this limit. There, the bombs had produced numerous large secondary explosions which showed that the enemy, believing that B-52 aircrews were forbidden to bomb within three kilometres of 'friendlies', had moved men and munitions inside the supposed 3,300yd safety zone. Marines at Khe Sanh were aware that the NVA was excavating a trench network, often digging 1,000ft in a night to approach the perimeter. Although USMC Commander Lt Gen Robert E. Cushman asked for a minimum two-mile bombing radius to protect his men the NVA entered this too. Gen Momyer reassured him that a three-quarter mile bombing radius was safely achievable and a single B-52 demonstrated this on 26 February. From then on *Arc Lights* included 101 genuinely CAS missions within 1,700yd of the base. One aircraft, *Yankee 37*, put its bombs only 1,400yd from the perimeter and triggering secondary explosions which lasted two hours. There were devastating consequences for the NVA, particularly when they were hit on open ground or at night. One attack, on 19 March, apparently caused 1,000 fatalities and 300 soldiers deserted the battle in acute shock. When they eventually retreated from the incessant pounding Gen Westmoreland proclaimed that, 'The thing that broke their back basically was the fire of the B-52s'.

The ceaseless demand for munitions kept 'U-T's' personnel busy loading B-Bay racks of Mk 82 LDGP bombs in 1969. USAF via Thurlow

The B-52's complex undercarriage was considered a major secret in its early days and it was airbrushed out of the first company photographs showing take-offs and landings. On B-52D 56-0617, the units are beginning to swivel through 90 degrees to lie flat, a procedure which took about ten seconds. Frank Mormillo

Into Cambodia

Perhaps the most contentious of America's interventions in S.E. Asia was in Cambodia. Tenuously neutral under Prince Norodom Sihanouk, the country had condoned military activity by both North and South Vietnam on its soil to preserve that neutrality. Throughout the 1960s its eastern border with Vietnam had enclosed an extension of the Ho Chi Minh Trail (the 'Sihanouk Trail') supplying the Viet Cong. After 1967, a half of all USAF sorties in S.E. Asia were flown in an attempt to stop this leakage southwards. During Johnson's presidency the Pentagon had resisted the possibility of attacking VC sanctuaries in Cambodia, which expanded considerably in 1968-69 to include training camps and supply dumps, in preparation for an invasion of the South as soon as the USA withdrew its forces from Vietnam. Within weeks of taking office President Nixon responded to the Viet Cong shelling of Saigon in February 1969 by allowing B-52 attacks on Cambodian base areas. These began on 18 March 1969 and were kept secret in order to protect Sihanouk. All were officially recorded as targets in South Vietnam.[12] One of the first of these *Arc Lights* may well have destroyed the HQ for NVA border operations into South Vietnam, a target which was revealed by an NVA defector. Within a year, 3,630 *Arc Light* sorties were flown over Cambodia in an extension of the war which lasted into August 1973, long after the main S.E. Asia conflict had subsided. In all, over 16,500 sorties were mounted.

involved a sequence which ran from *Breakfast* to *Supper*) began in March 1969 to prepare the way for cross-border incursions by 90,000 ARVN troops supported by the US Army. By May 1970, over 4,300 *Arc Lights* had contributed to this process. As in Laos, the degree of success against the presumed locations of NVA base facilities was often unknown except when large secondary explosions occurred or follow-up BDA by ground units was possible. Missions elsewhere yielded more tangible results. B-52s flew 804 sorties against NVA forces besieging a Special Forces post at Ben Het, eventually driving them off. In April 1970, Westmoreland's replacement, Gen Creighton Abrams, began Operation *Patio*, an extension into May of *Menu* strikes into Cambodia and Laos, which put even more pressure

left the briefing room! The NVA had moved war materiel real close to the border and was stockpiling it in massive quantities – I remember viewing the intel photos of this. We struck at targets not far from the South Vietnam/Cambodia border, some within fifty miles of Saigon itself. In all my 178 missions I never again saw secondary explosions of the magnitude of those occurring on that first day over Cambodia – they were incredible. We continued strikes for several days and gradually the secondaries subsided as we continued to destroy what was left.

During the two months that the troops remained in Cambodia, 763 *Arc Light* sorties were flown, many ranging deeper into the country than the eighteen-mile limit set for the troops.

With up-flexed wings and sooty wake, a 22nd BW B-52D takes to the air. Frank Mormillo

Under pressure from *Arc Lights*, the NVA moved deeper into Cambodia putting increasing pressure on its government until March, 1970 when Sihanouk lost control and fled into exile (possibly encouraged by the CIA). The American public was then informed that over 100,000 tons of bombs had been deposited on this neutral country by B-52s. His successor, Marshall Lom Nol supported increased US intervention from June 1970 onwards, by which time Nixon had begun to send US and ARVN troops into Cambodia to search out the NVA safe havens, with *Arc Light* support. Operation *Menu* (so-called because its various stages

on the *Arc Light* force. Six missions were aimed at targets in the *Parrot's Beak* and *Fish-hook* areas of Cambodia to prepare the way for army advances. Don Campbell, who flew some of those April sorties recalls,

Prior to the first mission the Commander of the 3rd AD, Lt Gen Alvan Gillem (who was an outstanding leader and highly respected by all) briefed the personnel directly involved in the pending operation. But before doing so he ordered all of the Wing staff out of the Andersen briefing room and informed us that we were going into Cambodia. Boy, were they mad and tried to find out where we were going when we

Meanwhile, Operation *Good Look* kept the B-52s busy in Northern Laos with 2,580 sorties right through until April 1973 as the US repelled constant NVA/VC incursions, while simultaneously attempting to reduce its own forces, hand over the war to the South Vietnamese and walk out of the war.[13] The consequent run-down in USAF assets in the area meant a reorganization of the B-52 force. On 1 April 1970 the 3rd AD was inactivated and *Arc Light* operations came under 8th AF control (3rd AD was part of the 'Mighty Eighth' during World War II). SAC's influence over the use of its B-52s had increased since Gen John D. Ryan ('Three Fingered Jack'), a SAC man, assumed control of USAF operations in the Pacific. He and 'Spike' Momyer had managed to speed up the cumbersome decision-making chain required for *Arc Light* target approval.

From April 1970, the rotation system was changed so that individual crews were sent to the two war-waging Provisional Bomb Wings on six-month detachments, with seventeen weeks at Andersen and the rest at U-Tapao. By the war's end it was hard to find a SAC B-52 crew who had not completed a Vietnam deployment, and many had made five or more. Mission totals of up to 400 were not uncommon for individuals.

Arc Light operations from Guam ran down in September 1970, as they did at Kadena, and U-Tapao took over the task. Partly this reflected the reduction of USAF numbers but it also enabled considerable savings in B-52 logistics.

B-52 losses up to 1971 were minimal and none was directly due to enemy action though the North had tried hard to down one. It was discovered that new MiG airfields had been built within flying range of Northern Laos in an attempt to shoot down a 'BUFF' (the nickname which came into use during 1968, based on the epithet 'Big Ugly Fat Fellow', with variations on the final word). The 306th BW suffered two B-52D casualties during its brief stay at Kadena, both caused by fires on or before take-off. Capt Robert F. Newton describes the crash of B-52D 55-0103: 'He couldn't get enough speed and tried to abort take-off, but by that time he was going too fast and went off the end of the runway, coming to a sudden stop. The fuel tank behind the ECM operator's bulkhead burst and fuel spilled into the cabin, soaking the crewman. His suit caught fire and he burned to death, though the rest of the crew got out safely. Fortunately none of the weapons went off during the fire as base housing was very close to the end of the runway.' U-Tapao was the scene of a particularly unfortunate accident on 19 July 1969 when B-52D 55-0676 of the 70th BW aborted its take-off and skidded off the end of the runway. The crew of an HH-43 rescue helicopter arrived over the burning wreck with their suspended ball of fire retardant, not realizing that the bomber's occupants were all safely out. When the B-52's bombs cooked off the explosion engulfed the HH-43 and its brave crew.

Although the overall total of B-52 sorties in 1971 fell to 12,554, U-Tapao's forty-two aircraft were extremely busy. *Arc Lights* in support of the big *Lam Son 719* operation began on 6 March with attacks on troop concentrations near Tchepone. Between 8 February and 24 March, 1,358 sorties were flown over the Laotian panhandle, dumping 32,000 tons of munitions, sometimes within 1,000yd of ARVN forces who came to rely on the B-52s whenever they encountered opposition. A change of weapon configuration was introduced at U-Tapao for this period too, giving a 108-bomb total payload. The wing pylons were loaded with twenty-four Mk 117s in place of Mk 82s and 84 Mk 82s were carried in the bay in place of the usual 42 Mk 117s. On one mission with this devastating warload, when a large force of NVA was identified, the subsequent body-count was thought to be 1,700. Another enemy force was caught on 21 February as it assembled to attack ARVN soldiers occupying a hill, and 698 bodies were left in the wake of an *Arc Light*. Four days later another of the bombers detonated four tons of ammunition and left 142 dead. ARVN troops developed a technique of engaging the enemy and then withdrawing just before an *Arc Light* was due. Sometimes this meant bombs falling only 300ft from friendly forces, but the consequences for the persistent NVA regiments were appalling. They were decimated by over 150 tons of bombs from an unseen, unheard force seven miles above them. On other occasions, *Arc Lights* were used merely to clear forest and prepare landing sites for helicopter-borne infantry – a quick but costly way of creating an airfield. A further push by US/ARVN troops attempted to regain communist-held sections of Cambodia later in 1971, with U-Tapao aircraft dropping 1,000 tons of ordnance on 20 September, the first day. As 1971 came to an end *Arc Light* strikes were the USAF's main contribution to the war effort.

B-52D 56-0677, with one of the biggest shark grins in the business. Another Guam-based B-52D, 56-0582, was similarly adorned. Paul Minert via Greg Spahr

CHAPTER FOUR

Linebacker

Send in the B-52s

In 1972, Richard Nixon decided to force North Vietnam to negotiate a peace settlement, beginning with a gradual increase in B-52 pressure. The North proved equally determined in attempting to capture as much of South Vietnam as possible, aiming to destroy the ARVN and undermine President Thieu's fragile government. Unusually heavy movements on the Trails necessitated increases in *Arc Lights* from 1,000 to 1,200 monthly from 8 February and the despatch of twenty-nine B-52Ds to Guam to take the sorties to 1,500. At the time, Andersen had reverted to stand-by nuclear status with a few 60th BS aircraft but the 43rd SW infrastructure was in place to support the extra 'iron bombers'.

Within the five stages of *Bullet Shot*, Guam's 'BUFF' force was steadily rebuilt, beginning with crews from the 7th BW, 96th BW and 306th BW in February. Representatives from the other SAC units were gradually added to comprise the 63rd BS (P) and in July the 72nd BW (P) formed with the 64th BS (P), 65 BS (P) and 486th BS (P), all flying the B-52G. The 2nd BW alone deployed 1,461 personnel and 23 bombers in April 1972. With fifty 43rd SW B-52Ds also on Guam, and U-Tapao's eventual complement of 54, it was necessary to draw on a hundred of SAC's nuclear-alert B-52Gs to face the threat of a large-scale North Vietnamese invasion of the South. Inevitably, this stretched the B-52 SIOP, increasing the number of nuclear targets assigned to each remaining Alert aircraft. Meanwhile, SAC tanker squadrons also deployed to S.E. Asia in support of Operation *Constant Guard* and *Young Tiger*, placing additional strains on their resources.

Accommodation at Andersen came under severe pressure with large tent cities and a 'Tin City' of steel dormitories for the 12,500 personnel on base at the peak of the *Bullet Shot* build-up. Operations continued round the clock, with night-shift maintainers attempting to sleep in Tin City where temperatures hit 110 degrees without air-conditioning. The predominance of the B-52D in the war zone meant that numerous crews had to convert to this model with Castle AFB's CCTS, the 329th BS. Crews from the B-52F, 'G' and 'H' units were processed through the 'D-Difference' course. Converts from those models, with powered controls, found the 'D' physically demanding to fly, especially with underwing bomb-racks. Its reduced power also required some familiarization and it usually took at least four sorties for a crew to qualify on the aircraft whose handling qualities Gen McCarthy described as 'like an eighteen-wheel truck without power steering, air brakes or automatic transmission in downtown Washington during the rush hour'.

With up to 200 B-52s at the two bases, enabling a huge increase in sorties to be made to 3,150 monthly, formidable strains were placed on the support organizations. At Guam, the 303rd Consolidated Aircraft Maintenance Wing (CAMW), known as 'The Bicycle Works' (perhaps in deference to the B-52's unusual undercarriage) had responsibility for fuelling (two million gallons daily) and pre-flighting each aircraft inside four hours – half the peace-time rate. With only two 'nose-dock' hangars for maintenance, plus another pair for Boeing-supervised, mid-cycle PDM, most of their work was done outside in all weathers, day and night, including major inspections. The 303rd's engine maintenance shop inspected and repaired 120 of the thousand resident jet engines per month, a 250 per cent increase in its customary workload. Each inspection required 250 man-hours at the 1,200 hour-point. With each aircraft making several fourteen-hour flights per week this figure was often reached.

As communist activity increased through February 1972 most tactical air opposition to it was flown by SVAF units. However, under the full weight of artillery, infantry and (for the first time) T-55 main battle tank assaults on positions in Quang Tri province from 30th March, ARVN resistance quickly collapsed. North Vietnam had been able to increase its fighting capability immensely during the US bombing 'pause' since 1968. Heavy cloud cover prevented most tactical air support and *Arc Lights* were the only way of tackling 40,000 NVA troops and their armour. A three-pronged assault was aimed at taking Quang Tri City, An Loc and Kontum. From 30 March to 6 April 132 *Arc Light* sorties pounded the advancing army and missions continued through May. Although Quang Tri fell, 300 NVA soldiers were killed by the bombing. Two cells were called in by an FAC to bomb a section of Highway 1, which was in their target box, destroying thirty-five tanks en route to Quang Tri City. Continued bombing enabled ARVN platoons to set up solid defensive positions, blunting the NVA advance. The US Army policy was to let ARVN troops hold a position long enough for enemy forces to mass near it in large enough numbers to make a suitable *Arc Light* target. There is no doubt that such massive losses weakened and disrupted the attempted North Vietnamese invasion.

Further south at Kontum, a large NVA regular force, advancing east out of Laos, besieged the town. Once again, Stratofortresses saved the situation, crushing the NVA and eventually driving them back on 6 June. It took all of 2,262 sorties to hit the 795 targets identified around Kontum in a 22-day onslaught, causing enormous NVA losses. The third prong of the attack speared due south against An Loc in the Saigon area. A strategy of in-depth B-52 strikes had already been planned for this eventuality and it went into action on 6 April as the communist forces approached out of Cambodia. An Loc had seen heavy fighting in the summer of 1969 when *Arc*

Lights helped to disperse a VC threat. In 1972 it took 10,000 tactical sorties and 254 *Arc Lights* to save An Loc. Ninety-one targets, including a group of thirty-five tanks were devastated by the bombing, which was often placed within 650yd of South Vietnamese units. (NVA soldiers used to say 'hang on to the American soldier's belt in order to fight him'). During April-June 1972 the two B-52 bases recorded over 6,000 take-offs by bombed-up B52s, which undoubtedly turned back the invasion. At the height of the battle for An Loc B-52s appeared every hour for thirty hours, with each mission taking a serious toll of the invaders. Gen Westmoreland's view that military units caught in the open could be destroyed or demoralized by *Arc Lights* was at last shown to be true. They had a decisive role in the situation at An Loc. Two missions were targeted on NVA soldiers who were trying to prevent an ARVN regiment from relieving the city. The enemy formation was shattered by the rain of bombs (one cell could drop 188,000lb with a 500ft CEP inside two minutes) and An Loc was restored to ARVN control. With the typical irony of war, the city they regained was already virtually destroyed. In the words of the local US Commander, Gen John R. McGiffert, the B-52 'became the most effective weapon we have been able to muster; absolutely central to the successful defence effort against the invading force. Its massive firepower has made the difference in such key areas as An Loc and Kontum.' Above all, Saigon had been saved from immediate danger allowing the US withdrawal to proceed safely.

Linebacker I

Meanwhile, Nixon began to use B-52s north of the 20th parallel 'bomb-line' to force Hanoi into meaningful negotiations. Operation *Freedom Train* began these attacks in April 1972 and developed into *Linebacker I*. Beginning with the mining of Haiphong harbour by USN jets, and later by B-52s, the operation was the opening round in the heavy strategic bombing of the North which many military leaders had recommended since 1965. For many senior USAF officers the belief in strategic bombing as a means of winning wars, rooted in World War II, had always been a basic principle. However, the spectre of possible B-52 losses re-emerged more strongly since the North's defences had been massively increased. Although occasional SA-2s had been launched against B-52s over the Trails in 1967 none had come within range. SAC's best bomber was now pitted against the most heavily defended targets in military history. Inevitably, much faith was placed in the aircraft's very powerful internal ECM with extra support from the two USMC EA-6A Intruder 'jammer' squadrons at Da Nang.

The first SAM hit was taken by a B-52D in the opening *Freedom Train* mission on 9 April. Twelve jets bombed a railhead and underground POL site at Vinh and one took a hit which blew off most of an external wing-tank. It managed to recover safely to Da Nang. Three days later, eighteen aircraft attacked the MiG airfield at Bai Thuong, hitting several fighters, AAA sites and runways. A similar formation struck a railyard and POL store near central Hanoi on the 16 April, causing fires, the reflections of which, from the cloudbase, could be seen from Task Force 77 ships 100 miles away. On that occasion the bombers tested the main ring of SAM sites around Hanoi and Haiphong, drawing thirty-five missiles which all failed to inflict damage. This was attributed in part to some excellent flak suppression by

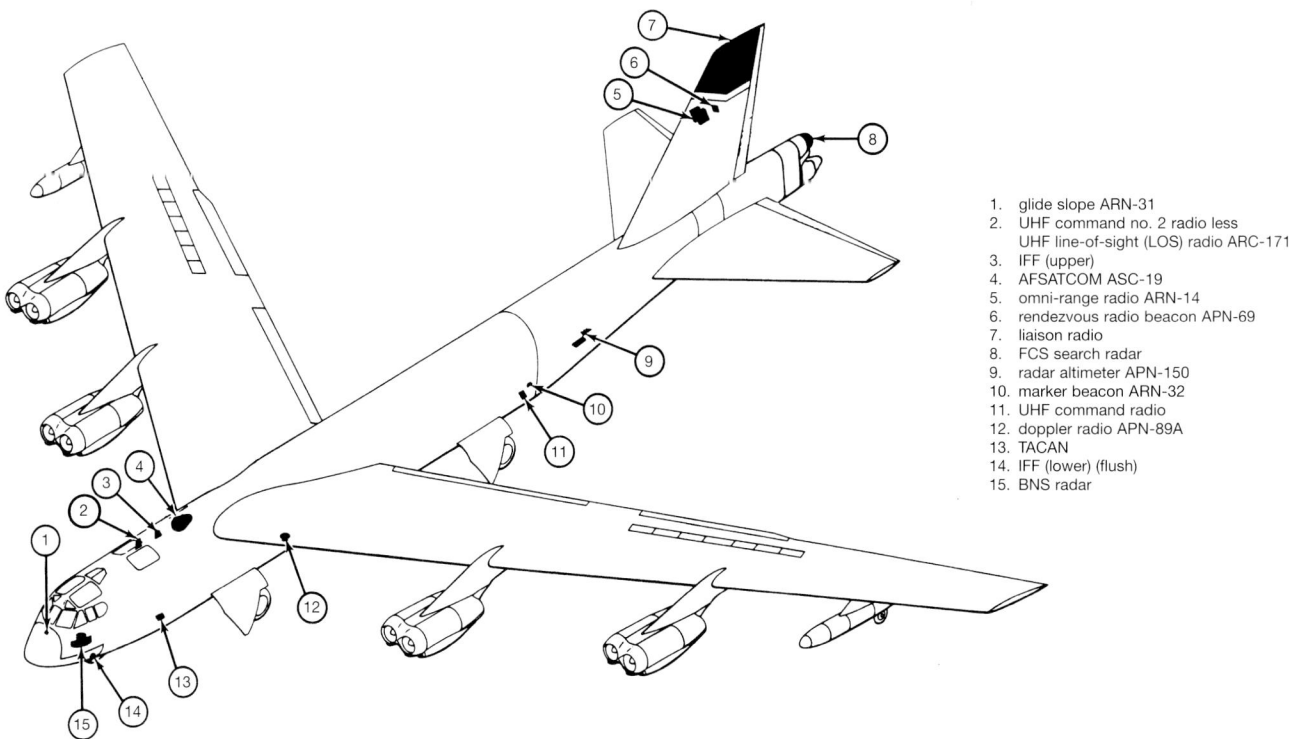

1. glide slope ARN-31
2. UHF command no. 2 radio less UHF line-of-sight (LOS) radio ARC-171
3. IFF (upper)
4. AFSATCOM ASC-19
5. omni-range radio ARN-14
6. rendezvous radio beacon APN-69
7. liaison radio
8. FCS search radar
9. radar altimeter APN-150
10. marker beacon ARN-32
11. UHF command radio
12. doppler radio APN-89A
13. TACAN
14. IFF (lower) (flush)
15. BNS radar

Antenna locations (except ECM).

F-105Gs, A-7B Corsairs and F-111As ahead of the raid.

The *Freedom Train* rolled again on 21 and 23 April with eighteen-ship formations bombing the Than Hoa area on both days, blasting railways and a thermal power plant. Fifty SAMs sped aloft, but only one 'BUFF' was caught in a lethal burst of shrapnel. It headed for Da Nang with two engines out and the other pair on the same wing failing. Capt Alward attempted a landing using a 'hot and high', sniper-avoidance approach and touched down at mid-runway, but his damaged brake 'chute failed to blossom. Worried by the minefield which he knew to be off the end of the runway he managed to haul the half-dead B-52 around for another approach and successful landing. Groundcrew counted over 400 holes in the airframe, many of them streaming fuel.

There had been particular concern over the survivability of the B-52D compared with later versions. It had ten independent hydraulic systems with four AC generators, powered by small hot-air turbines using 250 degree C bleed-air from the sixteenth-stage compressor of the J52 engines. The hot air was ducted along pipes which often ran parallel to oxygen and fuel lines, and control runs. Even a small shrapnel hit in a hot pneumatic line could ignite fuel and melt control cables. In practice the extremely low temperatures at 35,000ft reduced the chances of this happening. One advantage of the system was that the pneumatic supply could be drawn from any engine. On the B-52G the loss of an engine killed any electrical or hydraulic systems which it powered.

Freedom Train continued until the *Linebacker I* operation took over on 8 May and lasted until October. Its main purpose was to disrupt the huge rail network whereby North Vietnam received supplies and weapons from China, rather than trying to interdict those items on the Trails network leading from North Vietnam. *Linebacker I* cost 46 US aircraft losses for 155,548 tons of bombs dropped but the B-52s escaped without loss despite having over 200 SAMs fired at them. The first casualty came during the bombing 'pause' which Nixon called in November to give Hanoi time to negotiate. *Arc Lights* below the 20th parallel continued and on 22 November B-52D 55-0110 *Olive 2*, flown by Capt Norbert J. Ostrozny from U-Tapao was involved in a particularly heavy raid on troops around Vinh. SAMs were not

A cell of B-52Ds rolls out at U-Tapao for a mission in September 1972.
USAF via Thurlow

expected there but a missile exploded close to '110' starting fires in the wings and rear fuselage. The crew elected to try to make part of the 400-mile return journey before baling out and Ostrozny managed to hold the flaming aircraft aloft for a hundred miles with an F-105 *Iron Hand* escort before ordering the crew out. All the engines wound down at 10,000ft and part of a wing fell away in flames. Their bale-out took place just over the Thai border near Nakhon Phanom. Luckily one of that base's HH-53 helicopters was airborne in the vicinity and it located the crew before they touched down. They all survived and Ostrozny received a Silver Star but the North Vietnamese had scored their first B-52, after 100,000 sorties.

There was also heavy B-52 involvement in the fight against NVA and Pathet Lao in Northern Laos in November 1972. The combined bombardments from B-52s and F-111As overwhelmed communist forces besieging Long Tieng, allowing relief to reach the town. *Linebacker I*[14] and innumerable *Arc Lights* continued the strict SAC tactics established early in the war. Each three-ship cell had a colour-code and a 'wave' comprised several cells. During *Linebacker I* around twenty-two cells were

launched each day. A 'trail' of bombers included two or three waves, separated by an hour or more. Bombing at 30-35,000ft the formation maintained a speed of about 430kt over poorly defended target areas and 470kt over SAM-infested environments. Usually, all cells used the same altitudes, headings and departure routes. Separation between cells was maintained by using the aircraft's radar and the lead aircraft navigated. In the event of a radar failure the Bonus Deal tactic was employed. Some of the more rigid SAC procedures were unpopular, such as the testing of ECM and ALE-24/25 chaff dispensers (holding a total of 1,125 chaff packages per B-52) at a set time before bomb release. This gave the enemy clear radar warning of the intended target.

Linebacker II

When President Nixon curtailed *Linebacker I* on 23 October it was because chief US negotiator Henry Kissinger was convinced that 'peace was at hand'. Sadly, by 13 December the Paris talks collapsed once again and Nixon faced the grim realization that he would have to hit the

Bonus Deal

Maj Gordon Rees Williams (Ret) flew 208 combat missions from Guam, U-Tapao and Kadena and piloted five different models of B-52s. He explained how Bonus Deal was accomplished:

One of the B-52's capabilities that impressed me greatly was the ability for three aircraft to fly in trail formation and drop conventional bombs in all weather conditions where only one aircraft had navigation or gunnery radar operative. Normally, in such a formation each trail aircraft would keep station by using its navigation radar. During conventional bombing in formation one method of selecting the point of bomb release would be for the lead ship to select the release point either from their own bomb/nav system, from a pathfinder aircraft or as a ground-directed release and the following B-52s would drop on the leader's command after adjusting for their trail position relative to the leader.

There were cases where the gunnery radar and navigation radar would fail in two of the aircraft in the cell. In that case the leader, the one with the functioning radar, would place himself in the middle position [in trail formation] and station-keep and navigate for the aircraft in front, using his good navigation radar. The middle aircraft's gunner would use his gunnery radar to position the third aircraft properly behind him. Thus the formation would be complete and able to drop bombs on the target. It required a lot of radio communication and skill for all concerned, but it worked. In fact it worked so well that it was possible to place a slight right and left offset of two of the aircraft so that the bomb pattern could be spread better. I know this was practised because I experienced it, both as the directing aircraft and the directed one, during bombing missions.

USAF and USN back-up was made available but it could provide only partial protection. A B-52 wave would be tracked from take-off, initially by the Russian 'trawlers' positioned off Guam. As it neared North Vietnam sophisticated early-warning radar and well-organized command and control could threaten every second of its time over hostile territory. The JCS released 210 B-52s, half of the SAC total for the operation and expected a 5 per cent loss rate. In

As Linebacker II progressed, and understanding of the North's radar techniques was refined, the B-52 crew put their faith in their own countermeasures much more than chaff curtains.

Most of the 'no-go' industrial and logistic targets which had escaped attack during Rolling Thunder were put on the hit-list. Eventually, the JCS settled on fourteen targets to be bombed over three days, with the rail supply network from

Representing Dyess AFB's 96th SAW as Big Country Bomber at the 1971 SAC Bombing Competition, B-52D 55-0061 was destroyed on a Linebacker II mission. Isolated from its wave by radar failure it survived a MiG interception but took a SAM hit over Bac Mai as 'Scarlet 1'. Authors' collection

North harder still to force a settlement. In the monsoon season the B-52 was the only aircraft capable of the sustained heavy attacks required. JCS Chairman, Adm Tom Moore, was told, at last, 'this is your chance to use military power to win the war'. Nixon had decided on the concerted strategic thrust which Washington had eschewed for seven years.

The planners of Linebacker II (as it was named on 16 December) faced considerable problems. A primary consideration was the massive increase in the North's self-defence capability. There were over 1,000 known SA-2s available on twenty-one launch-sites in the Hanoi/Haiphong target areas and no-one was certain that a B-52 force could penetrate the elaborate array of radar-directed missiles supported by thousands of AAA weapons and a fighter force. Substantial

crude terms this meant thirty-six of America's main offensive weapons going down in flames over Hanoi. In relation to the 1,737 USAF combat losses during the war this may seem less than disastrous. Over a hundred aircraft were lost in VC attacks on American air bases alone. However, the symbolic significance of such a spectacle would have been immense, and very hard to explain to the American public.

For the first three nights great reliance was placed on the 'curtains' of chaff which were to be dropped by a phalanx of F-4 Phantoms ahead of the B-52 trail. This explained, in part, the need for a single approach route to the target, bounded by this metal foil protection. In fact, unpredictable winds often dispersed the chaff too quickly, even though the curtain was repaired by F-4s replenishing the supply.

China as the main objective. For the first night, 129 B-52s were scheduled in three waves, the first of which was targeted on three fighter airfields to keep the MiGs away. The VPAF was known to have received twenty-five MiG-19/Shenyang F-6s while building up its MiG-17 and MiG 21 force to around 170, some of which were all-weather PF/PFS versions. Although they were unused to night-fighting and hampered by the monsoon and US fighter CAPs the MiGs, under skilful radar control, were perceived as a real threat to the big bombers.

Although 15 December was the original start-date for the operation another three days were required to finish the complex planning, which was done in great secrecy. Targeting had to be absolutely precise to avoid American POW locations and

On a long overseas transit a B-52D opens its flight refuelling receptacle doors and moves into position for the 'boomer'. Robert F. Dorr

Many hours of combat flying have degraded 55-0101's paint job but loaded MERs indicate that another mission is imminent. The crew entry door on variants prior to the B-52G opened forwards. Via Robert F. Dorr

civilian casualties. It was also vital to ensure the best possible provision for defence suppression (SEAD) and other support aircraft, meshing them into the split-second timing of the B-52 waves exactly. The size of the support element increased as *Linebacker II* evolved, from thirty-six aircraft on the first night to 113 at its height, reflecting an increasing need for more effective protection from SAMs. For the period 18–29 December, 769 SEAD/support sorties were flown altogether.

On 17 December, 7th and 8th AF Commanders received the following message from the JCS: 'You are directed to commence at approximately 1200Z, 18 December 1972 a three day maximum effort, repeat maximum effort, of B-52/Tacair strikes in the Hanoi/Haiphong areas against the targets contained in the authorized target list. Object is maximum destruction of selected military targets in the vicinity of Hanoi/Haiphong. Be prepared to extend operations past three days if directed.'

The cockpit of a B-52D seen just before another Vietnam sortie. *Peter Kuehl*

SEAD and Support aircraft

In addition to its large force of tanker and reconnaissance aircraft the *Linebacker* B-52s received 'close-in' support from a variety of other specialist missions:

Grumman EA-6A Intruder Unit
VMCJ-1, USMC, Da Nang. Provided ECM support, particularly for the B-52G which often required up to eight EA-6As with their AN/ALQ-76 jammers to provide adequate protection. Its jamming capability against I-Band radar, introduced to the North Vietnamese at this time, was particularly valuable.

Grumman EA-6B Prowler Units
VAQ-131 (USS *Enterprise*), VAQ-132 (USS *America*), USN with four aircraft each. Began *Arc Light* support from 10 November 1972 and throughout *Linebacker II*. Three Prowlers took up station off-shore fifteen minutes ahead of the B-52 TOT. The B-52s internal ECM seriously degraded the Prowler's ALQ-99 suite, blotting out its detection of *Fan Song* radars in the 2,900-3,200 MHz range. Prowler crews tended to concentrate instead on lo-band early warning/ground control frequencies and COMJAM, denying the enemy his command, control and communications network and disrupting SAM and MiG co-ordination. This was particularly effective on 23 December when EA-6Bs were deployed in strength for the first time in support of *Linebacker*, resulting in fewer SAM firings. They were particularly successful in jamming the *Spoon Rest A* early-warning radar used by SA-2 sites.

Douglas EB-66C/E Destroyer Unit
42nd TEWS, 388th TFW, Korat RTAB. Provided *Tiny Tim* support for *Arc Lights*. With up to twenty-three internal jamming devices and VHF com-jam, plus an ALR-26 SAM-launch warning receiver and ALQ-71 ECM pod, the EB-66 accompanied every *Linebacker II* mission.

Douglas EA-3B/EKA-3B Skywarrior Unit
VAQ-130, USN. Dets. on USS *Ranger* and USS *Oriskany*. Provided ECM support with off-shore jamming of early-warning radars.

Vought A-7B/C/E Corsair II Units
Thirteen TF77 USN squadrons flew Corsairs which, from 26 December flew *Iron Hand* SAM and flak suppression alongside USAF F-105s. Pairs of A-7Bs were armed with AGM-65 Shrike anti-radiation missiles while other A-7 units attacked coastal AAA batteries near Haiphong.

Republic F-105F/G Thunderchief 'Wild Weasel' Units
17th WWS and 561st TFS, 388th TFW, Korat RTAB. F-105Gs with QRC-380/ALQ-105 ECM blisters, APR-35 RHAW and Standard ARM Mod 1 equipment could carry two AGM-78B Standard ARM (more effective than Shrike as an anti-radiation missile) and two or four Shrikes. After 20 December, flights consisting of two F-105Gs and two CBU-carrying F-4E Phantoms (replacing F-105Fs) operated as hunter-killer teams, doubling the strike rate against SAM sites.

McDonnell F-4C Phantom 'Wild Weasel IV-C' Unit
67th TFS, Kadena (TDY to Korat RTAB). Eighteen F-4Cs had ER-142/ALR-53 direction-finding sensors, APR-25/26 RHAW and Shrike, though they could not carry the AGM-78B Standard ARM. F-4C/WWs flew 406 missions from October 1972 to January 1973 for *Linebacker*.

General Dynamics F-111A Units
429th and 430th TFS, 474th TFW, Takhli. Flew up to twenty-five sorties per night hitting airfields, AAA and SAM sites with CBU and bombs ahead of the B-52s. Nine targets hit on Night One. Attacked several SAM storage sites. Apart from USN A-6A Intruders, which flew similar missions, no other tactical aircraft had the all-weather capability to fly these missions and all others were grounded throughout the operation apart from one eleven-hour break.

McDonnell F-4D/E Phantom Units
8th TFW, Ubon RTAB (F-4D/E) and 388th TFW, Korat RTAB (F-4E) provided MiG CAP and close-in B-52 escort which included protecting damaged bombers leaving the target area. USAF F-4s laid chaff corridors or clouds ahead of the bomber stream, using ALE-38 chaff pods each containing 320lb of metal-foil strips. Chaff-bombers flew in line-abreast formations of up to eight aircraft (twelve after Night Three) at reduced speed, escorted by other Phantoms which flew a four-ship 'element-weave' two miles in trail with the 'chaffers'.

On Nights One to Three high winds blew most of the chaff away leaving all but three cells of B-52s unprotected by it. In all, 125 tons of chaff were dispensed during the campaign, occasionally upsetting the radars of F-111A and A-6A strikers which were also at work in the vicinity.

McDonnell F-4B/J Phantom Units
Various TF 77 USN squadrons provided fighter MiG-CAPs, and USMC F-4 unit VMFA-232 'CAPped' for the tankers from Takhli RTAB which stood by for fuel-hungry fighters. USAF F-4Ds and USN Phantoms scored four MiGs during late December 1972.

56-0584, seen here with racks full of Mk 82s, became a Linebacker II casualty on Boxing Day, 1972. After a SAM hit, Capt Jim Turner nearly made it back to U-Tapao. His aircraft, Ash 1 crashed on approach and only two of the crew escaped the flames. Authors' collection

(Below) 'Quad 50' guns equipped B-52s for almost two decades before being used in anger over Vietnam. Above this B-52D's guns are the bulge of the MD-9 search radar and the transparency for the back-up periscope sight. Frank Mormillo

Detailed planning covering routes, defences, support aircraft and targets had begun at 8th AF Directorate of Operations Plans (8AF/DOX) in August 1972 and mission 'frag' folders were ready. One crucial task was the selection of radar offset aimpoints, which had been undertaken by photo-interpreters examining miles of reconnaissance photography. Imagery from four *Senior Crown* SR-71s was particularly valuable. Flying from OL-8 at Kadena AB from March 1968 and following a period of activity by the similar Lockheed A-12 Oxcart reconnaissance vehicle, the Mach 3 'Habu' ventured over Hanoi and Haiphong at least once weekly capturing the finest detail on its OBC cameras and always evading SAMs. These had to be fired at least thirty miles ahead of the spy-plane's track to stand a chance of reaching its altitude in time.

Mission folders were issued to B-52s through Andersen's *Arc Light* Centre. The target area was divided into 'low threat' and 'high threat' areas depending on the numbers of SA-2s and the risk from MiGs. It was a shifting scenario because of the mobility of SAM launchers, making timely reconnaissance all the more vital. At U-Tapao the 307th SW under Col Donald M. Davis adopted the 'press on' philosophy which meant that the B-52s continued to their targets whatever the threat level. At Andersen the same approach was generally employed except on the third night when losses to the B-52G with their less capable ECM equipment made the recall of two cells of 'G'-models necessary. Mission planners often flew as extra crewmen on combat missions in order to acquaint themselves with tactics but the risk of SAMs and the lack of 'passenger' ejection seats ruled this out for most of *Linebacker II*. Underlying all B-52 tactics, including the 'press on' doctrine, was the need for cell integrity. It was vital for each trio to maintain trail formations at exact separations and altitudes. Three aircraft created a large 'aura' of interference to enemy radars, jamming both the guidance beam from the *Fan Song* guidance radar and the uplink/downlink UHF radio signal between the missile and its controllers. The radar signature of individual bombers was hidden in this interference pattern. However, if an aircraft moved out of its cell its smaller area of jamming became visible on enemy radars and a missile operator could select 'track on jam', aiming his missile at the source of the interference and probably scoring a damaging near-miss. EWOs in single B-52s could operate their countermeasures to defeat single missiles but they were hard pressed to identify and individually jam missiles fired in a salvo, as they often were. After a few days of *Linebacker* SAM crews learned to use radar data from outlying warning radar posts and sent salvos of up to twenty SA-2s, set to explode at altitudes determined by these 'out of town' sites. The B-52D's Phase V *Rivet Rambler* ECM fit was at that stage unable to cope with jamming dispersed radars data-linked together in this way, although the 'Wild Weasel' support aircraft soon got their measure. When a B-52 became detached from its cell, weakening its combined jamming power, the other two aircraft were also put at greater risk. If this occurred because of an abort by one aircraft before take-off the 'roll forward' principle was used whereby the No. 1 aircraft in the following cell moved up to occupy the gap, and was himself replaced by his No. 2, with a ground-spare as No. 3. Andersen's taxyways were so narrow and crowded during a mass-launch B-52 'elephant walk' that spare aircraft could not overtake the queue to fill gaps. The crew of a 'rolled forward' bomber usually had to re-brief themselves for a different mission 'frag', consulting the three large black briefcases full of information which were delivered to each bomber shortly before departure. On a thirty-aircraft launch, six extra B-52s were prepared for 'abort' standby. Each had to be prepared to fill in for any of three other cells and each therefore received nine 'frag' briefcases. With up to 150 aircraft involved in a *Linebacker II* mission the task of delivering the right material to each 'tail number', in the dark, was in itself a major feat.

In order to maintain the sortie rate the 'bag-drag' system was also used. Ground-spare B-52s were pre-flighted up to the 'engine start' point. One was allocated to each cell and its crew attended the cell's briefing. If a primary aircraft developed a fault its crew, with their briefcases, tech manuals, food, survival gear and heavy high-altitude flying clothes piled into two pick-ups and were driven to the spare aircraft which would by then have its engines running. Normally a crew could be strapped in, checked out and ready to roll within ten minutes of evacuating their sick bird. On one night a crew had to make five successive 'bag drags' before finding a healthy aircraft but they still managed to join their cell for the mission.

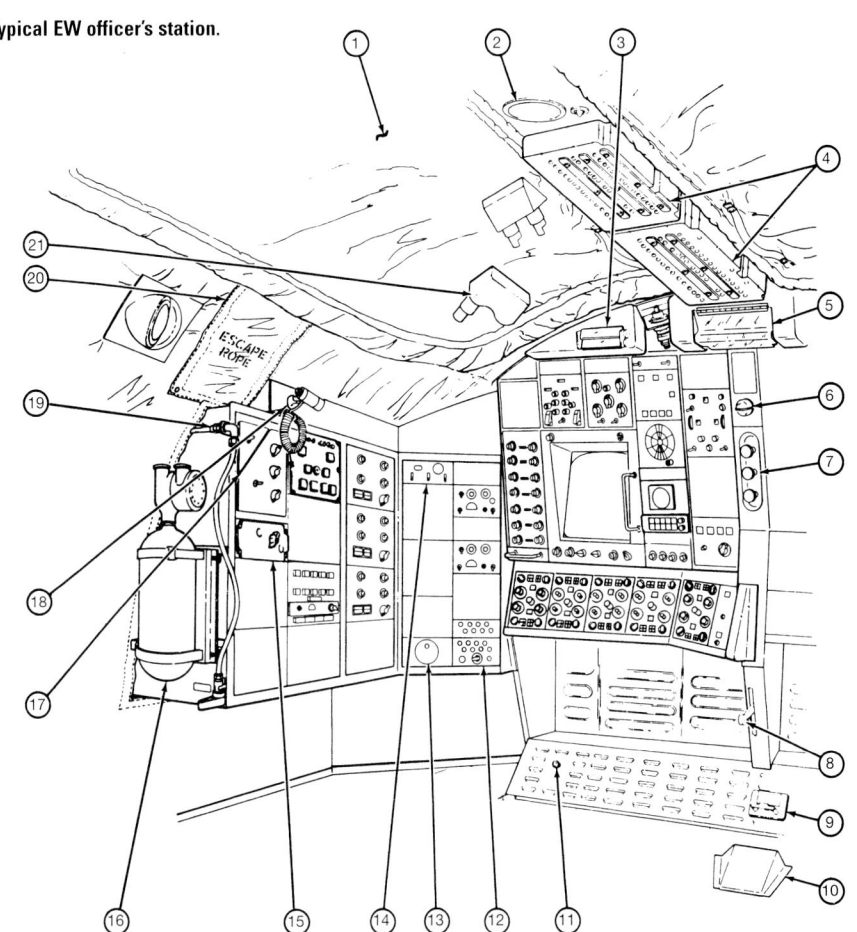

Typical EW officer's station.

1. escape hatch
2. upper aisle and entry light
3. upper air outlet
4. ECM circuit breaker panel
5. AGM-69a lock-unlock switch panel
6. emergency alarm light
7. temperature control panel
8. refuel valve emergency control lever
9. special weapons manual lock handle stowage bracket
10. special weapons manual lock handle
11. interphone foot switch
12. interphone control panels
13. ashtray
14. oxygen regulator
15. main console light control panel
16. portable oxygen bottle
17. lighting control panel
18. spotlight
19. oxygen bottle recharger
20. escape rope container
21. side-panel flood lights

As an additional constraint to preserve the mutual ECM power of each cell a 'no manoeuvring' order was in place. This reduced the possibility of mid-air collisions, maximized the interference pattern and enhanced bombing accuracy in a scenario where the slightest error would be fully publicized in the world's press. B-52 bombing computers required an absolutely straight and level approach and for the first missions crews had to maintain that approach for at least four minutes before dropping their ordnance. If radar navigators were not entirely sure of their targets at this point they were instructed to abort their drop.

Holding the aircraft steady while its RHAW system gave clear warning of approaching SAMs required considerable nerve and more than one pilot did just that, knowing that a SAM hit was almost inevitable. In a few cases a pilot who was tempted into an evasive manoeuvre by missiles during his bomb run missed his target or degraded his cell's ECM resistance, resulting in a lost bomber. Despite all these precautions ECM integrity could be compromised in two situations. If aircraft were required to overfly, rather than skirt round SAM sites, as they did later in the campaign in order to bomb them, *Fan Song* radars were powerful enough to 'burn through' the cell's jamming at such close range, giving the operators a clearer image to aim at. Also, bombers became vulnerable as each cell made its big post-target turn (PTT) on to its escape heading. As the B-52 banked at 45 degrees the intensity of its downward jamming transmissions was reduced by the slant angle allowing the SAMs time for a tracking solution. This was to be a major cause of B-52 losses, particularly to the B-52G, and six losses on the first three nights were on PTTs.

Crews were therefore under great pressure to maintain strict discipline for these missions even though normal safety rules had to be overlooked to some extent. Aircraft were not allowed to turn back for many of the standard reasons. As long as they could remain airborne, loss of radar or up to two engines had to be accepted. In fact, the abort rate at Andersen was negligible. One aircraft returned having lost four engines on one side soon after take-off. Its pilot, Capt Goodman, managed to land safely. Another suffered a refuelling system failure outbound. On 'Night One' a crew which lost an engine were told to push up the power, stay with the formation and pick up extra fuel on the return leg.

Target Hanoi

On 18 December, the planning for SAC's first strategic jet bombing mission was complete and crews crammed into Andersen's briefing rooms to hear Gen James McCarthy tell them, 'Gentlemen, your target for tonight is Hanoi'. At U-Tapao the crews of forty-two B-52Ds received similar news from Col Davis. Crews for the second wave prepared to receive their briefing as the first wave climbed from their fifty-one crew buses and clambered through the entry hatches of their black-bellied bombers. At 1451 local time Maj. Bill Stocker, who had already logged 300 B-52 missions, led the ungainly procession of bombers down Andersen's undulating runway in the first of 129 B-52s to lift off that day. Every ninety seconds another shark-tailed bomber hauled off the strip leaving eight wakes of smoke.

The North Vietnamese would have found the B-52s' approach route familiar from *Rolling Thunder* days; a long swing towards the Chinese border and then an approach from the north-west along the Red River Valley and Thud Ridge. U-Tapao's aircraft made the first strikes.

As the B-52Gs of Ebony cell, last in the trail, popped their brake-chutes on Guam, engines were being started for the second night. There was no time for a post-mortem on the opening night, let alone changes in tactics following from that experience. Mainly it was evident that 94 per cent of the aircraft had dropped their weapons on target. A few had lost their radars and resorted to *Bonus Deal* tactics. The strike force had 200 SAMs fired at it (causing considerable radio-oversaturation with warning calls) and a few had found their mark, mainly because winds had dispersed the chaff curtain too early.

The loss of B-52G 'Charcoal 1' was particularly galling. Its pilot, Lt Col Don Rissi, had been preparing to go home at the end of his tour but a delay in replacing him obliged him to fly the mission. He and his gunner, M Sgt Walt Ferguson, died from an SA-2 hit seconds before bomb release. Three of the crew became POWs, Maj Dick Johnson suffering the humiliation of a street parade through Hanoi for the benefit of the world's news bulletins. 'Peach 2', victim of a close SAM explosion, lost a wing tank, two engines, LOX and cabin pressure, part of a wing-tip and most instruments. It left the target with a raging fire in its left wing but its pilot managed to man-handle it as far as the Thai border so that the crew could be rescued by a Nam Phong 'Jolly Green'. MiG activity was less than expected. There were only two attempted interceptions and one of these fell to the tail-guns of 'Brown 3' in Wave 1's second cell.

A general problem was unexpectedly strong headwinds which ran the fuel reserves of the leading cells down to

---

First Night – 18/19 December

TOTAL B-52 SORTIES: 129.

WAVE 1	U-Tapao	307th SW	seven cells of B-52D (Snow, Brown, Maple, Gold, Green, Purple, Walnut) TOT: 1243Z.
	Andersen	43rd SW	three cells of B-52D (Rose, Lilac, White).
	Andersen	72nd SW (P)	six cells of B-52G (Rust, Black, Buff, Charcoal, Ivory, Ebony).

TARGETS:
Hoa Lac airfield (15m west of Hanoi) for Snow and Brown.
Kep airfield (north east of Hanoi) for Maple, Gold, Green.
Phuc Yen airfield (north of Hanoi) for Purple and Walnut.
Kinh No storage area (north of Hanoi) for Rose, Lilac, White, Rust, Black, Buff.
Yen Vien rail yard for Charcoal, Ebony, Ivory.*

* Colour codes were similar each night and are not repeated here, to save space.

RESULTS: B-52D 'Lilac 3' (56-0678) hit near cockpit by SAM. Unable to bomb so diverted to U-Tapao. B-52G 'Charcoal 1' (58-0201) downed by two SAMs. Another B-52G badly damaged. Seventeen SAMs fired from eight sites. Forty-five B-52s bombed successfully. One MiG-21 shot down by S/Sgt Turner, 'Brown 3'.

WAVE 2	B-52D	43rd SW	four cells.
	B-52G	72nd SW (P)	six cells. TOT 1700-1726Z: two minutes between cells.

TARGETS: Kinh Lo storage area, Yen Vien rail yard, Gia Lam.
RESULTS: B-52G 'Peach 2' (58-0246, 72nd SW) hit by SAM. Crew, including observer Lt Col Hendsley R. Connor, baled out over Thailand after Maj Cliff Ashley and Capt Gary Riches flew the burning aircraft for 250 miles.

WAVE 3	B-52D	307th SW	seven cells. TOT 2143-2158; two minutes separation.
	B-52D	43rd SW	four cells.
	B-52G	72nd SW (P)	two cells TOT 2207-2215.

TARGETS: Hanoi railway repair centre. Gia Lam. Radio Hanoi.
RESULTS: B-52D 'Rose 1' (56-0608) hit by SAM on PTT. Four crew POW. Two attempted MiG intercepts. One B-52D, 'Rainbow 1' (56-0583) slightly damaged. 61 SAMS fired at this wave; 200 in all.
SUPPORT AIRCRAFT:
39 (F-4 chaff/escort, F-105 *Iron Hand*, EB-66).

MiG Killers

S/Sgt Samuel O. Turner, on TDY to the 307th SW from March AFB, was gunner in B-52D 56-0676. Just after bomb release on the first night his crew received a MiG warning for their area and soon discovered that the fighter had them on its radar. His combat report described the encounter: 'As he closed in on us I also picked him up on my radar when he was a few miles from our aircraft. A few seconds later the fighter locked on to us. As the MiG closed in, I also locked on to him. He came in low in a rapid climb. While tracking the fiirst MiG I picked up a second enemy aircraft at 8 o'clock at a range of about 7.5 miles ... allowing the other fighter to conduct his run first. As the attacking MiG came into firing range I fired a burst. There was a gigantic explosion on the rear of the aircraft. I looked out the window but was unable to see directly where the MiG-21 would have been. Except for the one airplane out at 8 o'clock there was nothing and within fifteen seconds he broke away'.

Airman 1st Class Albert E. Moore was tail gunner on 307th SW B-52D 55-0083 bombing the Thai Nguyen rail yard on 24 December. He picked up a MiG-21 closing fast, notified the crew to dispense chaff and flares and locked on to the 'bogey' at 4,000yd. He opened fire with 0.50 cal at 2,000yd, shooting until the MiG 'blossomed' on his radar scope and vanished. Another gunner saw the MiG falling away in flames.

Three other MiG-21s were claimed by B-52 gunners but rejected by the USAF Claims Evaluation Board. MiG-killer B-52D 56-0676 was the last B-52D to remain in the active inventory when it reached retirement on 1 October 1983.

Danny Burnett recalled the B-52D gunners' valued role: 'The people who flew the *Linebacker II* missions swore by the extra eyes in the tail and that was one more reason why the D-model was preferred for 'going downtown', plus the ECM advantage over the B-52G'.

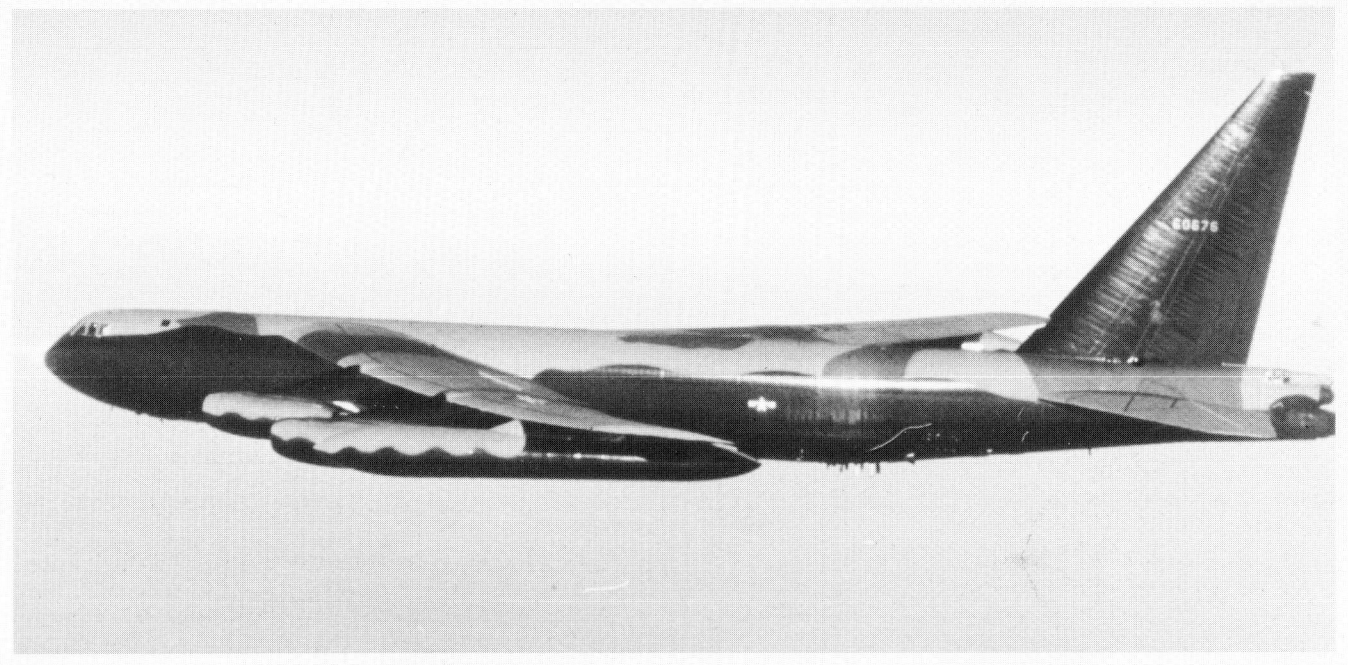

One of the two MiG-killer B-52Ds of Linebacker II, **56-0676. S/Sgt Sam Turner felled one of a pair of MiG-21s on Night One in the first wave. The bomber survived the campaign and was displayed at Fairchild AFB.** USAF via Chesneau

dangerous levels. Only one flight-refuelling, outbound, had been allowed for. The thirsty bombers were directed towards extra 376th ARW KC-135As from Kadena on the return trip, adding four hours to the trip but saving the day.

Crews in the second night's launch, led by Maj Tom Lebar, were understandably concerned about duplicating the pattern of Night One's attack after hearing of the two losses and there were some vociferous complaints about such predictable tactics. Wave 1 was instructed to maintain strict cell discipline. However, it was possible to signal to Wave 2, following four hours behind, that its crews were allowed to perform modest SAM-evasion manoeuvres as a cell, as long as straight and level flight was resumed to allow the computers to

Second Night – 19/20 December

WAVE 1	B-52D	43rd SW	four cells.
	B-52G	72nd SW(P)	three cells. TOT 1309-1322Z.
TARGETS:	Kinh No railyard.		
RESULTS:	All bombed successfully. No aircraft damaged. Sixty SAMs launched.		

WAVE 2	B-52D	307th SW	five cells.
	B-52G	72nd SW9(P)	seven cells. TOT 1309-1322.
TARGETS:	Hanoi Radio, Bac Giang trans-shipment centre.		
RESULTS:	Minor damage to B-52G 'Hazel 3' which had strayed from formation and lost ECM transmitters. B-52D 'Ivory 1' (56-0592) had SAM damage to engines and tail; Capt John Dalton diverted to Nam Phong USMC base.		

WAVE 3	B-52G	72nd SW(P)	two cells.
	B-52D	43/307th SW	ten cells. TOT 2210-2222Z.
TARGETS:	Thai Nguyen thermal power plant (nine cells); Yen Vien storage area (three cells).		
RESULTS:	90 out of 93 B-52s bombed successfully. 150 SAMs fired but no losses, partly due to better cell integrity and excellent 'Wild Weasel' work. One B-52 did evasion manoeuvre, bombed four seconds late and hit Gia Lam Airport.		

B-52Gs mix with 'tall tails' on Andersen's crowded taxi-strips prior to a Linebacker II mission. The 'G's retained full SIOP camouflage for battle. USAF

stabilize for the bomb run. This was possible because analysis of the first night's radar film showed that all offsets and targets had been correctly identified.

The final part of the original three-night onslaught dovetailed into Night Two, leaving insufficient time for significant tactical changes apart from a few target and threat-assessment revisions. Night Two's formation had only two cases of minor damage, apparent justification of the basic strategy. Such a complex operation could not be 'unpicked' with less than forty-eight hours notice. Importantly, EWOs received data which improved their performance against multiple SA-2 threats, thanks to some urgent tests at AFSC, Eglin AFB.

Six losses were obviously a severe challenge to CINCSAC Gen John C.Meyer who had to consider public reaction, crew morale and the wisdom of pressing on against such formidable defences. Two B-52Gs and a B-52D were lost on the PTT.

With its bow-wave nudging at the KC-135's rear end a B-52D takes on fuel. The operation required extremely accurate control movements and judgement. In darkness or bad weather it could be a nightmare for the inexperienced.
USAF via Robert F. Dorr

Third Night – 20/21 December			
WAVE 1	B-52G	72nd SW(P)	four cells.
	B-52D	307th SW	seven cells. TOT 1300Z.
TARGETS:	Yen Vien rail centre, Ai Mo warehouses (nine cells), Gia Lam railhead (two cells).		
RESULTS	B-52G 'Quilt 3' (57-6496), A/C Capt Terry Geloneck, lost two ECM transmitters and was shot down on PTT. Four POW, two KIA. B-52G 'Brass 2' (57-6481) A/C Capt John Ellinger, hit on PTT, lost four engines and crew baled out over Nam Phong, Thailand. B-52D 'Orange 3' (56-0622) A/C Maj. John Stuart, hit by two SAMs just before bombing while rest of cell on PTT and exploded. Four crew MIA, two POW. Many MiGs reported.		
WAVE 2	B-52G	72nd SW(P)	two cells (recalled en route to target).
	B-52D	43rd SW	five cells.
	B-52D	307th SW	four cells. TOT 1700Z.
TARGETS:	Thai Nguyen thermal power plant, Bac Giang and Gia Lam rail/trans-shipment centres.		
RESULTS:	No damage to aircraft; all bombed successfully.		
WAVE 3	B-52D	43rd SW	three cells.
	B-52G	72nd SW(P)	four cells.
	B-52G	307th SW	four cells.
TARGETS:	Kinh Noh complex. Gia Lam rail centre.		
RESULTS:	B-52D 'Straw 2' (56-0669) hit on PTT after losing two ECM transmitters. Five crew bailed out over Laos, one MIA. First 43rd SW loss. B-52G 'Olive 1' (58-0198) A/C Lt Col Jim Nagahiro, hit on PTT. Four KIA, three POW including Deputy Mission Commander Lt Col Keith Heggen who died in captivity. B-52G 'Tan 3' (58-0169) A/C Capt Randall Craddock, hit by two SAMs as it left formation due to radar loss. It exploded and gunner S/Sgt Jim Loller was the only survivor. B-52 'Brick 2' (55-0067) badly damaged but returned. Despite 90 successful sorties this was the worst night. Four unmodified B-52Gs and two B-52Ds were lost, with seventen men KIA or MIA and nine POWs. Missiles were often fired in salvos of ten to fifteen, with 220 in all.		

Wreckage of a B-52G remains in the community pond at Ngoc Hi, North Vietnam. US Navy

(Below) **A combat-worn B-52D, 56-0587, under tow with empty racks after a mission.** Via Robert F. Dorr

A new threat involved the use of MiG-21s which 'hid' in the B-52's ECM blanket, pacing the leading cells and reporting their heading and altitude to their controllers. SAM operators allowed those cells to pass and salvoed their missiles at the following cells while they made their vulnerable bomb-runs, using the MiGs' information. Inevitably, doubt was cast upon the efficacy of the B-52G. All four losses of this model were from the half of Guam's B-52G contingent without Phase V ECM updates: four AN/ALT-22 modulated CW jamming transmitters in place of four AN/ALT-6B unmodulated units, plus two underwing ALQ-119(V) pods in some cases.[15]

Already at a disadvantage because of its smaller internal bomb-load (27 M117s against 42 in the B-52D) and frequent bomb-release problems, the B-52G had sustained six out of the ten losses. When two unmodified B-52Gs had gone down from Wave 1, 8th AF HQ rapidly decided to recall two cells from Wave 2, which then returned unscathed. However, the twelve B-52Gs in Wave 3 could not be spared and two (unmodified) aircraft went down, one in an area where it was in 'burn through' range of seven SA-2 sites. Later analysis of 'Habu' imagery showed a new radar array near Hanoi which was more resistant to B-52 jamming, possibly including the T-8029 system which could switch rapidly between low band (Echo) and high-band (India) frequencies.

Early in the three-day thrust the JCS decided to prolong the operation, though the task was handed to U-Tapao while Andersen's B-52Gs temporarily reverted to Arc Lights – partly due to the T-8029 threat. Twenty-two Guam B-52Ds moved to 'U-T' on 23 December to assist. With the advantage of four-hour mission times requiring less internal fuel and no tankers, the 307th SW could sustain the pressure of two nights of thirty-aircraft missions. Their two losses happened due to cell disintegration, and on a bomb-run. Tactical changes enabled the cells attacking Hanoi to egress over the Tonkin Gulf, avoiding PTTs. Also, cells were more compressed together in time (from four to two minutes gap) and altitude.[16] Approach and egress routes were from the sea on Night Five, combined with some ingenious deception tactics. The formation approached on three tracks, then split into six directions, none of which headed directly towards Hanoi. At thirty miles out all six components simultaneously turned in towards their targets, saturating SAM radars.

Andersen returned to the fight on 23 December, tasked with attacks on three SAM sites which had escaped SEAD units. To counter the bombers' vulnerability while directly over these sites the four Andersen cells split, with single aircraft attacking each site, followed by one each from the next cell. The guess was that the SAM launchers would assume that the lead aircraft were headed elsewhere and merely use them to establish altitudes. Fortunately, the deception succeeded and the sites were hit hard despite the absence of the delayed SEAD fighters. Night Seven was a U-Tapao solo, noted for the second MiG kill during a rare interception attempt.

Fourth and Fifth Nights – 21–23 December

21/22 December 30 sorties by B-52Ds of 307th SW in ten cells. TOT: 0340.
TARGETS: Quang Te airfield, Bac Mai/Hanoi storage area and Van Dien warehouse complex.
RESULTS: B-52D 'Scarlet 1' (55-0061) A/C Capt Pete Giroux, lost bombing radar and became isolated from formation. Intercepted by MiG, without damage, then destroyed by a SAM over Bac Mai. B-52D 'Blue 1' (55-0050), A/C Lt Col Yuill, hit by two SAMs on bomb run, crew POW.

Andersen flew 30 *Arc Light* sorties.

22/23 December 30 sorties by B-52Ds of 307th SW in ten cells. TOT: 0450-0516.
TARGETS: Haiphong railway repair centre. Haiphong POL storage.
RESULTS: All bombed without loss. Support aircraft increased to 65 with particularly good *Iron Hand* by F-105s, reducing SAM firings to 43.

Andersen flew 28 *Arc Light* sorties.

B-52D 56-0604 returns to the Juliet revetment area at U-Tapao. Cichocki

For the last four nights of *Linebacker II* there were further revisions in tactics to counter the persistent SAMs. It had been noticed that sites kept only small missile reserves to avoid their destruction by *Iron Hand* aircraft. Urgent analysis of SR-71A photographs revealed the central SAM storage sites and these were added to the target lists from 26 December after a 36-hour Christmas truce. Recce information from SR-71As and BQM drones showed that severe damage was being

Sixth and Seventh Nights – 23–25 December

23/24 December 30 sorties by B-52Ds of 43rd SW (four cells), 307th SW (six cells). TOT 1910-1927.
TARGETS: Lang Dang rail yard (eight cells), SAM sites VN 537, 563 and 660 (two cells)
RESULTS: No losses. 40 SAMs fired. 70 support aircraft but SAM suppressors delayed.

39 *Arc Light* sorties also flown.

24/25 December 30 sorties by B-52Ds of 307th SW (ten cells). TOT:1950-2010.
TARGETS: Kep railway centre (four cells). Thai Nguyen rail yard (six cells).
RESULTS: Only 19 SAMs fired; no hits. Slight AAA damage to 'Purple 2', the only AAA damage to a B-52. MiG kill by 'Ruby 3' (A1C Moore). Sixty-nine support aircraft and 763 refuelling sorties by the local tanker force of only 194 KC-135s.

30 *Arc Light* sorties also flown.

The crew bus takes B-52D 55-0080's occupants off for debrief and a meal post-mission. Cichocki

Armourers and maintainers prepare B-52D 55-0110 for action at U-Tapao. This aircraft became the first loss to enemy action when it took an SA-2 hit while attacking troop concentrations around Vinh. The AC, Capt 'Oz' Ostrozny, won a Silver Star for saving his crew. USAF via Robert F. Dorr

B-52D 56-0604 rises from Andersen's runway in 1972 laden with bombs while a B-52G taxies out in the background. Via Robert F. Dorr

done to the North's war-making capacity and another all-out assault was planned to push the situation towards resolution. Seven waves with 120 aircraft were aimed at ten targets within a fifteen-minute timeframe, rather than over several hours. An intricate pattern of cells, approaching from seven directions and avoiding sharp turns was designed to swamp the defences and bomb at absolutely precise times and altitudes, ensuring deconfliction. Some more 'candle-burning' research at Eglin yielded further data on enemy radar frequencies for EWOs' benefit. Unmodified B-52Gs were targeted outside the main defence 'ring' and chaff bombers dropped clouds of chaff rather than corridors to give an overall 'blanket' effect.

The thunderous take-offs at Guam and U-Tapao marked SAC's biggest-ever B-52 launch. This time there were no long gaps between waves. Some prodigious organization by 'Charlie Tower', the Deputy Commander of Operations at both bases got them all aloft on time and provided experts on call for every emergency, including a satellite link to Boeing (Wichita). Bomb-loaders had worked around the clock heaving over 10,000 bombs on to racks. Refuelling each aircraft took two hours and even the preparation of 750 in-flight meals took considerable organization. Soon after take-off it was learned that the tanker force was twenty minutes late due to an emergency at Kadena, causing delays in refuelling the third wave. Its

A truck-load of M117s awaits a Linebacker II **B-52G (58-0193) at Andersen. This scene was re-enacted nineteen years later when '0193 flew thirteen missions in** Desert Storm. Paul Minert via Greg Spahr

B-52Gs with everything open receive outdoor maintenance on Guam during the Linebacker **campaign.**
Paul Minert via Greg Spahr

leader, Maj Lebar, elected to swing north to meet his KC-135As. His navigators then recalculated their flight-plans and the B-52s slotted back into the formation exactly on time. The alternative would have been to abandon the whole mission. Such a huge bomber trail impressed its participants. One described it as, 'like a highway at night – nothing but a stream of upper rotating beacons as far as I could see'. Needless to say, those beacons were extinguished if MiGs were reported.

Despite the B-52s' brief exposure over the target more than 100 SAMs were launched. Brig Gen McCarthy, in his famous account, logged twenty-six coming at the lead B-52 in which he flew as Airborne Commander, before losing count. A U-Tapao B-52D went down and another struggled back to that base with mortal damage, only to crash just short of the runway. Its tail broke away, saving the gunner, and the copilot, 1st Lt Bob Hymel was pulled clear of the wreck by Capt Brent Diefenbach who had just landed his own B-52. The rest of the crew perished in the flames. Both aircraft had been in two-ship cells, the third aircraft having aborted, underlining the need for cell integrity. Two-ship cells were disallowed on Night Nine and these aircraft were required to combine with the cell ahead.

Haiphong was removed from the destination list on 27 December for lack of suitable targets. Time over target was further reduced to ten minutes, requiring

Bomb doors on this B-52G are raised as armourers shift a 'jammer' load of M117 into place. Paul Minert via Greg Spahr

A fine study in heavy metal. B-52G 57-6471 was the 'prototype B-52H' at a later stage, fitted with a set of TF33 turbofans. Boeing

U-Tapao RTAB, October 1968. A1C R. E. Brown captured this cell of B-52Ds returning from an Arc Light **mission.**
USAF via Robert F. Dorr

(Above) **For seventeen years B-52s 'fought' the Cold War with a combination of Hound Dog missiles and free-fall nuclear weapons. The Hound Dog's power settings could be controlled via a 'throttle wheel' on the co-pilot's side of the B-52 cockpit.** Boeing

(Below) **A B-52G departs with ear-shattering reverberations. The flying schedule for this July, 1989 morning stated that the fuel load was '270W'; 270,000lbs with a 'wet' take-off.** Tony Cassanova

(Below) **Under a heavy monsoon sky B-52D 56-0629 is prepared for another 1968 Arc Light at U-Tapao RTAB.** Jim Cichocki

On 9 May 1992, a pair of pristine Tu-95 Bear-H bombers and an An-124 Condor arrived at Barksdale AFB for a reciprocal visit. USAF/T/Sgt Fernando Serna

(Below) Since 'stealth' can't be added to the B-52 it has been added to some of its weapons. B-52H 61-0025 of the 410th BW banks over Primrose Lake during a captive-carry ALCM test on the Cold Lake Air Weapons Range in October, 1991. Canadian Forces/M/Cpl Bruce Dyck

(Bottom) Looking immaculate in its 'natural metal' and white scheme B-52H 60-0056 was photographed in August, 1966 with the 716th BS at Kincheloe AFB. Larry Milberry

(Below) **First Strike! was B-52G 58-0257, assigned to the 1708th BW at King Abdul Aziz Airport, Jeddah for** Desert Storm. Tony Cassanova

(Right) **Munitions maintenance personnel inspect the AN/ASG-15 FCS of a B-52G.** William A. Ford/AFA

(Below) **Many SAC bomber bases were situated near the United States' northern borders for quick access to the polar SIOP routes. Despite its location in the north-eastern USA, Griffiss AFB was technically too far south to be labelled a northern tier base: hard to believe in this view of 'Bravo' row at the base.** Tony Cassanova

With its weather-worn SIOP scheme B-52G 57-6501 taxies off the main runway, dragging its chute. Usually the nylon braking parachutes are dropped earlier so they don't snag taxi-way lights. Mike Valenti

(Above) Maintaining an excellent pattern a cell of B-52Gs makes a twelve-second 'dry power' MITO. During such a launch the lead position is the place to ride it out while the rest of the cell fans out to avoid the active turbulence from preceding aircraft. Tony Cassanova

(Above right) Special Delivery II **59-0170** was assigned to the 801st BWP at Moron AB, Spain for Desert Storm. Tony Cassanova

B-52G moves away after a fuel offload in 1989. Strakelets were fitted to G models' wing-root leading edges under the SALT II treaty to identify cruise missile-capable B-52Gs. They also offered a two per cent improvement in aerodynamic efficiency. Larry Milberry

Travelling at 275kts a KC-135R feeds fuel to a 92nd BW B-52H. The principal limiting factor on the B-52's global capability is its need for tanker support: two KC-135Rs are said to be needed for every three BUFFs. Jim Benson

(Right) A B-52H comes around to line up for its bomb-run over the Yakima firing range in Washington State. The BUFF's long wingspan makes wingtip clearance in very low-altitude turns quite critical. A 40deg bank puts the wingtip 55 feet closer to the ground than the fuselage would be. Jim Benson

(Below) JB-52C 0 53-0399 is adorned with the insignia of the Aeronautical Systems Division on its nose in this 1966 shot. The 4950th Test Wing flew it for most of its life, including fourteen test-drops of the Rockwell B-1A crew escape module. Larry Milberry

With 'chute fully blossomed a 5th BW B-52H arrives at Nellis AFB for a Red Flag exercise. To facilitate the stopping of a BUFF in a 5,000ft run on dry concrete, eight hydraulic, segmented rotor-type disc brakes are fitted to each main wheel. Ted Carlson/Fotodynamics

(Below) **During 1997 the US Senate directed the USAF to retain all 94 B-52Hs in FY98. Although on paper there are 48 assigned to the 2nd BW there is funding for only 36: the remaining dozen are rotated to even out flying hours.** Guy Aceto/AFA

(Top) **The B-52H is currently the USAF's principal cruise missile carrier and it also bears 80 per cent of the US nuclear bomber role.** Jim Benson

(Above) **In aesthetic terms the B-52 was at its best in the early 1960s with its 'natural metal' and white finish. B-52H 60-0043 is depicted at Homestead AFB on 28 December, 1966.** Larry Milberry

A 92nd BW B-52H stands ready after a generation exercise to demonstrate for the benefit of Russian satellites that SAC could rapidly 'generate' the balance of its forces in a crisis. Twenty ALCMs would take roughly three hours to upload. Jim Benson

The fuellers fill B-52D 56-0625 at Andersen. It returned to McCoy AFB after Arc Light duties and crashed on an overshoot in March 1972. Cichocki

(Above) The B-52D's immense flap area is evident here. So is the pollution. Frank Mormillo

Maintainers uncock the tail guns of a 'BUFF' post-mission and repack its drag 'chute container. Cichocki

meticulous co-ordination. Each of two waves divided into three smaller streams, re-forming into a single stream just before reaching the target. Two B-52Ds were destroyed including 'Ash 2' which had to overfly two SAM sites, successfully bombing the first but taking a hit from the second, a notoriously accurate team known as 'Killer Site VN 549'. Capt John Mize kept the lacerated B-52, with all the engines out on one wing, airborne for forty-eight minutes, enabling his wounded crew to bale out safely over Laos. For this action he was awarded the Air Force Cross. A short while later, Cobalt leader took a hit only seconds before reaching the target, preventing bomb release. The B-52 went down with only four survivors – the last casualty of *Linebacker II*.[17] The losses were partly reduced that night, when many SAMs were fired, including 31 against one cell, by DECM emissions from a passing SR-71A. Lt Col Darrell Cobb and Capt Reg Blackwell overflew the target at bomb release point, collecting ELINT and blanketing the area with their own jammers.

For the final two nights, SAM sites which had eluded the *Iron Hand* units were bombed, as were rail choke points. In a further refinement of tactics it was possible to release bombs from three cells simultaneously, using three waves in an elaborate cross-over pattern. SAM evasion manoeuvres were perfected, including a synchronized 'dip' by a five-ship cell. But there were few missiles left to launch after their storage depots had been located and destroyed. When Capt Vic Putz landed the last B-52G on 30 December it had completed the 729th sortie. 150,000 tons of bombs had fallen on North Vietnam, 75 per cent of them from B-52s. Andersen's bomb-loaders had manhandled 58,000 bombs during the operation. As Cdr Rollins, a VAQ-132 EA-6B crewman noted, a single wave of B-52s delivered as much ordnance as twenty-seven USN *Alpha Strikes*. Undoubtedly the campaign forced a settlement in Vietnam, albeit temporary. It also achieved its aim of minimizing collateral damage, though one late bomb damaged Bach Mai hospital near a MiG base. BDA indicated heavy damage to the rail network. It was estimated that a quarter of the North's POL reserves and 80 per cent of its electrical generating capacity had been destroyed. Of the thousand SAMs launched only twenty-four had found their targets, bringing down fifteen B-52s and damaging ten others. The overall loss-rate equated to 2 per cent, far less than expected, though it did reach 4 per cent over the most heavily defended targets. Fourteen crewmen died and the same number were MIA, with thirty-three taken prisoner. Of the thirty crew who made it to Thailand or Laos only twenty-five lived. The North Vietnamese estimated their own civilian casualties at 1,600 dead. *Linebacker II* was SAC's last big 'gravity bomb' operation before a new generation of PGMs appreciably redefined the nature and accuracy of strategic bombing once again.

The aircraft bore little evidence of their prodigious efforts. Mission scores were not

---

Final Phases – 26–30 December

26/27 December 120 aircraft in seven waves (three failed to make the TOT).

B-52D	43rd SW	eleven cells.
B-52G	72nd SW(P)	fifteen cells.
B-52D	307th SW	fourteen cells. TOT 2230-2245.

WAVE 1 B-52D led by Maj Bill Stocker in 56-0680 with Gen James McCarthy as Airborne Commander. (Snow, Slate, Cream, Lilac, Pinto, Cobalt cells from Guam).
WAVE 2 B-52G led by Maj Louis Falck (Opal, Lavender, Wine, Sable, Lemon from Guam and Walnut cell from U-T).
WAVE 3 B-52D led by Maj Tom Lebar (Rust, Maroon, Amber, Silver, Red from Guam and Gold cell from U-T).
WAVE 4 B-52D 307th SW (Pink, White, Ivory, Yellow, Ebony, Smoke cells).
WAVE 5 B-52D 307th SW (Black, Ruby, Rainbow, Indigo, Brown, Ash cells).
WAVE 6 B-52G led by Maj Woody O'Donnell (Paint, Brick, Grape, Purple, Copper cells from Guam).
WAVE 7 B-52G led by Maj Glenn Robertson (Maple, Hazel, Aqua, Bronze, Violet cells from Guam).
TARGETS: Thai Nguyen, Duc Noi, Hanoi, Haiphong and Giap Nhi rail centres, Kinh No complex, Van Dien vehicle centre, Hanoi POL storage, Haiphong power transformer, SAM site VN 549. Collateral damage to civilian housing in Kham Trien St. Hanoi.
RESULTS: Over 100 SAMs fired. Chaff bombers very effective. B-52D 'Ebony 2' (56-0674) hit by SAM. Four crew POW. B-52D 'Ash 1' (56-0584) A/C Capt Jim Turner, hit by SAM and crashed on approach to U-Tapao. 1st Lt Bob Hymel (copilot) and TSgt Spencer Crippen (gunner) the only survivors. Minor damage to B-52s 'Cream 1' and 'Cream 2'. Support aircraft made 113 sorties, including F-4s in five functions. (*see* SFAD Box)

27/28 December

B-52D	43rd SW	three cells.
B-52G	72nd SW(P)	seven cells.
B-52D	307th SW	ten cells. TOT 2259-2312.

TARGETS: Lang Dang rail yard (seven cells), Duc Noi (three cells), Tring Quang rail centre (four cells), Van Diem supply complex (two cells), SAM sites VN234, 243, 549 (one cell each).
RESULTS: 120 SAMs launched. B-52D 'Ash 2' (56-0599), A/C Capt. John Mize, hit by SAM ten seconds after bombing SAM site. Whole crew injured; baled out over Laos. B-52D 'Cobalt 1' (56-0605), A/C Capt Frank Lewis, hit near forward wheel-well. EW and RN both MIA, rest of crew POW. One of these aircraft was part-claimed by a VPAF MiG pilot, Pham Tuan.

Guam flew 54 *Arc Lights*.

28/29 December

B-52D	43rd SW	five cells.
B-52G	72nd SW(P)	five cells.
B-52D	307th SW	ten cells. TOT 2215-2239.

TARGETS: Lang Dang rail yard (eight cells), Duc Noi, Hanoi (four cells), SAM support facilities, Hanoi (four cells), SAM sites VN 158, 266 (one cell each).
RESULTS: No losses. Only 27 SAMs. Support aircraft flew 99 sorties.

28 *Arc Lights* flown.

29/30 December

B-52D	43rd SW	six cells.
B-52G	72nd SW(P)	four cells.
B-52D	307th SW	ten cells. ('Wine 3' aborted with refuelling problem.) TOT 2320-2344.

TARGETS: Phuc Yen SAM support facility (nine cells), Lang Dang rail yard (six cells), Tra Cam SAM storage area (five cells).
RESULTS: No losses. 'Gray 3' evaded nine SAMs but took 119 shrapnel holes. One attempted MiG interception. Support aircraft flew 102 sorties.

B-52G/H Conventional Weapons

B-52D 'Big Belly' Stratofortresses were unique in being able to carry internal bomb-bay clips housing a total of 108 bombs. The B-52G/H models' internal capacity comprises two four-bomb or up to three nine-bomb clips. Conventional internal loads comprise one of the following types, normally using one type of munition. Bracketed designations indicate sub-variants:

27   SUU-30H/B (CBU-52, -58, and -71); Mk 82 (LDGP, SE, AIR, and Mk 36 DST and Mk 62 QS mines); M117 (conical fin, R, and AIR); CBU-72/B (FAE).

18   British 1,000lb bomb* and M129 leaflet bomb.

8   Mk 84 (LDGP, AIR, and Mk 41 DST mine); AGM-86C CALCM; Mk 55/56 mines, Mk 60 Captor mine, and Mk 63/65 QS mines.

6   TMD (CBU-87 and CBU-89)

*Between September and December 1990 Lear Siegler and USAF teams modified 39 B-52Gs to carry Royal Ordnance 1,000lb bombs at SAC HQ request since they could be fitted with UK960 fuses and provide an area denial weapon which could not be matched by US weaponry.

Pylons

Two types of external wing pylons are used. The longer one was originally used for carriage of the AGM-28 Hound Dog missile. The shorter one was designed for conventional weapons carriage and is known as the 'Stub' wing pylon. It is only compatible with aircraft not modified for carriage of air-launched cruise missiles (ALCMs). There are two types of mounting hardware attached to the pylons for carriage of conventional weapons. The most common is the I-beam rack adapter to which two multiple ejection racks (MER-1-6 or -6As) are attached. This arrangement allows the carriage of a dozen weapons from each pylon, comprising twenty-four each of the SUU-30H/B (CBU-52, -58, and -71), CBU-89, Mk 82 (LDGP, SE, AIR, Mk 36 Destructor, and Mk 62 Quickstrike), M117 (conical fin, R, and AIR), MC-1, CBU-72, Mk 20 Rockeye II, and M129 leaflet dispensers. Because of stores weight only twenty-two CBU-87 CEMS can be carried, with the aft centre station on the forward left MER and the forward centre station of the aft right MER being left empty.

For stores too long and too heavy to be attached to MERs the Heavy Stores Adapter Beam (HSAB) is used. This permits carriage of up to nine weapons from each pylon, depending on weapon size and weight. HSABs can only be used with the stub pylon and were never used with B-52Fs. Normally, only one type of bomb was carried per mission. However, M129 psychological warfare leaflet dispensers can be interspersed within loads of GP bombs (for example, a single M129 on a forward left HSAB station with 17 Mk 82 LDGPs on the rest during some *Desert Storm* missions).

HSAB pylon carriage comprises one of the following arrangements, using one munition type:

4   AGM-142 Popeye (or three Popeyes and a data-link pod) mounted on fore and aft centre HSAB stations.

8   AGM-84 Harpoon, AGM-84E SLAM, or GBU-10. Mounted on fore and aft shoulder stations.

10   Mk 84 (LDGP, AIR, and Mk 41 DST mine) or Mk 60 Captor mine. Mounted on fore and aft shoulder and centre middle stations.

12   GBU-12, or Mk 55/56 mines. Mounted on shoulder stations only.

18   Mk 40 DST mine, British 1,000lb bomb, or any bomb carried on the I-beam. Full HSAB employment.

24   CBU-87 (including six internally) or twenty-eight with AGM-28 type pylons fitted. 24CBU-89 (including six internally) or thirty with AGM-28 type pylons fitted.

For *Desert Storm* sorties typical loads were: (Total with MERs) fifty-one M117 or Mk 82, or fifty-one Mk 52/-58/-71 CBU. (Total with HSAB) forty-five of the above. CBU-87/-89 was also used (*see* table above).

B-52D 56-0057, preserved at Ellsworth AFB in June 1987, provides a sinister reminder of eight years of B-52 combat in Vietnam. Ron Thurlow

B-52D 55-0090 with a new coat of paint post-war.
Frank Mormillo

usually painted up, partly because crews were not assigned a particular aircraft but mainly, as a 43rd SW RN put it, because, 'It wouldn't be SAC to do it. Our style's cooler'. In any case, their job was far from complete. *Arc Lights*, which had continued at a high rate throughout *Linebacker*, were flown until 15 August 1973 over Cambodia, where *Freedom Deal* took B-52s ever deeper into the country in search of Khmer Rouge insurgents. In May and June Operation *Scoot*, with 763 sorties, provided targets in the outskirts of the capital, Phnom Penh, though the bombing only delayed the city's fall by a few weeks. In Laos, missions supporting the Trails war continued, right up to the cease-fire on 21 February, 1973 with additional sorties thereafter in response to breaches of that agreement. The final total of Laotian *Arc Lights* was an astonishing 33,000 sorties.

Duxford BUFF

At 8am on the cold, grey morning of 8 October 1983 B-52D 56-0689 loomed over the closed-off M11 motorway. Pilot Lt Col Jim Nerger, used to 12,000ft SAC runways, made three circuits and put the bomber down in about 3,500ft of Duxford's 4,800ft strip. It was probably the shortest-ever landing by a B-52. Twelve days later CINCSAC Gen Bennie Davis flew in from Offutt AFB to hand over the aircraft to ACM Sir David Craig, AOC RAF Strike Command. In exchange, the USAF received three Vulcan bombers for display in the USA. Lacking space to display the B-52D the RAF donated it to the IWM Museum, Duxford.

This B-52D was only the second to be put on display (after 55-0100, the *Arc Light* Memorial on Guam) outside the USA. A brief account of its 15,000-hour flying career illustrates the hard-working life which these 'bodacious BUFFs' had completed when they were retired in the early 1980s. Boeing Wichita delivered it to the USAF on 11 October, 1957 for service with the 28th BW at Ellsworth AFB. It then served with the 4128th SW (Amarillo, Texas), the 95th BW (Biggs AFB), 494th BW (Sheppard AFB), 509th BW (Pease AFB) and in 1966, Douglas Aircraft borrowed it for contract work. It then returned to operational use at Glasgow AFB with the 91st BW before its first visit to Guam in September 1966 for war service. Back in the USA with the 91st BW in March 1967 it moved to Westover AFB and the 99th BW in July 1967 and then completed another six months of *Arc Light* missions from Guam and U-Tapao, interrupted by a stay at March AFB with the 22nd BW. A brief period with the 306th BW at McCoy AFB led to a return to battle at Guam in June 1968 where it was progressively rotated from the 454th BW to the 509th BW and then to the 99th BW at U-Tapao. After a short respite at Westover AFB it was back with the 43rd SW at Andersen AFB, Guam in November 1971, then at U-Tapao, with a further Andersen stint in the 96th BW before moving to Carswell AFB in November 1972. Recalled to Andersen's 99th BW in December 1972 for *Linebacker II* it survived and transferred to Carswell AFB in July 1973. Further TDYs with the 307th SW, U-Tapao and 43rd SW, Andersen, occurred in 1974-75 with a final Guam visit in June 1978 after further service with the 7th BW (Carswell) and 96th BW (Dyess AFB). It saw out its SAC service with the 7th BW at Carswell, one of the last B-52D units, in 1982. After such prodigious activity with a range of units, many of whose names and bases are already half-forgotten, the noble survivor has become the centrepiece of the new American Air Museum at Duxford.

Short-landing expert Jim Nerger also delivered a B-52D to the Yankee Air Museum, Ypsilanti, Michigan.

CHAPTER FIVE

SIOP 'BUFFs'

Low-level flight puts immense strains on the B-52G airframe which necessitated a series of costly rebuilding and modification programmes. Boeing via Thurlow

If the B-52 is synonymous with the USAF, then preparedness is what the USAF is about. The two are inseparable institutions and there is no doubt that the 'BUFF' provided by far the greatest contribution towards both the psychological and physical strength of America's aerial nuclear deterrent force for nigh on four decades. It is a tasking it enjoys to this day, albeit eclipsed by the new B-2A Spirit and a pronounced shift towards conventional bombing with precision-guided munitions (PGMs), to which it has adapted and continues to excel.[18]

Some B-52Fs wore SIOP camouflage including 57-0045 in 1971. Ron Thurlow

SIOP – the Master Plan

Ground alert quickly became the dominant pattern of SAC operations during the 1960s, punctuated by exacting ORIs (Operational Readiness Inspections) to test readiness and seldom less gruelling Bomb Competitions, with the machine kept well-oiled by constant upgrades to avionics and weapons systems and related training. At the apex of SAC, nuclear strategy hinged upon what was known as the Single Integrated Operations Plan (SIOP), which wove together SAC's bombers, tankers and even reconnaissance assets to guarantee maximum striking power in the event of a crisis. Its origins lay with the creation of the Joint Strategic Target Planning Staff (JSTPS), created by Secretary of Defense Thomas S. Gates Jr on 16 August 1960 to coordinate all American nuclear forces. Composed of representatives from all the services, the JSTPS was made responsible for the task of preparing and maintaining a

National Strategic Target List and a SIOP, with the staff collocated at SAC Headquarters at Offutt AFB, Omaha, Nebraska. A series of coded (coloured) Defense Readiness Conditions, or DEFCONs, were put into play, which might climax with DEFCON One, or 'Red', calling for massive nuclear retaliation. Some may be surprised to learn that, for most of its tenure, SAC was usually on 'Yellow alert' – just a couple of stops away from nuclear Armageddon.

1960 also witnessed the introduction of 'Short Order', a new single sideband HF radio communications system linking SAC HQ and its three numbered Air Force headquarters to *Chromedome* or post-launched bombers en route to their targets under what was known as Positive Control. Without receipt of the special 'go code', bombers would RTB – return to base. Further control of the nuclear bomber force was provided by EC-135 'Looking Glass' airborne command posts, which commenced round-the-clock operations from 3 February 1961, after a six-month trial, and rapidly built into a large fleet dotted around the Globe. Using long-range communications they could link with any of the Joint Chiefs of Staff, any SAC base and any SAC aircraft in the air. The technology was expanded upon throughout the ensuing thirty years, adding a National Emergency Airborne Command Post or NEACP (pronounced kneecap), designed to take the President or his stand-in aloft. Newer communications arrays included AFSATCOM (Air Force Satellite communications, fitted to the B-52G/H's gunner's station and later moved to the Nav console and being upgraded to Milstar), and a netted computer system for 'real time', encrypted communications, which began as the ARPAnet and evolved into the Milnet.[19] The US Navy similarly expanded control over its submarine assets, adding TACAMO (Take Charge and Move Out) aerial nuclear battle controllers. It represented a colossal investment, but ensured that a tight rein was always in place. There was no room for 'wild cards in the pack'.

It was against this background of command and control technology that the B-52 force stood on vigil, cocked and ready to launch, around the clock for 365 days a year, for over thirty years. Targets and timing were contained in the SIOP War Orders but with much of the detailed mission-planning being furnished by the Bombing-Navigation and Operations Branches of the Wings, prepared on a contingency basis.

SAC Bomb Competitions kept troops sharpened up, including the crew members of this B-52G at the 15th AF Shootout **event at March AFB. Note the copious baggage waiting to be inspected and loaded aboard.** USAF via Thurlow

But no matter what rank or status, 'pulling' alert meant the same to everyone – when the klaxons hooted, Alert crews stopped what they were doing, finished suiting-up from their standby tasks or recreation, and ran or drove out to their aircraft.

Later, Quick Fix cartridge start-up meant all eight B-52 engines would be turning over amidst a cloud of soot as the last of the crew clambered onboard, strapped in and ran through their launch checklist, setting switches, although the aircraft would have already been 'primed' as far as was practicable by the 'tech troops' and aircrews. Alert aircraft received maximum preening before they were pulled from the duty, to be duly replaced by freshly serviced 'BUFFs'.[20] According to the crews, 'Cart start takes approximately thirty seconds [as] we have the capability to start all eight engines simultaneously'.[21] For less time-critical launches, a combination of cartridge and pneumatic start would be employed, using cartridges in engines four and five only. 'One, two, three, six, seven and eight are started from bleed air [taking] approximately one minute, thirty seconds.' It is still an impressive statistic compared with an average tactical aircraft, which can spend up to an hour between start-up and roaring down the runway.

Aircraft were pre-heated during the winter months to make things a little more comfortable – primarily for the avionics and engines, rather than the besuited crewmen. H-1 heaters were employed routinely, but later procedures introduced JP-4 fuel into the mid-body fuel tank for aircraft sitting alert at temperatures below freezing point, allowing engines to be started as low as –20 degrees. Low flashpoint fuel has advantages when you want to get moving in a hurry!

MITOs and *Marshmallows*

Whether war or an ORI, the idea was to get off the ground as quickly as possible. Col Phil Rowe described the procedure beautifully in a piece he titled *MITOs and Marshmallows*:

> What makes a helluva lot of noise, spews clouds of black smoke and draws huge crowds? Answer: A MITO. So what in the heck is a MITO, you ask? Well, it's a mass launch of a bunch of airplanes with minimum (M) interval (I) between Take (T) offs (O). And it is a truly spectacular thing to behold. It's even more exciting to participate in a MITO. And what's all this got to do with marshmallows, you ask? That's just a bit of gallows humour, an inside joke amongst flight

crews. The MITO's for practice were usually scheduled events that crews and others on SAC bases knew about up to a week in advance. Those mass take-offs were so spectacular and interesting that folks used to drive their cars, loaded with family, friends and neighbours, to the perimeter road around the base and park there to watch the MITO event. Some crew members joked that the spectators were there with their marshmallows, ready to roast them in the fire of a potential crash. Sick, eh? The interval between planes taking off, as many as a dozen or so at a time, depended upon the size of the runway, its width, and the airplanes, their wing span. Large birds, like B-52s could not take off side-by-side down the runway, so they'd be spaced just a few seconds apart, typically at fifteen-second intervals. [Relatively] small planes, like B-58s or FB-111s could be staggered, left and right, down wide runways. They could go at seven and a half second intervals. There were attempts to make the big planes go at the smaller interval, but that didn't always work out.

The reason for MITO's in the first place was to get the war-loaded Alert airplanes off the ground as quickly as possible. The advent of enemy submarine-launched medium-range-ballistic-missiles (MRBMs) gave flight crews much shorter times to get their airplanes out of harm's way. Before MRBMs there might have been twenty or thirty minutes warning time, but that was cut in half with the new threats. Hence a technique for quickly launching all available Alert airplanes, the MITO, was developed. And MITOs are not all that easy to do, hence practice launches were conducted from time to time.

Imagine that you are in the cockpit of a MITO-launching airplane. If you're in the lead spot it would be a normal launch with nobody up there just in front of you. But back in the pack you get a different view. It's analogous to what the sled dogs view of those up front. There ain't much scenery, but you'd better stay in your place.

The second, third and remainder airplanes get a lot of smoke in their faces, considerable noise in the cockpit and quite a bit of turbulence from those jet engines spewing out high-velocity hot gases. You kinda hope for a light crosswind to minimize your discomfort and improve forward visibility by sweeping the crud aside. And, of course, you hope like the dickens that the fellows in front of you don't have a problem. For if they blow a tyre, lose engines or otherwise slow down unexpectedly, you've got a real problem. That's why it's 'pucker time' for everyone except the lead ship. But then too, if you are in the lead ship and suddenly slow down, you've got a bunch of roaring monsters on your tail. And then what do you do? For the ground observers, those folks along the runway perimeter road with the marshmallows, the MITO is exciting, a truly awe-inspiring sight. So now, dear reader, you know what a MITO is, even if you still don't appreciate the marshmallow factor.

On the Apple at the ARIP

B-52s do not 'rotate' on take-off but 'elevate' off the ground, using the aircraft's built-in eight degrees of wing incidence; the 'BUFF' can thus build up speed before attempting to climb more rapidly, sometimes with an apparently alarming nose-down attitude as they cross the runway threshold in level flight! With a potential maximum take-off weight of 488,000lb as specified in the Dash-1 manual for the turbofan-powered B-52H model – 'the maximum weight the landing gear, brakes, hydraulics and associated bulkheads are stressed for' – the sight, sound and smell of the launch was and remains awesome, as 136,000lb (605kN) of thrust fought to push the whole ensemble along. Masks would be worn to protect the crewmen from the hazards of nuclear flash on the assumption the base or environs might be under ICBM or SLBM rocket attack: 'PLZT, Lead Lanthanum Zirconate Titanite flash blindness protection equipment is donned prior to take-off. During daylight conditions, pilots will, time permitting, use thermal flash blindness [curtains] and PLZT goggles during taxi, take-off and climb-out, turn thunderstorm lights and other required interior light to full bright to make the flight instruments easily visible while wearing PLZT'. Cumbersome, but essential.

Clambering for height with just black streaks from the water-injected engine take-offs etching a charcoal claw mark from the runway to the horizon, the first item on the agenda was to top up the fuel reserves to the brim at the ARIP (aerial refuelling initial point). At night the twinkling of navigation beacon lights would have faded before the thunder. ARIPs comprised prearranged coordinates all mapped out in the SIOP mission folder, where the KC-135A or 'R tankers' launch patterns would be interleaved with the B-52s, so that all strikers could guarantee replenishment.

B-52s, on the same heading and 1,000ft below, would rise towards a 'contact point' some fifty feet behind the tanker, and then 'ease in', using the tanker belly's lights to get into position. 'On the apple' – the fluorescent green extension point of the boom – signified the 'boomer' had control and transfer rates were up to 6,500lb (2,945kg) fuel a minute. The copilot was responsible for 'fuel management', beginning with the wings, then fuselage, bringing the B-52H up to an impressive all-up weight of 566,000lb (257 tonnes), all borne by the flexing, long-suffering wing which could travel some seven feet (2m) up at its tips.[22] AAR altitude would be around 28,000ft, and maintaining the hook-up was a tricky affair at gross weight – there was 'one gulp club' for pilots and copilots able to stay 'on the boom'. 'Fuel burn rate varies greatly with gross weight and altitude. Since we fly a wide variety of low and high altitude missions at different gross weights, there is no "average" fuel burn rate. For example, a 400,000lb aircraft at 30,000ft and 0.75 Mach would burn 20,000lb/hour.' All-up machines with a belly stuffed with a nuclear cargo would burn about 26,000lb/hour, which diminished as more fuel was burnt, in turn reducing aircraft weight and allowing the aircraft to fly higher – a classic 'cruise climb profile'.

'Go Code'

Heading north for the ice cap – the quickest Great Circle route to the Soviet Union – the SIOP War Orders dictated a set course and strict timing, keeping the navigators fully occupied. Undoubtedly the most crucial stage in a nuclear mission would have been the Positive Control point – a set position away from enemy territory where the crews would receive the 'go code' (or be asked to maintain a holding pattern, or be recalled), and where the Emergency Action Messages included codes for arming the nuclear cargo. Without these enabling codes, the bombs effectively remained inert. This was and remains the supreme advantage of the bomber – it is recallable.

Usually, all aircraft in a given strategic strike package (and there were several, designed to ingress enemy airspace at different locations to maximize survivability, based on a constantly updated electronic order of battle or 'threat map' of the enemy's integrated air defence system or IADS) would arrive at their inbound points within a two-minute time gate. By this stage individual formations would

Phase VI ECM

In the post-Vietnam years the B-52's ECM became highly automated, featuring 'power management' to apportion available electrical 'juice' to priority threats, while also introducing revised displays which featured alphanumerics (the threats indicated as simple symbols) on individual displays.

'Jamming Strategies' for the systems also became flightline-programmable, based on Sigint derived from SAC's extensive fleet of RC-135 'ferrets', the U-2 Dragon Lady and SR-71 Blackbird, garnered and processed by the 9th SRW at Beale AFB, California, and 55th SRW at Offutt AFB, Nebraska, and their FOL (Forward Operating Location) detachments. This ensured that ECM was finely-tuned to the latest Soviet radar threats. EWOs, later known as 'E-Dubs', attended regular briefings where they would be brought up to date on preferred countermeasures strategies.

Rivet Ace was the kick-start to Phase VI. By 1970 electronic warfare had become so sophisticated that another expensive update was deemed necessary for the B-52G/H SIOP fleet. Initially, under ECP-1151 it was to have been Phase VI of the evolving 'BUFF' countermeasures evolution, but it continued at a slower pace through Phase VI+ under ECP 2519, into the 1990s. The project was given the green light in December 1971 at a projected cost of $362.5m, although the eventual cost has been well over four times that. Installation of the initial components took several years, with B-52G 58-0204 serving as testbed for much of the equipment. The main problem in installing all the items, which eventually totalled more than 6,000lb in weight, was lack of space. Boeing had to add an extra 40in (1m) to the rear fuselage aft of the rudder to accommodate new equipment racks. This work took place between 1970 and 1977 when aircraft became due for depot-level maintenance and an early casualty was the transparent blister on the extreme tail originally used for the TV camera link to the tail gun AN/ASG-15 FCS. The first B-52H with Phase VI updates was delivered to the 319th BW at Grand Forks, North Dakota, on 24 February 1974. The enormous array of devices, based on the original programme, evolved to comprise:

Type	Supplier and Function
Passive receivers	
These 'sniffed' the airwaves and alerted the crew to threats. The B-52's own radars were programmed to avoid interfering with these:	
AN/ALR-20	Tasker Inc. This is a panoramic 'all seeing' display showing threats within a selected band-width. It became the E-Dub's main instrument for helping direct 'man in the loop' control over jamming and pyrotechnics.
AN/ALR-46	Dalmo-Victor. This replaced the earlier AN/ALR-25 and provided digital processing. It analyses and displays threat information to the E-Dub (and gunner) in audio, and alphanumerics on little 'dart-board' compass-rose screens.
Active receivers	
AN/ALQ-153	Westinghouse. A 'terminal threat' tail-warning pulse-Doppler radar designed to detect and identify closing fighters or missiles. It was linked to pyrotechnics to command automatic release of chaff and flares, if authorized. Retrofit completed late 1984.
Power-managed jammers	
Most of the following devices were designed to apportion available power to enemy radars using 'power management', replacing manually-tuned jammers used previously and increasing Effective Radiated Power.	
AN/ALQ-117	ITT Avionics. One of the key Phase VI components. Two sets were installed initially, mainly to work against high-frequency threats, including monopulse radars. Later superseded by the AN/ALQ-172. AN/ALQ-122 Motorola. Smart Noise Operation Equipment (SNOE). A false target generator, it employed two AN/ALT-16A transmitter/amplifiers searching for low band signals: early warning radars, height-finders, acquisition and GCI radars, denying them range and bearing. AN/ALQ-155 Northrop. AN/ALT-28 replacement. Ten units receive, and twelve transit noise jamming signals across a broad frequency range, using power management.
AN/ALQ-172	ITT. Active 'smart' jamming system developed under the *Pave Mint* project. The fit of two units was later expanded to three units per aircraft after experience in *Desert Storm*, and memory capacity also increased by 400 per cent.
AN/ALT-16A	Hallicrafters, updated by Northrop, Raytheon and Litton. Amplifies signal from AN/ALQ-122, denying the enemy range, bearing and identity of the B-52.
AN/ALT-32B	Barrage or spot noise-jamming in high or low frequency bands, designed to jam enemy communications.
Pyrotechnics	
These comprise the 'disposables', ejected from the tail and mid-wing to foil 'terminal threats'.	
AN/ALE-20	Dynalectron. Twelve flare dispensers in underside of tail with sixteen AN/ALA-17 flares each, doubling capacity to 192 from 96 cartridges. The number of flares 'shot' and intervals can be programmed at spacings ranging from twenty secs to full salvo.
AN/ALE-24	Lundy. Four chaff dispensers per wing, ejecting from four slots at mid-wing. Chaff packets can be dispensed in pairs, fours or sixes (1,125 total). Wing turbulence helps to spread chaff rapidly. It was built into the B-52H on an ab initio basis and retrofitted to the B-52G.

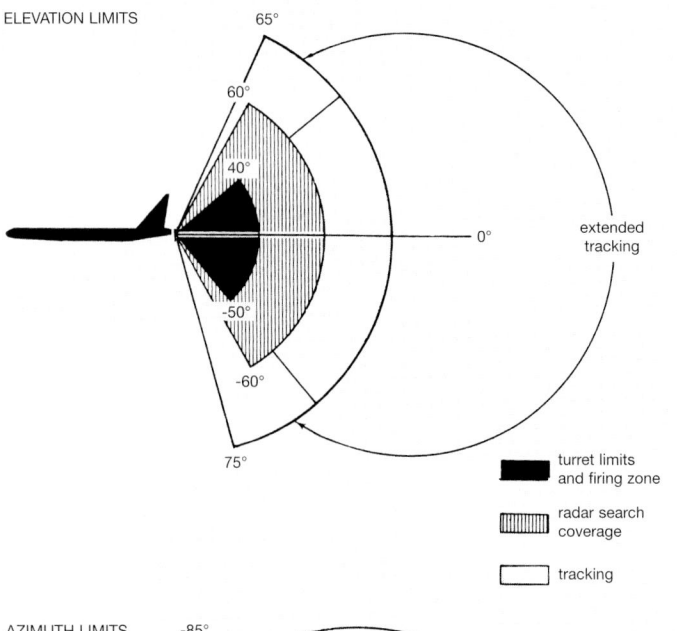

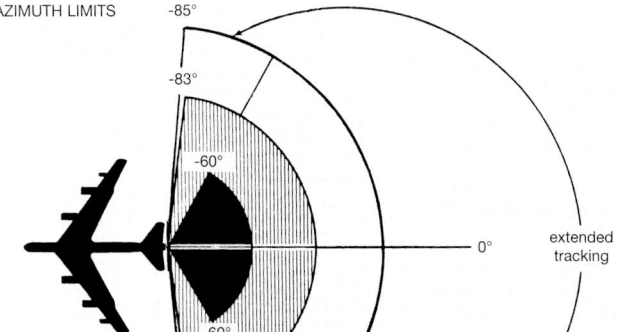

Angular coverage of ASG-15 FCS

A hard-working B-52G, 58-0204 was used for the Rivet Ace (Phase VI) ECM tests, with appropriate nose-art and an ALQ-153 test installation on the left stabilizer. This tail warning system was finally installed in the vertical stabilizer. '204 also took part in AGM-86B vs AGM-109 ALCM fly-off trials, later returning to squadron service and Desert Storm. Boeing

have fanned out a few miles apart, and would be preparing to duck down below the enemy radar umbrella, with weapons cocked and the electronic countermeasures blasting out 'music' under the skilful management of the EWO, known latterly as the 'E-Dub', based on a predefined 'start countermeasures' point. This way, the enemy's radars and communications could be swamped with jamming and decoys.

The Cold War era Soviet IADS was formidable, embracing thousands of SAMs and fighters linked to a huge radar multiplex. SAMs became abundant during the 1960s and were constantly improved while day fighters gave way to all-weather, radar-equipped interceptors during the 1970s so that by 1986, it boasted aircraft like the MiG-31 'Foxhound', capable of using 'look down' radar with long-range missiles in formation sweeps. SAMs had evolved to lethal packages such as the Model 9M83 (SA-12A 'Gladiator'), Model 9M82 (SA-12B 'Giant') and S-300PMU (SA-10 'Grumble'), linked to the S-300V mobile radar systems. Each of these sophisticated, expensive SAM systems is capable of monitoring 200 targets and tracking seventy of them, and supplying two dozen of those tracks to four separate missile batteries – enough to hack down down any unprotected aircraft or air-launched missile at ranges of 6–75km (3.75–47 miles) and altitudes between approximately 80ft (25m) up to 80,000ft (25,000m), closing in at speeds of up to 1.7km/sec!

With threats like these, ECM and low-level terrain-hugging flight alone was seldom adequate and strategies were evolved to 'roll back' the enemy IADS using nuclear missiles. Even if the weapons did not achieve a direct hit, the shockwave would knock out radars for tens of miles and the electromagnetic pulse created by nuclear detonations could be employed to 'fry open' a corridor through the enemy's electronic screen by disabling his sensitive electronics. Hound Dog, which was retired from the inventory during June 1975, could be employed in this capacity but there existed only two per B-52. By contrast, its successor, the Boeing AGM-69A SRAM (Short Range Attack Missile) was bountiful, with the B-52 capable of accommodating up to twelve externally, not counting additional, internal 'revolver loads' of the missiles. It was the perfect antidote to a burgeoning air defence system.

Modifying the 281-strong B-52G/H fleet for SRAM cost $400m and began in October 1971, with the first aircraft redelivered to the 42nd BW at Loring AFB, Maine the following March. Operational capability was achieved by the 42nd BW on 4 August 1972, six months after the first production SRAM had been delivered to the base. By August 1975 there were nineteen B-52G/H Wings operational with the missile. It remained very much part-and-parcel of the SIOP mission until its withdrawal from service during June 1990, under orders from Defense Secretary Cheney, but helped to keep the B-52 viable for eighteen years!

Short-range Attack Missile AGM-69A

The Boeing SRAM-A packed a 200kT W69 warhead in a 2,230lb, 14ft-long slender airframe. After release, SRAM fired an XSR-75-LP-1 two-pulse solid-fuel rocket motor. Maximum speed was Mach 2.8–3.2, and the range varied from 35 to 105 miles, depending on the mission profile, steering with three tail fins. Equipped with a Delco computer and Singer-Kearfott KT-76 Inertial Measurement Unit, it was fed target coordinates by the B-52's SRAM Carrier Aircraft Equipment and could be launched in one of four different modes: 'inertial', wherein the missile was launched at a set altitude and bearing to the target for optimum accuracy; 'terrain sensor', in which SRAM employed a radar altimeter to skim over the topography to avoid detection; 'combined' inertial and terrain-following; and 'semi-ballistic', in which the weapon was lobbed at the target in a ballistic rocket trajectory, when range counted for more than pinpoint accuracy.

First in the league was the B-52G-equipped 42nd BW which received its initial operational missiles on 4 March 1972 and fired their first round a trimester later on 15 June, over White Sands, New Mexico. The last of 1,521 SRAMs was delivered in August 1975, going to Mather AFB, California. The missiles were originally carried on the wing pylons in clusters of six, with a further eight on an internal bomb-bay rotary launcher. External carriage ceased when OAS-modified B-52s arrived, and from April 1988, the new Common Strategic Rotary Launcher (CSRL) came into use, of which Boeing supplied 98 units.

After a successful eighteen-year career stretching to 7 June 1990, by which time some 300 inert missiles had been expended in training, it was withdrawn from Alert under the express orders of Defense Secretary Richard B. Cheney. Concerns existed regarding the integrity of the rocket motors, which had begun to leak. The weapon's intended successors, the Boeing SRAM II and tactical nuclear SRAM-T, were cancelled in September 1991 as part of the ongoing cutbacks to the strategic arsenal.

An AGM-69A rotary launcher suspended in its ADU-317/E adapter is moved into position beneath a B-52G. Test rounds of AGM-69A SRAMs are in place and the bomb doors have been raised out of the way. Boeing via Thurlow

When SRAMs were safely installed the bomb bay doors were lowered and their retractors reconnected. Tony Cassanova

This SRAM-loaded B-52H's Crew Chief supervises its preparation for a mission. Boeing via Chesneau

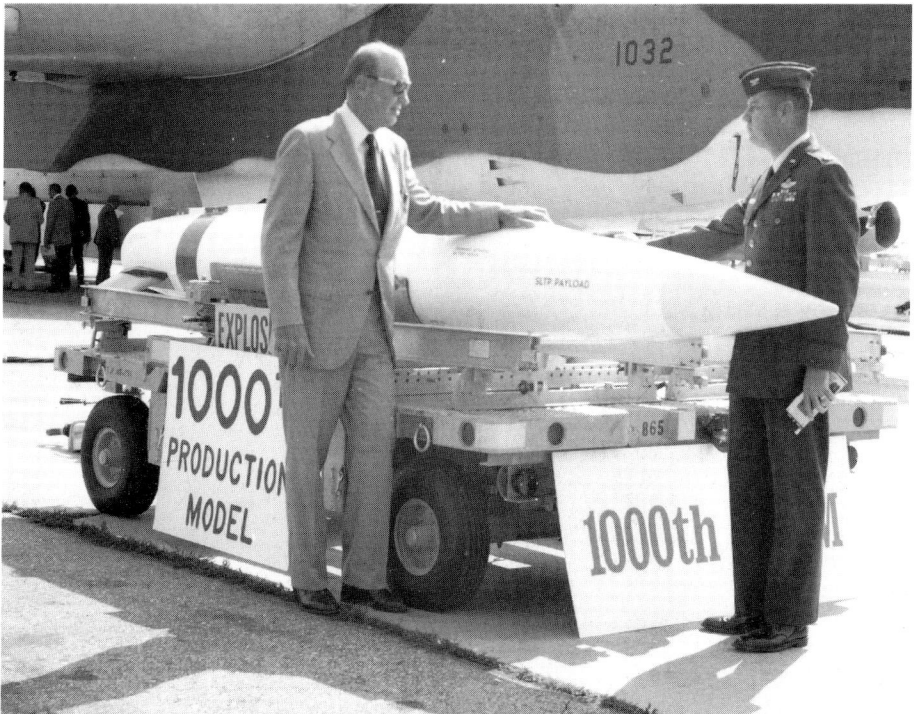
Handover of the one thousandth Boeing AGM-69A SRAM in its MHU-69 cradle, with the 17th BW's B-52H 61-0032 behind. B-52G/Hs could carry up to twenty SRAMs.
Boeing via Thurlow

EVS: New eyes

Alongside SRAM carrier aircraft equipment, the SIOP fleet also began to receive a substantially updated navigation and offensive avionics, beginning with the External Viewing System (EVS). The first aircraft to receive EVS was B-52H 61-0031, inducted into the modification line at the San Antonio PDM line at Kelly AFB, Texas, in October 1972 and delivered to K. I. Sawyer AFB, Michigan, the following 24 June, according to Boeing. EVS was a huge boon to the crew, massively increasing situational awareness for low level operations. The programme was completed during 1976.

The ASQ-151 EVS comprised two steerable sensors carried in two prominent fairings under the radome, the port one containing Westinghouse AN/AVQ-22 Low-Light-Level Television (LLLTV) and the starboard unit Hughes AN/AAQ-6 Forward-Looking Infra-Red (FLIR). The

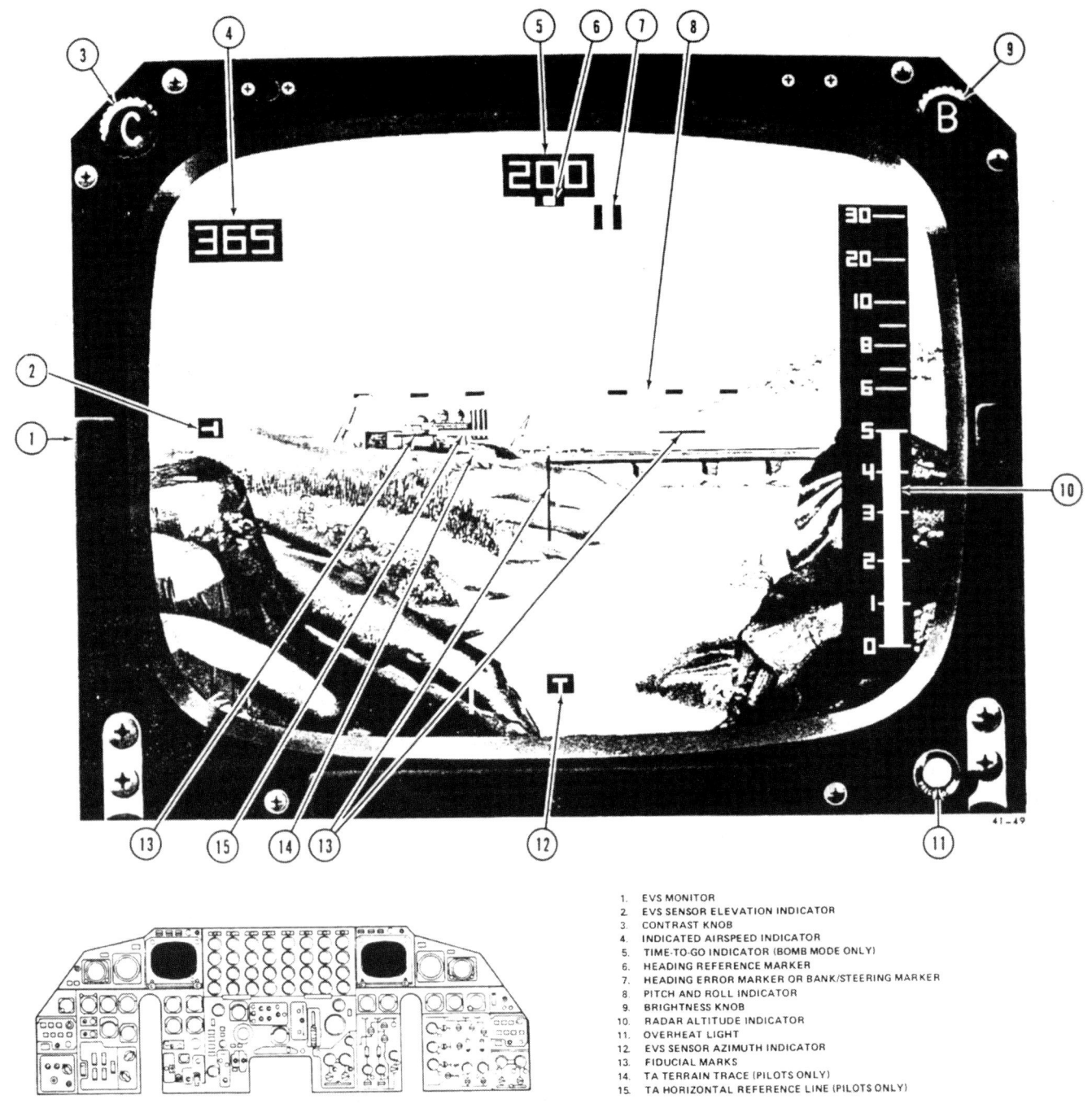

1. EVS MONITOR
2. EVS SENSOR ELEVATION INDICATOR
3. CONTRAST KNOB
4. INDICATED AIRSPEED INDICATOR
5. TIME-TO-GO INDICATOR (BOMB MODE ONLY)
6. HEADING REFERENCE MARKER
7. HEADING ERROR MARKER OR BANK/STEERING MARKER
8. PITCH AND ROLL INDICATOR
9. BRIGHTNESS KNOB
10. RADAR ALTITUDE INDICATOR
11. OVERHEAT LIGHT
12. EVS SENSOR AZIMUTH INDICATOR
13. FIDUCIAL MARKS
14. TA TERRAIN TRACE (PILOTS ONLY)
15. TA HORIZONTAL REFERENCE LINE (PILOTS ONLY)

monitor view.

sensors were designed to feed information on to new Conrac Corp ten-inch displays screens used by the AC/pilot and copilot, and also both navigators. Data that can be presented on these screens includes an overlaid terrain avoidance profile trace in both LLLTV and FLIR modes, alphanumeric symbology which includes a height reading from the radar altimeter and Time-To-Go before weapons release, as well as indicated airspeed, heading error and bank steering, artificial horizon overlay and attitude and position of the sensor in use. Each sensor has its particular merits, with the FLIR the preferred choice in total darkness or for cutting through haze in daytime, while the LLLTV would work better in high humidity and when there were low solar grazing angles, such as at dawn and dusk, creating imagery akin to black and white domestic television. The

AN/ASQ-15 EVS fairings on a Loring B-52G. The opaque germanium window of the AN/AAQ-6 FLIR is on the left and the AN/AVQ-22 steerable low-light TV turret is to the right. Authors

(Below) **The B-52G pilot's panels with the two EVS monitor screens, eight sets of engine gauges (*centre*) and eight 'poker chip' throttles. The drag 'chute control is just right of the throttle quadrant and the complex fuel panel fills the lower section of the copilot's instrument area (*right*).** Boeing

sensors can be driven in unison or individually through an area 45 degrees either side of the nose, up 15 degrees and down 45 degrees, with each crew member opting for their preferred display. The EVS was linked to the bomber's IBM bomb-nav system and terrain radar, helping the pilots avoid obstacles, the navigators to cross-check points being tracked in their radar crosshairs, while supplying all four men with a view outside the aircraft laced with essential basic flight information. A 3:1 zoom was also available. The fairing introduced a drag penalty shaving two per cent off the bomber's range, but this was negligible. It was and remains – in updated sensor format – a very popular upgrade.

OAS: New Brains

Safe and accurate low-level navigation and target ingress was also assisted by other improvements in the pipeline during the latter half of the 1970s, prompted by the need to replace the by then antiquated Q-38 OWS. Dan Lapham, a B-52H bomb-nav technician at K. I. Sawyer AFB, Michigan, remarked that the 'ASQ-38 was a real Pandora's Box of hybrid electro-mechanical and electronic components. IBM from the fifties and updated. It was not easy to maintain. I observed some system failures and fixes that defied any logic. In reality, it was so tough to work on that it took years for most guys to get a handle on it – many never really did. Then they worked the hell out of those able and willing to do the job. Many found taking leave very difficult with the heavy workload. I was no superman, but I ended up selling many weeks of leave that I never got to take.' Navigators, too, were burdened by the system, invariably finding themselves serving as in-flight maintenance folk, clambering aboard their aircraft with screwdrivers, pliers and spare vacuum tubes and fumbling about with hard-to-read radar displays. It was distracting.

The solution, spurred on by the availability of up-to-date solid-state electronics which would serve the B-52's expanding arsenal of sophisticated nuclear missiles, was the AN/ASQ-176 Offensive Avionics Systems (OAS) update programme. The first B-52G scheduled for the upgrade arrived at Boeing Wichita for rework on 7 December 1979, and was flight-tested beginning on 3 September 1980. The first operational delivery ensued when the 416th BW at Griffiss AFB, New York, received B-52G 58-0247 during August 1981. Principal items – evolving through the 1980s – included a Mil.Standard 1553 databus linking the subsystems, chief among them the AN/AYQ-10 ballistics computer, Honeywell SPN/GEANS inertial navigation set, Honeywell AN/APN-224 radar altimeter, Lear Siegler AN/ASN-134 attitude heading reference system, Teledyne-Ryan AN/APN-218 common strategic Doppler radar and OY-73 radar group, amongst other items.[23] From 1985, B-52Hs and some B-52Gs, received the Norden AN/APQ-156 multimode Strategic Radar as a further update, which introduced photo-like synthetic aperture radar imagery modes. It is all a bit of a mouthful, but in essence the OAS linked the computers, radar and INS to provide virtually automatic navigation and weapons release, allowing the navigators to focus on target acquisition and tweaking the weapons. The package was also hardened against nuclear interference.

For the purposes of executing emergency war orders with the new OAS, actual missions developed at the JSTPS at SACHQ in Omaha were sent to the Wing in question where the Bombing-Navigation Branch and Operations Plans 'cut mission tape' (prepared data transfer unit cartridges or DTUCs), using a Mission Data Planning System. This would also be accomplished on an ab initio basis for routine, day-to-day training, when relatively innocuous sets of practice missions could be drafted and filed on standby.[24] 'When the crews prepare for a real or simulated launch, the navigator carries four DTUCs in a container resembling a large fishing tackle box. He puts them into the OAS system. The first cartridge has the B-52 mission profile; the second contains all the data concerning the simulated [missile launches] for that day; the third cartridge holds the executive program, which basically tells the OAS computers that they are OAS computers and not word processors; and, finally, there's the recorder or 'stool pigeon', which records inputs about most of the important aspects of the flight for later use in maintenance and operations analysis. It also records certain types of crew errors – hence the nickname.' The ballistics system knows the characteristics of the gravity thermonuclear weapons as well as the later missiles which gradually became the dominant weapons in the strategic scenario.

Busy luggage

Routine training missions took crews out on low-level navigation and weapons delivery exercises over what was for a long time known as the Olive Branch Strategic Training Route Complex with its approved Instrument and Visual Rules corridors, encompassing 250,000sq miles within the Dakotas, Montana, Nebraska and Wyoming, climaxing in a pretend 'drop on target'.

Far more realistic training could be obtained at Nellis AFB, Nevada, as part of *Red Flag* mock adversarial combat and *Green Flag* electronic combat wargames. There, to this day, crews may employ 'ballistic training shapes' such as the BDU-38/B or BDU-46/B, which emulate the flight characteristics of the B61 and B83 gravity weapons, respectively, engage simulated and live electronic defences with ECM and their missiles, and fly as low as 400ft (120m) AGL, descending to 200ft (60m) when under mock attack. Although long-time adversaries for former Aerospace Defense Command interceptors across the 'States, B-52s began training at Nellis in the mid-seventies, beginning with *Red Flag 76-3*. Radar-nav Col Robert McAnally (retired) was there and flew the inaugural B-52 mission. His account is particularly revealing:

> They [TAC] thought it was going to be somewhat easy to 'shoot down' B-52s! SAC participation during *Red Flag 76-3* involved a total of six B-52 wings, flying some 36 sorties – six apiece.
>
> Well at SAC, we planned all our missions fairly extensively down to the last detail, and this exercise was to be no exception to the rule. We did some intelligence work and figured out where they had most likely positioned their anti-aircraft artillery and missile sites. Taking this into consideration, we planned to employ our Short Range Attack Missiles (SRAM) ahead of us in the air defence suppression role, which is exactly what they were designed for.
>
> For our inaugural mission it was decided to go it low-level, really low. I was a member of an exceptional crew, so we planned for 50ft (15m)! Now fifty feet at about 460 knots over the desert is fairly exciting at times to say the least. The pilot, who is actually flying the plane has to basically sit there with arms extended to apply forward pressure on the yoke to keep the aircraft down, because we're flying over what's commonly called ground effect. At this altitude in a 'BUFF', the aerodynamic force below the wings becomes so powerful that you almost can't force

SIOP Gravity Bombs

In 1968, the thermonuclear bomb prefix 'Mk' was replaced by 'B'-for bomb, but the two remained interchangeable, the number always reflecting the installed warhead (W). Compared with the pioneering weapons of the fifties, later generations of gravity devices offered in-flight adjustable yields and arming by means of electronic FUFO (Full Fuzing Options). FUFO included the facility to prime the weapon for a specific delivery mode from the cockpit, including low-altitude parachute-retarded 'laydown' (immediate contact or delayed surface burst), or higher altitude freefall or retarded air or ground burst. Airburst would be used for attacking sprawling facilities while ground burst was aimed at 'taking out' pinpoint targets, particularly underground facilities or hardened targets. The weapons were preloaded in twos or fours as 'clip-in assemblies', with the latest versions being employed on the Boeing CSRL up to eight at a time. Nuclear gravity weapons were always carried internally. 'Ballistic training shapes' which behave just like the real thing in the air, and 'handling shapes' used for ground crew training, are available for both these devices for day-to-day training purposes.

B28 Entered atomic stockpile in August 1958. Some 4,500 examples constructed in five key versions through 1966. Carried in quartets in a MHU-14/C 'clip' in B-52 forward bay (alongside four ADM-20 Quails aft, and two external Hound Dog missiles). 1.2mT yield, using the same W28 warhead employed in the Hound Dog. Three versions for the B-52: B28IN Entered stockpile 1958. 8ft long and weight approx 1,980lb. No retard parachute and fuzed for either ground or airburst. Withdrawn by 1980.

Four B-61 nuclear weapons in a B-52G of the 68th BW at Seymour-Johnson AFB.
Ron Thurlow

B28RI. Entered stockpile 1960. 11ft long and weight approx 2,230lb. Included low-altitude delivery retard parachute, with fuzing for ground or airburst. Withdrawn by 1980.

B28FI. Entered stockpile 1962, with retarding parachute and FUFO fuzing options offering a selectable 70–350kT yield. 12ft long. Retired from 1984 and completely phased out by 1991, replaced by the B61 Mod 7.

B41 Entered atomic stockpile in September 1960. Weight 10,670lb, yield demonstrated at 8.9mT during developmental TX-41 Hardtack Oak test drop at Eniwetok atoll on 29 June 1958. 500 constructed through mid-1962 and withdrawn in July 1976. Two in the bomb-bay.

B43 Entered stockpile in April 1961. Weight approx 2,300lb and 12-ft long with yield varying up to low megaton range. B-52 carried four in a 'clip'. Primarily a theatre forces nuclear weapon, but B-52-compatible. Retired mid-1991.

B53 Based on the W53 warhead used in the Titan II ICBM missile. 340 constructed between August 1962 and June 1965, and phased-out through 1987 when they were recalled into the inventory for possible use against deeply-buried Soviet command and control facilities, for use in immediate or delayed surface burst. Yield 9mT, weight approx 9,000lb, it was the last of the 'heavyweights', measuring some 5ft in diameter. 'Ballistic shape' Bomb Dummy Unit was the BDU-13.

B57 Primarily a US Navy nuclear depth charge measuring some 10ft long and weighing approx 500lb, yield varied between 5 and 20kT. 3,000 assembled by the spring of 1967, having first entered the stockpile in 1963. Delivery options included freefall or retarded airburst, laydown delayed surface detonation or retarded depth bomb.

B61 Entered stockpile in December 1966. 11ft long, weight approx 700lb, with later models offering full Class F FUFO facilities with yields ranging between 10kT and half a megaton. Four carried in a 'clip'. 'Ballistic shape' is the BDU-38, backed by BDU-36 and BDU-39 load training shapes. Some 3,150 were built in all, with roughly half being assigned to Strategic forces (which retain the lion's share following START dismantling of earlier Mod types). Several versions existed all of which offered retarded and freefall contact burst or airburst, and retarded laydown. The chief subtypes introducing new technology comprised:

Subtype Notes

Mod 0 17ft nylon chute for 200ft laydown, 4-digit PAL B (Permissive Action Link) switch.

Mod 2 In production from March 1975. New 6-digit multiple code PAL D switch.

Mod 3 In production from May 1979. New 24ft nylon/Kevlar chute for 50ft laydown. 12-digit multiple code PAL F switch and FUFO microelectronics.

Mod 7 In production from September 1985 to replace the Mk/B28FI. Yield is variable, between 300 tons and 300 kT.

Mod 11 Newest version, which has replaced the B53, based on modified Mod 7 bombs using Sandia Laboratories 'field kits' to add a steel penetrator nose and revised tail 'fin box', but retaining the original 'physics package'. Its energy is directed downwards, destroying everything buried beneath it to a depth of 700m. In development since 1987 and test-dropped in June 1997 (the project was placed on 'hold' for eight years through to 1995). Effectively, this is a new weapon designed for 'bunker busting', weighing some 1,210lb.

B83 Entered stockpile June 1983. Weight approx 2,400lb, with variable yields of 1–2mT. Over 1,000 constructed, B-52 carries up to eight on a CSRL. 'Ballistic shape' is the BDU-46. Probably the last all-new thermonuclear gravity weapon to be developed for the USAF.

the aircraft any lower, so you're basically riding on a cushion of air beneath you that is literally trying to force you up. The only problem is that if you are going to make a turn, climb first. To climb, the pilot would relax his arms and the plane would climb up to 300ft (90m) within seconds. The aerodynamic force would pop you up; you'd start your turn roll up and then go back down.

During this flight we'd simulated a SIOP profile. We kept well below the radar's coverage for the entire flight. As we approached our intended target, we did a PUP manoeuvre, a pull-up, pushover for a low altitude drop of a BDU-38. About the only time the range would have been able to track us was if we climbed above 1,500ft (450m), and the only time we were above this was when we climbed over an 8,500ft (2,550m) ridge after hitting our target, after which we exited the range. Now this occurred long before aircraft exercising over the ranges were instrumented [with ACMI pods] as they are today, so tracking an aircraft's movements was impossible. The TAC guys were adamant that we never got near our intended target, because they stated that a triple-A site had a good look at us; [however] we informed them that we had simulated a double SRAM launch against Tolicha Peak, where there was a known gun site situated. The TAC guy didn't seem to realize that we had the ability to launch defense suppression ahead of us.

During the mission, we did get some indication that there were fighters around and in fact, during a post flight debrief, an 'aggressor' F-5E pilot, who coincidentally had previously flown 'BUFFs', did say that he had stumbled upon us. He commented that he thought he was low at 800ft (240m), until he looked down and spotted us flying beneath him. What had caught his attention was our trail of dust! It was overcast that day so there was no projected shadows, however we were so low that we were kicking up a storm behind us. He said that he took his eyes off while climbing to make a turn in an attempt to come after us, but was unable to reacquire us again. He also noted that the-then new three-tone SIOP paint scheme was very effective and worked well in the desert.

However, the story is not over yet. It seems that during our ingress to the target we flew directly over a van parked out in the middle of nowhere. It was a simulated mobile SAM site. We pretty much popped up from behind a sand dune and were as surprised as those working the site. As we approached the van, its antenna was

---

Flying the Systems

Otto Pernåtto was the first OAS-qualified navigator at Barksdale on B-52Gs, before upgrading to radar navigator. Here he describes using some of the systems introduced during the SIOP period.

The change from the ASQ-38 to OAS was like night and day: ASQ-38 had typical aviation instruments, radars, gauges, etc: OAS instead used four large multi-functional displays. Each of the navigators 'downstairs', called the Offense team, had two of them. There were other standard instruments such as altimeters which were still on OAS but the radar displays and EVS screens were the primary navigation displays for the Offense team. The changes in workload for the crew was phenomenal. I only had one ASQ-38 ride, taking an airplane to the factory to get modified to OAS standard and the amount of work the two navs did was amazing. There was very little idle time for them whereas on the OAS it was much more laid back.

The EVS was an excellent system for either confirming a target or data waypoint or just watching the landing. It provided a view to the world, which although surreal because everything had a green tint, gave us something to look at. Prior to each flight the Nav had to sign out a large briefcase housing a number of very expensive data transfer modules. One was the OAS system cartridge which we used to say told the OAS it was navigating a B-52 and not running a refrigerator, and the others held waypoint and targeting data. After take-off the Nav team confirmed the validity of the overall navigation system which included two separate Inertial Navigation Systems. These integrated with other inputs to give one primary system, which is what the pilots flew from. The R/N's job was to keep updating and evaluating the system using a series of radar 'fixes' or using the EVS for much-reduced accuracy. One of the final and absolutely worst-case system updates was using a visual overflight update. This was where you found something on the map; a road intersection or a building – anything the Pilot team could see. They flew over that area and called out when we were over that spot. The R/N's bread and butter was massaging the system to accurately guide you to a good weapons release. One of his jobs was to prepare the weapons, whether they were conventional or nuclear, for delivery. He also had to have the AC and EWO perform certain actions. This provided the consent which prevented any one crew member from acting alone.

During a low-level exercise everyone got their 'game face' on. Flying at 300ft at 350kt in a thirty-year old airplane with a 185ft wingspan kept up your attention! Most of the mishaps B-52s had were from some sort of inattention down low or during landing or take-off so your concentration was intense. Crews that had been flying together and who had good crew co-ordination could tell by the inflection in each others' voices how well things were going or if something was amiss. Throughout the low-level phase the Nav team frequently talked on 'Private', an intercom channel that allowed them to talk about waypoints or coordination without disturbing the other crew members. As the Initial Point got closer (the point at which you are flying prior to the target and a term used as long as there have been bombers) the crew coordination became intense because that was where the enemy's defences would be greatest. It was also where SAC had set up Strategic Tracking Ranges (STRs) with simulated SAMs and anti-aircraft defences. It got to be a busy intercom with the EWO and gunner shouting out simulated missile and gun attacks while the Nav team gave the pilots directions. All the while the crew was running the bomb-run check-list and the pilots continually reminded the R/N of critical checklist items so that the plane would get the bombs off. During the final twenty seconds of an STR run the copilot turned on a radio tone which sent a signal to the site. Upon bomb release the tone cut and the STR gave back their bombing score.

After release the crew would clean up the checklist and prepare to come out of the low-level. Occasionally crews flew against two or three STR sites during a few hours. These long runs were particularly brutal as the crew was down low, usually at night, midway through a twelve or fifteen-hour mission and particularly vulnerable to fatigue. Your sleep cycle was often out of alignment and yet you had to be at peak attention to detail.

Otto recollected that even this gruelling regime had its lighter moments:

The B-52 had six ejection seats but could carry an additional four crew members who had to jump out of the Navs' hole wearing parachutes. For this manoeuvre you needed 500 feet, or so they said. We were also worried about banging into the landing gears or the many antennas the 'BUFF' had underneath. We were convinced we'd all have antennas stuck in our bodies if we made it. One very different part of our ejection seats was leg restraints that came slamming up when released. Whenever we got new crew members or flyers from different planes we sat them in our seat and then watched their horror when they accidentally hit these restraints, releasing them with a loud 'bang' as the restraints grabbed their lower legs. It was actually pretty scary because you didn't know if you had somehow armed the seats. Another joke we played on brand new copilots was the 'Voice Actuated Throttle Cables'. Down in the Navs' 'hole' we actually had the throttle cables running overhead, past our seats. In flight the IP would tell the unsuspecting copilot about a 'new modification that hadn't made it into the study materials yet'. He would then say over the interphone, 'Throttle Number Four – increase'. We would then slowly move the cable. Then, when it came time for the copilot to try, we wouldn't do anything. The IP would advise the copilot to work on a deeper voice so that the 'computer' would recognize it! In fact, many of the guys had heard about this one so it didn't always work.

quickly swivelled in our direction and as it attempted to track us, the momentum of this action, coupled with our jet exhaust at 50ft (15m) and the ground effect, toppled the van on its side. Luckily no one was hurt, but the electronics were shaken up. To put it mildly, TAC was not amused!.

While *Flag* exercises are still part and parcel of the training repertoire, even more sober evaluations of crews and their nuclear arsenal are conducted annually under the *Busy Luggage* programme. This originates from 1975, following a memorandum between the Air Force, the Department of Energy, and Sandia National Laboratories which provided for joint testing of nuclear weapons. The programme is 'intended to verify weapon system capability to function in a variety of stockpile-to-target environments after stockpile exposure' and will soon embrace the full threat scenario. In essence, it is a quality assurance check for stored nuclear ordnance, without any 'big bangs'. 'Sortie profiles attempt to mirror a War Order mission. During a test, aircraft are generated to Alert status. A typical flight profile can include air refuelling, low level navigation, and target ingress and egress scenarios using operationally realistic weapon delivery techniques. Release profiles are mixed between freefall airburst, freefall ground burst, and low altitude laydown. Average duration of the flight is ten hours.' Some five *Busy Luggage* test missions are scheduled each fiscal year, split between the B-52 and B-2A (the B-1B Lancer no longer having any nuclear strike capability).

Weapons are randomly selected from Air Combat Command stockpiles and converted into Joint Test Assembly (JTA) units – payloads with a telemetry unit installed in lieu of the warhead. Test aircraft are similarly selected on a random basis from operational units with a nuclear tasking. Any quirks encountered during the tests are noted by the SIOP planners and subsidiary tacticians.

Air-launched Cruise Missiles

Dropping bombs on somebody's head, even at high speed and low level using 'laydown' techniques, was and remains a highly dangerous business. Although gravity bombs still formed a big part of the B-52's nuclear arsenal well into the late 1970s, the weapons have given way gradually to long range stand-off missiles, primarily the Boeing AGM-86B Air Launched Cruise Missile (ALCM) and its follow-on, the stealthy General Dynamics AGM-129 Advanced Cruise Missile (ACM) which bypass completely the need to overfly heavily defended targets and are exclusive to the B-52. The 416th BW at Griffiss AFB was the first to get to grips with the AGM-86B ALCM, with production models arriving during April 1981. Four months later the Wing received its first ALCM/OAS-modified B-52G, although B-52G 58-0204 was the first to be equipped with ALCM mission-identifying wing-root strakes, during June. These were added to comply with the conditions of the SALT II treaty, which put a ceiling on the number of operational ALCM platforms. The treaty was never properly ratified and in February 1982 the Air Force announced it would modify all B-52Hs for AGM-86 carriage, with the first entering service in this revised guise during July 1985. As a result, in November 1986 (just after SAC had taken delivery of its last ALCM), the arrival of B-52H 60-0055 at Carswell AFB, Texas, breached the SALT II – it was the 131st bomber modified for ALCM duties and was appropriately named *Salt Shaker*! 194 B-52G/H aircraft were eventually rendered ALCM-capable.

The early service introduction at Griffiss AFB was 'an incredible effort' according to Lt Col Don Campbell (retired).

We had personnel that went over ninety days without a day off. It was as if there was no one in charge of the little things! All the big stuff worked just fine. I don't think there was a single piece of equipment we had in the integrated maintenance facility that had a plug that fitted. And of course, it was all nuclear certified, so you just couldn't cut the plug off a device and replace it with another, even if it was just an electrical forklift or something seemingly simple like that. I remember the first uploading demonstrations we had with the ALCM lift trailer. It was the first MHU-179 trailer in the field, as all the rest were on the production line. The MHU-179 was designed specifically to mate the pylon, complete with ALCMs, to the wing of the B-52G. It had a hand-held control unit with a long cord so an operator could stand back and manoeuvre the trailer unit. Well, the day before the demo an operator screwed up and ran over the cord, crushing it. Now, we had all these DoD dignitaries due in the following day to see the trailer at work. I received a frantic call at my office stating the situation, so I immediately called the manufacturer in Maryland and asked if they had a spare cable. The answer was no, but they could take one off a unit that was on the line.

B-52G/Hs could carry six AGM-86Bs on each pylon and another eight on the internal CSRL. AGM-86B was designed with the B-52 as sole user. Boeing via Chesneau

Cruise Missile

AGM-86B ALCM
Neé the Boeing SCAD (Subsonic Cruise Armed Decoy), an air-breathing missile designed to replace Quail, this rapidly evolved into a full-fledged nuclear strike Air Launched Cruise Missile offering a range of 745 miles. Test flown as the AGM-45A from 5 March 1976 (the SCAD testbeds distinguished by their sharkmouths), it was soon realized that this decoy-cum-weapon could be developed further with double the range of the original model, and staggering precision when matched to TERCOM (terrain contour matched) guidance. TERCOM works by comparing radar altimeter (height above ground level) and barometric pressure (height above mean sea level) to deduce both missile altitude and the elevation of the terrain below; these electronic notes are then compared with position and a database or digital contour maps, and through this cross-reference process the missile can deduce exactly where it is, enabling it to maintain a safe terrain-avoidance profile as it journeys to target, with detonation being based on terminal target coordinates and timing. The subsequent AGM-86B was essentially a 'stretch' from 14ft to 19ft, doubling fuel capacity, powered by a Williams F107 turbofan offering 600lbst. Pop-out wings deploy on weapon release.

Development was kick-started by President Jimmy Carter concurrent with his cancellation of the B-1A programme. Commensurate miniaturization in the guidance systems as microchip technology came to the fore also enabled the designers to maximize TERCOM. The ALCM concept was thrown open to competition between the AGM-86B and General Dynamics' AGM-109A Tomahawk during 1979. While the US Navy/GD model went on to be perfected as the hugely successful ground-, ship- and submarine-launched Tomahawk series, Boeing won the contract to develop its AGM-86B specifically for SAC's big bombers. CEAs (Circular Error Averages) were stated to be in the order of 100ft, trifling for a nuclear warhead. However, those figures were in fact bettered during *Desert Storm* by Secret *Squirrel* conventionally-armed derivatives. The ALCM's nuclear warhead was the W80, offering a 200kT yield.

Deliveries began to the 416th BW at Griffiss AFB, New York, in January 1981, and the last and 1,815th ALCM, was delivered to SAC in October 1986. With the introduction of the AGM-129 ACM, many AGM-86Bs have been adapted to conventional applications (described in the next chapter). Loading is accomplished by means of heavy-duty MHU-179/E trailers, which lift the pylon and missiles into place in about ninety minutes (previous, non computer-aided loading taking a meticulous four–eight hours).

Internal carriage is as for SRAM and the B61/83 bombs, using a CSRL capable of carrying eight weapons, with external carriage being the principal mode.

Tacit Rainbow
A Northrop programme based on cruise missile technology designed to harass and suppress enemy radar defences, AGM-136 Tacit Rainbow came out of the closet in October 1986. B-52s would have been capable of carrying up to thirty of these air-breathing, winged missiles, which would have loitered in enemy airspace for up to ninety minutes and engage any radars that came 'on the air'. Early design configurations resembled the AGM-86A SCAD, but the project was cancelled in 1990.

AGM-129 ACM
Successor to the AGM-86B, the General Dynamics (now Hughes) Advanced Cruise Missile employs the same warhead (classed as the W80-1) and emerged from the secret 'black world' in 1988, having first flown in July 1985. The first training ACM was delivered to the 410th BW at K. I. Sawyer AFB, Michigan in December 1987, followed by the first production version in June 1990. A total of 500 of the 2,750lb missiles was built, including 29 development and trials rounds, and 461 production examples, the last of which was delivered to the 5th BW at Minot AFB, North Dakota, in August 1993.

Powered by a Williams F112 turbofan generating 900lbst, the ACM has a staggering range of more than 1,800nm (3,320km). Guidance is based on GPS/inertial systems with a laser radar (Ladar) sweeping ahead during the terminal phase of attack to cross-check the terrain and target profile, preprogrammed into the weapon. It is carried externally only on the B-52. An AGM-129B conventionally-armed version is available, packing a high-explosive unitary warhead.

All versions are 'stealthy'. Angular geometry to deflect radar waves, coupled with lightweight non-metallic composites or reinforced polymers that allow radar waves to pass through them with minimal reflection to render the ACM with a massively-reduced radar cross-section (RCS). For example, the Tomahawk, designed in the 1970s and utilizing the simple low observable technologies then available, proffered an RCS of some 0.05 square metres. It is extremely difficult to locate using radar or infrared sensors and is the most potent weapon in the B-52H arsenal.

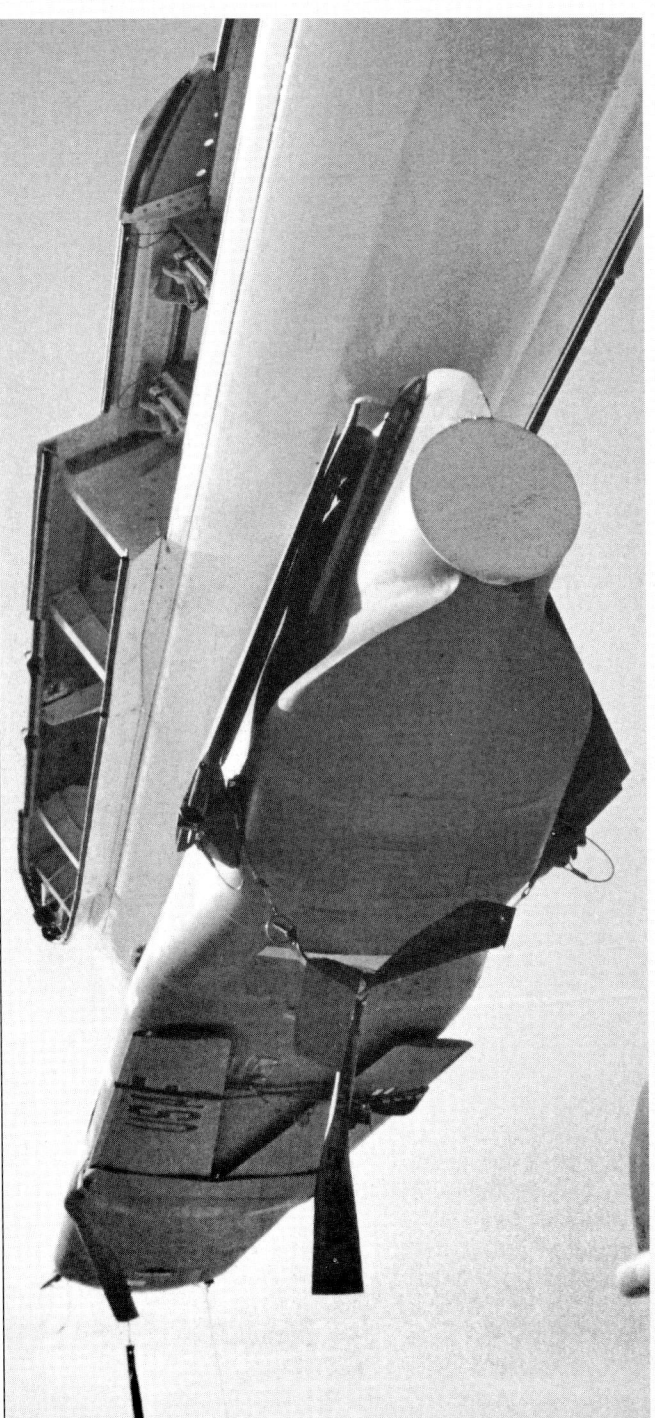

This rear view of an AGM-86B shows its folded wings and tail surfaces, also the covered jet efflux for the Williams International F107 turbofan.
Frank Mormillo

Engine start time on a bomb-laden Griffiss B-52G. Greg Paprocki

Fitting the 4,450lb ALCM pylon with six missiles on MAU-12 ejector rails requires a specialized ADU-318/E loader adapter, and plenty of manpower. Boeing via Chesneau

Now keep in mind that this is long before the advent of FedEx etc. So they bought the cable a seat on an Empire Airlines flight and it was flown from Baltimore International Airport to the nearby O in Utica, New York. The next day the demo went off without a hitch.

He also noted that the first flight of twelve ALCMs on a B-52G 'was out of Griffiss, not at Edwards or any place like that'.

Loading the weapons required transferring fuel, installing the weapons and then filling-up the tanks, and this meant hours of elaborate pylons for the ALCMs. I thought to myself that there was no guarantee that any of those would fit. It was a nightmare – it took filling, sheet metal and much more. [Eventually] we kept a record of which pylon was mated to which aircraft. The old 'BUFF' wasn't to spec anymore.

Once installed and pigtailed in place, it was a formidable weapon system, and gave the SIOP force some extra arm's length. The AGM-129 ACM upped the stakes with its stealth technology (ALCMs were retrofitted with 'stealthy' nose radomes at the same juncture), making it a much harder target to shoot down. ALCM, however, was and remains an external weapon only. The 410th BW at K. I. Sawyer AFB, Michigan, was the first to be declared operational with the ACM, in January 1993, and it currently forms the principal thermonuclear weapon in the B-52H arsenal at Minot and Barksdale. The pre-launch procedures for ALCM and its successor, and indeed the earlier SRAM, have remained very similar, as all employed common systems. Amongst these are the Environmental Control Unit (ECU) or Missile Conditioning System (MCS) which serves to provide pressurized, conditioned air to the weapons to give them a controlled temperature environment for reliable operation. Without this, the missiles are apt to malfunction.

A second key component is the Weapons Control Panel, which controls weapon power-up, prearming and jettisoning. With the OAS in display format 7, ALCM (or SRAM) missiles are arranged as Bays 1-8 as

Sea mines are among the less familiar occupants of the B-52's weapons bay and HSAB. They include the Mk 52 and Mk 55 2,000lb 'bottom' mines and the Mk 56 moored mine. *Frank Mormillo*

painstaking work. The heavy-duty SUU-67 ALCM pylons also presented a challenge in themselves, as Boeing had manufactured them to original specifications.

When I first saw [them], I thought back to the trouble the Air Force encountered when trying to mate pylons with MERs on the D-models – nothing fit! These G-models had been bashed around, the wings had been flexed all over the place and now the Air Force had come up with these big placed on a bomb bay rotary launcher, and ALCM or ACM in sets of three on the wing pylons; format 7XY allows the radar-navigator to isolate individual missiles and check on their status: cautions and faults which alert the crew to a 'down' missile.

The final item on the pre-launch agenda is the TAL or Transfer Alignment Manoeuvre. TAL was initiated between two and fifteen minutes prior to SRAM launch (half an hour for cruise missiles) to

AGM-84D Harpoon, of which twelve could be carried by the B-52H. Thirty B-52Gs were modified for the missile though only eight were carried due to interference from the J57 efflux on the aft 'shoulder' position missile station. In practice, B-52Hs also normally carry eight. McDonnell Douglas

give the missiles accurate velocity information, lunging the aircraft for six seconds or more. The B-52 was kept straight-and-level for a minute at either end of the manoeuvre. For SRAM also, a Launch Point Fix (LPF) was established to torque its guidance system. The OAS would then transfer INS coordinates to the missile during its five second launch countdown. Missiles would then be fired automatically or manually, with all weapons releases invoking an oral five-second countdown through to weapons release. During this time the R/N was effectively 'steering' the B-52 through the OAS while the pilot merely held wings level.

For ALCM, which was and remains highly dependent on the B-52 OAS, after activation the weapon downloads the target data from the appropriate DTUC after reading the B-52 Mission Data, while its onboard clock is harmonized with the aircraft. After release, described as a 'loud clunk', ALCM descends to its first commanded altitude and the steers towards its first waypoint. Autonomous TERCOM terrain contour matching then takes it to its preplanned target coordinates. ACM works on similar procedures but uses GPS Navstar and a laser radar for terminal navigation as its principal means of guidance.

While the navigators would be checking missile and OAS status just prior to launch, a key job for the copilot would be to start pumping fuel from the aft tanks to the wings to maintain the B-52's centre of gravity, as ALCMs are launched – a single SUU-67 pylon with six ALCMs weighs as much as an F-16 fighter!

Bombs Gone?

Weapons away, and having egressed enemy airspace the crew would have aimed to land at a preplanned (with diversions) friendly airfield, normally planned so that they would have been minimally reliant on tanker support. Radio communications would have been resumed and the crew attempt as normal a recovery as is

B-52H 60-0048 taking part in the Joint Service Exercise Bright Star '85 **which took three Ellsworth AFB 'BUFFs' to Egypt in August 1985.** USAF via Thurlow

Sgt Alan Wilkin of the 2nd OMS guides Ack-Ack Annie **(58-0214, 62nd BS) to the flight line during Exercise** Proud Shield '88. USAF via Thurlow

practicable. In a SIOP scenario it is anyone's guess what the outcome would be, though that fortunately has now become an academic exercise.

On 27 September 1991, Bush's Presidential Order came down the hotlines ending thirty-four years of round-the-clock ground alert. Capt Grantham of the 92nd BW wrote 'Like leaves falling in autumn, munitions came off Alert aircraft and crew scattered as winds of world's change swept Fairchild. While bomber crew members took steps to complete the necessary action for their aircraft, tanker crew members already off Alert doused each other with champagne in celebration.' Col David Young, 5th BW commander at Minot, announced the stand-down at 1.31am that Saturday. By 2pm, 'the Alert aircrews were driving out of the area. Lights flashing and sirens wailing accompanied them out of the containment area between the two security fences, along with waving and victory hand signs.' The Cold War had been won.

The following June, SAC was dis-established after forty-six years, and the B-52 force passed to Air Combat Control at Langley AFB, Virginia. With this came an obvious shift in emphasis. As American Chief of Staff Gen Colin Powell ably surmised shortly after the cessation of hostilities in the Persian Gulf, and as one USAF officer reiterated, 'In anything short of a general war, or need for a nuclear retaliation, conventional PGMs are as capable at target destruction, and much less controversial.'

A SIOP-camouflaged Wurtsmith B-52H, in for maintenance. TF33s are a little cleaner to work on than J57s. Maintainer Keith Kimmons recalled that, 'removing the sailboat fairing from the back of the J57 pod was a nasty job since it was usually coated with oil and carbon'. Ron Thurlow

More recently, in a speech made in Washington in February 1998, former CinC Gen Lee Butler (retired) reflected on the insanity of the Cold War era. Deterrence, he opined,

A 23rd BS B-52H lifts off from Eielson AFB, Alaska during Exercise Giant Warrior '89. USAF via Thurlow

(Above) City of Goldsboro **(B-52G 58-0214) was the last to leave Seymour-Johnson AFB in October 1982 ending twenty-three years of 'BUFF' flying there. Its aircraft moved to Grand Forks AFB, replacing B-52Hs.** Ron Thurlow

B-52Hs line up at K. I. Sawyer AFB with the 410th BW in 1980. Fourteen years later, their last B-52H, 60-0026, departed ending thirty-three years of B-52 operations at the base. Ron Thurlow

failed completely at setting rational limits on the US and Soviet nuclear arsenal, and he went on to state that 'preparedness became... a formula for unmitigated catastrophe. It suspended rational thinking about the ultimate aim of national security'. He concluded that 'we cannot at once keep sacred the miracle of existence and hold sacrosanct the capacity to destroy it'.

Although there are some who would disagree with his sentiments, there is no doubt that the B-52 has survived a dangerous and exciting epoch and adapted to wholly new requirements. While ACM will remain a B-52 capability for many years to come, the machine and its crews have shifted decisively towards conventional bombing using a host of new PGMs under the Conventional Enhancement Modification (CEM) effort. The OAS and Strategic Radar package, aided by GPS Navstar (and vastly improved communications systems) now lend the Stratofortress a precision strike capability that was unimaginable forty years ago. Today, the philosophy of the B-52 is that of a weapon that shoots right between the eyes, rather than wielding a sledgehammer.

CHAPTER SIX

Desert Destroyer

The striking, barbed arrowhead profile of the F-117A Nighthawk is probably destined to be the most lasting visual image of the Gulf War. Its protagonist role in the media coverage of the war ensured that. Consequently, few would have placed the B-52 among the most memorable contributors to the Coalition air campaign which returned Kuwait to the Kuwaitis. Like the F-111 Aardvark, also a dominant warplane in that conflict, the B-52 was not new enough to attract major media coverage or proper recognition from a defence establishment which wanted to 'push' funding for new technology. Once again though the worthy, nuclear, 'BUFF', proved that it was also an indispensable part of the USAF's conventional capability and adaptable to the needs of the day.

In percentage terms the forty-two F-117As made up 2.5 per cent of Coalition fighter/bomber aircraft in the Gulf. B-52Gs, amounting to seventy-four aircraft at most (64 Primary Aircraft Authorized plus ten to cover potential attrition and 'downtime' for maintenance) constituted 3 per cent. Nighthawk pilots logged 1,296 attack sorties; 2 per cent of the total, dropping over 2,000 tons of PGMs. All but forty-nine of these sorties struck targets which Gen Norman Schwarzkopf's CENTAF Offensive Campaign Plan listed as 'strategic' – an ambivalent term in relation to Desert Storm. The B-52G's sortie total was rather higher at 1,624, but the total ordnance tonnage was 27,000 (or 72,000 weapons), 42 per cent of the total weight of bombs delivered by USAF aircraft and nearly 30 per cent of the Coalition's total. However, only 15 per cent of B-52 bomb-loads, (compared with 96 per cent of the F-117A's), fell on conspicuous, high-value strategic targets. Most of the remainder were rained on to the hapless Iraqi Republican Guard's armour in Kuwait, far away from CNN's cameras.

By Vietnam standards the bombing statistics were miniscule – less than 1 per cent of the ordnance dropped in that earlier war, some of it by exactly the same B-52Gs. Just as they had done nineteen years before, cells of B-52Gs flew many of their missions from a distant island base. In this case it was Diego Garcia in the Indian Ocean rather than Guam, with an initial deployment of fourteen B-52Gs from the 42nd BW on 12–13 August 1990. Just as they had in Vietnam they attacked troop concentrations

Gulf Weapons (Bombs)

Bombs dropped by B-52Gs during Desert Storm (tonnage)

Type	Jeddah	Diego	Moron	Fairford	TOTAL
M117	22,532	10,398	9,527	2,193	44,650
Mk 82	8,261	6,225	2,632	560	17,678
CBU-52	2,122	360	457	nil	2,939
CBU-58	3,278	979	1,674	nil	5,931
CBU-71/87/89	387	162	nil	255	804
UK 1,000lb	nil	287	nil	nil	287
TOTAL:	36,580	18,411	14,290	3,008	72,289

The landing gear doors are almost closed on Blythville Storm **(58-0237) from Castle AFB as it pulls up into an English winter sky as 'Arbor 33' on one of its ten combat missions from Fairford. Underwing MERs hold twenty-four Mk 82 bombs.** Authors

with Korean War-vintage M117 bombs, relying on a large support force of tankers (including KC-135s), SEAD and fighter escorts. A further similarity, and one which added to the lack of recognition of the B-52's role in the Gulf, was that accurate BDA from the kinds of targets they attacked was often hard to acquire. Paradoxically, visibility over the target areas was sometimes as poor as in monsoon-soaked S.E. Asia. On several occasion after 6 February B-52Gs flew missions when 'tacair' types were 'weather-aborted'.

However, the crews were a new generation. As Griffiss AFB's Chief of B-52 Training at the time, Lt Col Charles Chiesa (with 5,200 hours on type) told the authors, 'We deployed our most experienced crews but the fact remained that we

Memories of Vietnam were re-created too by the renewed ambiguity over the B-52's 'strategic' role. Once the decision had been taken to use the B-52s primarily against the Republican Guard in the Kuwait Theatre of Operations (KTO) responsibility for providing their targets passed to the KTO targeters and the B-52s were regarded as a part of the total tactical air assets from mid-January onwards. After Vietnam the bombers had quickly reverted to their clearly-defined nuclear, strategic posture. As a Congressional Report[25] on the Gulf War concluded, SAC had assumed that, 'B-52s would operate autonomously, flying alone or with a few other bombers at high altitude'. 'Thus there was no emphasis on operating with fighter support packages provided to help

integrated cells. That meant flying with the same wingman, for example, time after time. At Loring they flew in no special order so that was a new concept for them, especially when combat began.

In *Desert Storm* SAC flew its first conventional bombing missions since 1973. However, a proportion of the B-52 fleet was well-prepared for this. In May 1988 SAC decreed that four B-52G units were to be tasked primarily with this role. Two of them, the 320th BW and 43rd BW were inactivated by 1990 leaving Loring's 69th BS, 42nd BW and the 62nd BS, 2nd BW at Barksdale as SAC's 'iron bombing' specialists (though all SAC B-52G units were training for conventional bombing by this time). Their expertise was invaluable to crews from other B-52G units who were

Hauling a load of CBU, B-52G 58-0194 Buffasaurus from Wurtsmith, stirs up the sand at Jeddah on 6 February 1991 as it embarks on one of its forty-seven missions. USAF

had to prepare the rest of the squadron for deployment later on down the road. Most of the guys were young and any Vietnam era veterans of iron-bomb dropping were as rare as moondust. With a lot of help from my colleagues at Griffiss and throughout SAC we started flying lengthy fourteen hour sorties to the Utah Test and Training Range where we could drop real iron under the operational code-name *Desert Warrior*. We carried out low-level training with NVG and bombed targets every which way.'

defeat the threat.' However, most SAC crews were used to composite force operations with AWACs and tactical fighters or *Red Flag* and NATO exercises. The 'lone wolf' SIOP role had to be shelved and long-forgotten concepts of conventional formation bombing re-established. Even the word 'cell' had lost currency in some quarters, though as 1st Lt Peter J. Bloom pointed out, 'Those of us from Griffiss had one advantage over crew from Loring. They didn't stand Alert, while we did and because of this we were used to flying in

called to action, particularly from SIOP-orientated squadrons, and all bases contributed personnel to the war.

In Vietnam, B-52 squadrons had spent most of their time flying 'tactical' sorties against actual or suspected soft targets. In Iraq, once again, the roles were reversed in some respects and smaller fighter-bomber types were directed to the majority of the high-value fixed targets. The reasons for this originated from the overall target plan devised by the brilliant strategist, Col John A Warden and initially called *Instant*

Thunder. Echoing the wishes of the White House, his objectives were to attack Saddam Hussein's power-base[26], not the Iraqi population as a whole. Casualties to Iraqi civilians and to Coalition forces were to be minimized. He devised ten sets of targets with Saddam's regime as the central objective. Second was C3 (Command, Control and Communications), with electrical generating capacity and oil storage third and fourth. Nuclear, biological and chemical warfare facilities came next, followed by rail transport, air defence, naval forces and airfields. Two others were added before the outbreak of hostilities: the Republican Guard and road/rail bridges. Although the B-52s were given some targets within the original ten they were regarded as particularly suitable for attacks on the Guard.

When Gen Schwarzkopf incorporated Warden's suggestions into his integrated air and ground war plan he saw the B-52s coming into their own, particularly for Phase III of that plan. After neutralizing Iraqi defences and gaining air superiority in the first two Phases the third, beginning on Day Two, was aimed at 'preparing the battlefield' for the land campaign. The Republican Guard, which he described as the 'Iraqi centre of gravity' and vital to Saddam's survival, had three divisions in Kuwait. Their elite Tawakalna Mechanized Division was located near the border with Saudi Arabia, blocking a potential Coalition thrust into the country. Nearer to the Iraqi border were the Hamurabi Mechanized and Madinah Armoured Divisions. Their armour was well dug-in, dispersed and extremely numerous making a difficult target for tactical strikers with small bomb-loads. To Schwarzkopf it was the ideal opportunity for what he called 'carpet bombing'. Recalling the destructive force of the *Arc Light* missions of the 1960s he decided to reserve the big bombers for that job.

In so doing he reduced the B-52's role against other types of targets. Clearly there was no possibility in any case of re-staging the massive *Linebacker*-type attacks. SAC's total bomber force of 625 B-52 and FB-111As at the end of the Vietnam period (FB-111As had been bought to replace the retiring B-52E/Fs) had been reduced by 1991 to around 300 including the B-1B Lancer squadrons. Only 122 B-52Gs remained in service when the war began and a mere twenty of those were under direct CENTAF control on 1 January 1991. B-52H units were required for SIOP tasking although they could have been made available if the war had continued. The B-1B, much criticized for its absence from the Gulf action, was also vital for the SIOP shield. In any case its conventional weapons clearance trials had only progressed as far as the Mk 82 bomb and its training programme had not encompassed much iron bombing, whereas many B-52H crews could have performed that task.

There were other reasons for restricting the B-52G's use against Col Warden's 'ten sets'. The Baghdad area, where many of the prime targets were located, was considered to be seven times more heavily defended that Hanoi was in 1972. Although the characteristics of Iraq's French and Russian radars were well known to Coalition planners the sheer weight of its 7,000 AAA

SAC Time was B-52G 58-0164 of the 416th BW, attached to the 1708th BW (P) at Jeddah for a total of thirty-three missions. USAF via Thurlow

guns and 16,000 SAMs might have daunted even the most effective SEAD intervention. B-52s would have been at risk despite their recent ECM updates.

Brig Gen 'Buster' Glosson, commanding USAF Wings in the Gulf, stated that B-52s were not used against heavily-defended targets during the first twenty-four hours of the war because the Iraqi air defence network had to be significantly degraded first. He was sure that aircraft would otherwise have been shot down when the intention was to minimize US losses. Iraqi fighters were not regarded as a major problem. The skies over Iraq were soon full of Coalition fighter pilots itching for combat. After the first two nights, Iraqi fighters were effectively removed from the fight. Even if they had challenged the 'BUFFs', one EWO told the authors that he, 'could have gone on pumping out chaff long enough to run the fighters out of gas'.

Gunner Brad Martens almost had a chance at one. 'We were part of a cell attacking when AWACS informed us that first two, and then four fighters were hot on US! I was pretty excited at this point, figuring that I would finally have a chance to fire my guns and see if all that training was worth it. But then it turned out that friendly fighters chased off the hostiles. AWACS told us that we had permission to go forward at our discretion but there would be no fighter cover available. Capt David Ross, the AC, took a quick poll and we all decided to do it. As we approached the target the AAA got very heavy – the other guys in the cell said it looked like one of those military weddings where the bride and groom walk under a bunch of crossed swords. The AAA was criss-crossing overhead so Capt Ross [later recommended for a Silver Star] took us directly under the fire and right down the middle of the target. The rest of the cell was unable to get through as the fire got even more intense.'

Capt Ross explained, 'I knew that at that low level – about 250ft – their gunners couldn't touch us. An oil refinery on the opposite bank of the river had been hit moments before and the whole area was lit up for about fifteen miles. I could see a real good route between the tracers and we just followed that and dropped our bombs.

Coming off target, we were just yelling and carrying on!'

On the fighter threat, Capt Timothy W. Mers added, 'One of the most serious problems we had was the danger of being shot down by our own fighters. The F-15s were keyed up and were dying to get a kill. We were part of a six-ship cell over Baghdad when AWACS notified us that we were being challenged by F-15s. AWACS told them who we were but they stayed on our tails. Finally, one of the B-52s turned on his lights and showed very clearly what he was.'

for the B-52 crews, using their *Pave Tack* laser/FLIR pods. Although this might have been a quick way of clearing away static tanks the tactic wasn't adopted.

The B-52G's accuracy with 'dumb' bombs actually made Schwarzkopf's 'carpet bombing' terminology rather inappropriate for situations where the bombers could be given precise targets. Under the $1.6 billion Offensive Avionics System (OAS) improvement programme, completed in 1987, the B-52G's weapon and navigation fit had been significantly

'Chuck' Horner, overall commander of USAF units in the Gulf, complained that B-52s were, 'hard to move around the sky. We could re-target most of our other assets in seconds' but with B-52s, 'it was three minutes'. Clearly, a B-52 could not be expected to act like an F-16.

An outstanding demonstration of the B-52G's accuracy and of its unique strike capability, was offered in the first few hours of the war. Because of the secret nature of the weapons used for this mission its success was not made public for exactly a year,

A Desert Storm **flightline includes two 42nd BW B-52Gs, 58-1257** First Strike **which flew fifty-six missions and 59-2585** Swashbuckler **with twenty-two. The latter was flown at Mildenhall Air Fête in May 1990 where Capt Randy Rushworth demonstrated a nose-down take-off. Both aircraft were among the six which transferred from Diego Garcia to Jeddah on 17 January 1991, hitting targets en route.** USAF

High on the Coalition priorities list was the need to avoid collateral damage. Obviously, precision-guided munitions were the best way to achieve this. While the B-52G could have acted as an LGB dropper there was no need to risk it in that capacity. If the battlefield preparation phase had continued beyond CENTCOM's requirement to eliminate around half of Iraq's armour and artillery before beginning the ground war, B-52s could have been involved as 'tank plinkers'. There were contingency plans to arm B-52Gs with GBU-10 or GBU-12 Paveway III LGBs and fly them with F-111Fs which could laser-mark tank targets

updated with new digital components. However, OAS was optimized for low-level delivery and although B-52Gs flew low for the first couple of days of the war they were required to bomb from above 30,000ft for the majority of their later sorties, causing some difficulties in re-programming their bombing computers to ensure accuracy – and, incidentally, a temporary shortage of high altitude bomb fins at Diego. The complexity of the system compared with that of single-seat fighters also caused some delays in re-routing or re-targeting B-52Gs mid-mission in the light of a changing tactical situation. Lt Gen

denying the B-52G a stellar role in the guided weapons 'airshow'.

B-52s made a second marathon attack on 18 January. Ten aircraft (a four-ship and two three-ships) from the 379th BW at Wurtsmith AFB made a direct attack from their base, with four aircraft releasing weapons on the Republican Guard's Tawalkana Division in Southwest Kuwait as a show of force while the others landed at Jeddah with weapons still aboard.

At the beginning of *Desert Storm*, B-52s were very much involved in the massive air action from 0239 to 0525 (local time) on the opening night, which delivered lethal

Global Reach – Global Power

In July 1986, as part of its enhanced conventional bombing capability, SAC funded tests on a non-nuclear version of the AGM-86B ALCM. Partly, the initiative was a response to Operation *El Dorado Canyon* in April 1986. F-111Fs with LGBs had flown a thirteen-hour mission to attack Libya. However, for a variety of unpredictable reasons the bombing results were degraded to the point where USAF planners began to examine other alternatives for long-range conventional attacks using stand-off weapons. Boeing replaced the W80-1 nuclear warhead of the AGM-86B with a 1,000lb blast-fragmentation version at the expense of some fuel capacity and therefore the 1,500-mile range. With the new warhead, the missile had better penetrating power against hardened targets than the AGM-109 Tomahawk TLAM. GPS navigation replaced the contour-matching (TERCOM) version in the ALCM.

Absolute secrecy in developing this conventional air-launched cruise missile (CALCM) under Project *Senior Surprise* had to be maintained because arms-control negotiations with the USSR were at a sensitive stage. The missile's external similarity to the AGM-86B helped in this. It was referred to as the XLRB (extra-long-range bomb), or *Secret Squirrel* after a cartoon character (the 'crusader against evil'). Aircrew had their own *Secret Squirrel* patches made up. Flight tested from August, 1987 and operational with the 2nd BW in January 1988, CALCM or AGM-86C was designed exclusively for the B-52G/H. The AGM-137 tri-service stand-off missile (TSSAM) was cancelled in the early 1990s by which time the USAF requested up to 300 additional conversions of the total production of 1,815 AGM-86Bs to CALCM configuration, but only about forty had been delivered by January 1991 when the 8th AF combat tested them on the longest bombing mission in history. It was a flight which made the Falklands-era *Black Buck 1* Vulcan mission of 15hr 45min seem relatively brief.

CALCM's availability at the start of the *Desert Shield* phase of the Gulf War, before US forces were in place to protect Saudi Arabia, enabled the US to make what Gen 'Buster' Glosson called a 'political statement'. However, the small numbers of CALCMs meant that their use for a decisive first strike would have been limited. In the event, Saddam held back from Riyadh, a massive US deterrent was emplaced rapidly and *Secret Squirrel* became one part of the crushing air assault on the first night of *Desert Storm*.

At 06.35 CST on 16 January 1991 seven B-52Gs of the 596th BS, 2nd BW departed from Barksdale AFB in heavy rain after a briefing by Lt Gen Ellie 'Buck' Shuler, 8th AF Commander, in which he compared their mission to the Doolittle Raid of 1942. They headed for the first of four flight-refuellings, near the Azores and another by Moron-based KC-10s over the Mediterranean. Each aircraft was to spend a total of two hours 'on the boom', longer than many complete tactical sorties! Using the *Doom* call-sign (routinely used on training sorties by the 596th BS) the formation carried thirty-nine AGM-86Cs in all, with three or four to each SUU-67/A ALCM pylon. The missiles had been stored in Barksdale's 'igloos' for three years and fifteen crews had received some rapid training in their use during the latter part of 1990. Secrecy had been preserved throughout, though there had been comments about the unusual asymmetric loading of the CALCMS. Normally, six ALCMs were carried on each pylon. Overflying Egypt and avoiding Libya for fear of 'sounding the alarm' among Saddam's allies before the first F-117A strikes hit Baghdad the 'BUFFs' arrived at their launch-point, according to the Mission Commander, Lt Col Jay Beard, 'within fractions of a second' of the deadline after a fifteen-hour flight. From a point about a hundred miles south of the Saudi/Iraqi border, thirty-five CALCMs were successfully fired over ten minutes. Four others could not be launched because of software problems. The missile carriers then swung away for the return journey, eased only a little by the presence of an 'augmentee' pilot and navigator in each crew. Col Beard, the 596th BS Commander, had been unable to supply his 'crewdogs' with hot meals following their 3am awakening because secrecy ruled out any non-routine requirements at Barksdale's catering facility. They had to make do with regulation low-residue, low-gas in-flight lunches and water. Inflatable mattresses and sleeping bags replaced the usual instructor seats but on the lower deck a catnapping crewman had to suspend his feet or his head over the lavatory in order to fit into the tiny rest area.

One aircraft (57-6475 *Miami Clipper II*) had flown the whole mission with one engine shut down due to oil-pressure problems on take-off and a second B-52 lost an engine later in its sortie. On the return leg Col Beard's crew listened in to the BBC on AM radio hoping to pick up news of the night's results. It was an exhausting flight. They met unexpectedly severe 140mph headwinds, requiring another tanker 'plug' by Moron's KC-10s (as the Azores-based KC-135s were grounded by weather) and adding six hours to the mission. A final additional 'fill' was given by two tankers from Robins AFB over the US coast. When they trundled back down Barksdale's runway the 'BUFFs' had completed thirty-five hours in the air and covered 15,000 miles.

All the missiles were timed to hit simultaneously at 11am, shortly after the opening strikes of the first night of the war. Coalition aircraft were landing back at their bases so that the B-52 attack maintained the pressure on Iraq without causing further 'deconfliction' problems between the CALCMs and earlier strike elements. Some targets were in northern Iraq, an area which was beyond the unrefuelled range of Coalition tactical aircraft until F-111E missions from Incirlik were cleared with the Turkish Government for Day Two. Relatively soft targets; hydro-electric and geothermal power generation facilities at Mosul, and Basrah telephone exchange in the southeast were among the eight successfully attacked by the thirty-one missiles which made it to their objectives. Overall, the success rate was estimated at 85–91 per cent. The Williams F107 turbofan on one CALCM failed to develop power on launch, one failed to explode and had to be destroyed later and a third may have been shot down. A year and day after the mission all the crews involved were awarded Air Medals by Lt Gen Martin J. Ryan, 8th AF Commander and the mission was revealed to the public.

The B-52G's introduction to the war, at least, was definitively 'strategic' and its long-term effects as a demonstration of the battle-worn bombers' power projection were profound.

B-52Gs used in Senior Surprise

Sortie number	Serial	Aircraft name	Aircraft Captain	Crew Number
1 (Doom 31)	58-0177	Petie 3rd	Capt Michael G. Wilson	S-91
2 (Doom 32)	59-2564		Capt John P. Romano	E-54
3 (Doom 33)	59-2582	Grim Reaper II	Capt Charles E. Jones Jr	R-53
4 (Doom 34)	57-6475	Miami Clipper II	Capt Bernard S. Morgan	E-83
5 (Doom 35)	58-0238	Miss Fit II	Capt Marcus J. Myers	E-81
6 (Doom 36)	58-0183	Valkyrie	Capt Alan W. Moe	S-92
7 (Doom 37)	58-0185	El Lobo II	Capt Stephen D. Sicking	S-93

blows to Iraq's defences. Five of the strike packages involved B-52Gs from Diego Garcia and from King Abdul Aziz International Airport, Jeddah from which the Saudi Arabians had agreed, two weeks before the war, to allow a limited number of B-52s to operate. A week before the 'Storm' broke twenty B-52Gs arrived from the 42nd, 93rd and 379th BWs, with a few additional migrants from the 2nd BW at Barksdale and the 416th at Griffiss. Among the 93rd BW's contingent was 58-0203, *Black Widow*, which ended the war with a record fifty-seven missions marked up on its venerable jowls. These indicated an average of two missions daily throughout the war. Squadrons generally used the 'hard crew' policy, keeping crews intact and balancing personnel to ensure that the talent was spread evenly through the unit. Although they seldom flew the same B-52s this created few problems. As a Griffiss pilot told the authors, 'All "BUFFs" smell the same'.

Diego Garcia, over 3,200 miles from Baghdad, received around twenty aircraft, from the same units as Jeddah, though a small number of 668th BS aircraft had arrived during *Desert Shield*. Capt David

Loring's Thunder Struck, 58-0126 (with fearless crew) racked up twenty-two combat sorties.
Authors

Ross: 'On 13 August I was on a tanker bound for Loring. Within an hour of arrival we were getting ready to fly a fully-laden B-52G, armed with forty-five bombs, to Diego. I had never flown a plane as loaded with live ordnance – the most I had ever flown a plane as loaded with was four or five. We got to refuel with a KC-10 for the first time on the trip over from Loring. It was more aerodynamically stable than the '135' and I was pretty impressed. We didn't have a clear idea of what we would have to do but we were pretty psyched'. During the early stages of *Desert Shield*, with the exception of Langley's F-15s which were in Saudi, we were kind of "it". We were pretty nervous and just kept hoping Saddam would hold off. We studied real hard, spending a lot of time on the new tactics we were going to use'.

Both bases' aircraft were managed by a new Provisional Air Division, the 17th AD (P) and given Provisional Bomb Wing status. Diego Garcia's tenants became the 4300th BW (P) while the B-52s baking at Jeddah were the 1708th BW (P). Peter Bloom arrived at Diego to find, 'There was little space. Maintenance and other support people had to sleep in tents by the runway, so with the planes taking off around the clock you can imagine that they didn't get much sleep'. From these two bases the majority of the B-52 missions were flown, with the 1708th delivering about half the bombs, largely because of its comparatively short distance from the battle front. Diego Garcia's aircraft were used for the first night's onslaught on the 16–17 January. Fourteen were targeted against four major forward airfields and a 'highway strip' dispersal base just northeast of the Saudi–Iraqi border, eight of them carrying British 1,000lb GP bombs which were considered to be particularly effective against airfield targets. It was feared that these bases might be used as launch-pads for fighters to intercept the crucial AWACS aircraft orbiting to the south of the border, or to lay chemical or biological weapons on Coalition troops massed there. Maj Ron Funk flew on SAC's first-ever low-level combat mission:

We received word shortly before dinner time that the war was a 'go'. Once the crews were notified all the primary crews and airborne/ground spares boarded buses for the Operations building where we assembled for the mission briefing. We received our mission packages and were briefed by the Operations Planning Team concerning our mission specifics. Each crew was already intimately familiar with their particular mission as we had been able to review the packages during the week. After the briefing we collected our gear and proceeded out to the aircraft, which had been 'prepped' with our wartime weapons and fuel loads for some time. During the previous week the crews had been given the opportunity to 'prep' the jet with professional gear and perform advanced pre-flights to check systems. The events of the first evening were a surprise to no-one. The first aircraft took off shortly after 10pm local time on 16 January.

Three B-52Gs were targeted against each major airfield, two loaded with 'UK-1000s' with delayed action fuses and one with CBU-89s, with two against the highway strip carrying CBU-52s or -58s. All aircraft flew low-level attacks, as low as 400ft depending on the load-out. My aircraft was one of eight assigned to release at 400ft AGL over the target. The attack was accomplished by performing multi-axis attacks with time control over the target area providing the critical de-confliction. It is my understanding that all of the targets were guarded by radar-guided and unguided AAA, small arms and MANPADS (hand-held SAMS). The CBU carriers were required to fly at slightly higher altitude to achieve weapons parameters. The overall objective of these missions was essentially disruption and area denial of the fields for a specific amount of time.

A target in northern Iraq was also slated for B-52 attention on the second night

Gunner Danny Burnett at 30,000ft over Idaho demonstrates the B-52G's ASG-15 fire control system. The control unit which he is operating stowed away flush with the other panels so that the gunner could eject safely. The system was not used in anger in *Desert Storm*. Danny Burnett

when two aircraft made a low-level strike on the Al Sahra Undergraduate Pilot Training airfield and Air Force Academy. The bombs exploded on target, embarrassingly close to Saddam's Tikrit home territory. It was one of relatively few deep penetrations of Iraqi airspace by B-52s but there were other attacks by packages of bombers with F-4G, EF-111A Raven and fighter support on industrial targets, communications centres and railways. Nuclear, biological and chemical (NBC) warfare stores and manufacturing plants also received visits, and several strikes on suspected missile sites at H-2 and H-3 airfields in western Iraq were flown as part of the SCUD-hunting campaign to eliminate Saddam's long-range missiles.

In one action, somewhat reminiscent of the siege-busting *Arc Light* sorties in Vietnam, B-52s pulverized assault forces supporting three Iraqi armoured brigades who were massing to occupy the Saudi coastal town of Khafji on 29 January. A major component in the first three days' air activity was the temporary removal of Iraq's electrical generating capacity. A pre-war study had calculated that a single strike by B-52s and TLAMs on the Ajaji power plant near Baghdad could have knocked out 60 per cent of the city's electrical power. The mission was eventually entrusted to TLAMs and fighter-bombers. However, a two-cell strike wiped out the North Taji Logistics Centre and an ammunition plant, whose fifteen SAM sites had been comprehensively removed by F-117As ahead of the strike, while three cells bombed part of Baghdad's radar early

---

Ground Attack

Captains Tony Monetti (copilot) and Jonny Iverson (EWO) flew seventeen *Desert Storm* missions with B-52G Crew E-13 from Diego Garcia and Jeddah, including a memorable low-level sortie.

Before our first mission on 18 January, we became familiar with the threats by way of the Intel folks and crews who had flown Nights One and Two. The main threat seemed to be AAA. The reason we were going low level was the air-to-air threat. We knew that they had a very significant air element, consequently the main threat against the 'Flying Barn', as we call the B-52, was air-to-air. On the evening of our first mission – Night Three of the war – ten aircraft were readied, of which two were spares. The eight primary bombers were split into two cells of four. Our cell's target was an oil refinery south of Baghdad, near As Samawah. Our aircraft was No. 4 and we, along with No. 3, were going to attack the storage tank farm, while lead and No. 2 took out the control facility.

We soon descended to low level over Saudi and discovered the entire region was fogged in. We had envisioned a 200ft ingress altitude but we were at 400ft because the terrain avoidance set wasn't working. The radar beam was skipping off the sand. In addition, the NVG we were wearing were ineffective due to fog. The plan for our four-ship cell was to split into two-ship elements and prosecute a multi-axis attack on the target to confuse the enemy. The timing was very close so it was critical that we released our weapons on time and on the proper axis of attack. Otherwise the cell might 'frag' itself. When the lead ship of our element dropped out with radar problems we were directed to make up lead's time, meaning a 100 per cent power setting. We also had to cut a few corners which made it very challenging for the navigation team. The only thing we were flying off was the radar altimeter – which was crazy. As soon as we'd see it get a little low, we'd pull up. I even said to the AC, 'The regs say we don't go'. He replied, 'The regs don't apply in combat'.

The bomb run was very short and began with a right turn roll-in IP. Because of a tall tower in the middle of our attack axis we couldn't execute less than 30 degrees of bank in the final turn from the roll-in IP, but if we exceeded this the radar altimeter would break lock and we'd be flying off nothing but the regular pressure altimeter. To get us on the proper axis the Nav said, 'I need you to come right and give me 45 degrees of bank'. There was a very tense exchange between the pilot and nav at this point, one trying to save the bomb run, while the other tried to save the aircraft. Both were right. We had corrected too far right of track.

The crew were forced to abort their attack and they loaded the co-ordinates for the secondary target. Then the Airborne Commander of the cell came over the radio to say we could return to the target as they had encountered no threats. The Iraqis had just had over 100 bombs dropped on their heads, so I was sure they were up now. The AWACS came back and replied, if you guys are up for it, go ahead! So we did a 180 degree turn and a nineteen-minute 'racetrack', just like in the movie *Memphis Belle*. As we came in with eight seconds to go the sh*t hit the fan. I [Capt M] remember seeing red tracers coming at us from the right and within seconds of that, the AC yells, 'I've got AAA at nine o'clock!'. All you could see were these red things coming through the fog. I thought for sure we were taking hits. It was now 4, 3, 2, 1... release. I had never dropped fifty-one 750lb-bombs in my life and during the release the aircraft shook pretty violently as if we were driving over a rough road.

I [Capt I] actually thought we were taking hits! I just looked at the gunner as if to say, 'God, this is it!'. We both reached for our ejection handles, then we shared a seemingly psychic experience when we simultaneously realized it was the M117s coming off the jet.

As we continued through the AAA I [Capt M] was still wearing my goggles and the fog was now starting to burn off due to the excessive heat from the fires. I could now see the tanks ahead of our aircraft as our weapons began going off behind us. Suddenly it was like a nuclear detonation! I'll never forget this, the fog lit up like a bright light and the AC and I were temporarily blinded. About five seconds later the 'E-Dub' [EWO] calls out: 'Pilot, SAM, hunker!'. The way we operated the 'BUFF' at low level is that one guy flew it while the other controlled the throttles. I was the 'speed' guy while the AC was the left-right- up-and-down guy. The AC pushed the nose down and the countermeasures worked as the missile locked on to either our chaff or flares. And this is the point where we almost hit the ground. I saw my radar altimeter start to bottom out so I grabbed the yoke, wrapped both arms around it and pulled it back. I thought for sure we were going to hit when the altimeter locked on at 50ft. People facing near death have said that time slows down and it did, but during this period I didn't think about my wife and children, I thought about what a priest had said to me earlier that evening – 'God would never abandon me'. So, I was at peace. However everyone was screaming out, 'Climb, climb!' We did start to climb and as the AC looked over at me I could see there were beads of sweat pouring off his face and he was as white as a ghost! I grabbed him by the arm and asked if he was all right. He replied that he couldn't let go of the yoke; he had a death grip on it. Then the AAA started up again.

They managed to re-enter Saudi airspace in search of a tanker, but their problems were not over. Capt Iverson: 'It was freezing in the back of the cabin so I asked Tony to turn up the heat. He responded to the whole crew with, "Hey, we've got a fire light!". That statement quickly re-tightened our sphincters and we started a whole new pain-in-the-ass adventure on this sortie from hell.' Capt Monetti: 'As we were exiting Iraq and climbing out of low level I started to turn on the instrument lighting and I immediately got the fire warning light on engine number five, so we shut it down but the light stayed on. I figured it was because we took hits so, as a precaution, we shut down the adjacent engine.' He passed an emergency message to the AWACS via another member of the B-52 element, but was not to know that the AWACS had already gone off duty. The crew then had to find their way to Jeddah, unable at first to find its coordinates as they did not know the full title of the base (King Abdul Aziz Airport) and, guided by a Saudi controller with little English, and someone who warned them not to overfly Mecca or they would be shot down. Finally, the SAC Runway Supervisory Officer at Jeddah talked then in. Upon returning home I spoke to a few Boeing engineers regarding our ordeal of almost impacting the ground and they are convinced that the large underwing surface and ground effect cushioned the aircraft that night. This, plus the right angle of attack saved our lives. We obviously pulled up at just the right time.'

Surprisingly, in view of the damage caused to their target, none of the crew ever received a commendation for this mission.

warning network. Jeddah-based B-52s also hit an important weapons-storage area near Basrah. In another night raid two cells, attacking on different axes, devastated a refinery and POL storage area. Targets covering a large area such as the Al Qaim industrial and chemical complex proved to be particularly vulnerable to the wide bombing 'coverage' of a B-52 attack.

The huge number of sorties brought inevitable de-confliction problems; some of them avoidable. Peter Bloom: 'My scariest mission was in a four-ship cell going after a railroad centre, vectored by an AWACS. Suddenly, the AWACS controller vectored us out of the formation (it turned out that she was in training and may not have known exactly what she was doing). We were two or three minutes behind the cell when we were vectored 90 degrees into the target area, or so we thought. We were told that that cell was ahead of us and we were clear to drop. Unfortunately we were given bogus information and the rest of the cell was directly underneath us. We almost dropped our load on to the plane beneath us'. For Capt Brooks R. Lieske, 'The most dangerous part could have been the return flight home. We usually had to return as part of a six-plane cell that had to air-refuel in bad weather. That was dangerous!'

The low-level missions of the first three days resulted in some damage to B-52s. Several received shrapnel damage from AAA or hand-held SA-series missiles. The authors were told of one which returned to Diego Garcia with bullet holes in its wings from hits which weren't noticed until the post-flight inspection was well advanced. Several hits were taken by high-flying 'BUFFs' too. One B-52G returned with sixty-five holes, many streaming fuel, from fragments of two near-misses by SAMs which holed its wings, spoilers and fuselage. The rapid defeat of Iraq's radar defences and fighters meant that Coalition aircraft could fly fairly safely above the reach of AAA and smaller SAMs (the scourge of the low-level A-10As and AV-8Bs) after Night Three. B-52Gs then pursued their attacks on the Republican Guard from altitudes above 30,000ft, although these had begun on Day Two. Responding to Gen Schwarzkopf's wishes, Gen Horner asked for attacks on the Guard every three hours for the rest of the war. This task accounted for 85 per cent of B-52 sorties and confined the aircraft to the KTO. To the DoD's analysts the Republican Guard were so vital to Saddam that they were regarded as a 'strategic' target. In many ways they had become a fixed military target in that they remained in place, thereby making targeting easier. Schwarzkopf wanted them locked into Kuwait for this reason and began the bridge-busting campaign partly to prevent their escape or re-supply. B-52 attacks on them then intensified.

There was no shortage of targets, or of attackers. Timothy Mers recalled, 'On one mission we were waiting to get into our "kill zone". The waiting line consisted of a

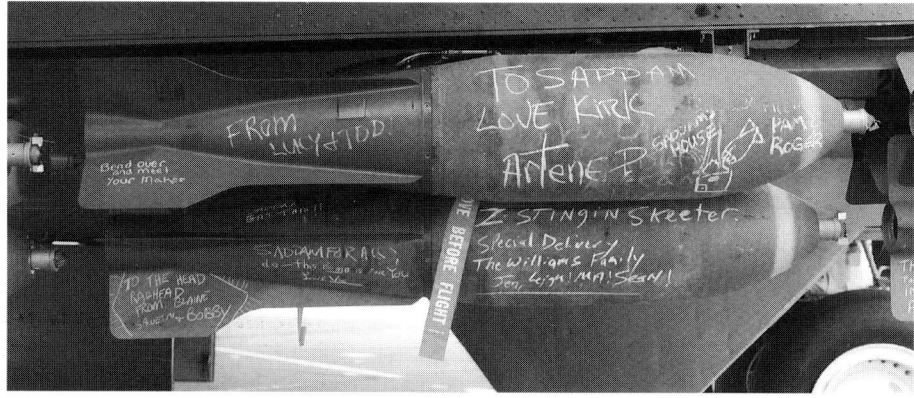

Bomb graffiti, as seen on this cluster of M117s with low-drag tails, was inspired as much by the frustration of being away from home as it was by animosity towards the foe. Tim Perry

---

SAM Salvo

Capt Brad Rupert was an Instructor Navigator with the 416th BW and flew ten sorties in *Desert Storm* with seven different crews.

My most memorable mission occurred on 3 February when I was involved in an attack on an armour marshalling yard. The plan was a multi-axis bomb run in which my three-ship cell would break up and attack from different points from about 30,000ft. Two would make a head-on bomb run which provided a better 'stick', or run of bombs over the target area. As we approached our break-up point our F-4G 'Wild Weasels' reached a critical fuel state and had to fly off to a tanker. Within minutes, our EWO detected an enemy search radar that was actively searching. Here, I give full credit to our R/N for suggesting that I plot the location of the signal. Within seconds, the EWO called out that he had a missile launch. The AC was now screaming out that he had a visual on two missiles and the aircraft was banked real hard to the right – we pretty much did a ninety degree turn. As we banked, the AC reported viewing the missiles as they went by the cockpit window and exploded well above the aircraft.

At the time it seemed like a big *Red Flag* exercise, so it didn't really dawn on me that the danger was genuine. However, my adrenaline was pumping but not for the obvious reasons – the fact that my crew and I had almost been blown out of the sky. No, I was incensed because someone down there was shooting at us and had screwed up my timing. If you had asked me before the incident how I would have reacted I would probably have replied that I would have freaked out and not been able to accomplish my job. But I guess that the massive amounts of training provided by SAC really paid off. Then again, had I been able to actually see the missile, the story might have been different.

As we broke to our right, four more missiles were launched in our direction, but EWO did his thing and countered them. Before the launch of the second salvo I was once again able to plot an approximate location of the radar source, and by using our coordinate in the air I was able to draw another line and now I had an intersection.

After delivering our fifty-one M117s we made a 180 degree turn towards Saudi. While heading back, the entire crew agreed that they were interested as to what it was we had encountered during ingress to the target. The AC then enquired how everyone felt about getting close enough to the area to view it with our EVS and still stay out of danger. I had no problems with this as the crew was made up of very proficient StanEval members from Castle AFB. We then flew the aircraft almost directly at the suspect area and sure enough, right there in the centre of the TV and FLIR was the unmistakable pattern of an SA-2 site. Again, the same signal came up so now I had a third line, and using our present position I was able to create a line of intercept. We then immediately changed course and called up AWACS which tasked a pair of Strike Eagles to take out the site. Apparently it had been there for a while and had remained dormant until we flew over it.

B-52 cell, an F-16 cell, another B-52 cell, a cell of A-10s and finally our cell of B-52s'. Peter Bloom added, 'The situation was ever changing up there, so much so that by the end of the war we had basically quit mission briefing before take-off. We simply waited for word from the ground. Targets were everywhere and there was not much they could do to stop us'.

The sheer numbers of Republican Guard positions forced targeters to adopt the 'kill box' method of dividing up the battlefield. Each box was thirty miles square and divided into quadrants. Cells of B-52Gs were directed systematically to active kill-boxes where they dropped their ordnance causing a strip of destruction 1.5 × 1 mile in area. Even with one or two cells of B-52Gs the cumulative tonnage was considerable. On 30 January, 470 tons were dropped in twenty-eight sorties and 1,240 tons fell in a three-day period later in the month. Each aircraft could carry up to fifty-one M117R bombs or a similar number of CBU-58, CBU-87 CEM or CBU-89.

Reconciling President Bush's directive to keep Iraqi troop casualties as low as possible with this relentless 'strip-bombing' was a dilemma, but its psychological effect was considerable. Many Iraqi prisoners were unanimous that the B-52 was the most feared weapon in the KTO. Often, they were troops who had not been bombed, but they had seen and felt the effects of up to 300 bombs landing without warning on positions close to their own. In all, the Republican Guard was attacked in 5,600 sorties during the war. Several battalions were bombed continuously for up to six weeks. Casualties were inevitably heavy, but considerably reduced by desertions, which often amounted to 40 per cent of Iraqi strength, particularly among officers. This process was encouraged by leaflet bombs slipped in among the live ordnance. B-52s were also used for 'breaching' operations, blasting gaps in the Iraqi fortifications to ease the progress of the counter-invading Coalition ground forces.

Bombing results from these essentially Battlefield Air Interdiction (BAI) sorties were less predictable. Direct hits were needed to destroy dug-in tanks and the well-constructed bomb-proof revetments put up by Iraqi engineers. The impact of many bombs was absorbed by the desert sand. Even so, when the cease-fire came their armour had been reduced by the requisite 50 to 60 per cent margin and damage to regular Iraqi Army artillery often approached 90 per cent.

Desert Storm presented B-52 crew members with many new challenges. Capt Brad Rupert was a B-52G instructor navigator at Griffiss AFB, where GPS was not in use before the war. 'During my ten missions I flew seven as lead navigator, which meant I was aboard a GPS-equipped 'BUFF' as these aircraft led all cells. This was interesting because I had never worked a GPS before. I was provided with a manual and instructions but my first hands-on experience was in-theatre. As a matter of fact, on one mission we actually bombed off the GPS. About a minute from weapons release we flew through some flak and simultaneously lost our radar, FLIR and LLTV. I thought we had taken some hits, but we hadn't. Our R/N just got the altitude [to the GPS] and bomb from it. On another mission we lost radar while attacking an airfield. One of the offsets was the control tower. As we ingressed the target the R/N slaved the FLIR and LLTV to where the offset should have been, and there plain as day was the tower, dead centre with its beacon still flashing. The GPS had worked as advertised'.

The volume of bombing which was required in Kuwait meant drawing in B-52G missions from other sources. The B-52's nuclear mystique made the Saudis rather sensitive about their presence in large numbers at Jeddah, and Diego Garcia was at full stretch. Consideration was given to Cairo West as a fairly convenient location for another Provisional Wing, but Gen Schwarzkopf was quickly made aware of the Egyptian President's political reservations about B-52s on his territory.[27] Instead, the 801st BW (P) was established at Moron de la Frontera near Seville in

One of thousands of leaflets dropped on Iraqi positions warning of the probability of B-52 strikes, using a Vietnam-era photo. USAF

Spain and the 806th BW (P) at RAF Fairford, England. Both bases were maintained on a 'standby' basis. Each was a Provisional Wing of the 8th AF (hence the numbering) under the overall control of the 17th AD (P) at Riyadh, which also managed the Saudi and Diego Garcia operations. Moron's aircraft and personnel came mainly from the 2nd BW and were commanded by Col Ronald C. Marcotte.

Capt Brooks Lieske left for Spain on 13 January, 'with the full knowledge that the 15 January deadline was coming up. Because of the political sensitivities involved, and because of Spain's reluctance to base bombers on her soil prior to the start of hostilities, we used KC-10 call signs on our seven-hour flight to that country. We also entered Spanish air space after diverting from our regular destination of Aviano in Italy. Personnel from the 2nd BW had been in place for about two weeks and I could not believe how quickly things had come together. Within three days of arrival we were involved in local procedures training. Finally, on Day Five of the war we flew our first combat mission. We all did some pretty stupid things in the earliest missions, based on inexperience. For example, for the first two weeks we flew our missions low-level through Turkey until we reached the Iraqi border, at which time we climbed to avoid AA fire. But this meant we were climbing right into the fire and we were endangering ourselves. During the last few weeks of the war B-52s flying out of Fairford took all the northern routes while bombers from Spain, Jeddah and Diego flew the southern routes. We flew eleven missions, dropping primarily 750lb iron bombs'.

Numbers at each of the four Provisional bases fluctuated slightly as aircraft sometimes launched from one base and recovered at another, as they sometimes had done between Guam and U-Tapao in the 1960s. Moron had up to twenty-four aircraft by late January while Fairford received the first of eight B-52Gs at 7am on 5 February.

One of the criticisms of the use of B-52s was their reliance on support and tanker aircraft. Aircraft based out of theatre used up 40 per cent of the KC-10A's (and a quarter of the entire tanker fleet's) offloading capacity. However, SEAD and fighter cover were indispensable for most of the other strike aircraft too. Their success in helping to protect the B-52s was evidenced by the total lack of combat losses. B-52G 59-2593 from the 69th BS was the only operational casualty. Returning from

Armament specialists ease another Mk 82 from its perch on the MJ-1 'jammer' at Diego. Andy Evans

B-52G 58-0204 Special Delivery **(formerly the** Rivet Ace **testbed) developed hydraulic problems on its 17 February mission, jettisoned its bombs north of Sicily and diverted to Palermo. In 1979 it flew in the ALCM fly-off competition, was the first B-52 with OAS and wing strakelets and flew in** Big WIP **at a record 567,000lb with air refuelling.** Authors

an 18-hour mission on 3 February it suffered major electrical failure and crashed into the sea only fifteen miles short of Diego Garcia. Capt Jeffry J. Olsen and 1st Lt Jorge Arteaga and Eric Hedeen died in the crash. It is thought that they may have delayed their bale-out too long in an attempt to save the old warrior. A second B-52G (58-0248) was hit by an SA-8 missile in the extreme aft end of the fuselage, losing its gun turret and some ECM gear and sustaining numerous holes in its tail area. Apart from realizing that the tail guns and radar were not working the crew were unaware of the hit until dawn broke on the return flight and a following B-52 reported the damage. '248 recovered to base safely and was repaired using parts from 58-0234, grounded at Guam with a wing spar crack. Although SA-2 and SA-3 missiles were used, Lt Col Brian Rogers told the authors that, 'most of us never saw anything bigger than an SA-8 or SA-9 or -13 and they were miles below me. I think a few guys got looked at by SA-6s but that was about it. There were so many 'Wild

'BUFFs' on Ice

Operating from the snow-sprinkled RAF base at Fairford, UK the 806th BW (P) existed from 1 February until 5 March, 1991. Its first aircraft arrived on a chilly February morning, its wing-tanks white with ice from its high-altitude transit flight. Within days the Wing was in action against targets in Iraq and Kuwait after the French Government gave permission to overfly France. Although the Fairford Wing flew only sixty Gulf sorties (compared with 846 from Jeddah and around 400 from each of the other two bases) its operational tally gives some idea of the organization involved in mounting B-52G Provisional Wing operations. (An equivalent account for operations at Jeddah or Diego Garcia would fill an entire book!)

Commander: Col George I. Conlan with staff from the 97th BW, Eaker AFB and 1,100 personnel.
Designated as 806 BW (P): 5 February 1991.
First B-52 arrived: 5 February.
Munitions arrived: 6 February – 2,000 tons of M117, Mk 82 and CBU of which 1,158 tons used.
Operational from: 8 February.
First mission launched: 9 February.
Sorties flown: 60.
Total Flying Time: 975.7 hours.
Average sortie time: 16.3 hours.
Turnaround times between missions reduced from peacetime 5.5 hours to 1.5 hours using the Integrated Combat Turnaround (ICT) for rapid refuelling, arming and replenishment which the USAF introduced in the mid-1980s.

B-52Gs used, with parent units, arrival and departure dates and missions flown:

57-6498	416th BW	5 Feb – 8 March	11
58-0168	379th BW	23 Feb (from Moron) – 28 Feb (to Moron)	2
58-0182	379th BW	5 Feb – 9 March (at Moron 22–27 Feb)	6
58-0204	379th BW	5 Feb – 5 March	6
58-0231	416th BW	5 Feb – 8 March	6
58-0237	93rd BW	6 Feb – 9 March	10
58-0245	2nd BW	5 Feb – 9 March	9
58-0247	379th BW	6 Feb – 9 March	4
59-0579	379th BW	24 Feb – 9 March	2
58-0589	379th BW	6 Feb – 1 March	9

Missions

Date	Number of B-52Gs	Call-sign
9 Feb	four + one air-spare	LUXOR
10 Feb	three + one air-spare	LUXOR
11 Feb	three + one air-spare	LUXOR
12 Feb	four	WRATH
13 Feb	three + one air-spare	LOBO
14 Feb	four + one air-spare	SHACK
15 Feb	four + one air-spare	NOVA
16 Feb	four prepared but mission cancelled	
17 Feb	four	PLACID (58-0204 *Placid 73* had hydraulic problems, jettisoned its bombload in the Mediterranean and diverted to Palermo, returning to Fairford on 19 February)
18 Feb	four	BELLE (58-0231 weather-diverted to Mildenhall)
19 Feb	four	ARBOR
20 Feb	four	YALE
21 Feb	four	LISA (All diverted to Jeddah, flew the next day's 'Fairford' mission from there and returned to Fairford on 23–24th February)
22 Feb	mission cancelled	
23 Feb	three + one ground-spare	TUSK
24 Feb	four	JENNY (Weather-diverted to St Mawgan)
25 Feb	four	ERIE
26 Feb	four	BARB (Mission cancelled)
27 Feb	four	ELKO (59-2579 diverted to Jeddah)

Tanker Support: 807th AREFS (P) at Mont Marsan (BA 118), France
803rd AREFS (P) at Athens-Hellinkon
Istres-le-Tube (BA125) was a weather-diversion base and Malpensa Airport, Milan could provide refuelling support.

Provisional Wings for Desert Storm, Deployments and Parent Units

Unit of Origin/Base	to:1708 BW (P) Jeddah, Saudi	to:806 BW (P) Fairford, England	to:4300 BW (P) Diego Garcia	to:801 BW (P) Moron, Spain
2nd BW, 62 BS and 596BS Barksdale, LA	–	1	–	7 LW
42nd BW, 69BS Loring, MA	4	–	16 LW	–
93rd BW, 328BS Castle, CA	5	1	4	–
97th BW, 340BS Eaker, AR	crews	LW	crews	–
99th SWW	crews	–	–	crews
379th BW 524BS Ellsworth, SD	5	6	–	9
416th SW, 668BS Wurtsmith, MI	LW			
Griffiss, NY	3	2	crews	9

Notes

1. These figures show maximum numbers of aircraft which appeared at the bases. Primary Aircraft Authorized figures for the basic establishment at each base were: 20 at Kiego, 16 at Jeddah, 20 at Moron and 8 at Fairford. Rotations and diversions caused numerous fluctuations. Sometimes missions started at one base and ended at another.
2. LW indicates the parent Bomb Wing which was tasked with providing the core organizational infrastructure for reach Provisional Wing, and its Commander.
3. The Moron deployment ended 17 April 1991.
4. Wurtsmith sent five 379th BW aircraft, all ALCM-modified with Strategic Radar, ALQ-172(V)1 ECM, AGM-28 pylons and MERs. All had the famous 'Triangle K' fin flash. They were 57-6492 *Old Crow Express*, 58-0194 *Bufasaurus*, 58-0173 *Let's Make a Deal*, 58-0159 *Alley Oop's Bold Assault*, 58-0175 *Viper*. Five were 93rd BW were all so-called '777' jets with enhanced conventional capability. Strategic Radar, ALQ-172(V)1, GPS and stub pylons with HASBs (that is non-ALCM aircraft). They were 58-0192, 58-0203, 58-0218, 59-2570 and 59-2598. Of those, '192 and '218 were Loring jets which had been in PDM and were delivered to Castle. The other three were AGM-142 'Have Nap' capable, though those missiles were not used during the Gulf War. Diego Garcia-based aircraft were all '777' jets. Jeddah initially had eleven '777s' and five AGM-28/MER-equipped jets. Moron and Fairford aircraft were all AGM-28/MER-equipped.

Weasels' hanging about the tri-border areas; those few SAM sites that survived the first couple of days didn't act very aggressively. I was shot at by SA-2s and SA-3s on missions to H-2 and Al Quaim, but nowhere else. I don't remember seeing any missiles over Taji any of the three times I was there'.

In some areas the threats remained palpable right to the end. Capt Lieske: 'On the last night of the war we were flying a mission over an airfield and we were assured that most of the threat was gone. Suddenly we got indications that we had a missile right behind us. My EW guy did his

(Above) Ace in the Hole **(57-6498, 416th BW) bombed-up for its ninth mission on 20 February 1991. Its iced-up wing tanks show that the temperature had stayed below freezing since its mission the previous night. This was one of the ALCM trials B-52Gs.** Authors

(Left) **Transferred to the 2nd BW,** Ace in the Hole **still retains its nose-art and mission markings. It was scrapped on 19 July 1995.** Andy Evans

B-52G 58-0247 had its High Plains Drifter **nose-art crudely obliterated but retained its 'crew' nameplate – Dream Warrior. It air-aborted on its second mission, diverting to Bentwaters.** Authors

thing and all of a sudden it was gone. It seemed to happen real quick'.

When President Bush decided that the time had come for a cease-fire on 28th February a proportion of Iraq's Republican Guard units still remained substantially intact, particularly those which had remained on or near the northern border. The Divisions further south which had been under constant attack, were devastated by the B-52s. Once again, the bombers' enormous ordnance capacity had been decisive, wiping out years of expensive Iraqi military development in a matter of days. An independent study group, commissioned by the USAF in August 1991 to analyse the effects of airpower in the Gulf War, concluded that the B-52 was 'one of the most sought-after aircraft by ground commanders for strikes against Iraqi forces'. For some of the longer-serving B-52 crews, or their sons, those were familiar words. In a new theatre of war the old symbolism was reasserted: B-52 = Airpower.

When the Sand Settled

Retirement of the B-52G had already begun by the summer of 1990 with around thirty-five in the boneyard, while the rest pounded Iraq and Kuwait. First to go were the 320th BW at Mather AFB followed by the veteran 43rd SW at Andersen, both flying Harpoon-modified B-52Gs. In 1991, the 416th BW retired its B-52Gs and re-equipped with B-52Hs drawn from around the Command. Two more Wings lost their aircraft in 1992, the SIOP orientated 97th and 379th BWs. Withdrawal accelerated that year as the 2nd Wing took over B-52Hs from the inactivating 7th BW at Carswell, Texas in October–December 1992.

June 1, 1992 marked the end of Strategic Air Command after forty-five years of managing America's airborne nuclear deterrent. Total redesign of the USAF's airpower organization, necessitated by a receding Cold War threat, dictated an amalgamation of SAC with Tactical Air Command in a unified Air Combat Command (ACC). With it came a revision of the combat Wing structure. As a prelude, all SAC bomber Wings had dropped their 'BW' or 'SW' nameplates from September 1991, becoming simply Wings (for example 2nd Wg) SAC's ICBMs were absorbed by Space Command and its tankers passed to the newly-created Air Mobility

Command. Within the reorganization the establishment of ACC's first Composite Wing brought the B-52 into a mixed arrangement of fighter and SEAD units, drawing on the success of the Composite Wing which had pursued the war against Iraq from Incirlik, Turkey. Based at Mountain Home AFB with single squadrons of F-16C, F-15C and F-15E Strike Eagles, plus a squadron of EF-111A Ravens the 366th Wg was designed for rapid reaction 'power projection' and was referred to as the Air Interdiction Composite Wing. Its 'MO' coded B-52G component was the 34th BS which remained with its tankers at their Castle AFB home. The squadron was reactivated on the B-1B Lancer at Ellsworth AFB on 4 April 1994, but remained part of the Super Wing. At Loring the 42nd BW gradually shed its B-52GS shortly after receiving 'LZ' tail-codes and the restoration of its 'BW' titles in 1994. By the end of that year the 93rd BW at Castle had lost its 328th BS B-52Gs and prepared for closure. Ironically, they won top awards for their Class during *Gunsmoke '93* at Nellis AFB. The last of the old soldiers gradually faded away as the year ended, leaving only the 'Cadillac' B-52H model to carry the tradition of that illustrious late-1940's design forward to the end of the Century and into the next.

A standard I-Beam rack adaptor allowed two MER-1-6/6As to carry a dozen weapons, as on this Diego Garcia-based example. Andy Evans

(Below) **The 416th BW's distinctive Statue of Liberty tail-art, obliterated on SAC orders for Gulf missions, had long been a bone of contention with the senior management. Post-war, on a gunship grey example, it is slightly reduced in size. Former 416th BW Commander Col Loughran explained to the authors that the logo says, 'We fly big bombers. We're in New York State, the Statue of Liberty is here in the Empire State, it's big, not some wimpy little landmark'. Each visit by the SAC Inspector General resulted in the 416th being written up for 'Egregious violation of the rules of decorum'. The markings stayed.** Andy Evans

Desert Strike

When the US Government chose to warn Saddam of the inescapable might of US airpower as a reprisal for his invasion of Kurdish territory in August 1996, the same CALCM missile was used but the B-52H was given its combat initiation. Col Floyd L. Carpenter, who was Commander of Barksdale's 96th BS, explained to the authors how Operation *Desert Strike* was mounted. On Friday 30 August 1996 he had been waterskiing with his family:

> The phone rang almost immediately after we came in the house; it was my boss, Col Duke Evans, the 2nd Bomb Wing's Operations Group Commander. I put on a flight suit and went to his office where he informed me that my squadron might be tasked to fly a sortie against Iraq. We met with a few of the Group mission planners and Brig Gen Dave Young, 2nd BW Commander before seeing Lt Gen Ford, 8th AF Commander who made it clear that we would have to fly west. Diplomatic clearances would not be granted to fly an easterly route or launch missiles that would require flying over foreign soil, except Iraq.
>
> I immediately went to my squadron and began looking at the personnel necessary to accomplish the mission. We had decided to deploy four aircraft though it was fairly certain that only two would fly the mission. Eventually, six were loaded with weapons though only four went to Guam. I left the flightline that night around 2400hrs to get some rest as the word was out that we would launch the next day. Unfortunately, after arriving home and crawling into bed I received four phone calls up to 0400hrs. Finally giving up on sleep, I returned to the flightline about 0530hrs on 31 August and by the time I left at 1200hrs we had four aircraft ready to launch and a C-5 on the runway ready to load personnel and equipment. The decision to go to Guam had been made and take-off was to be that afternoon around 1700hrs.
>
> Also, at Offutt the missile mission planning effort was well under way. The CALCM missions are originally 'built' at Offutt on the same system that produces the mission tapes for the ALCM, then transported to the unit or transmitted to our deployable mission planning system and then converted to Data Transfer Unit Cartridges (DTUCs) that are used in the aircraft. We took the deployable system with us to Guam and Diego Garcia and though the original missions were built before we left, several changes were made and transmitted to us in Guam. In-flight changes were also made during the mission which the navigator teams had to manually input into the system.
>
> We launched two separate two-ships, my take-off being just before 1700hrs that afternoon. En route to Guam was 15.8 hours with two air-refuellings, the first just off the West coast and second around Hawaii. Arrival at Guam was at midnight and at 0400hrs next morning we made it to our rooms to sleep. I awoke about 1030hrs and went over to where our planners were working. Col Evans was there with his staff and they asked me why I was there since I should be in crew-rest for the coming afternoon's mission. That was the first I knew that we were launching a combat strike against Iraq.
>
> Three aircraft were to launch with the best two continuing on to launch missiles. We did minimal route and target study before proceeding to the aircraft and we launched at 1900hrs on 1 September, nineteen hours after landing at Guam. Our first refuelling was with five KC-135Rs and immediately afterwards the third [airspare] B-52H with Capt Bill Bilton in command turned back to Guam. The second refuelling, sharing the offloads of one KC-10 [the other had gone unserviceable] put us behind on our required fuel plan. For that reason, when two more KC-10s showed up to refuel us south of the Persian Gulf, I decided to take on as much as possible and both aircraft refuelled above the 448,000lb max inflight weight.
>
> As we approached the Straits of Hormuz we began receiving radio calls asking for identification. We gave the standard response of US military aircraft on a routine training mission. These radio calls persisted, warning us that we were nearing a firing zone. Eventually, two Mirage interceptors were launched and gave chase but by then we were into the Gulf and Navy F-14 Tomcats assigned as our cover came to discourage these guys from harassing us. The flight up to this point had been fairly routine, although with a voice satellite radio on board we were getting inputs from Barksdale, Guam and CENTCOM which made for more confusion than anything. This radio also made it possible to receive updates to target priorities, offering greater flexibility but problems too. As we prepared to launch missiles the navigators had realized that the assigned targets now resided on two different tapes, meaning that we would have to 'reboot' the system in the middle of the launch which would require an extra three minutes while the system 'timed out'.
>
> As we approached the southern coast of Kuwait we separated our formation and began launching missiles. Our first three launches were uneventful but we then had to change tapes and the missiles were not ready for launch before reaching the end of our launch box. We had to turn back, having only launched half our loads. There was complete silence and dejection in the aircraft and at 8 AF too as our EW had already radioed back our launch. Sitting in the IP seat I casually mentioned that we should turn around and launch the rest of our missiles as they were now 'timed out' and ready to go. A cheer went up and as the EW radioed back our intentions the pilot continued his turn back to bomb run heading and we launched the remainder of our CALCMs. My aircraft [60-0054 *Mud Buff*] launched six and the other B-52 launched seven.
>
> We reversed our course and headed back out of the Gulf with our Navy escort still in place – those guys did a great job for us. Exiting the Gulf we received the same threatening phone calls and interceptors were launched again but never got within forty miles of our position. Because we had taken on so much gas we still had plenty to recover to Diego without air refuelling. So when a KC-10 showed up with 180k pounds of available fuel I instructed my wingman to take the entire offload and proceed on to Guam where the majority of our maintenance personnel and supplies were still located. Shortly after we had separated the formation another KC-10 from Diego arrived with another 180k. I took the entire offload and headed for Guam myself.
>
> As we neared Thailand the weather turned very bad with thunderstorms everywhere and there were moments when I questioned the wisdom of the decision as our fuel began to dwindle. It turned out I had nothing to worry about as this airplane seems to 'make' gas as it gets lighter and altitude is increased accordingly. We dodged thunderstorms around Vietnam and even talked to some commercial airliners who congratulated us for the mission – I assume they had already heard about it in the news. When we arrived back we did simultaneous approaches on the parallel runways at Andersen AFB, touching down together at dawn; the closest thing to a formation landing a B-52 can do. Everyone was out to meet us, maintenance personnel and officers in formation, saluting us as we taxied in. Though we were tired from the 33.9-hour, 13,600-mile trip everyone was excited about the successful mission.

Col Carpenter and the other thirteen aircrew were awarded the Mackay Trophy for 'the most meritorious flight' of 1996.

Lt Col Floyd L. Carpenter at the controls of the 96th BS 'flagship' B-52H which flew the Desert Strike *mission.*
Lt Col Carpenter

CHAPTER SEVEN

Going Grey

What of the future of the B-52? In reply to a request from the former chairman of the House Committee on Armed Services, the US GAO reviewed the Air Force's *Bomber Roadmap* in its own paper, *Strategic Bombers: Adding Conventional Capabilities Will Be Complex, Time-Consuming and Costly* (February 1993). It concluded that 'if the Air Force retires the B-52Gs in 1994, it will be retiring its most capable conventional bomber before any other bomber will have the equipment that the Air Force says will be needed to attack the [1,250 postulated] high-priority targets... in one or two major regional conflicts'. It fell on deaf ears. The Pentagon proceeded to phase out the remaining B-52Gs as it had planned, with Congressional approval granted on the promise of the new PGMs being just around the corner, permitting the USAF to 'recapitalize' and upgrade its remaining, newer aircraft. The last B-52G departed service in Spring 1994. However, the debate nevertheless highlighted the B-52's potency and drew attention to many of the quarter-century newer B-1B Lancer's teething troubles, making fascinating comparisons between the two.

The svelte Lancer offers fighter-like performance, made possible by its FCGMS (Fuel and Centre of Gravity Management Subsystem) and SMCS (Structural Mode Control System), pushed along by its quartet of GE (USA) F101-GE-102 afterburning turbofans. The swing-wing Lancer can keep pace with modern fighter strike packages and conduct automatic terrain following (based on F-111 experience), giving a glassy-smooth ride to its crew. Lancer apparently possesses a radar cross section which is 1 per cent of the mighty B-52's. However, the B-1B fell short of the 'BUFF' on several counts. Most worrying was its ALQ-161A defensive jamming system, which remains tailored to programming for a single, specific nuclear mission scenario and is not adaptable enough to counter the diversity of threats that would be expected in a medium-to-high intensity conventional war. The B-52 *Pave Mint* and related RWR devices have that flexibility and were recently upgraded to enhance their memory by a staggering 400 per cent!

Countercritics contend that the B-1B 'Bone' would use low level evasion and its low RCS to evade enemy anti-aircraft threats. ECM would be used as a last resort, rather than as the first line of defence, as in the B-52. The truth is that long-range PGMs, already offering up to fifty miles stand-off range (discounting the B-52 with exclusive cruise-missile capability) will very soon mature into 300-mile stand-off weapons. Penetration is an obsolete art which has given way to stealth technology. Moreover, a good ECM package is essential at countering look-down, track-while-scan aerial intercept radars.

Lancer turnaround rates and aircraft availability are also much lower at the time of writing and there are intolerable operational restrictions on the bomber which do not affect the truly all-weather B-52. The B-1B's lack of an anti-icing system for its engine inlets restricts the aircraft from operations 'when moisture is present and when the temperature is below 48 degrees F', otherwise ice tends to accumulate on the inlets and chunks are hoovered up, damaging the engines. Also, pending the incorporation of the new generation of wind-corrected, GPS-aided *Bomber Map* weaponry, the B-1B was really only capable of delivering one type of weapon accurately – the 500lb Mk 82 AIR, at low level, and that too has presented enormous challenges.

The Lancer's three weapons bay Conventional Bomb Modules have an impressive combined capacity of eighty-four Mk 82s, but are complex and time-consuming to install in a pre-loaded format as was originally conceived. The GAO discovered that loading took something like 28-29 hours to accomplish – compared with just one or two hours to load up fifty-one Mk 82s in a B-52, which can employ common Aerospace Ground Equipment such as the ubiquitous

Single-point refuelling of B-52H 60-0013 using the Meyering Pantograph rig, June 1995. Authors

When the USAF decided to phase out B-52 guns and gunners in October 1991, the M61 cannons and related systems were put in storage. A cheesegrater panel covers the boot aperture, with holes to equalize pressure in the rear fuselage. Authors

Long Rifle

Over forty years after its service entry, the B-52 was still setting world records. *Long Rifle*, flown on 25 August 1995, took B-52H 61-0019 from Edwards AFB to Adak Naval Air Station and back in 11hr 23min at an average speed of 556mph. Gulf War (*Secret Squirrel*) veteran, Capt Russ Mathers, and his crew took off at 6am and headed for Greenland but high winds forced them to change course to Atka Island, Alaska instead. Sustained by roast-beef sandwiches the five aircrew returned to Edwards, dropping nineteen inert 500lb ballutes at low level on the Edwards Precision Impact Range Area before landing at 5.38pm. Aboard the B-52 was Ray Lutz, representing the Federation Aeronautique Internationale, who was able to confirm new speed records for an aircraft in the 440,000 to 550,000lb class, carrying an 11,000lb-payload over 10,000km (6,200 miles) unrefuelled. In all, six new records were set, earning the crew the 1995 Curtis E. LeMay award.

Lancer has a lot of catching up to do simply because of time, but the B-52s offer very smooth weapons release whereas the Lancer's turbulent shock-wave causes all sorts of problems. The same was true when the aircraft delivered ostensibly similar Mk 82s, its original mainstay weapon. This problem surfaced at all altitudes, but was especially irksome at low level in deliveries between 200–500ft AGL. During a dozen test drop sorties flown between April and July 1990 using inert Mk 82s, a staggering 294 out of 631 bombs collided after release. The only solution was to increase bomb release intervals to 120–150 milliseconds minimum. The B-52, by contrast, can release its weapons safely at 85–90 millisecond intervals in a similar scenario, enabling it to place them in a much tighter 'box' and achieve greater striking power against smaller targets with less risk of collateral damage. High altitude drops by B-1Bs at 24,000ft and above (calculated to be beyond the range of AAA) resulted in at least one weapon going nearly two miles astray.

B-52 conventional weapons accuracy and diversity was by contrast highly praised in the GAO report. At its zenith the now-retired B-52G could be configured with eight types of general purpose bombs, two special purpose weapons (bullsh**-bombing leaflet canisters), six varieties of CBUs, a dozen sorts of sea mine, two chemical bombs and two Paveway LGBS. And to that could be added ALCM-C, Harpoon and *Have Nap*! Much of this capability has been transferred to the B-52H force already under the CEM (Conventional Enhancement Modification) programme. If B-1Bs employed larger-category stores such as the Mk 84 they would be released from rotary launchers, but at 4–7 second intervals. This implies eight passes on the target, dropping two or three Mk 84s at a time – clearly a ludicrous scenario.

Some serious work has ensued to bring the B-1B's capability up to par, beginning with the addition of CBU delivery capability. The type will still continue to lag behind the B-52 until the new range of precision weapons comes on line at the turn of the century and adequate countermeasures are fielded. There was, after all, a twenty-year gap between the delivery of the last B-52 and the first B-1B. The 'BUFF' an obsolete

'jammer' bomb-loader. Techniques have been sharpened, of course. In a *Lancer Joust* loading competition held at Ellsworth AFB in September 1992, expert bomb assemblers and loaders managed the task in five hours, and nine hours should be a possible goal for regular munitions handlers. However, with only a hundred modules to go round, even with just two-thirds of the inventory active most Lancers would fly with just two modules and an extra fuel tank in lieu of the third, giving them no greater bomb capacity than the valiant 'BUFF', despite the pseudo-'Big Belly' hoopla about the B-1B.

The B-52 also holds its head high when it comes to actual weapons employment, both in terms of diversity of weapons and ordnance release itself. In all fairness, the

Seemingly about to suffer a multiple bird-strike this B-52H made a safe landing. Authors

> ### Rolling around the World
>
> Two B-52Hs of the 96th BS completed a round-the-world flight during 1–3 August 1994 for *Global Power 94-7*. Brig Gen George P. Cole, 2nd BW Commander, led the pair, piloting B-52H 60-0059 *Laissez le Bon Temps Roulez* (*Let the Good Times Roll*), re-named for the mission, *New Orleans II*, after the original world-circling aircraft *New Orleans* of 1924. The other aircraft, 60-0008 *Lucky Lady IV* had the 2nd OG Commander, Col James A. Hawkins at the controls for their 20,000-mile marathon, lasting over 47 hours. Perhaps surprisingly, this was only the fifth non-stop flight around the world. The first, by a B-50A, which also bore the name *Lucky Lady*, won its crew the 1949 Mackay Trophy. Three B-52Bs of Castle AFB's 93rd BW made the second Mackay-winning circumnavigation (45hr 19min) in Operation *Power Flite*, January 1957. In March 1980, a brace of B-52Hs from the 410th BW (61-0028 and 61-0034) also won the Mackay award for a trans-global flight of 45hr 30min, conducting sea control operations en route. *Coronet Bat*, a *Global Power* flight by a pair of 7th BW B-1Bs in June 1995 marked the first world 'circuit' for the Lancer bomber. The only other similar flight so far has been that of the ultra-lightweight trimaran aircraft *Voyager* in December 1986, though it took a total of nine days of non-stop, unrefuelled flight. *Global Power 94-7* required a total of five refuellings by KC-135R and KC-10A tankers from bases in the USA, Japan, Saudi Arabia and Abu Dhabi. *Lucky Lady IV* had a flight surgeon, Capt David R. Nabert aboard to study the effects of fatigue on the crews during the longest jet sorties in aviation history. Most of the crews managed only six hours sleep out of the forty-seven. For Brig Gen Cole it was the last mission before his retirement on 12 August 1994.

old crate? Hardly. At the very worst it provides a vital stop-gap until those new weapons are available in 2000–2004 while also handling the lion's share of the airborne element of America's USSTRACOM nuclear strike force, a tasking since removed from the B-1B altogether. However, it may remain the only viable sea mine sowing platform well into the future and it will be similarly unique in being able to launch an impressive armoury of ALCM-C derivatives. These have been developed with an expanding range of non-destructive ALCM-C 'warheads' capable, for example, of shorting out electricity generating stations by covering them in a ton of wire wool. With a 350-mile stand-off range, ALCM-Cs may help to make the B-52 the ultimate weapon of diplomacy well into the first decade of the twenty-first century. The mere threat of depriving an enemy's hub of activity of its electrical power, or gluing its armour to the ground at staging depots by covering it in tacky chemicals which require over twenty-four hours to clean off, creates a range of non-lethal options which could generate useful diplomatic pressure.

As far as the even newer B-52 replacement, the B-2A Spirit is concerned, in the words of more than one contributor to this book, 'that trillion dollar machine has all but annihilated the Air Force'. It is unlikely to fly from anywhere but its home base (Whiteman AFB) on round-robin Global Reach missions, with occasional refuelling or crew-change stops and very infrequent short deployments. Its cost and the vulnerability of its delicate

> ### The B-52 Renegades: 93rd BS, 917th Wing
>
> Barksdale's 93rd BS is unique in being the only Air Force Reserve Command unit ever to fly heavy bombers. The 917th Wing's two squadrons were formerly A-10A equipped but on 1 October 1993 one was replaced by the 93rd BS with the B-52H. One of the longest-established USAF units, the 93rd and its distinctive Indian Head insignia originated at Kelly Field, Texas in August 1917 flying 157 combat missions with its Spad XIIIs over the trenches in the First World War. It was re-constituted in October 1939 to fly the B-18 Bolo, then the B-17 (including the famous *Suzy Q*) and B-24 with a period of service from Australian bases. Conversion to the Boeing B-29 took the unit into action in the Far East on 16 January 1945. Subsequently it transitioned to the B-47 at Homestead AFB, Florida, moving to the 4239th SW at Kincheloe AFB, Michigan and the B-52 from November 1961 to 1 February 1963.
>
> In mid-1997, the Squadron's 450 personnel and nine grey B-52Hs were assigned a full range of roles including strategic attack, interdiction, Offensive Counter Air (surface), SEAD and minelaying. Its forty-six Reservist 'crewdogs' had daytime jobs ranging from computer programming to teaching, business and roofing. Twenty-one were airline pilots. However, their combined B-52 experience was impressive – pilots averaged 2,060 hours on the type, navigators 2,140 and EWOs 1,910. Over half of them had combat experience.
>
> AFRC rules required crews to fly at least thirty-six sorties a year, though some managed up to eighty in 1996. A typical Flight Duty Day required a crew 'show' three and a half hours before take-off for mission planning, briefing and loading on the coffee and doughnuts for a sortie lasting four to five hours. This was followed by a ninety-minute post-flight and de-brief making a total of nearly ten hours. In the words of the 'squadron scribe' the sortie began when:
>
> > They're out the door and throw more gear on the bus than a family of ten would haul on a vacation to Disneyland. At the aircraft they are met by the world's best maintenance troops who assure the flyers that the fluid dripping from the No. 1 engine is merely morning dew. The bomb-laden behemoth rolls down the runway and finally pushes the earth away, roaring engines painting the sky black. Bombers following in formation grasp at thin air. The first activity after take-off is typically lunch ... ya gotta set your priorities. Next the crewdogs run checklists in preparation for air refuelling. Extra fuel is not normally necessary due to our long legs and short sortie duration, but for purposes of proficiency we rendezvous with the tankers. This is where pilots earn their pay – the good ones fly in contact smooth enough to lull the crew to sleep.
>
> During an actual refuelling the 'boomer' in a KC-135 engages all four of his aircraft's fuel transfer pumps for B-52 link-ups, passing a ton of fuel every twenty seconds during the ten-minute encounter.
>
> > Next comes bombing, the radar navigators' bread and butter. Of course, the enemy's defences are concentrated in the target area so the EWO gets a workout defending the aircraft. Total crew co-ordination and situational awareness are essential for bombs-on-target and safe escape from the threat. The EWO does his magic and support aircraft are called in – the sky is again momentarily still as the threat is suppressed. '5-4-3-2-1-Hack! Bombs away!' Now make for the border. As they say, the mission's not complete until the paperwork is done. The flight home offers time to do all that and make sure you've finished your in-flight lunch – there's never enough. Now comes the endless 'crashes and dashes' in the pattern until the pilots have had their fill of transition work. After your final landing you're off to the Trough Bar for a cold one and to talk about that bounce on the copilot's last touch and go.
>
> The *B-52 Renegades* flew their first sortie on 27 January 1994 and reached combat readiness the following May. Since then they have taken part in some demanding exercises including ACC's *William Tell*, Cannon AFB's *Pecos Thunder*, *Long Shot*, *Coronet Sentry* and several joint exercises with the US Navy. They were Top B-52 squadron at *Gunsmoke '95*. Overseas deployments have included *Pitch Black* in Australia where they successfully evaded F/A-18 Hornets on several occasions. *Blue Harrier* at Fairford, UK in June 1995 brought two B-52Hs (using the squadron's usual 'Scalp' call-sign), one of which (61-0008) was delayed at the end of this 'bare-base' exercise. Lacking the usual ground-start facilities the crew attempted a battery start but the aircraft's battery overloaded and a spare one had to be flown in. On 18 July 1995 a *Renegades*' B-52 flew the first AFRES *Global Power* sortie, joining a Minot B-52H in a twelve-hour flight which included simulated bombing on a range in northern England. By mid-1997, the 93rd had also participated in two other *Coronet* Exercises; *Coronet Voyager* to Andersen AFB and *Coronet Radar* to Moron AB, Spain. In all, the unit averages nearly 2,500 flight hours annually, costing the taxpayer over $23m and playing a vital part in the USAF's *Global Power* strategy. A particular strength was the ability to offer both nuclear and conventional weapons capability as part of the concept which SAC called the 'Twin Triad'.

Although the first production B-1B flew in July 1985, twenty-three years after the last B-52H was delivered, both bombers are crucial elements in the 1998 AAC line-up. B-52H 60-0003 belongs to the 93rd BS, B-52 *Renegades*. Authors

RAM coatings preclude longer TDYs. Although the threat of its stealthy attacks is, no doubt, a deterrent, diplomacy is usually about being *seen* to offer a palpable deterrent. The minute number of B-2As also tends to reduce its credibility in this respect. However, to counter rising criticism the USAF plans to demonstrate deployability of the Spirit and has fabricated eight portable shelters in which RAM repairs can be undertaken away from home. Partial loss of RAM due to erosion from the elements is not seen as a major problem because the grinding-down of enemy defences as a conflict progresses would allow the aircraft sustainable periods of action between major repairs. More resistant RAM coatings are being developed.

Perhaps the ultimate accolade the 'BUFF' has received is that increasingly-heard comment: 'When the last B-1B is retired its crew will fly home in a B-52'. The B-2A, which soaks up money like a sponge, may also be retired when the USAF has its deployable F-22 Raptors with stand-off strike munitions. Possibly, the crew of the last B-2A, having plonked their 'flying wing' in the desert scrub, might well be seen hitching a ride ... in a Boeing B-52 Stratofortress!

Storage – and the Crunch

Preservation
Until the early 1990s, most retired B-52s, in common with other American military aircraft, were dispatched to Davis-Monthan AFB, and the Arizona-based Aerospace Materiel and Reclamation Center (AMARC) for long-term storage and eventual scrapping, after a period in which they might be re-activated for service duty or refurbished for sale overseas.

Before an aircraft is stored it goes through a meticulous preservation process. First, AMARC workers remove guns, ejection seat pyrotechnics, classified equipment and 'pilferable items' (the original Boeing nameplates on B-52 control wheels were a particularly 'mobile' collectors' item). Workers then drain the aircraft's fuel system and pump it full of light oil, which is then drained leaving an oil film to protect the fuel system.

Engine intakes and exhausts are covered, and any gaps or cracks in the upper surface of the airframe are sealed with paper and tape. Workers then spray these areas and other vulnerable surfaces such as fibreglass radomes and cockpit transparencies with a vinyl compound called Spraylat. To prevent condensation within the aircraft the underside remains unsealed to allow free circulation of air. Spraylat, applied in two coats, uses a black coating to exclude dust and water and a white topcoat which is a heat-reflector. Summer temperatures inside unprotected aircraft can reach 200 degrees F causing deterioration of rubber, fabric and electronics. Spraylat keeps internal temperatures within ten to fifteen degrees of those outside. AMARC also uses large plastic bags on some of its 'inmates'.

'BUFFs' get the chop
The 1991 Strategic Arms Reduction Treaty (START) counted 479 B-52s, including operational B-52s. Many of these were 'tall-tails' – including 29 B-52Cs, 92 B-52Ds, 49 B-52Es and 58 B-52Fs – removed from service years ago but not yet reduced to scrap under previous Strategic Arms Limitation Talks (SALT) reductions. In addition to preserving 'BUFFs', AMARC was designated to accomplish the much greater task of eliminating approximately 365 such aircraft over a forty-two month period to comply with START's conditions. B-52G bombers ceased nuclear missions by the end of 1992 and by early May 1994 all were retired and had been (or were about to undergo) 'processing'. The first was broken up on 17 August 1992. The remaining 'tall-tails', which had been something of a tourist attraction for years, underwent the same ignominious fate.

To comply with START, strict procedures were established on how to destroy a heavy bomber, for safety and verification purposes. Destruction had to be conducted in the open so that Russian satellites could plainly see and count each bomber. Once the hazardous fluids, re-usable parts and engines were removed a 13,000lb guillotine blade was hoisted by Linkbelt crane 80ft above the B-52 and dropped on the tail section, severing it from the fuselage. Often, more than one drop was needed to cut through the strong longitudinal fuselage beams. The Damoclean blade was then used to separate wings from fuselage and, just to be sure, the remaining fuselage section was cut into three distinct pieces, leaving the proud bomber looking like a giant dead locust with its wings at its side.

The process left about 100,000lb of scrap, which at 20 cents a pound, yielded around $20,000 in reclaimed alloy per B-52. The treaty also specified that the remains should be visible to satellite observation for a ninety-day period after which the remains could be trucked away. So far, thirty-seven B-52s have escaped the guillotine by becoming museum exhibits.

Lucky **13**'s luck runs out as the scrap men move nearer.

(Below) **A small part of the B-52G fleet awaiting destruction at AMARC alongside venerable early relics still in pre-SIOP paint schemes.** USAF via Jerry Fugere/Ron Thurlow

APPENDIX I

B-52 Production

MODEL	SERIALS	C/N	FIRST/(LAST) DELIVERY	FIRST FLIGHT	QUANTITY
XB-52-BO (Model 464-67)	49-0230	16248		15 April 1952	1
YB-52-BO (Model 464-67)	49-231	16249		2 October 1952	1
B-52A-1-BO (464-201-0)	52-001 to -003	16491-493		5 August 1954	3
RB-52B-5-BO	52-004 to -006	16494-496	3 March 1955	25 January 1955	3
(generic Model No. 464-201-1/4)					
RB-52B-10-BO	52-007 to -0013	16497-503			7
RB-52B-15-BO	52-8710 to -8715	16838-843	June 1955		6
RB-52B-20-BO	52-8716	16844			1
RB-52B-25-BO	53-0366 to -0372	16845-851		August 1955	7
B-52B-25-BO	53-0373 to -0376	16852-855	9 November 1955	7 July 1955	4
(generic Model No. 464-201-3)					
RB-52B-30-BO	53-0377 to -0379	16856-858	3 November 1955 (last)		3
B-52B-30-BO	53-0380 to -0387	16859-866			8
B-52B-35-BO	53-0388 to -0398	16867-877	31 August 1956 (last)		11
B-52C-40-BO	53-0399 to -0408	16878-887	14 June 1956	9 March 1956	10
(generic Model No. 464-201-6)					
B-52C-45-BO	54-2664 to -2675	17159-170			12
B-52C-50-BO	54-2676 to -2688	17171-183	22 December 1956 (last)		13
B-52D-1-BW	55-0049 to -051	464001-003	26 June 1956	14 May 1956	3
(generic Model Number 464-201-7)					
B-52D-5-BW	55-0052 to -0054	464004-006			3
B-52D-10-BW	55-0055 to -0060	464007-012			6
B-52D-15-BW	55-0061 to -0064	464013-016			4
B-52D-20-BW	55-0065 to -0067	464017-019			3
B-52D-20-BW	55-0673 to -0675	464020-022			3
B-52D-25-BW	55-0676 to -0680	464023-027			5
B-52D-55-BO	55-0068 to -0088	17184 -204	1 December 1956	28 Sept 1956	21
B-52D-60-BO	55-0089 to -0104	17205 -220			16
B-52D-65-BO	55-0105 to -0117	17221 -223			13
B-52D-70-BO	56-0580 to -0590	17263 -273			11
B-52D-75-BO	56-0591 to -0610	17274 -293			20
B-52D-80-BO	56-0611 to -0630	17294 -313	1 November 1957 (last)		20
B-52E-85-BO	56-0631 to -0649	17314 -332	7 October 1957	3 October 1957	19
(generic Model No. 464-259)					
B-52E-90-BO	56-0650 to -0656	17333 -339			7
B-52D-30-BW	56-0657 to -0668	464028-039			12
B-52D-35-BW	56-0669 to -0680	464040-051			12
B-52D-40-BW	56-0681 to -0698	464052-069			18
B-52E-45-BW	56-0699 to -0712	464070-083	3 December 1957	17 October 1957	14
B-52E-90-BO	57-0014 to -0022	17408 -416			9
B-52E-95-BO	57-0023 to -0029	17417 -423	2 July 1958 (last)		7
B-52F-100-BO	57-0030 to -0037	17424 -431	18 June 1958	6 May 1958	8
(generic Model No. 464-260)					
B-52F-105-BO	57-0038 to -0052	17432 -446			15
B-52F-110-BO	57-0053 to -0073	17447 -467	25 February 1959		21
B-52E-50-BW	57-0095 to -0109	464084-098			15
B-52E-55-BW	57-0110 to -0130	464099-119			21
B-52E-60-BW	57-0131 to -0138	464120-127	28 May 1958 (last)		8
B-52F-65-BW	57-0139 to -0154	464128-143	14 June 1958	14 May 1958	16

B-52F-70-BW	57-0155 to -0183	464144-172	29 December 1958 (last)		29
B-52G-75-BW	57-6468 to -6475	464173-180	13 February 1959	31 August 1958	8
(generic Model No. 464-253)					
B-52G-80-BW	57-6476 to -6485	464181-190			10
B-52G-85-BW	57-6486 to -6499	464191-204			14
B-52E-90-BW	57-6500 to -6520	464205-225			21
B-52G-95-BW	58-0158 to -0187	464226-255			30
B-52G-100-BW	58-0188 to -0211	464256-279			24
B-52G-105-BW	58-0212 to -0232	464280-300			21
B-52G-110-BW	58-0233 to -0246	464301-314			14
B-52G-115-BW	58-0247 to -0258	464315-326			12
B-52G-120-BW	59-2564 to -2575	464327-338			12
B-52G-125-BW	59-2576 to -2587	464339-350			12
B-52G-130-BW	59-2588 to -2602	464351-365	7 February 1961 (last)		15
B-52H-135-BW	60-0001 to -0013	464360-378	9 May 1961	6 March 1961	13
(generic Model No. 464-261)					
B-52H-140-BW	60-0014 to -0021	464379-386			8
B-52H-145-BW	60-0022 to -0033	464387-398			12
B-52H-150-BW	60-0034 to -0045	464399-410			12
B-52H-155-BW	60-0046 to -0057	464411-422			12
B-52H-160-BW	60-0058 to -0062	464423-427			5
B-52H-165-BW	61-0001 to -0013	464428-440			13
B-52H-170-BW	61-0014 to -0026	464441-453			13
B-52H-175-BW	61-0027 to -0040	464454-467	26 October 1962 (last)		14

MODEL	TOTALS	MODEL	TOTALS
XB-52	1		
YB-52	1		
B-52A	3		
RB-52B	27		
B-52B	23		
B-52C	35		
B-52D-BO	101	B-52D-BW	69
B-52E-BO	42	B-52E-BW	58
B-52F-BO	44	B-52F-BW	45
B-52G	193		
B-52H	102		

NB Block numbers ending in BO indicate Seattle-built aircraft, while those ending in BW were Wichita-built. Generic Model Nos apply to all aircraft with the same letter suffix (for example B-52G).

APPENDIX II

B-52 Operational Units

In 1953, SAC intended to equip seven Bomb Wings with a total of 282 B-52s but this number rapidly rose to eleven Wings, each with forty-five B-52s, by the end of 1955. Ten of these Wings had operated the B-36 Peacemaker, with three Squadrons per Wing. At the end of 1957, five three-squadron B-52 Wings had been established and another three were re-equipping. From then on the policy of dispersing B-52 assets to reduce their vulnerability to ICBM attack introduced the Strategic Wing concept, the first of these being the 4123rd SW at Carswell AFB in December 1957. By mid-1962, a complex re-organization had yielded twenty-two Strategic Wings, each with a single squadron of fifteen B-52s. An exception was the 6th BW at Walker AFB, New Mexico which retained its 'big wing' three squadrons from 1957–63 and assumed a training role. Several other Wings controlled more than one squadron for short periods or for training purposes, particularly the 93rd BW 'Stratofortress College' training Wing at Castle AFB. In all, thirty-three squadrons were established by September 1961 and SAC planned another nine to accommodate its new B-52H production.

A further re-organization took place in 1963 with the replacement of Strategic Wings (SW) by thirty-eight Bomb Wings (BW), mainly those with nameplates which had powerful historical associations. Several remained as Strategic Aerospace Wings (SAW) to indicate 'ownership' of an ICBM squadron. Withdrawal of the early B-52 models began in 1965 and SAC's huge B-52 armada began to diminish with the inactivation of two squadrons at Loring and the 95th BW at Biggs AFB, Texas. More drastic reductions occurred at the end of the 1960s, despite Vietnam commitments, so that SAC had a little over 400 B-52s by the end of 1971. The retirement programme accelerated in 1978 with the withdrawal of the B-52Fs and many B-52Ds, leaving only eighteen active Bomb Wings. By the end of 1983 further reorganization and retirement left only the 263 surviving B-52G/Hs in fifteen Wings, of which three converted to the B-1B in 1986–88. Retirement of the B-52G between 1989 and 1994 eventually left only two Bomb Wings and a single AFRES squadron operating the sixty-five combat-ready B-52Hs between them.

UNITS

2nd BW *Libertatem Defendimus* Barksdale AFB, Louisiana
11BS   B-52H (July 1994–current)
20th BS   B-52F (April 1963–June 1965), B-52H (Dec 1992–current) coded 'LA'
62nd BS   B-52G (June 1965–Dec 1992)
96th BS   B-52H (Oct 1993–current) coded 'LA'
596th BS   B-52G (April 1968–1992), B-52H (1992–Oct 1993) coded 'LA'

5th BW *Kia-O-Ka-Lewa*
23rd BS   B-52G (Feb 1959–July 1968), Travis AFB, California. B-52H (July 1968–current) Minot AFB, North Dakota. Coded 'MT'
31st BS   B-52G (Feb 1959–Jan 1960) Travis AFB, California
72nd BS   B-42H (Jan 1995–Jan 1998). Coded 'MT'

6th BW Walker AFB, New Mexico
24th BS   B-52E (Dec 1957–Jan 1967)
39th BS   B-52E (Dec 1957–Jan 1963)
40th BS   B-52E (Dec 1957–Jan 1967)

7th BW *Mors ab Alto* Carswell AFB, Texas
9th BS   B-52F (June 1958–June 1968), B-52D (Dec 1971–1982), B-52H (1982–Aug 1992)
20th BS   B-52F (June 1965–1969), B-52D (1969–1983), B-52H (1983–Dec 1992) coded 'CW', but this was only applied
                     to B-52H 60-0007, the last B-52 to depart the unit for the 2nd BW
492nd BS   B-52F (June 1958–June 1959)

11th BW Altus AFB, Oklahoma
26th BS   B-52E (Jan 1958–July 1968)
42nd BS   B-52E (Jan 1958–June 1960)

17th BW
34th BS   B-52E (Feb 1963–July 1968), B-52H (Sept 1969–July 1975), Wright - Patterson AFB, Ohio
                     B-52G (Sept 1975– Sept 1976), Beale AFB, California

19th BW *In Alis Vincimus*
28th BS   B-52H (Feb 1962–July 1968) Homestead AFB, Florida. B-52G (July 1968–Oct 1983), Robins AFB, Georgia

22nd BW *Ducemus* March AFB, California
2nd BS   B-52B (Sept 1963–1966), B-52D (1966–Oct 1982), B-52E (1968–1970)
486th BS   B-52D (Oct 1966–July 1971), B-52E (1968–1970)

28th BW *Guardian of the North* Ellsworth AFB, South Dakota
37th BS   B-52H (July 1977–Oct 1982)
77th BS   B-52D (June 1967–1971), B-52G (1971–1977), B-52H (1977–1986)
717th BS   B-52D (June 1957–Feb 1960)
718th BS   B-52D (June 1957–Feb 1960)

39th BW Eglin AFB, Florida
62nd BS   B-52G (Feb 1963–June 1965)

42nd BW *Aetheria Nobis* Loring AFB, Maine
69th BS   B-52C (June 1956–1957), B-52D (1957–1959), B-52G (1959–March 1994)
70th BS   B-52C (June 1956–1957), B-52D (1957–1959), B-52G (1959–June 1966)
75th BS   B-52C (June 1956–1957), B-52D (1957–Oct 1959)

43rd SW *Videmus Omnia* Andersen AFB, Guam
60th BS   B-52D (March 1972–1983), B-52G (1983–April 1990)
63rd BS (P)   B-52D (June 1972–Nov 1973)

68th BW *Follow Me* Seymour Johnson AFB, North Carolina
51st BS   B-52G (April 1963–Sept 1982)

70th BW *Strength Through Unity* Clinton-Sherman AFB, Oklahoma
6th BS   B-52E (Feb 1963–1968), B-52D (1968–Dec 1969)

72nd BW Ramey AFB, Puerto Rico
60th BS   B-52G (Aug 1959–June 1971)

91st BW *Poised for Peace* Glasgow AFB, Montana
322nd BS   B-52D (Feb 1963–June 1968)

92nd BW *Duplum Incolumitatis* Fairchild AFB, Washington
325th BS   B-52D (March 1957–1971), B-52G (1971–85) Coded 'FC'
326th BS   B-52D (March 1957–April 1961)
327th BS   B-52D (March 1957–June 1960)

93rd BW Castle AFB, California
328th BS   B-52B (June 1955–1965), B-52D (June 1956–1958 and 1965–1974), B-52E (1957–1958 and 1967–1970),
                   B-52F (1958–1974), B-52G (1966–1967 and 1974–1994. Coded 'CA'), B-52H (1974–1983)
329th BS   B-52B (June 1955–1965), B-52D (June 1956–1958 and 1965–1971), B-52E (1957–1958 and 1967–1970),
                   B-52F (1958–Sept 1971), B-52G (1966–1967)
330th BS   B-52B (June 1955–1963), B-52D (June 1956–1958), B-52E (1957–1958), B-52F (1958–1963)
4017th CCTS   B-52B (Jan 1955–1956)

95th BW *Justice with Victory* Biggs AFB, Texas
334th BS   B-52B (1959–June 1966)

96th BW *Sempre L'Ora* Dyess AFB, Texas
337th BS   B-52E (Dec 1963–1970), B-52D (1969–1982), B-52H (1982–1985)

97th BW *Venit Hora* Blytheville AFB, Arkansas
340th BS   B-52G (Jan 1960–1992)

99th BW *Caveant Aggressores* Westover AFB, Massachusetts
346th BS   B-52B (1958–1959), B-52C (Dec 1956–1971), B-52D (1957–1961 and 1966–1972)
347th BS   B-52B (1958–1959), B-52C (Dec 1956–1961), B-52D (1957–1961)
348th BS   B-52B (1957–1961), B-52C (Dec 1956–1971), B-52D (1957–1961 and 1966–1972)

306th BW McCoy AFB, Florida
367th BS   B-52D (April 1963–Oct 1973)

307th SW   U-Tapao RTAB, Thailand
364th BS (P)   B-52D (July 1972–June 1975: non-operational July 1972–Jan 1973)
365th BS (P)   B-52D (July 1972–July 1974) non-operational July 1972–Jan 1973)

319th BW *Defensores Libertatis* Grand Forks AFB, North Dakota
46th BS   B-52H (Feb 1963–1982), B-52G (1982–1986)

320th BW *Strength through Awareness* Mather AFB, California
441st BS   B-52F (Feb 1963–1968), B-52G (1968–1989)

340th BW *Anywhere, Anytime* Bergstrom AFB, Texas
486th BS   B-52D (Sept 1963–Oct 1966)

366th WG Mountain Home AFB/Castle AFB
34th BS   B-52G (June 1992–mid 1994. Coded 'MO')

376th SW Controlled B-52Ds deployed to Kadena AB for *Arc Light* missions, Jan–Sept 1970

379th BW *Diligentia at Accuratio* Wurtsmith AFB, Michigan
524th BS   B-52H (May 1961–1977), B-52G (1977–Dec 1992)

380th BW *Strength and Confidence* Plattsburgh AFB, New York
528th BS   B-52G (June 1966–Jan 1971)

397th BW Dow AFB, Maine
596th BS   B-52G (Feb 1963–April 1968)

410th BW K. I. Sawyer AFB, Michigan
644th BS   B-52H (Feb 1963–Nov 1994 Coded 'KI')

416th BW *We Maintain the Balance* Griffiss AFB, New York
668th BS   B-52G (Feb 1963–1992), B-52H (1992–Nov 1994 Coded 'GR')

449th BW Kincheloe AFB, Michigan
716th BS   B-52H (Feb 1963–Sept 1977)

450th BW Minot AFB, North Dakota
720th BS   B-52H (Feb 1963–July 1968)

454th BW Columbus AFB, Mississippi
736th BS   B-52F (Feb 1963–1966), B-52D (1966–July 1969)

456th BW Beale AFB, California
744th BS   B-52G (Feb 1963–Sept 1975)

461st BW Amarillo AFB, Texas
764th BS   B-52D (Feb 1963–March 1968)

462nd SAW Larson AFB, Washington
768th BS   B-52D (Feb 1963–April 1966)

465th BW Robins AFB, Georgia
781st BS   B-52G (Feb 1963–July 1968)

484th BW Turner AFB, Georgia
824th BS   B-52D (Feb 1963–Jan 1967)

494th BW Sheppard AFB, Texas
864th BS   B-52D (Feb 1963–April 1966)

509th BW Pease AFB, New Hampshire
393rd BS   B-52D (April 1966–Nov 1969)

917th BW AFRES/AFRC Barksdale AFB, Louisiana
93rd BS   B-52H (Oct 1993–current. Coded 'BD')

3960th SW Controlled deployed B-52 operations from Andersen
              AFB, Guam (April 1955–March 1970)

4038th SW Dow AFB, Maine
341st BS   B-52G (May 1960–Feb 1963)

4039th SW Griffiss AFB, New York
75th BS   B-52G (Jan 1960–Feb 1963)

4042nd SW K.I. Sawyer AFB, Michigan
526th BS   B-52H (July 1961–Feb 1963)

4043rd SW Wright-Patterson AFB, Ohio
42nd BS   B-52E (June 1960–Feb 1963)

4047th SW McCoy AFB, Florida
347th BS   B-52D (Sept 1961–April 1963)

4123rd SW Carswell, AFB, Texas, and Clinton-Sherman AFB, Oklahoma (from March, 1959)
98th BS   B-52E (Jan 1958–Feb 1963)

4126th SW Beale AFB, California
31st BS   B-52G (Jan 1960–Jan 1963)

4128th SW Amarillo AFB, Texas
718th BS   B-52D (Feb 1960–Jan 1963)

4130th SW Bergstrom AFB, Texas
335th BS   B-52D (Jan 1959–Sept 1963)

4133rd SW Grand Forks AFB, North Dakota
30th BS   B-52H (April 1962–Feb 1963)

4134th SW Mather AFB, California
72nd BS   B-52F (Oct 1958–Feb 1963)

4135th SW Eglin AFB, Florida
301st BS   B-52G (July 1959–Feb 1963)

4136th SW Minot AFB, North Dakota
525th BS   B-52H (July 1961–Feb 1963)

4137th SW Robins AFB, Georgia
342nd BS   B-52G (Aug 1960–Feb 1963)

4138th SW Turner AFB, Georgia
336th BS   B-52D (July 1959–Feb 1963)

4141st SW Glasgow AFB, Montana
326th BS   B-52D (April 1961–Feb 1963)

4170th SW Larson AFB, Washington
327th BS   B-52D (June 1960–Feb 1963)

4228th SW Columbus AFB, Michigan
492nd BS   B-52F (June 1959–Feb 1963)

4238th SW Barksdale AFB, Louisiana
436th BS   B-52F (Aug 1958–April 1963)

4239th SW Kincheloe AFB, Michigan
93rd BS   B-52H (Nov 1961–Feb 1963)

4241st SW Seymour-Johnson AFB, North Carolina
73rd BS   B-52G (July 1959–April 1963)

4245th SW Sheppard AFB, Texas
717th BS   B-52D (Jan 1960–Jan 1963)

A number of Provisional Wings were also established temporarily to manage B-52s detached from other units for combat assignments in Vietnam and the Persian Gulf:

Unit	Location	Aircraft
72nd SW (P)	Andersen AFB, Guam	B-52G (June 1972–Nov 1973) including the 64th BS (P), 65th BS (P), 329th BS (P) and 486th BS (P)
801st BW (P)	Moron, Spain	B-52G (Jan–March 1991)
806th BW (P)	Fairford, UK	B-52G (Feb–March 1991)
1708th BW (P)	Jeddah, Saudi Arabia	B-52G (Jan–March 1991)
4133rd BW (P)	Andersen AFB, Guam	B-52D/F (Feb 1966–July 1970)
4300th BW (P)	Diego Garcia	B-52G (Aug 1990–March 1991)

NB B-52D squadrons often operated a number of B-52Cs as trainers in the 1967–71 period. Tailcodes were allocated with the introduction of Air Combat Command from 1 June 1992.

(Main source: SAC Command Historian)

APPENDIX III

Named B-52 Aircraft

For the first thirty-five years of the B-52's existence the tradition of naming aircraft was generally frowned upon by SAC, possibly out of deference to the nature of its nuclear deterrent mission, except to mark participation in SAC competitions. Names and accompanying nose-art began to appear on SAC FB-111As and B-1Bs in the mid-1980s, and B-52 units eventually followed the fashion. Towards the end of the 1980s CINCSAC Gen John T. Chain encouraged nose-art as a morale enhancer. In keeping with a trend throughout the USAF, names and designs were often of World War II origin as a matter of policy, sometimes using examples from the squadrons' own historical references. Others emulated the contemporary 'heavy metal' popular art styles with greater emphasis on names suggesting the aircraft's destructive power and rather less on pin-up or cartoon-based motifs. Names passed from unit to unit and from 'BUFF' to 'BUFF', sometimes following a crew. Verbal themes like 'midnight' or 'express' persisted, often reflecting the tastes of a particular squadron 'nose-artist'. Names and designs usually appeared beneath the pilot's cockpit window, although they were sometimes painted on the lower area of the nose in smaller letters in the 1960s. The fashion reached a climax, appropriately during the Gulf War period, but a change of policy soon afterwards saw much of the decoration disappear. It made a muted re-appearance on B-52s in the late 1990s.

In the following representative list names are shown with the 'owner' unit at that time in brackets, and changes of name/unit where appropriate. Participation in *Desert Storm* is indicated (DS) with mission totals where these are known.

NB-52A
52-0003	*The High and Mighty One*	(AFFTC)

RB-52B
52-0004	*The Tender Trap*	(AFFTC)
52-8714	*City of Riverside*	(22nd BW)

B-52B
53-0380	*Ciudad Juarez*	(95th BW)
53-0388	*City of El Paso*	(95th BW)
53-0394	*Lady Luck III*	(93rd BW)
53-0395	*City of Turlock*	(93rd BW)
53-0396	*La Vittoria*	(93rd BW)
53-0398	*Lonesome George*	(93rd BW)
	Island of Guam	(95th BW)
	Ciudad Juarez II	(95th BW)
	Lady Luck II	(95th BW)

B-52C
54-2673	*The Big Stick*	(99th BW)

B-52D
55-0061	*Big Country Bomber*	(96th BW)
55-0066	*City of Wichita Falls*	(4245th SW)
55-0067	*City of Forth Worth*	(7th BW)
"	*The Lone Star Lady*	(7th BW)
55-0071	*Calamity Jane*	(7th BW)
55-0072	*City of Austin*	(4130th SW)
"	*City of Orlando*	(306th BW)
55-0083	*Diamond Lil*	(7th BW)
55-0086	*What's Tapioca*	(99th BW)
55-0103	*Happiness is Home*	(99th BW)
55-0111	*Miss Patty J*	(99th BW)
55-0112	*Larson's Lucky Lady*	(4170th SW)
56-0581	*Spokane-City of Lilac*	(92nd BW)
56-0582	(large shark-mouth marking)	(43rd SW)
56-0589	*City of Burkburnett*	(494th BW)
56-0591	*Tommy's Tigator*	(4925th TG)
56-0600	*Nighthawk*	(7th BW)
56-0604	*East to Westover*	(99th BW)

56-0619	*First Lady of Glasgow*	(91st BW)	
56-0620	*Maverick*	(Special Weapons Center, Kirtland)	
"	*Deterrent II*	(Special Weapons Center, Kirtland)	
56-0658	*Cong Crusher*	(99th BW)	
56-0666	*The Beast*		
56-0672	*Night Missions...Blogh!*	(99BW)	
56-0675	*The Lavender Panther*	(92nd SW)	
56-0676	(shark-mouth and star, last B-52D at Andersen)		
56-0677	*City of Fort Worth, Clyde*	(7th BW)	
56-0679	*Yellow Rose*	(7th BW)	
56-0680	*Orlando – Where the Action Is*	(306th BW)	
56-0692	*Lone Star*	(7th BW)	
56-0695	*Early Riser*		

The following names were also applied to B-52Ds although serials are now known: *Amarillo's Pride* (461st BW), *The Sam Houston* (4130th SW), *Okie Special* (70th BW)

B-52E

56-0701	*The Enchanted Lady*	(6th SAW)	
57-0121	*Wings for Peace*	(96th BW)	

Other named B-52Es were *City of Roswell* (6th SAW), *The Lady Altus* (11th BW), *City of Forth Worth* (4123rd SW)

B-52F

57-0034	*Parker's Pride*	(320th BW)	
57-0042	*Hot Stuff*	(454th BW)	
57-0054	*Miss Magnolia*	(454th BW)	
57-0058	*Suzie Q*		

GB-52F

57-0071	*City of Wichita Falls*	(494th BW)	

B-52F

57-0072	*That's All Folks*		
57-0139	*Lady Luck*	(454th BW)	
57-0142	*Chain of Thunder*	(320th BW)	
57-0144	*Mekong Express*		
57-0152	*Casper the Friendly Ghost*	(320th BW)	
57-0153	*State of Louisiana*	(2nd BW)	
57-0163	*City of Sacramento*	(320th BW)	
57-0164	*Connie's Competition*	(320th BW)	
57-0169	*Thunder Express*		

Other named B-52Fs included *Pork Chop Charlie* (454th BW), *State of Mississippi* (4228th SW)

B-52G

57-6468	*Eldership*	(320th BW)	
57-6469	*City of Sacramento*	(320th BW)	
57-6470	*Screaming for Vengeance*	(93rd BW)	
57-6471	*Wolfess 2*	(2nd BW)	
"	*Tantalizing Take-Off*	(97th BW)	DS
57-6472	*Mad Dog*	(379th BW)	
57-6473	*Hard T' Get*	(2nd BW)	
57-6474	*Lone Wolf*	(379th BW)	DS (12)
57-6475	*Miami Clipper II*	(2nd BW)	DSC
57-6476	*The Black Swan II*	(93rd BW)	
57-6477	*A Certain Fury*	(93rd BW)	
57-6478	*Spirit of Solano County*	(5th BW)	
"	*Stars and Stripes*	(320th BW)	
57-6480	*The Big Stick*	(97th BW)	
57-6483	*Ragin' Cajun, Sweet Revenge*	(93rd BW)	
57-6484	*The Phoenix*	(42nd BW)	

57-6484	Express Delivery	(320th BW)	
57-6485	Miss Wing Ding II, Rebel Yell	(97th BW)	
"	Big Stick, We are the People II	(97th BW)	
57-6486	Wild Thing	(93rd BW)	
57-6487	Hoosier Hot Shot	(97th BW)	
57-6488	Shady Lady	(42nd BW)	DS (20)
57-6489	Express Delivery, Astro	(320th BW)	
57-6490	Phantom Four-Ninety	(416th BW)	
57-6491	Little Patches II, Little Princess	(2nd BW)	
57-6492	Old Crow Express	(379th BW)	DS (55)
57-6494 ?	Wabash Cannonball II	(2nd BW)	
57-6495	Dog Patch Express	(97th BW)	
57-6498	Ace in the Hole/Git Sun	(416th BW)	DS (11)
"	Invisible Stalker	(416th BW)	
57-6499	Against the Wind	(93rd BW)	
57-6501	Ragin' Red	(416th BW)	DS (15)
57-6502	Night Stalker	(42nd BW)	
"	Big Hog	(320th BW)	
57-6503	Superstitious Aloysius	(97th BW)	DS
"	The Grim Reaper	(2nd BW)	
57-6504	Snake-Eyes	(93rd BW)	
57-6505	Destination Devastation	(93rd BW)	
57-6506	Command Decision		
57-6508	Outhouse Mouse II	(2nd BW)	DS (5)
57-6509	Queen Andrea Hart	(2nd BW)	
"	Nine-O-Nine II	(2nd BW)	DS (32)
57-6511	Diabolical Angel	(2nd BW)	
57-6513	Memphis Belle II	(43rd BW)	
57-6514	Royal Flush	(93rd BW)	
	Cotton Boll Express III	(97th BW)	
57-6515	Mohawk Warrior	(416th BW)	
"	Ultimate Warrior	(416th BW)	DS (3)
57-6516	Ultimate Warrior	(416th BW)	DS (12)
57-6517	Buffalo Gal II		
57-6518	Leo	(2nd BW)	
"	Leo II	(93rd BW)	
57-6520	Ten-Hi	(2nd BW)	
58-0158	City of Goldsboro	(4241 SW)	
"	Boomerang II	(2nd BW)	
58-0159	Alley Oop's Bold Assault	(379th BW)	DS (47)
58-0160	Midnight Marauder	(2nd BW)	
58-0161	Bayou Belle	(4135th SW)	
58-0162	Surprise Attack		
58-0163	Dragon Lady	(93rd BW)	
58-0164	City of Goldsboro	(4241st SW)	
"	SAC Time	(416th BW)	DS (33)
58-0165	Rolling Thunder	(416th BW)	DS (24)
58-0166	Mission Completed	(2nd BW)	
58-0168	La Forteleza	(72nd BW)	
"	Treasure Hunter	(379th BW)	DS (2)
58-0170	Special Delivery	(28th BW)	
"	Special Delivery II	(416th BW)	DS (20)
58-0171	Li'l Peach II	(2nd BW)	
58-0172	The Negotiator	(43rd BW)	
58-0173	Let's Make a Deal	(379th BW)	DS (43)
58-0175	Viper	(379th BW)	DS (48)
58-0176	Heavy Metal	(416th BW)	
58-0177	Petie 3rd	(2nd BW)	DSC
58-0178	Phoenix II	(4134th SW)	
"	Old Soldier	(43rd BW)	
58-0179	Missbehavin'	(2nd BW)	

58-0181	The Witch II	(2nd BW)	DS (23)
58-0182	What's Up Doc?/Courage	(379th BW)	DS (8)
58-0183	Valkyrie	(93rd BW)	DSC
58-0184	Miss Ouachita II	(2nd BW)	
58-0185	El Lobo II	(2nd BW)	DSC
58-0189	Razorback	(97th BW)	
"	Special Kay	(379th BW)	
"	Midnight Madness	(320th BW)	
58-0191	Bearin' Arms	(93rd BW)	
58-0192	Good to the Last Drop	(93rd BW)	
"	East Coast Outlaw	(42nd BW)	DS (50)
58-0193	Iron Maiden	(416th BW)	
58-0194	Buffasaurus	(379th BW)	DS (47)
58-0195	Avenger	(42nd BW)	
"	Eternal Guardian	(42nd BW)	DS (47)
58-0198	California Star	(379th BW)	
"	Eternal Guardian	(42nd BW)	
58-0199	Specter	(93rd BW)	
58-0200	Wolverine Warrior	(379th BW)	
58-0203	Black Widow	(93rd BW)	DS (58)
"	High n' Mighty	(366th Wg)	
58-0204	Rivet Ace	(Boeing)	
"	Special Delivery	(379th BW)	DS (6)
58-0205	The Wild Hare 2	(2nd BW)	
58-0206	Cultured Vulture	(93rd BW)	
"	Texas Ranger	(42nd BW)	DS (13)
58-0207	City of Merced	(93rd BW)	
"	Special Delivery	(93rd BW)	
58-0210	Conceived for Liberty	(93rd BW)	
58-0211	Miss Ouachita	(97th BW)	
58-0212	Secrut Weapin II, Destroyer	(2nd BW)	
58-0213	Sunrise Surprise	(320th BW)	DS (26)
58-0214	City of Goldsboro	(68th BW)	
"	Ack-Ack Annie II	(2nd BW)	
58-0216	Thunder Struck	(42nd BW)	DS (22)
"	Night Mission II	(2nd BW)	
58-0217	The Liberator	(379th BW)	
58-0218	Night Rider	(42nd BW)	DS
"	Virgo II	(2nd BW)	
58-0220	Night Hawk VI	(93rd BW)	
58-0221	City of Blytheville	(97th BW)	
"	Command Decision	(93rd BW)	
58-0222	Triple Deuce	(97th BW)	
58-0223	Spirit of America	(93rd BW)	
58-0224	Sweet Tracy	(42nd BW)	
58-0225	Mohawk Valley	(4039th SW/416th BW)	
58-0226	Sudden Impact	(42nd BW)	
"	Wreckin' Crew	(42nd BW)	DS (38)
58-0227	Black Buzzard	(379th BW)	
58-0229	Sioux Warrior	(2nd BW)	DS
58-0230	Son of Kilroy	(320th BW)	
"	Black Widow	(42nd BW)	DS (22)
58-0231	High Roller	(416th BW)	DS (2)
58-0232	Disaster Master	(320th BW)	
58-0233	Chow Hound 2	(2nd BW)	
58-0234	Strangelove	(320th BW)	
58-0235	Spirit of Mount Rushmore	(28th BW)	
58-0236	Lucky 13	(2nd BW)	
58-0237	Daffy's Destruction/Blytheville Storm	(379th BW)	DS (8)
58-0238	Miss Fitt II	(2nd BW)	DSC
58-0239	Loring Moose Gooser	(42nd BW)	

58-0240	Silver Bullet	(42nd BW and 93rd Wg 'CA')	
58-0241	Pterodactyl Courier	(42nd BW)	
58-0243	Brute Force	(93rd BW)	
58-0244	Hellsadroppin'	(97th BW)	
58-0245	Equipose II	(2nd BW)	DS (11)
58-0247	Dream Warrior/High Plains Drifter	(379th BW)	DS (4)
58-0249	Urban Renewal	(379th BW)	DS (10)
58-0250	Surprise Attack II	(2nd BW)	DS (15)
58-0251	It's Personal	(42nd BW)	
"	Honey Suckle Rose	(43rd BW)	
58-0252	Maine DOWneaster	(4038th SW)	
"	Sagittarius II	(2nd BW)	
58-0253	Appetite for Destruction	(42nd BW)	DS (53)
58-0254	Damage Inc.	(93rd BW)	
58-0255	Guardian of the Peace	(42nd BW)	DS (56)
58-0257	Horsepower Ltd/Man o'War III	(2nd BW)	
"	We Make Nightmares	(42nd BW)	
"	First Strike, Dr Feelgood	(42nd BW)	DS (56)
58-0258	Claim Busters	(320th BW)	
"	Dog Breath	(2nd BW)	
59-2565	Killer Time	(320th BW)	
"	Big Shmoo II	(2nd BW)	
59-2566	The Wild Potatoe	(416th BW)	
59-2567	–		DS (21)
59-2568	Beast of the East	(416th BW)	DS (13)
59-2570	Ole Baldy II	(2nd BW)	DS (55)
"	Equaliser	(42nd BW)	
"	City of Bossier City	(2nd BW)	
59-2571	Duchess II	(97th BW)	
59-2572	SAC Time	(93rd BW)	
59-2573	Avenger	(42nd BW)	DS (16)
59-2575	City of Warner Robins	(4137th SW)	
"	Large Marge	(93rd BW)	
59-2577	City of Macon	(4137th SW)	
"	Majestic	(93rd BW)	
59-2578	Iron Fortress	(Sheppard TTC)	
59-2579	Sooiee	(97th BW)	
"	Armed and Ready/Make My Day	(379th BW)	DS (10)
59-2580	Arkansas Razorback	(97th BW)	
"	Sherriff's Posse No. 2		DS (16)
59-2581	Grand Illusion	(2nd BW)	
"	Mervin the Magician		
59-2582	Grim Reaper II	(2nd BW)	DSC
59-2583	Rushin' Nightmare	(416th BW)	DS (42)
59-2584	Memphis Belle III	(97th BW)	
"	Midnight Express	(93rd BW)	
"	Midnight Rendezous	(93rd BW)	
59-2585	Yossarian's Question	(320th BW)	
"	Swashbuckler	(42nd BW)	DS (22)
59-2586	The Final Decision	(2nd BW)	
"	Silent Arrrival	(NASA)	
59-2587	Stratofortress Rex	(93rd BW)	
59-2588	The Eagle's Wrath II	(2nd BW)	
59-2589	Darkest Hour/Big Bubba Does Baghdad	(379th BW)	
"	The War Bitch	(379th BW)	DS (10)
59-2590	Better Duck II	(2nd BW)	DS (20)
59-2591	Sweet Revenge	(379th BW)	DS (7)
"	Sudden Impact	(379th BW)	
59-2592	The Lavender Panther/Spokane, Washington	(325th BS)	DS
59-2593	–		DS
59-2594	Loaded Dice	(97th BW)	

NAMED B-52 AIRCRAFT

"	*Memphis Belle III*	(97th BW)	
59-2594	*Black Widow*	(93rd BW)	
59-2595	*Northern Howler*	(42nd BW)	
59-2596	*The Eager Beaver*	(43rd BW)	
59-2598	*Dangerous Toys*		
"	*Without Warning*	(42nd BW)	**DS** (49)
59-2599	*Wild Thing*	(42nd BW)	
"	*The Eagle's Wrath II*	(97th BW)	
59-2601	*Itzagoer, Tarheel II*	(68th BW)	
"	*Tarheel Triumph*	(68th BW)	
59-2602	*Yankee Doodle II*	(97th BW)	**DS** (6)*

* this aircraft may not have taken part in *Desert Storm* but carried these scores.
DSC indicates participation in the 2nd BW CALCM mission against northern Iraq in January 1991 (*see Global Reach – Global Power*).

The following names were also used on B-52Gs, although serials and/or units are not known in most cases:
American Maid (42nd BW), *Dream Weaver* (42nd BW), *Night Hawk* (28th BW), *Bomerang* (2nd BW), *Little Miss Mischief II* (2nd BW), *Boss Hog* (320th BW), *Godzilla* (320th BW), *Ground Pounder* (320th BW), *Forty Niner* (320th BW), *Northern Tier Howler* (42nd BW), *Phoenix, Black Buzzard* (379th BW), *Merlin, The Liberator* (379th BW), *Night Mission* (416th BW), *Equipoise* (2nd BW), *Miss Barbara M* (2nd BW)

B-52H

60-0001	*State of Michigan*	(379th BW)
"	*First Strike*	(7th BW)
"	*Memphis Belle IV*	(2nd Wg. 'LA')
"	*Black Magic II*	(5th BW)
60-0002	*Deuces Wild, Wilbur*	(17th BW)
"	*Urban Renewal*	(2nd BW)
60-0003	*Sheer Destruction*	(5th BW)
"	*Master Blaster*	(7th BW)
"	*Mohawk Valley II*	(416th BW)
60-0004	*Updraft, Baron Bugler*	(5th BW)
60-0005	*Monkey Business*	(416th BW)
"	*Warlord, Lobo*	(5th BW)
60-0007	*Dak Rat*	(5th BW)
"	*Maj H. S. Carswell*	(7th BW)
60-0008	*The Baron, Dragonslayer*	(5th BW)
"	*Lucky Lady IV*	(2nd BW 'LA')
"	*Dear Rocky, Not To Win Is A Very Bad Thing*	(19th BW)
60-0009	*Black Magic, Rolling Thunder II*	(5th BW)
"	*Bayou Bangel*	(2nd BW)
"	*Cloud Nine*	(7th BW)
60-0010	*Smaug's Revenge*	(7th BW)
"	*The Insti-gator*	(2nd BW, 'LA')
60-0011	*Cajun Dragon*	(2nd BW, 'LA')
"	*Wild Thang*	(5th BW)
"	*Snake Eyes*	(7th BW)
60-0012	*Bayou Bengal*	(2nd BW)
"	*The Big Stick*	(410th BW)
60-0014	*Intimidator*	(7th BW), Un-named: Pit bull
"	*Global Reach and Power*	(2nd BW, 'LA')
"	*Krewe of the Gemini*	(2nd BW)
"	*Victorious Secret*	(416th BW)
60-0015	*Special Delivery*	(92nd BW)
"	*No Antidote*	(5th BW, 'MT')
60-0016	*Red River Beast*	(2nd BW)
"	*The Baroness*	(5th BW)
"	*Spirit of Texas, Junkyard Dog*	(7th BW)
60-0017	*Bodcau Buzzsaw*	(2nd BW)
"	Un-named: Reaper art	(7th BW)
60-0018	*Guided Spirit*	(5th BW 'MT')

NAMED B-52 AIRCRAFT

60-0018	Darth Gator	(7th BW)
60-0019	Hell Razor	(7th BW)
60-0020	The Mad Bolshevik	(2nd BW)
60-0021	Black Jack	(7th BW)
60-0022	Yosemite Sam marking on tail	(319th BW)
60-0023	Warlord	(92nd BW)
"	Bomber Barons	(5th BW)
60-0024	Pride of the U. P.	(4042nd SW)
"	Guardian	(416th BW)
"	Six Pack-Free Delivery	(7th BW)
"	I'll Be Seeing You	(416th BW)
"	Snowbird	(410th BW)
60-0025	Atomic Dog	(7th BW)
"	Yosemite Sam (tail)	(319th BW)
"	Ol' Crow Express II	(2nd BW, 'LA')
60-0026	Rocky	(410th BW)
"	Red River Raiders	(319th BW)
"	Van Camp's Raiders	(319th BW)
"	Predator	(5th BW)
60-0027	Peace Persuader	(4136th SW)
60-0028	Opus	(5th BW)
60-0029	Athena	(5th BW)
"	Rocky	(5th BW)
60-0030	Luck o' the Irish	(410th BW)
"	Miss Liberty	(416th BW, 'GR')
"	Le France Libre	(416th BW, 'GR')
60-0031	War Goddess	(7th BW)
"	Yankee Rose II	(5th BW)
60-0032	MYAKINAS	(92nd BW)
"	El Lobo	(7th BW)
60-0033	Peace Maker	(410th BW)
"	Some Like it Hot	(416th BW)
"	Instrument of Destruction	(5th BW)
60-0034	Predator	(410th BW)
"	Slightly Dangerous	(410th BW)
"	Wise Guy	(5th BW)
60-0035	Land Scaper	(7th BW)
"	Special Delivery	(5th BW)
"	Louisiana Red Hawk	(2nd BW)
"	Louisiana Hot Turbin	(2nd BW)
"	SAC Time	(416th BW)
60-0036	Surprise Attack	(5th BW)
"	The Tagboard Flyer (D-21 mothership)	(5th BW)
60-0037	Black Widow	(5th BW)
60-0039	Spirit of '69	(319th BW)
60-0040	Peace Persuader	(4136th SW)
"	Watchman	(92nd BW)
"	Black Widow	(410th BW)
60-0042	Monster of the Midway	(2nd BW)
660-0043	Bridesmaid Becky	(410th BW)
60-0044	Better Duck	(92nd BW)
"	Radical Buff	(92nd BW)
"	Soo City Soo	(4239th SW)
"	Magnum Force	(5th BW)
60-0045	Ready for Duty	(92nd BW)
60-0046	Magicians-Best in SAC	(5th BW)
"	Iron Butterfly	(7th BW)
"	Aged to Perfection	(5th BW)
"	Red River Raiders	(319th BW)
60-0047	Classy Chassis	(410th BW)
60-0048	Stratofortress Rex, La Bomba	(410th BW)

60-0049	*Bayou Classic*	(2nd BW)
"	*City of Fort Worth*	(7th BW)
60-0050	*Dragon's Inferno*	(412th TS, Edwards)
60-0051	*Bear Hunter*	(7th BW)
"	*Prairie Warrior!*	(5th BW)
60-0053	*Nightstalker, Iron Eagle*	(7th BW)
60-0054	*El Lobo*	(7th BW)
"	*Ice Baby*	(5th BW)
"	*Mud Buff*	(2nd BW)
60-0055	*Midnight Magic*	(5th BW)
"	*SALT Shaker*	(7th BW)
"	*Old Crow Express II*	(5th BW)
60-0056	*Real Steel*	(410th BW)
"	*Taz*	(5th BW)
60-0057	*Knight Warrior*	(5th BW)
"	*Nemesis*	(2nd BW)
"	*Someplace Special*	(410th BW)
60-0058	*Great Balls of Fire*	
60-0059	*Whiplash*	(7th BW)
"	*Laissez le Bon Temps Roulez*	(2nd BW, 'LA')
"	*New Orleans II*	(2nd BW)
"	*Carswell Vice*	7th BW)
60-0060	*Diamond Girl*	(410th BW)
"	*Screamin' Genie*	(5th BW)
"	*Miss Liberty, Ol'Smokie*	(416th BW)
"	*Iron Butterfly*	(5th BW)
60-00061	*Paul Bunyan*	(379th BW)
"	*About Average*	(5th BW and 92nd BW)
60-0062	*Cajun Fear*	(2nd BW, 'LA')
61-0001	*Visibility Perfect, War Hawg*	(92nd BW)
61-0002	*Midnight Express*	(7th BW)
"	*The Eagle's Wrath III*	(2nd BW)
61-0003	*Miss Behavin'*	(92nd BW)
"	*Dragon Slayer*	(5th BW)
"	*Buff Bunny*	(5th BW 'MT')
61-0004	*Confessor*	(7th BW)
"	*Opus*	(5th BW)
"	*El Lobo*	(2nd BW)
61-0005	*Homestead's Hesperides*	(19th BW)
"	*Texas Two-step*	(7th BW)
61-0007	*Metal Mistress*	(92nd BW)
"	*Ghost Rider*	(5th BW)
61-0008	*Lucky Sherry/Strictly Loaded*	(92nd BW)
61-0009	*Wild Thing, The Albatross*	(92nd BW)
"	*Great Eagle of the North*	(410th BW)
61-0010	*Nightmares*	(7th BW)
61-0011	*Buff Rider*	(5th BW)
"	*Ragin' Cajun*	(2nd BW)
"	*The Heat/Tarrant County Sheriff*	(7th BW)
"	*Dressed to Kill*	(2nd BW)
61-0012	*Arnold*	(23rd BW)
"	*Ready to Strike*	(410th BW)
"	*Minot Magician*	(5th BW)
"	*Glory Days*	(2nd BW)
61-0013	*Real T. A., Warrior's Pet*	(410th BW)
61-0014	*Predator*	(2nd BW)
61-0015	*Peace Garden Princess*	(4133rd SW)
"	*American Eagle*	(416th BW)
"	*Yabba Dabba Deux*	(2nd BW)
61-0016	*Sweet 16*	(92nd BW)

61-0016	*POW/Bring 'Em Home MIA*	(7th BW)
"	*Batteries Not Included*	(2nd BW)
61-0017	*Renegade*	(92nd BW)
61-0018	*Homestead's Hesperides XII*	(19th BW)
"	*Christine*	(92nd BW)
"	*Dark Wing Duck*	(2nd BW)
"	*Griffiss 50th Anniversary*	(416 BW)
"	*Deadly Prescription*	(5th BW)
61-0019	*Jolly Roger*	(410th BW)
61-0020	*Nightstalker*	(410th BW)
"	*Deadly Prescription*	(5th BW)
61-0021	*Iron Eagle*	(7th BW)
61-0022	*Ridge Runner*	(92nd BW)
"	*The Intimidator*	(5th BW)
61-0023	*Sod Buster*	(5th BW)
61-0024	*Hell Razor*	(7th BW)
"	*Souris River Nymph*	(5th BW)
61-0025	*Shack Rabbit*	(410th BW)
61-0027	*Land Scaper II*	(7th BW)
61-0028	*Someplace Special*	(410th BW)
61-0029	*Renegade*	(5th BW)
61-0031	*Destiny Unknown*	(92nd BW)
"	*Old Crow Express II*	(5th BW)
"	*Ol Smokie*	(2ndBW)
61-0034	*Predator*	(410th BW)
"	*Vigilance*	(5th BW)
61-0035	*Freebird*	(2nd BW)
61-0036	*Skywolf*	(92nd BW)
"	*Balto*	(5th BW)
61-0038	*Dogs of War*	(7th BW)
"	*.38 Special*	(2nd BW)
61-0039	*Lone Star One*	(96th BW)
"	*Appetite for Destruction*	(5th BW)
61-0040	*Heavenly Body, Watchman*	(92nd BW)
"	*City of Fairborn*	(7th BW)
"	*Wonderful Lady*	(92nd BW)
"	*Spirit of Kitty Hawk*	(17th BW)

The following B-52H aircraft also received names: *City of Dayton* (17th BW), *WinterHawk* (92nd BW)

Nose art regulations

In common with Project *Warrior* which, from June 1987 set firm guidlines for nose-art on 20th TFW F-111Es, SAC policy on this topic was typically prescriptive. Designs were to be historical (that is, based on WWII precedents), or community/mission related and 'gender neutral'. All submissions from groundcrew had to be approved by the Wing Commander and a 10 × 8 photograph was required at HQ AFMC for their scrutiny. Even the colours were specified (FS 31136 red, 35109 blue, 37038 black, 30111 brown and 32169 orange). However, like all rules they were made to be bent and a glance at a selection of the results reveal a much broader palette. Rules on location were generally observed. Designs were to appear below the pilot's windshield, no larger than 4 × 4 feet. The use of cartoon figures required the unit to clear themselves for copyright infringements. Brightly coloured designs were to be painted out during deployments. For *Desert Storm* many deployed aircraft had some artwork on their noses and tails crudely obliterated, sometimes with black or dark red paint.

Additional data for this list supplied by Ron Thurlow and Brian Rogers.

APPENDIX IV

B-52 Deployments to the United Kingdom

1957–1966 Regular visits by B-52s to the UK began over forty years ago, with Marham, Brize Norton, Fairford, Greenham Common and Upper Heyford as the host RAF bases, partly because of their SAC-length runways. By July 1979, over 150 B-52s had made temporary deployments to these locations. The earliest recorded example was B-52B 53-0395 *City of Turlock* from the 93rd BW on 16 January 1957. It was involved in Operation *Power Flite,* an around-the-world non-stop flight by three other 93rd BW B-52Bs. In May 1958 Brize Norton hosted a week-long deployment by six B-52Ds, three of which (56-0584, -0599, -0674) were later to become *Linebacker II* casualties. A further six, this time B-52Es of the 6th BW, repeated the visit in April 1960 and the base recorded two visits by single B-52D and B-52F aircraft, while Greenham Common and Upper Heyford received their first callers; a B-52 (56-0589) and B-52F (57-0039) respectively. Additionally, B-52G 58-0248 (a *Desert Storm* participant thirty-one years later) overflew a number of RAF Battle of Britain Displays on 17 September 1960, giving the British public their first glimpse of the mighty machine.

The three bases received a total of eleven migrants in 1961 and six in 1962, the year in which Fairford had its first visit (B-52F 57-0052). The introduction of a SAC Initiative Training Programme late in 1963 brought sixteen B-52s, including a B-52H to the bases, excluding Upper Heyford, on long-distance solo navigation and orientation exercises. There was an even bigger increase the following year. Brize Norton picked up most of the B-52 traffic from Greenham Common when the latter closed as a *Reflex Action* SAC base in 1964. A total of seventy-eight singleton aircraft made the Atlantic crossing in 1964, a peak year for B-52 deployments. The flow diminished to ten for 1965, one of them being B-52D 55-0675 which already wore the 'O-for-obsolescent' prefix to its serial, and dried up altogether for 1966.

1967–1997 *Giant Strike/Double Top.* In mid-February 1967 B-52H 61-0040 spent a couple of days at RAF Marham, Norfolk evaluating the base's suitability as a fourth B-52 operating location. It was the first of forty-six B-52s to fly into Marham over the following fourteen years to take part in eleven RAF/USAF Bombing and Navigation Competitions which SAC called *Giant Strike* and the RAF knew as *Double Top.* The 'players' were the RAF's Strategic Vulcan and Victor tanker Force, B-52F, G and H bombers from all SAC units, and their supporting KC-135s. For *Giant Strike 3* a pair of SAC FB-111As also attended and flew the courses, although they didn't compete. The Competition ended with the withdrawal of the Vulcan from RAF service.

1967: *Giant Strike 1.* B-52F 57-0039 (93rd BW), B-52H 60-0008 (19th BW), B-52H 60-0049 (449th BW). *4th–20th March.*
1970: *Giant Strike 2.* Preparatory visit by: B-52G 57-6469 (2nd BW), 58-0158 (320th BW), B-52H 60-0037 (379th BW). Competitors: B-52G 58-0158 (320th BW), 59-2583 (2nd BW), B-52H 60-0037 (379th BW), 61-0016 (319th BW). *8 April–12 May.*
1971: *Giant Strike 3.* B-52G 57-6500 (320th BW), 59-2583 (2nd BW), B-52H 60-0019 (379th BW), 60-0024 (410th BW). *7–28th April.*
1972: *Giant Strike 4.* B-52G 57-6509 (2nd BW), 59-2580 (28th BW), B-52H 60-0013 (449th BW), 61-0002 (17th BW). *13 April–24 May.*
1973: *Giant Strike 5.* B-52H 60-0004 (319th BW), 60-0012 (17th BW), 60-0021 (5th BW) 61-0014 (410th BW). *28 March–9th May.*
1976: *Giant Strike 6.* B-52G 57-6505 (2nd BW), 58-0181 (92nd BW), 58-0207 (97th BW), 59-2589 (310th BW). *5 March–16 April.*
1977: *Giant Strike 7.* B-52H 60-0015 (410th BW), 60-125 (449th BW), 60-0030 (5th BW), 60-0054 (319th BW). *14 April–20 May.*
1978: *Giant Strike 8.* B-52G 57-6503 (92nd BW), 57-6517 (2nd BW), 58-0206 (379th BW), 59-2584 (2nd BW). *7 June–7 July.*
1979: *Giant Strike 9.* B-52H 60-0049 (28th BW), 60-0054 (319th BW), 60-0058 (410th BW), 61-0003 (28th BW). *5 June–21 July.*
1980: *Giant Strike 10.* B-52G 59-2577 (2nd BW), 58-0189 (379th BW), 58-0193 (68th BW), 59-2580 (97th BW), 59-2583 (320th BW). *23 June–2 Aug.*
1981: *Giant Strike 11.* B-52H 60-0057 (410th BW), 60-0026 (319th BW), 60-0046 (5th BW), 61-0022 (319th BW), 61-0028 (410th BW). *9 June–18 July.*

Busy Brewer/Mighty Warrior

Apart from the *Giant Strike* delegations the British bases saw virtually nothing of SAC's B-52s for over ten years from 1965. The exceptions were B-52H 60-0043 for Mildenhall Air Fête in 1971, B-52F 58-0159 at Upper Heyford and B-52F 57-0152 which spent three days at Brize Norton in November 1969. However, in September 1976 Upper Heyford welcomed four B-52Ds from the 7th BW for NATO Exercise *Teamwork*, initiating regular support for large NATO initiatives of this kind. As East–West tensions in the late 1970s increased it became US policy to add visible muscle to the USAF presence in Europe. Short-notice B-52 deployments (initially known as *Bush Brewer* exercises) were an easy way to demonstrate how quickly reinforcements could be provided. In Spring 1978 the USAF Chief of Staff stated that 'there are plans to use B-52s in Europe as necessary to offset the theatre capabilities of the Soviet Backfire strategic bomber'. Both RAF Lakenheath and RAF Sculthorpe were considered for additional B-52 rotations, and RAF Mildenhall was extended to provide extra tanker space. In September 1979 RAF Fairford commenced operations as a second KC-135 location. There was a big increase in B-52 deployments in the following two years, with *Busy Brewers* commencing in May 1979. In later years similar code names were used for B-52 deployments to the other forward bases. For example, *Busy Alley* took two 2nd Wing aircraft to Andersen AFB in September 1988. Deployed training to Moron, Spain began in October 1983 with Exercise *Eternal Triangle/Crispex.*

B-52 deployments normally involved about four aircraft, together with their tankers and logistical support transport aircraft, timed to coincide with a major exercise in Europe. *Teamwork'76,* for example involved 200 ships and 300 aircraft from the USAF, USN, USMC, RAF and other NATO partners. The following deployments to UK bases are representative of SAC (later ACC) commitment to NATO from 1976 to 1996 and indicate the changing patterns in B-52 sub-types involved, numbers, bases and in the composition of deployments.
Exercise *Teamwork* (Upper Heyford) B-52D 55-0090, 0673, 56-0671, 0672. (7th BW) 15 Sep–23 Sep 1976. Missions were flown daily during this period.
Busy Brewer Three 68th BW B-52Gs flew a 16hr practice bombing mission to Germany, non-stop in November 1978. This was followed by Exercise *Certain Sentinel* involving four B-52Ds of the 22nd BW on a similar

mission, and other flights of this kind in later years.

Exercise *Flintlock/Dawn Patrol. Busy Brewer* (Upper Heyford) B-52D 55-0677, -0107, 56-0659 (96 BW). 9–25 May 1979. The first (practice) B-52 contingency deployment to a foreign base since the Vietnam War.

Exercise *Cold Fire* (Marham) B-52D 55-0087, 56-0679, -0683 (7th BW) From 11 September to 8 October 1979.

Exercise *Open Gate* (Marham) B-52D 55-0071, -0080, 56-0694 (22nd BW) From 23 April to 19 May 1980. *Open Gate* exercises often involved sorties into Southern Europe.

Exercise *Cloudy Chorus* (Fairford) B-52D 55-0073, 56-0060, -0658 (7th BW). 10–16 June 1980.

Exercise *Priory/Busy Brewer* (Upper Heyford) B-52D 55-0677, 56-0585 (96th BW) 15–18 July 1980.

Busy Brewer (Brize Norton) B-52D 56-0606, -0617, -0671. (22nd BW) 25–29 August 1980.

Exercise *Teamwork/Cold Fire/Display Determination* (Brize Norton) B-52D 55-0677, 56-0659, -0676 [MiG killer] (96th BW) From 10 September to 15 October 1980.

Busy Brewer (Upper Heyford) B-52D 55-0090, 0113, 56-0698 (7th BW) 11–18 November 1980.

Exercise *Priory/Busy Brewer* (Brize Norton) B-52D 55-0105, 56-0585, -0686, (96th BW) 3–16 April, 1981 and B-52D 56-0600, -0679, -0690 (7th BW) From 24 April to 15 May 1981.

Busy Brewer (Upper Heyford) B-52D 55-079, -0088, 56-0606 (22nd BW) 6–26 June 1981.

Busy Brewer (Marham) B-52D 55-0075, -0079, 56-0606 (22nd BW) and B-52D 55-0107, 56-0689 (96th BW) 1–25 September 1981.

Exercise *Priory 3/81/Busy Brewer* (Fairford) B-52D 55-0069, -0070, 56-0690 (7th BW). From 20 October to 13 November 1981.

Busy Brewer (Marham) B-52G 58-0167, 57-6518, 59-2594 (2nd BW). From 27 May to 9 June 1982. Also three B-52D from 22nd BW from mid-April to 14 May 1982.

Exercise *Northern Wedding* (Fairford) B-52G 58-0172, -0192, -0197 (19th BW) and B-52G 58-0207, -0236 (42nd BW). From 7 Sept to late September 1982.

Exercise *Autumn Forge/Busy Brewer* (Brize Norton) B-52G 59-2588, -2596, -2599 (2nd BW). From 12 September to late September 1983.

Exercise *Open Gate/Busy Brewer* (Upper Heyford) B-52G 57-6478, 58-0213, -0250 (320th and 2nd BW). From 24 April to 18 May 1984. Included missions in the area of Spain and Portugal.

Busy Brewer (Fairford) B-52G 58-0253, 57-6520, 59-2599 (2nd BW). From 15 September to 12 October 1984. Included participation in NATO Exercise *Lionheart* in Central Germany.

Busy Brewer 85A (Fairford) B-52G 57-6489, -6506, 06512, 6519, 58-0201, 59-2586, -2599 (2nd BW). From 24 May to 20 June, 1985. Largest single B-52 deployment to UK up to this date; previous large deployments were 'staged' in batches of three or four aircraft.

Exercise *Ocean Safari* (Fairford) B-52G 57-6468, -6469, -6476, 58-0226, -0258, 59-2565, -2598. (42nd BW). From 6 September to 11 October 1985. Included Harpoon anti-shipping trials and a short deployment by three aircraft to Sidi Slimane, Morocco.

Exercise *Northern Wedding/Busy Brewer 86B* (Fairford) B-52G 58-0216, -0240, 59-2569 (2nd BW). 29 August–6 October 1986. B-52G 59-2570 (42nd BW) was at Mildenhall for continued Harpoon trials, 18–27 August 1986, under Exercise *Giant Quail*.

Busy Brewer 87/1 (Fairford) B-52G 58-0172, -0241, 59-2578 (42nd BW). *1–20 May 1987 and* B-52G 57-6510, 58-0202, -0240, (42nd BW) From 20 May to 8 June 1987. Included further Harpoon simulations with RN ships.

Exercise *Autumn Forge/Busy Brewer 87-2* (Fairford) B-52G 58-0172, -0224, 59-2596 (42nd BW and B-52G 57-6506, 58-0216, -0218, 59-2588 (2nd BW) From 1 September to 4 October 1987.

Busy Brewer 88-1 (Fairford) B-52G 58-0224, -0226, -0232, -0240, -0241, -0251, 59-2596 (42nd BW). From 29 April to 16 May 1988.

Exercise *Central Enterprise/Busy Brewer* (Fairford) B-52G 57-6476, 58-0212, 59-2569, -2588, -2595 (2nd BW). 3–17 June 1988.

Busy Brewer (Marham) B-52G 58-0241, 58-0251 (42nd BW) 13–24 June 1988 Harpoon Trials.

Exercise *Mighty Warrior* (Fairford) B-52G 58-0186, -0224, -0225, -0226, -0241, -0251, 59-2573 (42nd BW) From 29 July to 10 August 1988. First of SAC's *Mighty Force* detachments to the UK, providing crews with experience of 'bare base' operations. Developed from Rapid Shot deployments to Guam and in USA at bases such as Roswell.

Exercise *Giant Squid* (Marham) B-52G 58-0241, 0251, (42nd BW) 15–24 June 1988. In connection with RAF Kinloss-based exercise.

Exercise *Teamwork/Busy Brewer* (Fairford) B-52G 58-0213, -0226, -0235, -0255 (42nd BW). 2–19 September 1988.

Exercise *Busy Warrior/Open Gate 89* (Fairford) B-52G 58-0241, 59-2595 (42nd BW) 18–21 April 1989. Detached to Moron for *Open Gate* phase.

Exercise *Sharp Spear/Mighty Warrior* (Fairford) B-52G 58-0232, -0240 (42nd BW) and 58-0189, -0216, -0233, 59-2565, -2570 (2nd BW). The 42nd BW aircraft operated from RAF St Mawgan 11–21 September 1989 in support of Exercise *Sharp Spear*.

Exercise *Busy Warrior 90-1/Elder Forest/Blue Harrier* (Fairford) B-52G 58-0212, -0258, 59-2598 (2nd BW). 19–30 April 1990. Supporting UK air defence exercise. Involved 184 deployed personnel.

Mighty Warrior/Central Enterprise (Fairford) B-52G 58-0202, -0258, 59-2570, -2588 (2nd BW) 12–25 June 1990. Involved 263 deployed personnel.

The *Busy Warrior* deployment to Fairford for September 1990 was cancelled because of the situation in Kuwait/Iraq.

806 BW (P) Detachment (Fairford) B-52G 58-0237 (93rd BW), 58-0168, -0182, -0204, -0247, 59-2579, -2589 (379th BW), 57-6498, 58-0231 (416th BW). From 5 February to 9 March 1991. *Desert Storm* detachment.

Mighty Warrior (Fairford) B-52G 58-0195, -0206, -0216, -0218, -0226 (42nd BW). From 29 August to 14 September 1991.

Exercise *Elder Forest/Teamwork 92* (Fairford) B-52G 58-0195, -0216, -0226, -0230, -0255 (42nd Wg.). 6–19 March 1992.

Exercise *Central Enterprise* (Fairford) B-52H 61-0003, -0008, -0017, -0028, -0040 (96th BW). 16–29 June 1992. First B-52H deployment.

Exercise *Central Enterprise* (Fairford) B-52H 60-0024, -0030, -0060 (416th BW 'GR') 3–21 June 1993. *Coronet Comet*; flew missions into Europe *en route* to Fairford. Deployment shared with three B-1Bs of 28th BW. Between 19 and 30 April and April 20th BS B-52Hs also flew North Sea mining sorties in support of Exercise *Blue Harrier 93*.

Mighty Warrior (Fairford) B-52H 60-0012, 61-0015, -0020, -0021 (416th BW). 2–20 September 1993.

In 1994 a *Coronet Pluto* deployment of four 7th BW B-1Bs replaced B-52s for Exercise *Central Enterprise* from Fairford.

Exercise *Strong Resolve* (Fairford) B-52H 60-0017, -0020, -0032, -0049 (2nd BW 'LA'). From 17 February to 10 March 1995. B-52H 60-0001 also visited briefly, bringing the 2nd BW CO to inspect this *Coronet Capricorn* deployment.

Exercise *Salty Hammer/Central Enterprise* (Fairford) B-52H 60-0013, 61-0013, -0019, -0024 (2nd BW 'LA'). 6–26 June 1995. Deployment shared with eight F-111Fs from the 27th FW.

Exercise *Blue Harrier* (Fairford) B-52H 61-0008, -0029 (93rd BS AFRES, 'BD'). 26–30 April 1996. 'Bare base' exercise.

Exercise *Central Enterprise/Baltops '96* (Fairford) B-52H 60-0010, -0013, -0016, 61-0013 (2nd BW 'LA'). 4–21 June 1996. Deployment shared with five 28th BW B-1Bs (Coronet Catamaran) and designated 4611th Expeditionary Group (Provisional).

Exercise *Coronet Storm*, by three B-52Hs of the 2nd BW to Fairford for 6-13 June, 1996 was cancelled due to the situation in the Middle East.

Global Power (Mildenhall) B-52H 60-0015, -0018 (5th BW 'MT') 9–12 September 1996. *Global Power* missions usually involved B-52s in round-trip sorties to simulate attacks on European targets without landing at a base in Europe.

The 1997 *Central Enterprise* visit was by Dyess AFB B-1B Lancers.

Exercise *Central Enterprise/Baltops '98* B-52H 61-0022, -0008, 60-0003, 61-0029 (93rd BS AFRC 'BD') with six B-1B Lancers from 7th BW 11–26 June 1998.

APPENDIX V

B-52 Colour Schemes

The first B-52s appeared in natural metal finish which was soon replaced by an anti-erosion paint scheme for production aircraft from the B-52B onwards. Upper surfaces of wings, fuselage and horizontal and vertical stabilizers were finished in silver (aluminized acrylic nitro-cellulose FS 17178) though some metal areas of the fuselage were left unpainted. The rear third of all engine nacelles and exhaust fairings was light grey. Wingtips and upper fuselage radome areas were brown fibreglass and anti-glare panels appeared ahead of the windshield and behind the gunner's position in Black (FS 37038). HF antennas in the fin and some other antenna areas were unpainted plastic. The horizontal stabilizer wiper seal area (a rectangular patch on the fuselage adjoining the stabilizer) was wax finished. On camouflaged aircraft it had an extra anti-abrasion coating.

From 1956 onwards, beginning with the B-52C but affecting most B-52Bs, the undersides and wingtanks of all aircraft were painted in 'thermal reflective finish' (anti-nuclear flash) with a top coat of MIL-C-83286 White polyurethane (FS 17875). Lettering ('USAF', etc.) and SAC sashes, when used, were in Strata Blue (FS 15045) with sixty-inch national insignia, but none underwing. B-52s have not carried underwing markings since that time.

South East Asia Scheme
Initially the basic silver/white scheme was retained on *Arc Light* B-52Fs but the use of conventional rather than nuclear weapons meant that the undersides could be re-painted in Black (FS 37038) to reduce their visibility at night. When B-52Ds were prepared for S.E. Asian service in 1966, the entire B-52D fleet was camouflaged to T.O. 1-1-4 specifications despite the 400lb weight penalty of the paint. The B-52 scheme differed from the standard 'Vietnam' TAC camouflage, using a set pattern of Dark Green (FS 34079), Blue Green (FS 34159) and Tan (FS 24201 or 34201) on upper surfaces. The undersides, vertical stabilizer, wing tanks and fuselage sides were Black (FS 17038 or 27038). The tan shade had a greenish tint compared with the Tan (FS 30219) used on TAC aircraft. Anti-glare areas remained matt black but on the nose only. Smaller (eighteen-inch) gloss insignia were introduced on fuselage sides and the SAC nose 'sash' was usually omitted. Serial presentation on the fin was in Insignia red (FS 11136) with the 'last three' repeated in this colour or in white reflective tape on the nose. A reflective white stripe often appeared on the wing tanks and tips to help ground vehicles to avoid the aircraft on flightlines at night.

SIOP Scheme
With the shift to low-altitude operations from 1966–67 onwards, a new scheme was introduced after testing a variety of others. Prior to that, B-52G/H Stratofortresses had received the original silver/white SAC finish with the white extending over much of the rear fuselage on many examples. The new SIOP scheme used the same upper-surface colours as the S.E. Asia camouflage but in a revised set pattern which extended over the fuselage sides and vertical stabilizer. At first the white plastic radome was retained for maximum microwave 'transparency' but the entire nose area was refinished by 1990 in Dark Grey (FS 36081) as part of the colour pattern, extending under the nose and EVS area. Undersides were left in White (FS 17875). A wavy demarcation line between upper and lower surface colours was often used on nacelles and wingtanks. Full-colour insignia (sixty-inch upper wing and eighteen-inch fuselage) were kept but serial, walkway and other presentation were in black or dark grey. About thirty B-52Fs (eg. 57-0142) and several B-52Es (eg. 56-0701) received this scheme in connection with Hound Dog capability.

Strategic Scheme (from 1984)
A further revision for B-52Gs (and B-52Hs from 1988) brought the most elaborate scheme used on the bombers. A new pattern used IR Dark Green (FS 34086) and 'Euro 1 Grey' (FS 36081) on top surfaces covering the same areas as the SIOP scheme. Undersides had a disruptive pattern of Grey (FS 36081) and Gunship Quality Grey (FS 36118). 'Lo-viz' 18-in insignia appeared, using FS 34086 on an FS 36081 background and vice versa. USAF serial presentation was in black on the fin tip with the 'last four' below the pilot's windows in black. Pilot/aircrew names had to be centred under the pilot's window and crew chief/assistant names were in a 15x36-in block on the lower front fuselage. Exact locations (using fuselage 'station' numbers for reference, applied for Command, organizational and unit designators (badges). Walkways followed the two-colour style of the insignia or were overpainted in medium blue-grey. Although matt paint schemes on aircraft 'hangared' in the open air were expected to last six years the Dark Green (FS 34086) tended to discolour to a muddy appearance quite quickly. The same scheme was applied to the Rockwell B-1B.

Monochrome Scheme
A simpler (and cheaper) scheme was applied to B-52s as they passed through PDM from late-1988 onwards. Consisting of overall Dark Grey (FS 36081) the scheme extended over all exterior surfaces apart from some antenna areas in the rear fuselage and nose. Other markings were similar to those used in the Strategic Scheme.

Revised Monochrome Scheme
Towards the end of 1990, the B-52H scheme was once again standardized with the Rockwell B-1B's when the Dark Grey (FS 36081) was replaced during PDM by overall Gunship Quality Grey (FS 36118). B-1Bs were repainted from mid-1991. This is unlikely to be the last change. As an EWO remarked plaintively to the authors, 'We could use a coat of that stealth paint like the B-2A has!' Sadly, it takes more than a coat of paint to hide a B-52 from radar.

Interior Colours
Landing gear and wheel hubs tended to be silver-metallic until the mid-1980s when gloss white became standard. Cabin interiors, seats, bomb-bays, landing gear bays and door interiors were usually Interior Green (FS 24151) or zinc chromate, as were flap retraction bays in the wing and access panel interiors. During the 1980s, gloss white became more common for bay and door interiors with zinc chromate primer (FS 34151 approx.) inside flaps, wing-tip wheel wells and doors and other interior surfaces. However, areas of silver or interior green were often visible too. Cabin interiors were then usually Grey (FS 36231) with red headrests and black instrument panels.

Colour numbers are for Federal Standard FS 595A/B.

Postscript. A Tail of Two Tails: Us (416th BW) and Them (the rest of SAC)

(Col Mike Loughran, former Commander of the 416th BW, describes a long-running feud over the Wing's tail-art):

In the late 1980s the somewhat stodgy SAC actually started to loosen up a bit. The outward signs of the 'movement' were subtle in some cases; along the lines of the tail markings. First it was the tankers and the narrow band of coloured tail stripes that started appearing – with official approval, and the right amount of regulations and supervision, of course. Bombers, the real war machines, were not allowed to participate in this sort of frivolity. Anything other than the approved camouflage scheme would likely cause the loss of the free world – or at least a bomber crew's butt because all the sharp-eyed PVO Strany fighter pilots could see colours from 1,000 miles away.

Then came Gen John Chain as CINC-SAC. Virtually every piece of the Command's business felt the change of pace pick up dramatically. We trained more for conventional operations than we ever had. The challenges of that training increased – and the bombers started to get nose-art. Sometime around 1987 the 'BUFFs' were allowed to have markings on the tail of the airplane. In some cases the numbered Air Force Commander tried to bring back the World War II tail markings [for example the 379th BW's triangle K]. The 2nd BW was out in front of the nose-art programme. The unit dressed up some of the Vargas girl-based art for the nose and selected a rather nice, black, properly-sized fleur-de-lys for the tail in recognition of the French influence in their Louisiana home base. The guidelines from the Command on tail markings specified the colours (subdued) and sizes; roughly the upper third of the vertical stabilizer. The 'BUFF' had a huge vertical stabilizer which made a great palette for talented and not-so-talented artists. The 42nd BW at Loring spent a long time looking for a good depiction of a moose for their tail marks. I heard the Wing Commander offer his kingdom for a good picture of a moose. Of course, if you have ever seen a moose up close and personal then you can safely conclude that there are no good, becoming photographs, paintings or depictions of any moose that ever walked the face of the Earth!

One SAC unit rebelled on the whole issue of tail markings from the start; the 416th BW. Griffiss was not subtle in the way they violated the guidelines. Instead of using the upper third of the tail as their canvas that was the only area not covered by their chosen painting. The unit leader ship had absolutely no intent of taking action on this issue. I'll be willing to bet that several of my predecessors as 416th Commander might have enjoyed seeing the IG people in spasms of apoplexy over the tail markings. I sure did. [After a long running battle with the SAC Inspector General over infringement of regulations *Desert Shield* intervened and Col Loughran took over the 416th. He asked to review all tanker and bomber assets.] I wish I could remember the Chief's name who took me around the aircraft and walked through the forms. We had a great conversation. As we walked around the airplane I asked a question that I already knew the answer to; not a normal practice but appropriate in this case. We approached the tail and the rather prominent markings. My question was straightforward – are those markings in accordance with the 'reg'? The answer was absolutely professional – 'No sir, they're not'. And then a long pause with some shuffling of feet by the nearby maintainers. 'Well I like 'em and I don't want you to change them, OK? Anybody has any questions on that, tell him or her to call me'. And that word got out fast! The issue was not settled for the censors and those who say 'tsk, tsk' a lot are always lying in the weeds and looking for a way to get you to comply. As things heated up in the impending war it became clear that the 416th would not deploy as a unit to the theatre. Almost all the tankers were gone, about 1,000 people and some 'BUFF' crews went with jets to augment the other deployed Wings. We got to donate our last couple of warbirds to the 97th BW from Eaker AFB, commanded by an old friend, George Conlan. They were en route to RAF Fairford when the 8th AF Logistics staff called our planners and said to get full loads of bombs from Loring, load up our last three jets and give 'em to these strangers from a little base in Arkansas. Oh, and do it in January, quickly, this weekend... and paint out those damn tail markings!

My suspicion was that it was too cold to paint airplanes in Upper New York. So the word was that the painting was the lowest priority, check with the depot and see if it is too cold to do it. Amazingly enough, intuition was correct again as the DCM told me that it was in fact too cold. The paint would probably blow off due to improper curing, etc. All those reasons made perfect sense to me. The film on CNN of B-52s arriving at Fairford featured a magnificent shot of a taxiing Griffiss jet – what a sight! And only a couple of phone calls along the lines of, 'How could you not paint it? Etc, etc'. The 416th won again. Even though someone must have put the squeeze on because we got some of our jets back with crudely painted-over statues on the tail. Rumour has it that some Fairford types even used mops to wipe it out.

As time went on we restored the Statue of Liberty to the tails. One concession was not to do any G models that were painted out as we were converting to the H-model.

Shortly after the announcement that the 416th was to come off Alert duty after 30 years of it CINCSAC Gen George Butler made his annual visit to the base and inspected a B-52 in 'phase' (PDM), where he commented to Col Loughran about the tail markings.

My rejoinder was along the lines of saying something like 'If you're asking if the tail markings are authorized, they're not but we like them and are very proud of the symbol and what it represents'. His comment was something like, 'OK then they're approved now.' What a breakthrough! The CINC, a former SAC IG himself, just wiped out a six-year running battle with the shoe clerks at his own headquarters! Hell, the collapse of the Eastern Bloc paled in comparison with this. We were 'legal' and had just received absolution from the boss.

Well, the victory was short-lived. Someone decided that SAC should close down. Nose art was banned at the first Commander's Conference of the new ACC. The demise was a reaction to the debacle at the Tailhook event. Mind you, nose art did not get banned totally, just gender-related pictures on the planes. That edict covered it and really upset the aviators and maintainers. And the stake in the heart came next in the form of another edict from Langley in the form of the dreaded drive for standardization. TAC used tailcodes to identify bases and units. We, the former SAC recalcitrant on the nose art issue would now get our butts in line, so to speak. A message gave us the chance to select a two-letters code for the tail and gave a concession – the tail stripes were back! 'GR' seemed like natural choices for the tail letters. The tail stripe was a lot harder issue to work. Maybe it was a form of moping over the banished Statue of Liberty on the tail. The directive allowed for a symbol within a painted band on the fin. One of our local efforts was to scale down a Statue of Liberty to fit within the confines of the strip. No matter what our best and brightest painters tried, it just didn't cut it. Somehow, the marking when viewed from ground level to the top of the 40-ft tail always managed to look a bit like Bart Simpson. So the 416th ultimately caved in. A red stripe, bordered in yellow with a scripted GRIFFISS in 668th BS colours was it – except for just one jet in the world. If you go to Griffiss Technology Park today you'll find a B-52G parked there. She has the tail number '225, the first 'G to be assigned to the base over thirty years ago. When she arrived the nose art said *Mohawk Valley* in large red letters against shiny new silver skin. When she went on display the right side of the nose had the SAC *Time* nose art. That was until a certain three-star gave a clear, concise and very direct order to remove it. But on the tail, in all its full size multi-colour glory is the Statue of Liberty and the words GRIFFISS AFB. Maybe that beacon in the torch will stay on that plane a lot longer than those planes will fly. One can only hope.

B-52H 60-0009 with the 'missile that might have been', the GAM-87 Skybolt. USAF via R. Thurlow

APPENDIX VI

B-52 Attrition

SERIAL	UNIT	DATE	CAUSE/CIRCUMSTANCES
B-52B (Total losses 8)			
52-0009	93BW	8 Feb 1964	Crashed after hydraulic fire.
52-8716	93BW	30 Nov 1956	Crashed on takeoff from Castle AFB.
53-0371	93BW	29 Jan 1959	Attempted to abort takeoff without flaps at Castle AFB and crashed.
53-0380	95BW	7 April 1961	Accidentally shot down by F-100 with AIM9 (*see* text).
53-0382	93BW	6 Nov 1957	Landing gear accidentally retracted on touch down; crashlanding.
53-0384	93BW	16 Feb 1956	Electrical fire caused aircraft to disintegrate in flight.
53-0390	95BW	19 Jan 1961	High altitude turbulence caused catastrophic structural failure.
53-0393	93BW	16 Sept 1956	Crashed after severe inflight fire.
B-52C (Total losses 5)			
53-0406	99BW	24 Jan 1963	Structural failure caused by low-level turbulence.
54-2666	99BW	7 Jan 1971	Structural failure in flight caused crash into Lake Michigan.
54-2667	306BW	29 Aug 1968	Electrical system failure caused loss of engine power.
54-2676	Boeing	29 March 1957	Used as JB52C. Lost all electrical power and broke up in flight.
54-2682	99BW	10 Aug 1959	Lost nose radome and became unstable, crashed in New Hampshire.
B-52D (Total losses 41)			
55-0050	307SW	22 Dec 1972	*Linebacker II* loss (*see* text).
55-0056	307SW	4 Jan 1973	Hit by SA2 over Vinh, N. Vietnam and crashed in sea (*see* text).
55-0058	43SW	12 Dec 1974	Overstressed after instrument malfunction causing structural failure.
55-0060	484BW	13 Jan 1964	Structural failure while flying in turbulent air.
55-0061	307SW	22 Dec 1972	*Linebacker II* loss (*see* text).
55-0065	42BW	16 Sept 1958	Crashed in Wisconsin.
55-0078	22BW	30 Oct 1981	Crashed in mountainous terrain, Colorado, during night low-level sortie.
55-0082	42BW	10 Jan 1957	Crashed near Loring AFB.
55-0089	28BW	3 April 1970	Crash landed at Ellsworth AFB.
55-0093	42BW	29 July 1958	Hit ground on approach to Loring AFB in poor visibility.
55-0097	43SW	15 Oct 1972	Crashed at U-Tapao RTAB and subsequently scrapped.
55-0098	4170SW	15 Dec 1960	Broke up on landing after structural damage during mid-air collision with tanker.
55-0102	42BW	26 June 1958	Ground fire at Loring AFB.
55-0103	306BW	18 Nov 1968	Failed to become airborne at Kadena AFB. Burned out on runway.
55-0108	462SW	10 Nov 1964	Struck ground during night low-level sortie nr Glasgow AFB.
55-0110	307SW	22 Nov 1972	Shot down by SA2 nr Vinh, N. Vietnam.
55-0114	99BW	9 Dec 1960	Crew ejected on low-level sortie after navigator accidentally ejected.
55-0115	306BW	2 Dec 1968	Burned out in ground fire at Kadena AFB.
55-0116	307SW	29 March 1973	Recovered to Da Nang AB with severe combat damage and scrapped.
56-0584	307SW	26 Dec 1972	*Linebacker II* loss, crash landed at U-Tapao (*see* text).
56-0591	Boeing	23 June 1959	Structural failure in tail area during low-level turbulence.
56-0593	509BW	10 May 1969	Crashed into sea shortly after takeoff from Guam.
56-0594	22BW	19 Oct 1978	Crashed into sea after takeoff from March AFB.
56-0595	4133BW(P)	7 July 1967	Midair collision with 560627 (*see* text).
56-0597	92BW	12 Dec 1957	Crashed on takeoff from Fairchild AFB with stabilizer trim problem.
56-0599	307SW	27 Dec 1972	*Linebacker II* loss (*see* text).
56-0601	4133BW(P)	8 July 1967	Crash landed at Da Nang AB after electrical failure (*see* text).
56-0605	43SW	27 Dec 1972	*Linebacker II* loss (*see* text).
56-0607	92SW	1 April 1960	Destroyed in fire on takeoff after structural failure.
56-0608	307SW	19 Dec 1972	*Linebacker II* loss (*see* text).
56-0610	28BW	11 Feb 1958	Crashed on approach to Ellsworth AFB after iced-up fuel pumps caused fuel starvation.

56-0622	307SW	20 Dec 1972	*Linebacker II* loss (*see* text).
56-0625	306BW	31 March 1972	Crashed after several engines failed during overshoot at McCoy AFB.
56-0627	4133BW(P)	7 July 1967	Mid-air collision with 560595 (*see* text).
56-0630	70BW	27 July 1969	Crashed after structural failure soon after takeoff from Guam.
56-0661	92BW	9 Sept 1958	Mid-air collision with 560681 nr Fairchild AFB.
56-0669	43SW	21 Dec 1972	*Linebacker II* loss (*see* text).
56-0674	307SW	26 Dec 1972	*Linebacker II* loss (*see* text).
56-0677	307SW	30 July 1972	Struck by lightning over Thailand causing fire and loss of control.
56-0681	92BW	9 Sept 1958	Mid-air collision with 56-0661 near Fairchild AFB.

B-52E (Total losses 3)

56-0633	11BW	9 Dec 1958	Crashed on landing overshoot due to stabilizer trim problem.
56-0655	6BW	19 Nov 1963	Burned out on ground due to accident during maintenance.
57-0018	6BW	30 Jan 1963	Structural failure during high-altitude turbulence.

B-52F (Total losses 9)

57-0036	4228SW	15 Oct 1959	Collided with tanker during airborne alert, crashed with nuclear weapons aboard (*see* text).
57-0041	93BW	21 Oct 1969	Crashed on landing at Castle AFB.
57-0043	454BW	22 Dec 1963	Crashed during training mission.
57-0047	320BW	18 June 1965	Mid-air collision with 57-0179 during *Arc Light* mission (*see* text).
57-0149	93BW	8 May 1969	Crashed on approach to Castle AFB.
57-0166	4134SW	14 March 1961	Crashed after fuel starvation following cabin depressurization.
57-0172	93BW	8 Oct 1969	Crashed following control loss during overshoot circuit.
57-0173	7BW	28 Feb 1968	Crashed off Texas coast.
57-0179	7BW	18 June 1965	Mid-air collision with 57-0047 during *Arc Light* mission (*see* text).

B-52G (Total losses 28)

57-6479	92BW	17 Oct 1984	Crashed during low-level night sortie in Arizona.
57-6481	72SW(P)	20 Dec 1972	*Linebacker II* loss (*see* text).
57-6482	93BW	23 Dec 1982	Crashed after engine failure on takeoff.
57-6493	68BW	3 Sept 1975	Fuel leak from right wing caused unstable flight and loss of control.
57-6494	72BW	5 July 1967	Loss of control after crew life-raft inflated during takeoff.
57-6496	72SW(P)	20 Dec 1972	*Linebacker* loss (*see* text).
57-6507	319BW	27 Jan 1983	Fire in fuel tank during maintenance at Grand Forks AFB.
58-0161	19BW	11 April 1983	Hit ground during *Red Flag* sortie.
58-0169	72SW(P)	21 Dec 1972	*Linebacker II* loss (*see* text).
58-0174	456BW	8 Feb 1974	Several engines failed on takeoff from Beale AFB.
58-0180	72BW	2 Feb 1960	Crashed during touch-and-go landing after stabilizer trim problem.
58-0187	4241SW	24 Jan 1961	Crashed on landing with wing damaged by fatigue failure (*see* text).
58-0188	380SAW	21 Jan 1968	Crashed after fire in cabin on approach to Thule AFB (*see* text).
58-0190	2BW	20 July 1989	Destroyed by fire during PDM at Kelly AFB.
58-0196	4241SW	14 Oct 1961	Crashed into Atlantic nr Newfoundland during alert sortie.
58-0198	72SW(P)	21 Dec 1972	*Linebacker II* loss (*see* text).
58-0201	72SW(P)	18 Dec 1972	*Linebacker II* loss (*see* text).
58-0209	19BW	19 Aug 1980	Destroyed in ground fire at Robins AFB.
58-0215	42BW	4 Sept 1969	Crashed after several engines failed on takeoff.
58-0219	93BW	11 Feb 1988	Crashed after aborted takeoff at Castle AFB.
58-0228	2BW	18 Nov 1966	Crashed during a low-level sortie.
58-0246	72SW(P)	19 Dec 1972	*Linebacker II* loss (*see* text).
58-0256	68BW	17 Jan 1966	Collided with KC-135A over Palomares, Spain (*see* text).
59-2574	416BW	8 May 1972	Ran off runway at Griffiss AFB after aquaplaning on landing.
59-2593	4300BW(P)	3 Feb 1991	Crashed on return from mission during *Desert Storm* (*see* text).
59-2596	72SW(P)	20 Dec 1972	*Linebacker II* loss (*see* text).
59-2597	93BW	29 Nov 1982	Hydraulic fire after landing at Castle AFB.
59-2600	72SW(P)	8 July 1972	Crashed on takeoff from Guam.

B-52H (Total losses 8)

60-0006	17BW	30 May 1974	Crashed after failure of elevator and rudder controls.
60-0027	5BW	4 Oct 1968	Crashed on approach to Minot AFB with four fuel-starved engines.
60-0039	410BW	1 April 1977	Struck ground during landing approach to K. I. Sawyer AFB.

60-0040	410BW	6 Dec 1988	Crashed at K. I. Sawyer AFB after explosion during landing overshoot.
61-0026	92BW	24 June 1994	Pilot lost control during practice manoeuvre for Fairchild AFB airshow.
61-0030	319BW	2 Nov 1967	Two engines failed on instrument approach causing failed overshoot.
61-0033	5BW	14 Nov 1975	Ground fire in fuel tank at Minot AFB.
61-0037	5BW	21 Jan 1969	Stalled and crashed on takeoff at Minot AFB with incorrect trim.

Capt Donald C. Hedlund, Instructor Pilot, briefs his crew of the 4017th Combat Crew Training Squadron, Castle AFB, before taking off during training. USAF via AFA

APPENDIX VII

Laboured Landings

The 1976 Mackay Trophy and the Kaberer Outstanding Airmanship Award both went to Capt James A. Yule of the 337th BS, 96th BW for saving B-52D 56-0611 on 19 May 1976. On approach it became obvious that the forward landing gear units were not functioning properly. Yule flew the bomber to a 10,000ft holding pattern, left the pressurized crew compartment and entered the forward undercarriage bay. With the wind shrieking around him and a two-mile drop to the ground below he could see that the left gear was extended but the right unit had jammed part-way through its cycle. Hydraulic steering and braking systems were dead on all units. Despite this, Capt Yule brought the B-52 to a safe landing on a dry lake near Edwards AFB and '611 later returned to service (with the 379th BW).

Maj Robert M. Winn of the 379th BW brought a B-52H home in March 1969 with all four engines out on its starboard wing. One TF33 had exploded shortly after take-off, demolishing the No. 3 pod. As the blazing pod fell away, Maj Winn said it 'felt like dropping a bomb load'. The Nos 7 and 8 engines ran out of control and could not be shut down. A telephone call to Boeing, Wichita brought the advice to fuel-starve the runaway units. Winn then made a nose-high, no-flaps landing which he described as one of his best. Aircraft control on approach was severely limited. Maj Winn commented laconically, 'Since the aircraft could not be turned to the right, I elected to circle the field to the left'.

Landing at Edwards AFB the third and final B-52A (later NB-52A) 52-0003 is seen near the start of its long career as a test airframe. USAF via R. Thurlow

APPENDIX VIII

B-52 Maritime Operations

by Tony Cassanova

When one thinks of heavy bombers and the B-52 in particular, the first thing that comes to mind is its priority mission of delivering massive amounts of ordnance, (nuclear or conventional) over terra firma, on-time and on target. However, there is another side to this – MarOps; Mining and 'Harpooning' are all elements in a B-52's repertoire.

The 1947 National Security Act that established the US Air Force also charged it with training forces to interdict enemy sea-lanes, protect US shipping and conduct aerial minelaying, among its myriad other duties. The mission was a primary one and remained so until early the 1950s when it was relegated to a collateral role. During 1966, when the Department of Defense was gearing up to invest vast amounts in the navy's P-3 Orion programme, the USAF apparently viewed this as an opportunity to expand its budget. The overall thinking was that the B-52D, at the time earmarked for retirement in 1971, could also be employed as a maritime patrol aircraft. However, a SAC study later determined that it was not suited, although it was suggested that B-52Ds could drop weapons on command from other aircraft.

Over the years, several key documents were signed outlining the specific areas of the USAF's maritime participation. The first was during 1975 when the Air Force and the Navy signed the 'USAF-USN Collateral Functions Agreement', specifying that the USAF would train units for sea-control operations. The goal of the signing was increased cooperation between the two services. During September 1982 a Memorandum of Agreement on Joint USN/USAF efforts to further enhance the Air Force's contribution to maritime operations was also signed (approximately three months after the Falklands War ended) and again re-emphasized the mission. This document identified the missions of anti-surface ship warfare (ASUW), surveillance and targeting and aerial minelaying as areas in which the Air Force could provide valuable enhancements to Sea Lines of Communication (SLOCS) defence.

During 1984, the Air Force upgraded its maritime role from a collateral responsibility to a major mission again. The B-52 is able to carry out a maritime role with very little modification and technically it was fairly easy to equip. It can patrol the distant corners of the planet more effectively than any Navy aircraft, carrying up to eight AGM-84 Harpoon anti-ship stand-off missiles or a substantial payload of naval mines, and can perform sea surveillance on a massive scale due to its high-altitude, all-weather, day/night, long-loiter capabilities. Missions are limited only by crew fatigue and engine oil reserves.

Mine Warfare

This is the strategic and tactical use of offensive and defensive mines. The B-52H is currently the largest contributor in this role, establishing and maintaining control of vital sea areas by impeding the freedom of movement of enemy naval forces in areas such as harbours or chokepoints. On 15 January 1964 USAF Headquarters directed SAC to support Air Defense Command in providing an antisubmarine defence of the Continental United States. The principal US method of minelaying is by aircraft – the US Navy currently maintains no surface ship specifically tasked for the role – except in exercises for minesweepers. The B-52 has been performing this role since 1964, when the Air Force's maritime responsibilities were expanded. Only a few months were required to configure the 'BUFF' for the mission, and by September 1964 a B-52D had dropped eight types of aerial mines using tests at the Air Proving Ground Center at Eglin AFB, Florida. Due the fact that the B-52D was modified with a High Density bombing system, the 'Big Belly' aircraft, with its ability to carry up to 80 mines, proved to be the most capable minelaying aircraft ever.

During its involvement in South East Asia (1965–1973), the USAF's participation in 'true' maritime operations dwindled. However, during the Vietnam conflict there was discussion of employing the bomber to deliver Mk 36 or M117D Destructor mines in coastal waters, river deltas, and rivers as well as along roads and trails to interdict selective LOCs and to deny the enemy the use of his storage areas. It was thought that area-denial mines with delayed fuses would be more effective than hard bombs, especially during the monsoon season. The theory was that these 'dumb' mines with sophisticated fusing, capable of detonation by numerous means, would bury themselves within the saturated soil, swamps and ravines causing indiscriminate havoc. Although these aircraft were available at the time, when President Nixon ordered the mining of North Vietnam's harbours and river inlets during May 1972, Navy attack aircraft carried out the mission. There is evidence that the B-52Ds on Guam were in preparation to assist. By 1974, SAC had increased B-52 maritime training operations once more and in June of that year, a B-52D participated in the Navy's Atlantic Fleet Service Mine Test. In October, two B-52Hs flew a sea surveillance mission against a USN flotilla off Puerto Rico. By 1978, four B-52D Wings had been tasked with aerial minelaying in addition to their other missions, including the 7th BW at Carswell AFB; the 22d BW at March AFB, the 43rd SW on Guam and the 96th BW at Dyess AFB. Each crew was to fly at least one of these missions annually. Interestingly, the USAF does not own the mines it drops – the Navy does. Navy personnel complete assembly and then turn mines over to USAF munitions crews for loading. The mines are dropped just like conventional weapons but from an altitude of 3,000ft (914m) or less. Early models were derivatives of the Mk 80 series of iron bombs.

Eager to further demonstrate the B-52's capabilities, no location was too distant for SAC and that included Portugal. The 42nd BW was tasked with a minelaying mission, a daylight drop which was to be the centerpiece of a demonstration to a group of NATO naval officers and dignitaries in a little bay on the Portuguese coast. Naturally, the 'BUFFs' were on time and target for the relatively simple mine run. Re-usable mine 'training shapes' were equipped with echo locators so they could be located readily. Their target area was in shallow water, close to shore and prominent land returns were well within the range of the aircraft's radars, making the actual releases a 'piece of cake' for the crews. The ink had hardly dried on the congratulatory messages to the 42nd when the tone changed. It seems that no one could find the mines. Naturally, the first suspects were the aircrew. Radar film, photographs and documentation of the release were all sent to Navy Headquarters for an investigation – even though the drop was in broad daylight in front of a large crowd on ships and shore! The crews had no explanations or excuses. Controversy went on for a week and just withered away.

Currently the B-52H 'Dash One' manual lists twelve mines ranging from the shallow/bottom (max depth of approx 600ft or 182m) 500lb (227kg) Mk 36 DST or Destructor to the self-propelled, shallow/bottom 2,390lb (1,086kg) Mk65 Quickstrike. A number of medium-depth mines (down to about 1,000-ft or 305m) are also available. The Mk 36 is one of a series of converted streamlined general-purpose bombs. The larger Mk 65 is in the category of a smart weapon due to its state-of-the-art fusing that ranges from magnetic, seismic or pressure activated. A total of up to fifty-one Mk 36 (27/24) or eighteen (8/10) Mk 65 mines can be carried internally and externally. Another ingenious mine available to the B-52H is the 2,360lb (1,070kg) Mk 60 Captor (capsulated torpedo), which was designed exclusively with the submarine in mind. It is a deep-water (down to 3,000ft or 915m) weapon, which upon being laid is anchored to the ocean floor. While waiting up to several months, it ignores surface ship signatures (including submarines) until it acoustically detects the signature of a submerged submarine. Captor then launches a Mk 46 torpedo.

The accuracy tolerances for weapons release shrink considerably when dropping mines. If dropped with too much space in between, they will be ineffective: therefore release has to be extremely accurate. Mines must be placed precisely because friendly ships have to be able to pass through a minefield. In addition, after hostilities an accurate plan of their layout is needed for their removal – so it is critical that they are on target. During early missions, target areas were usually close enough to a point of land that a position fix could be taken, but because B-52s were operating over water more than ever, SAC brought back celestial navigation training. Today, with INS and GPS, it is unnecessary.

Also today, Sea Control is no longer a primary Air Force mission, nonetheless B-52 maritime operations seem to be on the increase. Starting in April 1983, ACC's bomb wings were tasked to fly a quarter of *Global Power* missions annually. The goal was to prepare the crews for the arduous, long flights as well as to profile the capabilities of their bombers. During the round-robin training missions flown outside the US maritime training has been practised as well as conventional general-purpose weapons. In fact, the Air Force is dropping mines as if they had just discovered the technique!

A somewhat typical *Global Power* exercise in which the B-52 showcased its aerial minelaying capabilities was during 1993 when B-52Hs from four bases participated. At the time it was said to be the largest mine-warfare exercise NATO had ever conducted. The target area was in Central Kattegat, the body of water between Denmark and Sweden, and two days of B-52 participation were included. Four aircraft were scheduled to lay ten mines during the round-robin missions. The flight from Griffiss AFB was eighteen hours, the K. I. Sawyer's flight was 19.5 hours, and Barksdale entry flew twenty-one hours, while Castle flew the longest at twenty-four hours.

Sea Surveillance

Sea surveillance is the systematic observation of ocean areas to detect, locate, and classify selected high-interest surface, and subsurface targets and provide this information to users in a timely manner. A target may be any hostile, neutral, or friendly platform. In the case of the 'BUFF', its focus is on the surface vessels. Because of its range and air refuelling ability, it is able to patrol distant corners of the world more effectively than any Navy aircraft.

After the success of the B-47's sea-surveillance missions during the 1962 Cuban Missile Crisis, the Air Force initiated testing of the B-52 for the role. During March and April 1965, SAC B-52s and KC-135s were tasked to carry out *Water Gap*, a sea surveillance exercise and the first extensive visual and photographic sea-search exercise for these two types. However, this was not the first time SAC had carried out a maritime surveillance mission. During the airborne alert missions and when over water, crew were instructed to look down periodically to check the surface for submarines – even though they were at 35,000ft (10,668m). Col. Phil Rowe: 'we actually did see a few subs – however, they were ours!' At the same time as 'BUFF' crews were increasing their mining capabilities, sea-surveillance missions were practised. While only four Wings were tasked to be proficient with mines, seven additional units were tasked with sea surveillance including those mentioned beforehand (except the 7th BW), plus the 19th BW, 42nd BW, 68th BW, 97th BW, 410th BW and 416th BW.

Initiated in 1975, SAC's *Busy Observer* exercises involved the tasking of B-52s to carry out sea surveillance training, and operational missions. *Busy Observer 1* missions were strictly training; 'BUFFs' worked with US Navy and NATO naval vessels on the high seas. It was an opportunity to test its tactics as well as the command and control procedures. During sea surveillance missions, the Navy is responsible for plotting all sightings, which are then forwarded to the USAF. A two-ship of B-52s would then fly to the approximate area and conduct a systematic radar search. Flying at a high altitude, almost 112,000sq nautical miles (208,000sq km) can be covered during a two-and-a-half hour search. Ships sailing the oceans cannot avoid being observed on radar, including suspected drug-running vessels whose descriptions would be passed to the B-52s. After the Air Force crews plotted the location of the surface contact, one B-52 usually mapped, stayed high and watched his wingman descend to about 3,000ft (914m) to identify it. Photographs were then taken by way of the vertical K-17/K-38 strike camera mounted on the underside of the aircraft. The 'BUFF' would again descend to 1,000ft (305m), this time for a few side-profile photographs via 35mm cameras. The two aircraft would then usually trade places to share the training.

However, *Busy Observer II* exercises were a different ball game altogether – they were operational and went after Soviet naval vessels. Any images obtained during these missions were passed on to the Navy, where they became part of their worldwide file on foreign ships. During one well-documented incident on 6 April 1978, a pair of B-52Hs from the 410th BMW intercepted the Soviet aircraft carrier *Kiev*, as it passed north of Scotland in the target-rich hunting grounds of the GIUK (Greenland, Iceland, UK) Gap. This gap would have been an ideal chokepoint in which to block an advancing Russian surface fleet trying to breakout westward into the vast Atlantic ocean in the event of hostilities. B-52s spent several hours with the fleet, photographing the ships involved in the manoeuvres. Flying some fifteen hours from their base, they were able to make contact in shifts for three separate peeks at the fleet. On another occasion a pair of 410th BW B-52Hs carried out a sea-surveillance mission in conjunction with the Navy while over the Indian Ocean during an around-the-world 43-hour, 19,353 nautical-mile (35,841km) flight. During the 14 March 1980 mission, each aircraft received close to 600,000lb ((272,155kg) of fuel.

Anti-surface Warfare

Anti-surface Warfare (ASUW) operations are conducted to destroy or neutralize enemy naval surface forces and merchant vessels. After looking at other weapons, SAC began modifying some B-52Gs in 1982 to carry the McDonnell Douglas (now Boeing) AGM-84 Harpoon anti-ship missile. First fielded by the Navy during 1977, this combination was a perfect match. A key factor for this re-thinking was the quickened pace of expanding Soviet naval forces during this period.

The concept of ASUW rests on a joint USAF – Navy maritime operation. A USN carrier battle group (CVBG) is a formidable striking force, yet the 'BUFF' Harpoon combination is able to enhance its capabilities. If assigned to the perimeter defence, it would allow the fleet to concentrate its force to an offensive strategy. The 1,145lb (519.36kg) AGM-84 Harpoon is an all-weather, anti-ship attack missile capable of airborne launch from a variety of aircraft. It is powered by a 600-lb (2.67-kN) thrust turbojet engine, and carries a 500lb (227kg) penetration blast type warhead. It has a low-level trajectory, active guidance, counter-countermeasures capability and contact-detonated high explosive, blast type warhead. The program was initiated during September 1982 and by early March 1983 the first B-52G had been modified to launch Harpoons. Several test launches were conducted by the 320th BMW between 15 and 28 March 1983 at a Pacific Missile Test Range. Directed by an E-3A AWACS, altitudes ranged form 30,000ft (9,144m) down to 700ft (213m). Three modified aircraft arrived at Loring AFB by September 1983 and the modification program, which made use of wiring originally installed for the SRAM, was completed during June 1985. The carriage of external SRAM was discontinued during the early 1980s due to the excessive drag factor.

The 42nd BW achieved a limited operational capability with Harpoon on 6 October 1983, followed by IOC with fifteen aircraft by the end of 1984. By June 1985, the only B-52 wing based outside the United States, the 43rd SW on Guam, was also fully operational. With two Harpoon-capable B-52G squadrons ready to provide operational support to both the Pacific and Atlantic fleets, the B-52G/AGM-84 integration that was carried out jointly by the USAF and USN in just eighteen months was hailed by both services as a cooperative success. While most B-52 wings had a single primary Design Operational Capability (DOC) of nuclear deterrence, both the 42nd and 43rd BW, after acquiring the Harpoon capability were dual-DOC units.

During May 1988, SAC announced that it was re-dedicating four B-52G wings (some 68 non-ALCM capable 'BUFFs') with a primary DOC of conventional operations. This involved a single squadron of the 2nd BW and those assigned to the 42nd, the 43rd and the 320th which were all to be Harpoon-capable. To enhance their capabilities, new OAS software and wiring modifications were installed, which when combined with the new GPS system, significantly improve bombing accuracy and weapons carriage capability. However, a sudden force reduction was announced and during July the 320th BW ceased operations and was inactivated on 30 September 1989, with the 43rd BW following on 30 September 1990. With the early retirement of all B-52Gs, a shortfall in precision-guided munitions capability loomed but the remaining Harpoon-dedicated B-52Gs were finally retired during 1994. The 'quick-fix' was a rapid conventional capability program, dubbed *Rapid Eight*. This program, which made interim modifications to eight B-52Hs, allowed half to employ the AGM-142 Raptor, and the rest the AGM-84, which was declared operational during September 1994. The 'Eight' later returned to Boeing to complete their 'production configuration', including the installation of GPS. Today, a new Harpoon Stores Management Overlay (SMO) and the Weapons Personality Adapter (WPA) allows any CEM aircraft with a WPA-equipped common pylon to carry Harpoon. The first B-52H to launch an AGM-84D Harpoon did so on 25 July 1995 at Roosevelt Roads – the first time the Air Force had launched a Harpoon since 1992.

Harpoons on the Buff

Col Michael F. Loughran (Ret), a former Commander of the 416th BW, arrived at Loring AFB just as the Harpoon was coming on line. 'As with everything else, there is a lot more to the whole story than one ever imagines. This chapter goes way back in the story of how the "BUFF" was issued a new weapon, the Harpoon. This author played a small role in the story and is friends with the other officer mentioned. I'm sure General Tom Goslin doesn't mind getting credit for what he did to make this happen. Today, Tom Goslin is a Brigadier and the Commander of the 509th Bomb Wing of B-2A Spirit fame. "Goose" Goslin and I were action officers in the Pentagon in an office called the Strategic Offensive Forces Division (XOXFS), part of the Directorate for Plans. Our collective chore was to develop force structure options for the leadership to debate about which way to go for the future. In actuality, we did a lot of busy work, but at least our force structure options were projected to be on board in the next ten or fifteen years, not tomorrow. There were lots of discussions with our SAC Headquarters' counterparts who just wanted the Air Staff to fund it all, because "the CINCSAC wants it." Hours and hours of time spent with budget types, analysts, contractors and writing papers did not allow for much freethinking.

However, every once in a while, an opportunity did pop up. None of us really thought that the war between the British and the Argentines would affect the capability of the B-52 fleet, but it did. The Air Force always had a collateral mission of assisting the Navy. In fact they were doing some training at the time in things like sea surveillance and mine laying, both missions that were pretty well matched for the "BUFF". Tom Goslin, then a Major, had the idea of resurrecting the B-52 as a Harpoon carrier, that Lt Col later General, H.T. Johnston had worked on in 1977 when he was an XOXFS AO, one day when we were discussing the Argentinean successes with the Exocet anti-ship missile. At the time, we may have been aware that the Argentinean AF did the whole thing as a "self-help" operation. Later writings in professional journals and after-action reports told how the Etendard pilots had never even shot a missile in practice and devised the whole program as a total *ad hoc* response to the situation. The reasoning was straightforward and can be summed up easily – an airplane is an airplane; the '52 carries a lot of stuff already; the Navy has Harpoons; let's borrow some, shoot 'em at something and see if it works. Makes perfect sense to a group of Majors in the Air Staff on an otherwise boring day. Since the "Goose" was the "bomber guy" and I was the "tanker guy", when it came to dividing up the workload, he got it! And he made it work. A sympathetic former B-52 crew member in the OSD [Office of the Secretary of Defense] staff had control of a large pot of money for research and development, including near-term added enhancements to the existing weapons systems. Easily convinced that it would work, he received some no-name, no-source advocacy papers that allowed him to convince his bosses and – surprise! A test program was born. In fact, some of us were so confident that the test would succeed that they basically told the Air Force to develop a limited operational capability. The USAF would have three 42nd BW airplanes and up to five crews ready to go in harm's way with the Harpoon by the end of September 1983.

Coincidentally, this author then received a dream assignment – except for the location: go to Loring AFB, Maine as the 69th BS Operations Officer and make that happen! The ops officer was responsible for the day-to-day flight training of the aircrews. Tom Goslin's reward was to stay at the Pentagon a bit longer and fight the really big battle in negotiating the memorandum of understanding with the Navy on Joint USN/USAF Efforts to Enhanced USAF Contribution to Maritime Operations.

The first work-ups in activating the Harpoon were typical of a new system's introduction to the field. Ground training classes explained to the aircrew and ground crew just what a Harpoon was. There was a large dose of help from our friends in the Navy for this effort, because they already had the knowledge of the weapon. It was, however, up to us to develop the Air Force tactics for use of the system. At first glance, we thought we'd solve this ship attack problem easily. After all, the 69th BS was to become one of the command's premier non-nuclear squadrons performing a wide range of contingency operations. Attacking something on the water would be like bombing in your backyard. Early thought centred on a mutual targeting scheme. Since B-52s were already flying ocean surveillance missions in pairs, we would use a hunter-killer arrangement. One aircraft would look at the ocean surface, pick out the bad guy's capital ship and the wingman would simply kill it with a missile. The plan was for the shooter to drop down low while the high bird would transmit coded messages updating the surface picture, or SURPIC (Surface Picture in Navy terms) – the first in a growing string of USN acronyms. Both aircraft would stay outside of SAM range: although search radar might acquire the high-altitude aircraft an engagement was not likely.

One of the earliest "test" flights of the Harpoon delivery tactic was a rather simple approach to the tactical solution. There was a Navy destroyer coming out of the yard at Bath, Maine after some sort of an overhaul. As I recall, they wanted us to try out some ECM gear against a cooperating target that had jamming capability. The *Fightin' 69th* got the call and added a couple of hours into one of our training missions with the promise that we could attack the ship at the end of the ECM testing period. The Bay of Maine was like a lake that day and you could easily spot the ship from altitude. Our "crows" [Electronic Warfare specialists] and their "crows" seemed to enjoy the jamming session, but the pilots and navs waited anxiously to try out a couple of Harpoon runs. Since we did not have any missiles yet, we had only just basically read the brochures – how fast, how far, how big, etc. The situation was a bit like reading an advertisement for a new car, walking up to a vehicle, jumping in and taking it out to explore the performance envelope. Our plan was simple – fly low, simulate a shot and then assume the missile's flight profile and home in on the ship. We knew the ship's position, its heading or MLA (Mean Line of Advance, in USN parlance) and, by straight dead-reckoning, figured a likely position where the "missile" would intercept the ship. There were a couple of key points involved; when would the ship detect us with our radar off; would the known azimuth of the missile's seeker acquire the ship, and an important question, when would the ship's fire control system be able to detect and engage the "BUFF"?

Of course, engagement by the ship was not a concern in an actual shot, because the missile launch point would be well outside the SAM and AAA envelope. The "BUFF's" huge radar cross section dwarfed that of the Harpoon, but it would be nice to know all this information. One added bonus was that it was chance to buzz the destroyer – legally. And I don't care what you say; buzzing a ship, a town, or a group of people is something every pilot looks forward to!

At 500ft (152m) and 300 knots, the ocean can be deceiving. The total lack of features, late in an otherwise grey, overcast day forces you to count on the radar altimeter for height information. We were at the flight parameters, well away from the destroyer on a heading that would make an intercept easy after we assumed the Harpoon's flight profile. I think the prediction was that the ship would not be able to see us until we closed to somewhere around twenty-mile range: problematic when the brochure said you could shoot from sixty miles away! And we did just that. After the launch point, speed was increased and altitude lowered a bit. At a point where the navigator calculated we should be able to see the ship off our nose, there she was. They had turned a bit from the last heading we had; yet the FLIR sensor picked up the destroyer at about 20 degrees off the nose. One short radio call let the ship know that we had them in a successful intercept. Since we had planned to fly over the "target" ship, I asked for their preference as to which side of the vessel we should "pass in review". Until that radio call was made to the destroyer's CIC [Combat Intelligence Center], they had no indication of our presence and had not detected us with their search radar. So, a missile would have flown for some forty miles before the target vessel would have a chance to detect it. A couple of small heading corrections and we were over the fantail, pulling a hard turn to fly down the starboard side, stern-to-stern. After a quick circle around the "target", it was climb power, pull up the nose and we were heading for "feet dry". The skipper came up on the frequency and passed on his compliments on the brief airshow.

In the next levels of discussions among the tacticians at the squadron, we generally agreed to a BFO (blinding flash of the obvious). A cooperating ship on a calm day was going to be a totally different situation than a Soviet Surface Action Group (SAG) that was capable of inflicting a lot of damage to the attacking aircraft. So, how did we propose to resolve this dilemma? Our Navy friends might be a useful source of information. Either through SAC Headquarters or through direct contact with a Navy P-3 unit, the 69th came up with some tools to aid in solving the attack problem. The vital piece of information would be the data contained in the SURPIC. This became a coded message from an aircraft that had "mapped" the surface ships on an area of the ocean. The targeting airplane would fly by an area of interest based on some external cueing from an intelligence source. The grouping of ships that were generally heading the same way in the open ocean areas were probably part of a formation out to do harm to someone. Plotting of that group, coupled with a little knowledge of the other guys' tactical formation would yield enough information to plan an attack.

For example, the MLA, speed and spread of the group was a clue as to the location of the capital ship. In US Ocean transits, SAGs would spread in a relatively predictable manner based on the activity at the time. The SURPIC would try to reconstruct that pattern and number the ships and therefore select a target. Suggested run-in headings would be developed based on the defensive spread of the formation. The attackers' objective would be to avoid the ships, which could engage the aircraft prior to the launch point. Of course, an egress route would also be part of the shooter's planning. Armed with this raw data, the approximate Harpoon launch point would then determine the routing also.

Well, that was the theory, now to the practice. Two "BUFFs" would try this approach as a lethal end game to the SAC's *Busy Observer* sea-surveillance missions. From time-to-time "BUFF" units would be tasked for these missions, usually a training sortie with just two airplanes, lots of open ocean and the chance to find ships, exercise the command and control reporting system and buzz the ships – legally, of course. On a *Busy Observer II*, our adversaries were out there and we had to find them. A good place to start was the GIUK gap. Soviet ships en route to Cuba usually passed through this gap and this Intel was passed on to USAF units. However, these sorties did come with a different set of rules of engagement. Usually, we loaded full chaff and flares as a defensive measure. On-board ECM gear was tweaked against the specific ship fire control radars as a prudent self-protection measure. The objective was to be fully prepared in the event that the Soviet skipper got really agitated and started some sort of firing solution involving the "BUFFs". Defensive actions were authorized if engaged by the ship's fire control radar. These exercises built up a modest experience base from which to further refine tactics applicable to the Harpoon mission.

The 69th's immediate task was to achieve a limited combat capability with the Harpoon by late 1983, which was defined as three airplanes capable of carrying the missiles and five qualified aircrews. Boeing sent two fight test engineers up to gather data on aircraft performance with various combinations of missiles loaded on the external pylons.

Generally, dummy missile were carried on these test flights; mass simulators that duplicated the shape, weight and drag of the actual missile. One early discovery was that there was unusual buffeting on some missile control surfaces causing delamination of the surface. The problem was most severe at the missiles at the bottom of both fore and aft stations on the racks. The ultimate fix was to limit carriage to only shoulder stations – four on each pylon, for a total capacity of eight missiles.

Aircrew training consisted of ground classes on system operation, weapons system control and operational procedure. The mechanical aspects, equipment operation and "nuts and bolts" was the straightforward part of the training and certification process for the crew members. Tactics were a true set of shifting sands because every flight led to a new idea and further refinement of the delivery method of the weapon. At one point, someone designed what was thought to be a universal targeting method to allow several platforms to search for targets, transmit the data to the shooters and ensure secure communication between the hunter and the killer. Probably the best example of how that system worked would be to visualize a wagon wheel centered over the target ship, the spokes using letters to identify the potential run-in headings to the launch point. The letter "A" was at true North and the circle was divided into segments based on the approximate number of degrees of the harpoon's seeker angle. Target course, or Mean Line of Advance, was an important piece of data. The message that was passed on to the shooter was encoded by various standard methods to ensure communication security. The ideal solution for the hunter was to use a platform that was optimized to perform that chore, such as an E-3 Airborne Warning and Control System (AWACS). At the time, E-3s were a heavily tasked with numerous real world commitments and a very limited availability for training, especially for a B-52 unit working out tactics to attack ships.

The 69th searched for times to practise our growing body of knowledge regarding the Harpoon system. The squadron looked for exercises that stretched the new "sea legs" and would think little of the time involved in flying two "BUFFs" from Maine to the Caribbean Basin for the chance to practise one Harpoon run. In fact, they would willingly be chewed but by F-14s attacking the B-52 as they would a Soviet Naval Aviation *Bear* trying to attack the carrier battle group. We learned a number of valuable lessons, including just how different the parts of the US Navy were from each other. As part of learning the business, the "BUFFs" would be under the control of USN E-2 Hawkeye. Navy lingo and jargon was probably as bad as ours grew to become. Generally speaking the Navy exercises that involved a carrier working up for deployment, was a non-productive mission for us. We thought that the Navy might like to shoot at some heavies that were simulating *Bears*. But the situation was fluid, and the demands of qualifying a carrier air group for a cruise, placed our request for a couple of Harpoon runs at the bottom of the navy's priorities, understandably; so we went elsewhere.

The first "shot" carried out with an AWACS turned out to be a thing of beauty. We briefed the E-3 crew by phone the day before the sea-surveillance and control exercise. We were headed just off the coast of Iceland and near the Greenland area. The objective was to search for a friendly destroyer who was trying to sneak through to engage friendly naval forces. AWACS was the airborne search asset; we were to be the shooter with a single ship using the tactic of looking at the target with a wagon-wheel grid superimposed over the ship. The AWACS weapons controller understood the plan perfectly.

After a couple of hours transit time from Maine, the solitary "BUFF" arrived in the agreed to area of operations. There was a bit of surprise when the AWACS answered with a different callsign. Things got a little more tense because it turned out to be a different aircrew too! The original jet broke and these guys took their place on the launch from England hours earlier. Now what? To our surprise, the AWACS folks did a beautiful job of passing the data from one crew to the other. Our replacement jet not only had it down pat; they had the target too. It turned out that the airplane controlling us was a B model with an update to the radar, which made it more effective over water. Information got passed, decoded and the attack started. The run-in to the Harpoon launch point was smooth with all crew procedures working well. Missiles were away at the right point and course, which the bomber took up to simulate missile flight and homing. From low altitude, there was no detection by the ship. Right on cue, the grey warship appeared at the 12 o'clock position, and since the ship did not have a helicopter, a quick pass over the stern was appropriate, in the "BUFF" crew's view.

The NATO planners started to read the literature on the B-52's evolving capability in the sea lines of communication attack role. Requests for the 69th to play in large maritime exercises started to arrive in the message traffic via CINCLANT [Commander-in-Chief, Atlantic Forces] from Norfolk, Virginia. Most of the training had absolutely too many commuting hours involved. No matter how you decide to travel to the coast of Iceland, Scotland or Norway, it's still a long way! Ultimately, the marriage of B-52s, Harpoons and a targeting platform may have reached its peak when the Royal Air Force Nimrods asked to take part in an exercise. No. 120 Squadron, RAF Kinloss, got the task. We found a large chunk of ocean and invited those guys over for a stay and a bit of aviation fellowship coupled with tactics development and information exchange. We learned more, I think, than we expected.

The Nimrod Mk II, was optimized for the sea surveillance mission – and it was a shooter too. So, these crews understood the end game better than our own people who had little to no experience in finding, classifying and engaging ships. Nimrod carried Harpoons, mines and torpedos for its submarine search and attack mission. Its on-board radar was optimized for sea search and was a quantum improvement over the "BUFFs" according to the guys who operated the B-52 radar. Flying on the Nimrod was a bit like being on the bridge of the *Enterprise* (the starship, not the carrier). We launched with a two-ship cell of B-52s and the Nimrod. During air refuelling, the RAF pilots just sat out a safe distance and enjoyed the view. It was an easy task to integrate the aircraft into a formation of B-52s en route to the search area off Nantucket. The eye-opening stuff happened at the merge, as they say when the fight's on. "BUFFs" went silent, peeled away from the Nimrod and the hunt was on. In short order, the RAF mission director found a warship. His systems could find and categorize ships, almost down to the specific name. Coded radio messages went out to the shooters and we just watched from the relative luxury of the suite of electronics aboard the Nimrod. By now, our tactical considerations had matured along with our thought processes on shooting the missiles.

The 69th's brains trust had done some significant homework in finding out the defensive capabilities and limitations of adversary's ships. Our objective grew to not just sending in a single shooter, but overwhelming the ship's fire control system with a barrage of missiles. A key point to keep in the forefront is that you did not have to sink the ship to make it ineffective – you could do that with a "soft" kill. By removing his combat capability (knocking out the phased array radars, for example) you effectively neutralized the ship as a combat platform. If you damaged and degraded the ship's combat information centre or its ability to command and control other forces, then you had a degree of success in the task.

Additionally, our aircraft equipment had improved significantly in the time since the squadron achieved limited initial operational capability in late fall of 1983. The Offensive Avionics System (OAS) was a big improvement in navigation and attack capabilities. Originally part of the modification to enable the B-52G to carry the Air Launched Cruise Missile (ALCM), the 69th's jets were the first non-ALCM aircraft to receive just the OAS modification. Along with this package came an improved databus to enable the aircraft to carry some of the soon-to-be-developed smart weapons. All of these capabilities, in practical terms, led to a much more precise weapons delivery platform. The aircraft now could arrive at a point in space and time within seconds of desired time. In fact, a bomb release could be controlled to the point of the weapon's impact, and detonation, taking place at the exact second the planners wanted. While these improvements were intended for the land attack role, they gave a better tactical use of the aircraft and the Harpoon in the ship attack role.

Thinking had evolved to where we essentially flew a three-ship of "BUFFs", line abreast with about a mile lateral separation, to a launch point; basically a circle centred on the target. Then each airplane would begin to salvo the missiles at very precise time intervals selected to overwhelm the ship's fire control systems. The missile's extreme low altitude flight profile, coupled with a small radar cross section and high speed, led to a high probability of penetrating the defences and hitting the ship, causing significant damage to its warfaring abilities. In the largest raid, we thought, that out of thirty-six Harpoons closing very low, very fast and nearly at the same time, some were bound to get through. But, did it work?

The mission with the Nimrod was very successful. Both the RAF crew and our folks were convinced that the tactic was sound, the missile would be effective and the "BUFFs" were a welcome addition to the problem of going after Soviet Surface Action Groups on the high seas. Of course, we were all airmen acting like a meeting where everyone was in violent agreement – not always the case in the real world. The optimists always said, "Of course it works. We thought of it". But that approach did not necessarily translate to success unless you tested yourself against a formidable opponent. An AEGIS cruiser and a battleship would do.

The USS *New Jersey*, an AEGIS cruiser and an oiler were crossing the Atlantic and looking for some training opportunities. We got wind of the request through our liaison with the P-3 Orion wing at Brunswick NAS in Maine. These guys were invaluable to us as they shared a great deal of their extensive overwater experience with the 69th. And, we even flew on one another's airplanes to understand the platforms better and exploit our capabilities in a mutual mission. The Orions were Harpoon-capable maritime aircraft that also aided us in targeting and fire control problem solutions. We probably flew as many missions with P-3s as we did with any other asset.

One of the flight commanders in the squadron attended a planning session in Norfolk for this "sink the Battleship" exercise. The B-52s would own a portion of time when the ships would practise defending against land-based aircraft attack. We were part of a larger force conducting separate attacks against the ships from Navy bases along the coast of New England. It seemed as though all the other jets were Navy attack squadrons flying A-6 and A-7 aircraft accompanied by EA-6B ECM platforms. Each type had a block of time with sterile periods to deconflict the air traffic over the ships. There was even an agreed attack corridor through which all the shooters would funnel as they approached the ships. We had a different idea, though. While the training objectives were to get the ships some air defence screen undetected, fly in as close as we needed to be to get the ships and not be exposed or engaged by the ships. As part of the agreement, the "BUFFs" could make two Harpoon attacks; three if there was time. We planned for a third attack, but did not tell anyone. The third set of Harpoon launch points were a piece of information we deliberately did not share with our navy counterparts. Why? Because, we had launched from where they weren't looking for us. In other words, we approached the ships from their blind side by circling around outside of the search radar range and making a run-in from the opposite compass heading from where the ships were looking. While they could detect aircraft coming from the seaside of the ship, they were expecting land-based airplanes to come in a reasonably straight line from their bases directly to the ship. The long legs on the B-52 did not limit us in the same way. In later investigations, it seemed as though the Navy doctrine led them to look in the shortest direction to a land base as the likeliest avenue of attack. It seemed like a very logical solution to a problem, but overlooked the flexibility inherent in long-range, land-based aircraft.

Attack number three was a success – they did not expect it, did not see it and, therefore, could not defend against the missiles with the close in guns. In the debrief session, the ship drivers were none too happy with the devious minds on the 69th Bomb Squadron. There was a lot of heated discussion about seeing every Harpoon missile, being able to shoot them down and besides, the little missile would just bounce off the armour on the USS *New Jersey* anyway. So, there, take that! At that point in the conversation, the Flight Commander, who was also one of the pilots on the raid, simply asked about their expected results against our third attack. Lots of blank stares, hard swallows and agitated Navy guns in that one!

The *Fightin' 69th* worked up to be the premier maritime attack squadron in the Air Force. Squadrons at Guam and Mother AFB followed and built on our early experience. Now, they're all closed. The body of knowledge is perishable and the time and energies have not been wasted. The B-52H now has the sea missions. Equipment from the venerable 'G-model was salvaged when the airframes went to the boneyard. Some of it sat in boxes somewhere until the service got around to installing the gear on to yet another B-52, thus sending Air Combat Command aircrews out to sea – in a "BUFF".

Glossary

AAA	Anti Aircraft Artillery	BDA	bomb damage assessment	EVS	external viewing system
ABCCC	Airborne Battlefield Command and Control Center	BS	Bomb Squadron	EWO	Electronic Warfare Officer
		BUFF	'Big Ugly Fat Fellow'		
AC	Aircraft Commander	BW	Bomb Wing	FAC	Forward Air Controller
ACC	Air Combat Command	BW(M)	Bomb Wing Medium	FCS	fire control system
ACM	advanced cruise missile	BW(P)	Bomb Wing Provisional	FLIR	forward-looking infra-red
ACR	advanced capability radar	CALCM	conventional air-launched cruise missile	FOD	foreign object damage
AD	Air Division	CAP	combat air patrol	FS	Federal Standard
AFB	Air Force Base	CAS	close air support	GCI	ground-controlled interception
AFFTC	Air Force Flight Test Center	CBU	cluster bomb unit		
AFRES	Air Force Reserve	CCTS	Combat Crew Training Squadron	GPS	global positioning satellite (system)
AFRC	Air Force Reserve Command	CEM	combined effects munition	HSAB	heavy stores adapter beam
AFSC	Air Force Systems Command	CEM	conventional enhancement modification	ICBM	intercontinental ballistic missile
AFSATCOM	Air Force Satellite Communications				
AGL	above ground level	CEP	circular error of probability	INS	inertial navigation system
AGM	air to ground missile				
AIR	air inflatable retard (bomb)	CENTAF	Central Air Force	IOC	initial operational capability
		CIA	Central Intelligence Agency		
ALBM	air launched ballistic missile	CINCSAC	Commander in Chief, Strategic Air Command	IP	Instructor Pilot or initial point (for attack)
ALCM	air launched cruise missile	COMJAM	communications jamming	IRAN	inspect and repair as necessary
ALE	airborne, countermeasures, dispenser	CONUS	continental United States	IRBM	intermediate range ballistic missile
ALQ	airborne, countermeasures, special purpose	CSRL	common strategic rotary launcher	JCS	Joint Chiefs of Staff
				JDAM	joint direct attack munition
AMARC	Aircraft Material and Reclamation Center	DECM	defensive electronic countermeasures	JSOW	joint stand-off weapon
AMSA	advanced manned strategic aircraft	DEFCON	defense condition	KIA	killed in action
		DMZ	de-militarized zone	KTO	Kuwait Theatre of Operations
APN	airborne, radar, navigational aid	DO	Deputy Commander (Operations)		
APQ	airborne, radar, special purpose	DoD	Department of Defense (USA)	LCO	Launch Control Officer
ARCP	air refuelling control point	DTUC	data transfer unit cartridges	LOX	liquid oxygen
ARVN	Army of the Republic of Vietnam	ECM	electronic countermeasures	MACV	Military Assistance Command, Vietnam
AWACS	airborne warning and control system			MER	multiple ejection rack
		ECP	engineering change proposal	MGen	Major General
		EPR	engine pressure ratio	MIA	missing in action

GLOSSARY

MITO	minimum interval between take-offs	POL	petroleum, oil, lubricants	SNOE	smart noise generating equipment
NASA	National Aeronautics and Space Administration	PTT	post-target turn	SRAM	short-range attack missile
		RCS	radar cross-section	SVAF	South Vietnamese Air Force
NVA	North Vietnamese Army	RHAW	radar homing and warning system	SW	Strategic Wing
NVG	night vision goggles	R/N or RN	Radar Navigator (bombardier)	TAC	Tactical Air Command
OAS	offensive avionics systems	RTAB	Royal Thai Air Base	TDY	temporary duty
				TOT	time over target
OMS	Organizational Maintenance Squadron	SAC	Strategic Air Command	TTC	Technical Training Center
		SAM	surface-to-air missile		
ORI	Operational Readiness Inspection	SAW	Strategic Aerospace Wing	USAFE	United States Air Force, Europe
		SEAD	suppression of enemy air defences	'U-T'	U-Tapao RTAB
PDM	programmed depot maintenance	SIOP	single integrated operational plan	VC	Viet Cong
PGM	precision guided munition				

Notes

CHAPTER ONE

1. The pronounced shift of emphasis towards bombing as the B-52's paramount tasking was spurred on by the Tushino Air Show in Russia in July 1955, which prompted fears of a huge 'bomber gap' which only later U-2 overflights were to dispel after bases had been photographed in minute detail. In fact, the same group of Soviet 'Bison' and 'Bear' bombers had been making repeated passes during the 'parade'! Originally, according to an Air Staff ruling of October 1951, all B-52s were to have had a reconnaissance capability.

2. In the late l950s, B-52 crews comprised cohesive teams who worked together for up to years at a time as a bomber crew, in the World War II or Korean War sense. The Aircraft Commander was the team leader, the boss and the one who wrote the effectiveness reports on all of his crew members. There was a definite hierarchy on B-52 crews, a tradition which carried over from B-29 and B-36 days. The AC was at the top, followed in order by the Radar Bombardier (Radar), Copilot (Co or Copilot), Navigator (Nav), misunderstood EWO (aka Extra Weight Onboard) and enlisted tail gunner (gun or gunner). The USAF navigator cadre peaked in 1957 with some 20,123 men, comprising 14.32 per cent of all Officers.

3. The nickname 'bubble chasers' originated from the antics of navigators who would pop bubbles that rose in the gooey tar that sealed the runway paving slabs on exceptionally hot days at bases in Texas and California. Sometimes these were tennis ball-sized and a firm stamp in solid boots created a gunshot sound that echoed around the flightline. ACs and Copilots flying B-52s had no desire to appear at all silly and eschewed such pastimes!

4. Described more fully in the Box, *Self-Protection: ECM*, Chapter 2.

5. Rising to forty aircraft in FY58 (twelve under *Harvest Moon* at Wichita and twenty-eight under *Yellow Rose* at SA-AMA); seventy-seven in FY59 (eighteen under *Wheat State* at Wichita and fifty-nine under *Gunsmoke* at SA-AMA); and to 123 in FY60 with the introduction of a new facility at Oklahoma City AMA, at Tinker AFB (thirty-one under *Jayhawk* at Wichita, eighty-four under *Alamo* at SA-AMA, and eight under *Big Chief* at OK-AMA). Air Materiel Command had designated the Oklahoma City facility as chief support depot as early as June 1952. However, depot work was established first at Kelly AFB under Project *Yellow Rose* because its 'super hangar', Building 375, could accommodate up to thirteen B-52s at a time. Additional in-service modifications were performed by field teams during this time under numerous projects, including *Baldie*, which encompassed some 200 safety modifications in the fleet.

6. Also comprising some 1,366 B-47s, 174 RB-47s, 745 KC-97s, 322 KC-135s, fifty C-124, six RB-57 and fifty-six F-86s, but excluding additional liaison aircraft and a fledgling force of U-2 spyplanes. Much of this force would dissipate with the B-52s replacing B-47s and KC-135s replacing KC-97s. SAC became exclusively bomber-tanker-recce as part of the new SIOP force structure introduced from 1960. *Ibid*.

CHAPTER TWO

7. KC-135 boom operators had precise settings for B-52 refuelling. The angle of elevation of the boom was 30 degrees with 0 degrees lateral (azimuth) deflection. Telescopic extension was 10ft of the maximum 18ft of boom. Automatic disconnection took place if the boom was moved more than 10 degrees laterally. At that proximity the B-52 created a 'bow wave' which could be felt aboard the tanker. B-52 pilots were required to do a refuelling every forty-five days at least and a night refuelling every ninety days to stay current.

CHAPTER THREE

8. Forty-six more B-52Fs received the same modifications in Project *Sun Bath* in June and July 1965. Both projects originated from an initiative by Robert S. McNamara early in 1964 to improve SAC's conventional war capability. This included tests to determine the best type of bomb and optimum release intervals to ensure maximum concentration of bombs on target.

9. Skyspot sites, each with a 200-mile radius were set up at Nakhon Phanom, Dong Ha, Pleiku, Da Lat, Bien Hoa and Bin Thuy.

10. One justification for *Arc Lights* in military circles was that they could theoretically result in heavy NVA/VC casualties. Whereas lost supplies and munitions could quickly be replaced by North Vietnam's many allies it was believed (wrongly) that heavy loss of life could be a factor in persuading North Vietnam to desist from infiltrating the South. However, one NVA leader, Major General Tran Cong Man, admitted that his troops had a 'deep psychological fear of the B-52s when they went into battle'.

11. The remains of two of the crewmen, Capt Charles H. Blankenship and 1st Lt George E. Jones, were returned to the USA for burial in 1997. In 1994 a joint US-Vietnamese investigation team followed a report from a fisherman who claimed to have found the remains of an aircraft and human bodies in 100ft of sea-water. DNA tests confirmed the identities of the two victims.

12. This system of false reporting was not made public until a former SAC officer, Hal M. Knight revealed it in July 1973, emphasizing that it had been ordered by the White House in 1969.

13. A recent study by the international Mines Advisory Group calculated that Laos was the most-bombed country in history. In 1998 a team of British volunteers was still dealing with 2,000 pieces of unexploded ordnance per week and estimated that over two million tons were dropped in total, the equivalent of one warload every eight minutes between 1964 and 1973. It also estimated that 30 per cent failed to explode, particularly CBU canisters.

CHAPTER FOUR

14. The code name was a gesture towards President Nixon's obsession with football.

15. The last batch of B-52Hs had pylons between the engine pylons on each wing for the AN/ALE-25 system and this was also retro-fitted to some B-52Gs. Using 1,000lb-pods, each loaded with twenty Tracor ADR-8 2.5in chaff rockets, the system would fire chaff clouds over a mile ahead of the aircraft. It was abandoned in the early 1970s with the introduction of the Phase VI ECM fit but the small pylons were retained and used to mount an AN/ALQ-119 pod under each wing for some situations.

16. The compression process usually happened off-shore when cells were shunted into their correct minimum spacing within the Wave. Close separations, to saturate the defences, were made safer by the use of Aldis lamps in B-52D rear turrets. Pilots could also check their position by viewing the eight glowing exhausts of the bomber ahead; a kind of flaming artificial horizon.

17. The final war loss was 55-0056, hit over Vinh by a SAM on 1 April 1973 and flown out to sea for a safe ejection. Another B-52D was written off after landing with severe battle damage in March 1973.

CHAPTER FIVE

18. Alert too, no longer has the same tempo. Today's USSTRATCOM (US Strategic Forces Command) pulls the force into line at twenty-four hours' notice ready for such a counter-strike – a comparatively leisurely affair compared with the tense, no-notice Cold War years. Nevertheless, the remaining B-52H force still flew 4,623 hours in Fiscal Year 1997 and 4,290 hours in FY1998, with the SIOP-style nuclear tasking accounting for a sixth of all training sorties.

19. What is widely known today as the Internet started life as an Advanced Research Projects Agency (ARPA) net, which subsequently split into its modern civilian guise and parallel military Milnet system. Milnet allows crews and technicians to

download information to assist with aircraft and mission preparation, as well as assisting in general communications.

20. The B-52H is currently subject to a 75-hour inspection schedule and a 300-hour Phase Maintenance inspection cycle, with full depot maintenance performed on all aircraft at 48-month intervals at Tinker AFB, Oklahoma. Average B-52H airframe time is 17,000 hours.

    Cannibalization of aircraft components 'is a fact of life for the B-52. Many of the commercial providers of essential aircraft parts have either gone out of business or are no longer willing to make parts in small quantities. We utilize a "Cann aircraft", or "Smart Canns" – that is, those required components that are not in supply channels or have a long-lead time for procurement. Aircraft are scheduled for "Cann" status and "set down" usually no longer than thirty days before another aircraft takes its place.' The current requirement is forty-five maintenance man-hours per flight-hour.

21. This and other unattributed quotes in this chapter are courtesy of the Public Affairs Offices at Minot and Barksdale AFBs, who very kindly conveyed some of the authors' questions to the crews.

22. The B-52G was cleared for this weight during Project Big WIP, performed in August 1980. This employed the Edwards, California-based test B-52G (58-0024) at an all-up weight of 566,000lb (following in-flight refuelling). Its weapons load included a dozen ALCMs externally, four Mk/B28s and eight SRAMs internally.

23. The update originated with IBM who had developed a new 64k computer and added a new Honeywell standard precision navigation gimballed electrostatic beryllium gyro aircraft navigation system (SPN/GEANS) for the B-52D, amongst other improvements. Flight-tested between October 1977 and April 1978, resulting in IBM being awarded the systems integration contract that August, eighty-eight digital systems were manufactured for the B-52D and installed at San Antonio ALC. It represented the first major avionics rework since the 1960s Big Four and Jolly Well ASQ-38 updates, though was short-lived. Most of the SPN/GEANS systems were gutted from retiring B-52Ds and reinstalled in Lockheed's F-117A Stealth fighters.

24. Since upgraded with the Air Force Mission Support System (AFMSS), a transportable 'desktop' suitcase system of mission-planning computers, which include access to satellite imagery, postulated solar angles and shadows for the purpose of delivering electro-optic weapons, and so on. Block 2 AFMSS provides the capability to plan nuclear weapons delivery, and Block 3 advanced planning with PGMs for the CEM force and their Mil.Std 1760 arsenal. This latter effort includes the addition of the Wind Corrected Munitions Dispenser (WCMD), Joint Direct Attack Munition (JDAM), Joint Stand-Off Weapon (JSOW), and the Joint Air-to-Surface Stand-Off Missile (JASSM), while maintaining compatibility with AGM-84 Harpoon, AGM-142 Raptor and the normal arsenal of 'iron' and cluster munitions.

25. GAO/NSIAD-93-138 Operation *Desert Storm*.

26. The US Constitution forbids the assassination of any Head of State.

27. In 1979, at the time of the US Embassy hostage crisis in Iran, Guam seemed to be the only base from which a B-52 attack on Tehran could be mounted, if required. SAC pointed out to the Pentagon that tanking problems would limit such a mission to only two aircraft.

Index

Bold type indicates illustrations.

A-3A Fire Control System 10, 30–1
A-7 Corsair II 82, 86
A-10A Thunderbolt II 129
ADU-318 loader 115
Advanced Capability Radar (ACR) 53, 60
Advanced Cruise Missile (ACM) AGM-129 113–14, 116
AN/ALQ-119(V) ECM pod 92
AN/ASB-4 Offensive Weapons System 32
AN/ASG-15 Fire Control System 31, 42, 104
AN/ASG-33 Fire Control System 31
AN/ASQ-38 Offensive Weapons System 32, 110, 112
Air Launched Cruise Missile (ALCM) AGM-86 113, **115**, 116–17, 125
alternators 20–1
AMARC 138–9
anti-surface warfare (ASUW) 166
AWACS 127–8

B-1A bomber 114
B-1B Lancer 113, 123, 133, 135–7
B-2A Spirit 101, 137–8
B-36 Peacemaker 12, 13, 19, 24
B-52 '777' modification 131
 depot maintenance 36–8, 62
 formation flying 73
 pre-flight procedures 25, 102
 radar bomb scoring 32–3
 reclamation 138
 structure 11, 16, 18, 27, 29, 40–3, 53, 57, 60–2
 undercarriage 78
B-58A Hustler 16, 39, 103
bag-drag system 77, 88
Battlefield Air Interdiction 129
Bay Assembly Transport (BAT) 69
Blodgett, Capt D. 38, 44–6
Bloom, 1st Lt P. 122, 126, 128–9
Boeing:
 B-29 137
 B-47 12, 32, 137
 B-52A 10, 11, **13**, 30, 41
  NB-52A 13, **37**
 B-52B 9, 12, 13, 14, **17**, **18**, **20**, 30, **33**, 38

 JB-52B 14
 NB-52B 37
 RB-52B 14, **19**, **20**, 31
B-52C 14, 16, **19**, 138
B-52D 14, 16, **21**, 23, **26**, **33**, 34, **36**, 39, 46, 60, 62, 63–100
B-52E **23**, **29**, 32, **35**, 39, 43
B-52F 27, **33**, 35, 47, 63–70
B-52G 31, 39–62, 81–120, 139
 JB-52G **53**
B-52H 7, 8, **39**, 41–62, 102–19, 123, 135–9
KC-97 **17**, 18, 20, 27
KC-135 22, 35, 38, 65, 75, 91, 103, 122, 134, 137
Model 462 10
XB-52 10, **11**, **12**
YB-52 **9**, 11, **12**
Bomber Map 135
bombs *see* weapons
Bonus Deal tactic 83–4, 89
braking parachute 42
Bugle Note tactic 76
Burnett, Capt D. 30, 42, 58–9, 90, 126
Busy Luggage tactic 113
Butler, Gen L. 119

Campbell, Lt Col D. 40, 65, 71, 76, 79, 113
Carpenter, Lt Col F. 55, 134
CBU weapons 68, 70, 99
Cheney, Defense Sec. 105
Chiesa, Lt Col C. 122
Cichocki, Jim 44, 71, 76, 79, 113
Clay, Gen L. 68
Cole, Brig. Gen G. 137
Combat Skyspot *see* MSQ-77
Common Strategic Rotary Launcher (CSRL) 106, **113**, 114
Conlan, Col G. 131
Conventional Air-launched Cruise Missile (CALCM or ALCM-C) AGM-86C 125, 134, 137
Conventional Enhancement Modification (CEM) 120, 136
COTS (re-engine programme) 7
Crumm, Maj. Gen W. 71, 73
Cuban Missile Crisis 44–6, 165
Cushman, Lt Gen P. 77

D-21 Tagboard, Lockheed 49–50
Data Transfer Unit Cartridge (DTUC) 110, 117, 134
DEFCON states 102
Diefenbach, Capt B. 96
Duxford, American Air Museum 100

E-2 Hawkeye 168
EA-3B Skywarrior 86
EA-6A Intruder 82, 86
EA-6B Prowler 86, 98
EB-66 Destroyer 76
EC-135 'Looking Glass' 102
Electronic countermeasures (ECM) 16, 29, 31, 41, 56–7, 74, 83, **88**, 89, 92, 104, 135
Enger, Maj 15, 27, 46–8, 58–9
Evans, Col D. 134
Exercises:
 Blue Harrier 137
 Bright Star '85 118
 Busy Observer 165–8
 Global Power 94–7 137
 Red Flag 110, 122, 128
 Water Gap 165
External Viewing System (EVS) 107–9, 128

F-4 Phantom 59, 67, 84, 86, 127–8, 133
F-5E Aggressor 59, 112
F-14 Tomcat 134
F-15 Eagle 59, 124, 126, 128, 133
F-16 Fighting Falcon 129, 133
F-100 Super Sabre 38, 61, 64
F-105 Thunderchief 72, 82–3, 86
F-111 Aardvark/Raven 73, 83, 86, 103, 121, 123–5, 127, 133, 135
F-117 Nighthawk 121, 125, 127
Fink, Col C. 18–20
Fisher, C. 60
forward-looking infra-red (FLIR) 107–9, 129
full fuzing option (FUFO) 111
Funk, Maj R. 126

GBU-15 glide bomb 70
Gillem, Lt Gen A. 79
global positioning system (GPS) 120, 129, 165
Global Power sorties 137, 165

Glosson, Gen 'Buster' 123
Goslin, Brig. Gen T. 166–7
gunner (tail-guns, B-52) 28–9, 42–3, 59
guns:
    M-3 10, 30, **47**, **87**
    M24A 30
    M61 53, 57–8, 136

Harpoon, AGM-84D **117**, 132, 136, 166
Hawkins, Col J. 137
heavy stores adapter beam (HSAB) 99
Hobbs, L.S. 15
Horner, Gen C. 67, 124, 128
Hound Dog, GAM-77 40–1, 46, 51–2, 105
Hymel, Lt B. 96

I-Beam rack adapter 133
inertial navigation system (INS) 112, 165
integrated combat turnaround 131
Iverson, Capt J. 127

J57 engine *see* P & W
Johnston, Tex 10

K-3A system 13
KC-10A Extender 130, 134
Kissinger, Henry 83
Kuehl, P.S. 69, 77

Laing, Don 73
Lapham, Dan 110
laser guided bomb (LGB) 124
Lebar, Maj T. 90, 96
LeMay, Gen C. 10, 24, 136
Lieske, Capt B. 128, 130–1
Loughran, Col M. 133, 166–9

MA-6A system 12, 26, 32
Mackay Trophy 41, 134, 137
Marcotte, Col R. 130
Martens, Sgt B. 123
Mathers, Capt R. 136
McAnally, Lt Col R. 40, 110
McCarthy, Brig Gen J. 81, 89, 96
MD-5 Fire Control System 10
MD-9 Fire Control System 30, 87
Mers, Capt T. 124, 128–9
Meyer, Gen C. 91
MiG-17 84
MiG-19 84
MiG-21 72, 90, 92
MiG-31 105
mines, minelaying **116**, 137, 164–5
minimum interval take-off (MITO) 102–3
Mize, Capt J. 98
Momyer, Gen 65

Monetti, Capt A. 127
Moore, A1C A. 90
MSQ-77 Combat Skyspot 64, 70, 76

napalm weapons 67
Nerger, Lt Col J. 100
Newton, Capt R. 11–13, 15, 27, 32–3, 40, 43–5, 71, 77, 80
night vision goggles (NVG) 122, 127
Nimrod, Hawker Siddeley 168–9
Nixon, President R. 81–3
nuclear weapons *see* weapons

offensive avionics system (OAS) ASQ-176 106, 110, 112, 117, 120, 124, 130, 169
Oil Burner training routes 33
Olive Branch training routes 33, 110
Operations:
    Arc Light 64–100
    Back Road 68
    Bullet Shot 81
    Chromedome 25–31, 102
    Clear Road 31
    Coverall 31
    Crested Ice 48
    Desert Storm 121–33
    Desert Strike 134
    Desert Warrior 122
    Flaming Dart 63
    Freedom Deal 100
    Freedom Train 82–3
    Good Look 79
    Harvest Moon 67
    Instant Thunder 122
    Lam Son 207 80
    Linebacker 64, 82–100
    Long Jump 44
    Menu 79
    Niagara 75–7
    Patio 79
    Pegasus/Lam Son 207 75
    Pink Rose 67
    Poker Dice 71
    Port Bow 75
    Quick Kick 18
    Redwing Cherokee 14
    Reflex 35
    Rock Kick 69, 71
    Rolling Thunder 64, 84
    Steel Trap 17, 26–7

P-3 Orion 167–9
P & W J57 engine 14, **15**, 43, **53**, **55**
P & W TF33 engine 53–5, **119**
paint schemes 14, 38, 70–1, 91, 112, 133, 139, 157–9
Palomares accident 47
periscope sextant 17, 22, 33
Pernatto, O. 112

PLZT goggles 103
Powell, Gen C. 119
Power, Gen T. 26
Project:
    Big Belly 70–1, 99
    Big Four 34, 60
    Big WIP 130
    Blue Band 22
    Fresh Approach 23
    Hard Shell 22
    Pacer Plank 61–2, 70
    Pave Mint 135
    Power Flite 19–20
    Rivet Ace 104–5
    Rivet Joint 62
    Rivet Rambler 62, **88**
    South Bay 64
    Quick Clip 22
    Quick Fix 102
    Straight Pin 60
    Sunflower 36
    Tagboard/Senior Bowl 49–50
    Try Out 23
    Watchtower 23
    Yellow Rose 38
Putz, Capt V. 98

Quail, ADM-20 45–6

Rapid Eight programme 166
Raptor, AGM-142 166
Rees-Williams, Maj G. 64, 67, 71, 73, 75, 84
Rogers, Col B. 6, 130
Ross, Capt D. 123–4, 126
Rowe, Col P. 16, 20–31, 67, 102, 165
Rupert, Capt B. 128–9

Schwarzkopf, Gen N. 121, 123–4, 128–9
sea surveillance 165–6
Shining Brass (bomb-damage assessment) 68
short-range attack missile (SRAM), AGM-69A 105, 106, 107
Skybolt, GAM-87 40, **51**, 52
SR-71/A-12/M-12 Blackbird 49, 87, 93, 98, 104
Stocker, Maj B. 89
Strategic Air Command Bombing Competitions 102
Strategic Arms Limitation Treaty (SALT) 113, 138
Strategic Arms Reduction Talks (START) 138
strategic tracking ranges (STR) 112
suppression of enemy air defences (SEAD) 86, 123, 137
surface-to-air missiles 63, 69, 74, 76, 82, 88–100, 105, 130

SUU-67 pylon 116

Tacit Rainbow, AGM-136 114
TERCOM 117
Thule Monitor 27
Turner, S/Sgt S. 90
Twin Triad concept 137

Underhill, Lt Col D. 70
USAF B-52 Wings:
   2nd BW 35, 60, 63, 81, 118, 122, 125, 130, 132, 134, 137
   6th BW 32
   7th BW 35, 64, 81, 132, 164
   11th BW 35
   19th BW 165
   22nd BW 14, 33, 73, 79
   28th BW 41, 71
   42nd BW 16, 19, 43, 105, 121, 122, 124–5, 133, 165
   43rd BW 81, 89–90, 164–5
   68th BW 47, 111
   72nd SW(P) 89–90
   92nd BW 16, 22, 119

93rd BW 9, 13, 18–31, 125, 133
95th BW 33, 60
96th BW 84, 163–4
97th BW 165
99th BW 60
306th BW 80
307th BW 87, 89–90
320th BW 64, 65, 122, 132
340th BW 63
366th BW 133
379th BW 124–5, 132, 163
410th BW 46, 55, 58, 120, 165
416th BW 110, 113, 132–3, 165–8
449th BW 51
454th BW 74
484th BW 71
801st BW(P) 129–30
806th BW(P) 130–1
917th BW 137–8
1708th BW(P) 123, 126
4123rd SW 38
4133rd BW(P) 71
4133rd SW 38
4135th SW 40

4200th ASS 49–50
4238th SW 27
4241st SW 61

Vulcan, Avro 52, 55, 125

Warden, Col J. 122
water injection, engine 43, 71
weapons, conventional 64, 66, 99, 135–7
   Gulf War 121, 124, 126, 128–9
   nuclear 7, 34, 47–8, 110, 111
Wells, E. 10
Westmoreland, Gen W. 64–5, 67, 72, 77, 82
Willgoos, A. 15
Winn, Maj R. 163
WS-110A proposal 39
WS-125A proposal 39

X-15, North American 37
XB-70, North American 40

Young, Brig Gen D. 7
Yule, Capt J. 163